KINGS
OF THE
KREMLIN

Sol Shulman was born in Belorussia to a medical family. After taking a degree in physics, he attended the Moscow Film Academy, graduating as a film-director. His pursuits include literature, and film-journalism. He has led film expeditions to distant corners of our planet, from the North Pole to the Australian deserts. His books *Through the Unknown Russia*, *Aliens Over Russia* and *Russia Dies Laughing* and other literary works have been translated into several languages.

Every nation has a government it deserves.

*Joseph de Maistre, French diplomat
and political philosopher.*

KINGS
OF THE
KREMLIN

Russia and its Leaders
from Ivan the Terrible
to Boris Yeltsin

SOL SHULMAN

BRASSEY'S

In Memory of my parents –
Efim Shulman and Nina Ufland
who shared all the hopes and tragedies
of Russia in the 20th century.

First published in 2002 by Brassey's

A member of **Chrysalis** Books plc

Brassey's
64 Brewery Road, London N7 9NT

North American orders:
Books International, PO Box 960, Herndon, VA 20172, USA

Sol Shulman has asserted his moral right
to be identified as the author of this work.

Library of Congress Cataloging in Publication Data available

British Library cataloguing in Publication Data
A catalogue record for this book is available
from the British Library

ISBN 1 85753 361 5

Translated by Alex Shulman
Edited and designed by DAG Publications Ltd
Designed by David Gibbons
Edited by John Gilbert
Printed in Great Britain by
Creative Print and Design (Wales), Ebbw Vale

CONTENTS

Author's Note, 7

Preface, 9

PART ONE

1 Barbarian Russia, 13

2 Wild Motifs of Distant Times, 24

3 The False Kings, 43

4 The Tragic Dynasty, 60

5 The Great Skipper, 71

6 'Moscow isn't the Home of the Czar,
  Moscow is the Home of Russia Herself!', 87

PART TWO

7 Leader in an Accursed Time, 93

8 The Country and the Despot, 123

9 The Jester and the King, 175

10 A Cult without Personality, 205

11 A Cop in a Dinner Jacket, 227

12 The Leader History didn't Notice, 241

13 Prince Hamlet on the Kremlin Stage, 249

14 The Guy from the Urals, 274

Bibliography, 327

Index, 329

AUTHOR'S NOTE

MYSTERY IS AN ANCIENT KREMLIN TRADITION, especially when it comes to the lives of the rulers who have lived there.

Kings of the Kremlin aims to uncover some of the mystery. It does not propose any complex academic or political goals: it is simply an account of the private lives and personal qualities of the people, who, ruling from the Kremlin fortress, determined the destiny and sharp turns of Russian and Soviet history.

For many centuries, the fate of the Kremlin was the fate of all Russia. By giving my own personal impression of what went on under its roof, I hope to give the reader an opportunity to understand better some of the patterns in the complicated and difficult fate of Russia – 'The secret of the Russian soul', as Russians themselves say.

I would like to express my gratitude to the friends and colleagues who have helped make this work a reality. The first of these is Andrew Stewart, the former president of the New York publishing association Stewart, Tabori & Chang, who stood at the idea's wellspring. A number of thoughts expressed in this book were suggested to me by my now deceased friend, the wonderful Russian writer and historian Natan Eidelman. We were preparing to write this book together, but fate decreed otherwise. My old friend, the talented Moscow artist Boris Zhutovsky helped me with photo-materials and personal recollections. My heartfelt thanks for their advice and assistance goes to my friends, the director of the Moscow Architecture Museum, Professor Vladimir Rezvin, and one of the most famous art-historians in all of Moscow, the now deceased Professor Boris Brodsky.

PREFACE

ON AN AUTUMN DAY IN 1147, the Russian Prince Yuri – known by his people as 'Longarms' for his ability to meddle deftly in the affairs of others and sink his long arms into their property – invited his neighbour, Prince Svetoslav, to 'come to see me in Moscow, brother, and the feast will be mighty!'

It is unlikely that this feast was in any way different from a host of similar revels of that time, but news of the event found its way into ancient Russian chronicles, where the word 'Moscow' was first mentioned. The hill upon which the Prince's farmstead stood, surrounded by a palisade, was the extent of Moscow at that time. It is from this hearty dinner that the chronology of the Moscow Kremlin begins.

While Europe was completing the magnificent palaces of Rome, while the Crusades raged on the fields of Palestine, and the philosophy of a new epoch was being born, the Russian princes lived in half-buried cottages which were heated by filthy, chimneyless stoves. The windows were covered with membranous cow bladders, and around them the great forest teemed with wild animals. European civilisation was unimaginably remote for the feasting princes, almost inconceivable.

To get a better idea of the backwoods where the Kremlin was born, it is enough to recount an episode, located in a forest more or less in the same region as this feast was being held, where a battle was due to take place between two large rival war-bands. The battle, however, was never fought, since both adversaries got lost in the dense forest. Unable to find each other, each was compelled to return home.

Despite many centuries of lagging behind the leading European civilisations of the time, history set aside a special role for the Kremlin. From its inauspicious beginnings as a little wooden stockade, almost lost in the backwoods, the Kremlin became the heart of Russia. It was here that Russian sovereignty was born, where the first Russian Czar, Ivan 'The Terrible', was crowned. Over its centuries-long history, the Kremlin either rose favourably in the eyes of Orthodox Christians to the spiritual levels of a Third Rome, or burned in the inferno of wars and fires, only to be born again. The 850-year history of the Kremlin is the history of Russia as a whole, its fate and culture concentrated on this one focal point.

Time has robbed many great citadels of their might. Once possessing limitless power, they have been transformed into imposing but moribund museums of human history. The Acropolis of Athens will, in our eyes, forever be populated by ancient Greeks, Versailles will always remain full of courtiers in powdered wigs. Only two edifices rightly belong to both past and present and have survived: the Vatican and the Kremlin. Only they, while remaining important historical centres of world culture, did not become dead museums: and both remain centres of real power to this very day.

It is doubtful whether a similar national centre, which has affected the fate of its people and as deeply as the Kremlin, could be found anywhere in the world. Napoleon did not try to take the Vatican when he held Rome. He did not demolish the Hofburg in conquered Vienna. He did try, nevertheless, to blow up the Kremlin, since in the form of this fortress he saw a manifestation of the spirit of the people with whom he was at war. The Emperor thought, with good cause, that without the Kremlin the history of Russia would be compelled to flow in a different direction.

And he was right. It is no wonder that the Kremlin has always been the place where Russian Czars were crowned, even in the Petersburg period. At the word 'Kremlin', the consciousness of the true Russian person reverts to a genetic memory mechanism, an understanding of autocratic power as the essence of Russia.

This is why I have limited the scope of this work to the Kremlin. My task here is not to unravel for the reader the entire history of the Kremlin and its political life. On the contrary: it is not my intention to touch on politics and wars any more than necessary. I intend only to draw personal portraits of key figures who lived in and ruled from the Kremlin during key periods of Russian history. For, it is worth repeating, the fate of the Kremlin, which depended so greatly on the personalities of its rulers, is the fate of Russia condensed to a single focal point.

PART ONE

PART ONE

1 | BARBARIAN RUSSIA

ONE OF THE MOST DIFFICULT CENTURIES IN RUSSIAN HISTORY was the thirteenth. From the east, from the Central Asian steppes beyond the Caspian Sea, in clouds of dust accompanied by war cries and the stamping of hooves, hordes of Mongol-Tatar nomads moved on Russia. They were led by the warrior Ghengis Khan, who had brought all the nomadic tribes under his sway. From the west, under the banner of the Crusaders, mail-encased German knights were stood poised. It was a time when Russia's very existence was being decided.

The Mongols had a rule: if the enemy submitted, they were spared. If they resisted, all were indiscriminately annihilated, from new-born babies to old men. Russia resisted valiantly, and as a result suffered devastation wherever the conquerors had been; barely one-tenth of the population remained. As one historian wrote:

> Russia was a terrible sight after the Mongol-Tatar pogrom ...
> Mounds of burnt-out ruins instead of towns and villages, bleaching
> bones of the unburied dead, fields choked with weeds ... Hundreds of
> thousands dead, tens of thousands taken captive ... The living envied
> the dead their peace ...

Russia remained under the Mongol-Tatar yoke for 240 years (1240–1480). All Russian people, from princes to peasants, were considered slaves of the Khan, who was considered to be lord of Russia's lands by divine right. Russia's princes ruled their own lands by his benevolence, known as the 'Khan's right'. Moreover, he could grant them dominion and power over other princes.

The problem for a far-sighted Russian politician of the time was to walk the razor's edge and, using cleverness and cunning, to manipulate Russia's relations with her foes in such a way as to ensure her survival. One man who assumed this task was Alexander Nevski, Prince of Novgorod. Nevski understood perfectly that a pillaged and butchered Russia could not, at that moment, even consider breaking out from under the Mongol yoke through force of arms. Russia was destined to take a different historical road. Meanwhile, it was necessary to bow to the will of the conqueror, especially since Khan Bhati himself summoned Alexander, promising to grant him power over other Russian princes.

Staying in Bhati's camp, and observing the lives of the Mongol-Tatars at close range, Alexander soon realised that their power was built upon monolithic unity, unquestioning obedience to superiors, complete indifference to the fate of the individual, fanatical belief and intense ferocity towards all opposition: these were the qualities that made them mighty conquerors. At the same time, they were very patient with those who submitted to their rule and acknowledged their power, never infringing on other faiths and practices, even freeing churches and monasteries from tithes. They declared the Christian Church's possessions to be untouchable; blasphemy against the Orthodox faith was punishable by gruesome death.

Alexander wisely understood that submission would not only help save Russia, but would also bring the Russian princes benefits they did not have previously. Never before had Russian princes been undisputed masters of their fiefs: They were rulers, but not masters, who, according to ancient Russian tradition, had to share power with a people's assembly, the Veche. With the arrival of the Mongols, the situation changed. The Khan found it easier to govern the conquered lands through the princes who had submitted to him, rather than through an unpredictable people's assembly. Hence, in any way he could, he helped to strengthen their power and to weaken that of the Veche.

Here the interests of Khan and princes coincided. Every Russian prince who came to the Khan's camp and 'beat his brow' was granted ownership of his own fief, thus becoming its sole master. Gradually, the power of the princes quashed the ancient right of the Veche. Inherited from the Mongols, harsh autocratic rule was long to be an enduring feature of Russian life.

Alexander Nevski died in 1263, leaving four sons. The youngest, Danil, was still a child, and his portion of the inheritance – Moscow, just a little village – was the least favourable. Prince Danil died in 1303, leaving Moscow to his own son, Yuri. In 1315, at the Khan's command, Yuri travelled to Orda*, the centre of the Khan's power. He lived there for two years, gained the Khan's favour and married his sister. Returning to Russia, Yuri became the Great Prince, senior of all princes, and settled in the city of Novgorod. Eventually he handed down Moscow to his younger brother Ivan whose miserly habits earned him the nickname Kalita (a money-bag).

* The Horde

The eighteen years of Ivan Kalita's rule constituted the first period of Moscow's ascendancy over other Russian fiefs. This was facilitated not only by the beneficial geographic location of the city – on a high hill, at the junction of two ship-carrying rivers, surrounded by other Russians' fiefs which protected it from surprise attack by foreigners – but also because Ivan Kalita remained on good terms with the Khan.

If, prior to his rule, the Kremlin and Moscow had, for all practical purposes, been one and the same, now, beyond the Kremlin walls, sprawled a flourishing fiefdom, with a port, traders' stalls and merchants' warehouses. Here, on market days, peasants from neighbouring villages gathered, craftsmen brought their wares, and barges laden with goods came from other Russian towns to dock. Commerce on the Moscow River was lively as boats plied up and down it until late autumn.

Seeing the rapid rise of the Moscow fief, many boyars (feudal lords, members of the aristocracy), having the right to move to and fro and, naturally, wishing to live where life was richer and better, abandoned their local princes and joined those of Moscow. In exchange for their loyalty, the Prince of Muscovy gave them lands. In the wake of the boyars followed freemen, who were good potential conscripts for military service. Finally, even foreigners, including Tatars, began to move to Moscow, converting to Orthodoxy and becoming Russians. This was how the Tatar Chet, ancestor of the Godunov family which was to produce Czar Boris Godunov, came to Russian soil.

At the time of his death in 1341, Ivan Kalita also owned five other towns apart from Moscow, as well as a number of villages. Unfortunately, all this wealth fell into somewhat incapable hands. Kalita's eldest son, Semeon, who ruled Moscow from 1341–53, did not distinguish himself in any way, and the youngest son, Ivan II, who ruled from 1353–59, was an out and out scoundrel. Only their departed father's authority and the Khan's traditional favour upheld Moscow's prestige during the rule of these two princes.

Ivan II's heir was nine-year-old Dimitri, known to history as Dimitri Donskoy. During this time, the Mongol-Tatars experienced great political upheavals, which heralded the end of their power. As a result of assorted murders and coups, the Khan's throne changed hands six or seven times. Thus began the division of the Mongol-Tatar Khanate. The leader of one of its offshoots was the future Khan Mamai.

The weakening of the Khan's power led to the mobilisation of independence movements in the Russian princedoms. The province of Moscow, supported by the majority of the Russian princes, was the main site of this movement. On 8 September 1380, on the banks of the Don River, upon the fields of Kulikov, a massive battle was fought between the Russians and Mongol-Tatars. Historical chronicles state that some 150,000 soldiers gathered under the Russian banners, while the Mongol-Tatar numbers were legion. At first, Prince Dimitri was reluctant to cross the Don to battle on the far bank, but the boyars persuaded him, advising him to cross the river so that the Russian soldiers would have no excuse for retreat. 'If we overcome the Tatars, yours, Prince, and everyone's, will be the glory. If they cut us down, we will all die one death.'

The day began overcast, but then the clouds parted and the sun shone through. The battle started at noon. According to the chronicles, it was a battle such as Russia had not previously known. Blood flowed like rainwater, corpse fell upon corpse – Tatar on Russian, Russian on Tatar. When it seemed to the Russians that all was lost, the outcome was decided by a detachment waiting in ambush which struck the Tatars from the rear. The decimation was complete. Even the obese Khan Mamai ran, having lost his horse.

Although victory at the battle of Kulikov did not have a decisive effect, and the Mongol-Tatar reign of Russia continued for exactly one hundred years more, it had huge moral significance. For the first time in a century and a half of slavery and humiliation, Russian self-esteem could be asserted. It was for this battle on the Don River that Prince Dimitri became known as Dimitri Donskoy.

In Soviet times, historiography, from patriotic motives, always portrayed the figure of Dimitri Donskoy in a positive light, elevating him to the status of a national hero, for which there was more than a little foundation. However, some Russian historians evaluate him more cautiously. Here, for example, is what Nikolai Kostomarov, in a classic of Russian historical science, writes about him:

> The personality of the Great Prince Dimitri Donskoy is presented via the chronicles as unclear ... a mixture of resoluteness and indecisiveness, valor and cowardice, intelligence and tactlessness, forthrightness and cunning.

Kostomarov's conclusions were drawn from and influenced by some pages from one of the old Russian chronicles, a piece of literary history entitled *The Tale of the Slaughter of Mamai*, in which the battle of Kulikov is described. Although Kostomarov maintains that this tale could in no way be taken to be an accurate historical document, he did draw certain conclusions from it. The story describes how, before the battle, Dimitri dressed a retainer in the bright mantle of the Great Prince, while himself changing into the clothes of a simple soldier, ostensibly so he could fight alongside his men. In fact, according to the tale, he chickened out. The retainer, wearing the prince's mantle, was killed in battle, whereas Dimitri was later found lying under a felled tree, covered in its branches, barely breathing from fear, but unwounded.

What is truth and what invention here is hard to say. History has its own peculiarities and chooses its heroes as it desires. However, regardless of the personal qualities of Prince Dimitri Donskoy, the battle of Kulikov was – and remains – a proud and important landmark in Russian, and possibly European, history, since it marked the beginning of the liberation of Russian lands from the Mongol-Tatars, thus halting their spread westward. As the great Russian poet Alexander Blok wrote in his famous poem *The Scythians*: 'We, like faithful servants, / Held a shield between two warring races, / The Mongols and Europe ...'

Dimitri Donskoy died in 1389 at the age of forty, leaving the princedom to his son Vasily (1385–1425), who, as the chronicles maintain, was somewhat more intelligent and cunning than his father. Vasily supervised the active expansion of Moscow's princedom at the same time as the Khanate fiefs continued to weaken and fragment due to internal conflicts. Muscovites even stopped paying tribute to the Khan, considering themselves independent of him. But in 1408 a Mongol army unexpectedly approached the walls of the Kremlin. They could not take the citadel, but thoroughly looted and pillaged the neighbouring towns and villages, demonstrating their capability for raids and destruction.

Prince Vasily's heir was his eldest son, also named Vasily. Not notable initially for intellect or force of will, he gained a reputation for guile. In 1446, Russia was embroiled in internal strife. At this time, while visiting a monastery, Vasily was captured by another prince, thrown into a dungeon, and blinded (which earned him his nickname, 'The Dark'). Public indignation, which in Russia always supports the victim, saw him freed from prison and restored to his princedom. If the sighted Vasily had been an ineffectual ruler, with the loss of his sight his reign was marked by intelligence, will and decisiveness. The most likely explanation is that the blind prince became more in need of assistance, and started listening to wise counsellors.

Vasily the Dark appointed his eldest son Ivan as co-ruler, with the title of Great Prince, on a par with his father. When he died, in 1462, he left Ivan III, often referred to, with just cause, as Ivan the Great, as sole ruler. Ivan was a complicated, contradictory individual, but in no way negligible. Indeed, he was a cold, calculating and cruel man, a worthy grandfather to the future Ivan the Terrible. Without knowledge of the course of Ivan III's reign, it is impossible to understand the evolution of Russia, since it was he who laid the foundation for many official policies and actions – uncompromising and often despicable – which were to take root in Russian soil for centuries to come.

As Ivan III's power grew, so did his cruelty increase. The prisons filled, horrible tortures became everyday events and shameful public floggings, unknown in old Russia, were staged for the first time. In time, Ivan III developed into a classic despot; he did not shirk from personally cutting the noses and lips off captives in order to inspire fear. Even the most influential of courtiers feared to cross the grim prince in the slightest particular, as his one glance could put heads on the block. The chronicles tell that women would fall into a faint at his ominous glare. During a feast, the highest nobles of the court, fearing even to fidget or cough lest they incur his wrath, would sit for hours in grave-like silence, slavishly waiting for the dozing prince to wake up and order everyone to begin celebrating again.

It was during the reign of Ivan III that Russian lands were finally freed from Mongol-Tatar dominion. Liberation arrived more or less peacefully, without bloodshed, thanks to the final disintegration of the Khanate, despite its plan for one further battle which, thankfully, failed to take place.

Although Khan Ahmat moved his army on Moscow in an attempt to restore his lost influence, this was by no means the fearsome Mongol-Tatar army of old. The Russian battalions, hardened by battle, were a good match for the enemy. Nevertheless, Prince Ivan was nervous. Rumours of ill omen spread among the people, who reported that at night the Moscow church bells had rung of their own accord, and that one church dome had collapsed.

Ivan panicked and returned to Moscow, leaving his generals in command of the Russian army that had moved to meet the enemy in the field. The people, who had feared but never loved Ivan, on seeing that he was not with his troops but in the capital, were overcome with rage. 'You, Lord, rule us and while all is quiet and well, you fleece us mercilessly, but when misfortune comes, you abandon us to it.' 'You fear death,' the archbishop told him angrily, 'but you are not immortal … If you are fearful, then hand your troops over to me. I may be old, but I will not spare myself. I will not turn my face when it comes time to stand against the Tatars.'

In reality, the Tatars were in even greater fear of the Russians. The Khan departed without giving battle, signalling the moment that Russia was finally freed of the Mongol-Tatar yoke.

Today, looking back from a distance of almost five centuries, two and a half centuries of Mongol-Tatar oppression represents, figuratively, a small trench choked with weeds, an historical scratch on the giant body that is Russia. In its time, this scratch appeared a gaping chasm, extending far beyond the horizon of time. Within the temporal space of 240 years, whole generations of Russian people were born and died. Many of them could only dimly imagine, through legends and stories, a distant time before Tatar rule; and none could glimpse a likely end, still many decades away.

To gain a better understanding of the historical period, let us move to Europe, then being shaken by dissent and civil war. The revolutionary ideas of men such as Martin Luther and John Calvin – particularly their rejection of the role of the Church as mediator between God and the Christian – gathered strength. Shaken to its very foundations, the Church armed its faithful, from the lowliest monk to the Pope, for the defence of its threatened doctrines. Executioners' blocks were set up in the squares of European cities. Priests and soldiers, lords and peasants, shouted battle cries to drown out the voice of freedom ringing from the heights of the Wartburg Castle, where Luther had taken refuge. Only Moscow, in its age-old, God-forsaken isolation, remained indifferent to these European storms. Russia barely noticed them. Only rarely did the hollow echoes of the distant struggle reach her gates.

At this point, a new danger loomed: Islam was preparing to advance on the Christian world. Fearful in the face of this new threat, Rome and Vienna, Venice and Geneva all looked for a new ally and turned their gaze upon the little-known town of Moscow. European diplomats began trying to build bridges to the distant barbarian tribes of Russia. This was no easy task, since Russians viewed Europe as an unknown and despised land. Chance came to the aid of both sides.

In 1471 Ivan III was widowed, and the Pope of Rome decided to arrange a match between him and Sophia Palaeologus, the niece of the Emperor of Byzantium. In 1453, the Turks had taken Constantinople by storm, bringing about the fall of the one thousand-year Byzantine Empire. Sophia was the last member of the imperial Palaeologus family. In Rome, where the Czarina-to-be was in hiding, she received a good education. She was intelligent and diplomatic. The Pope had every reason to believe that, with this marriage, he would forge sturdy links between Rome and Moscow. But he had no way of foretelling that the marriage would later give Russian Czars a foundation for proclaiming Moscow itself the Third Rome.

Although only a small portion of the Byzantine emperors' treasures could be saved, the dowry that Sophia carried to her fiancé in the Kremlin was not modest. The most valuable part of this dowry was the magnificent library of Byzantium, the rarest of hand-written books in massive golden bindings. As the *Chronicles of Livon* maintain, no court in Europe had such a library at its disposal, and comparable only to the Library of Ptolemy in Alexandria, the greatest library in the Old World until it was destroyed by fire. For example, Europe in its entirety could boast only 35 volumes of *History* by Titus Livius (Livy), while the library that was brought to the Kremlin boasted 140 volumes. The fame of the Roman poet Caius Calvus in the Ancient World rivalled that of Cicero, yet the libraries of Europe did not contain a single line of his writings, while the Byzantine collection contained his complete works. Of the twelve books of Tacitus brought to the Kremlin, Europe knew of only four. These literary treasures were placed in a special inner hall of the Kremlin where not a single foreigner was permitted entry for almost a hundred years. It was not until the reign of Ivan the Terrible that the scholar Johann Watermann was granted access to this library, and it is from his writings that we have received detailed information about it.

Later history of the library remains another Kremlin mystery. In 1571, the Crimean Tatars besieged and set fire to the Kremlin. The fire was so fierce that 'stone churches settled from the heat, and metal beams burnt through and broke'. In one version of this tale, about 80,000 people died in and around the Kremlin, but the library was saved. On the orders of Ivan the Terrible, the books were entombed below the Kremlin in an underground bolt-hole known only to a few people close to the Czar. These confidants, however, died in the fire. The Czar's family abandoned the Kremlin and moved to a residence in the outskirts of Moscow for a number of years. This was the period of Ivan's life when he most readily succumbed to drunken revels and bloodthirsty orgies. He had no time for books in foreign tongues he did not understand. The library was forgotten. When, after many years, the Kremlin was restored and new palaces rose out of its ashes, the library's subterranean hiding place had disappeared. Archaeologists have not given up hope of finding it: the search for it continues to this day.

The marriage of Ivan III to a Byzantine princess elevated him even higher in the eyes of his courtiers.

With Sophia's appearance in the Kremlin came Byzantine lavishness and new customs: for example, kiss the Prince's hand in greeting, bow to the very ground. Closer ties with the West were established, especially with Rome, although building such links was no simple matter, hindered by the lack of sufficient people who would make worthy representatives of Russian embassies abroad. Russian manners were so coarse that when sending an ambassador, the Prince had to include in their orders: don't carouse, don't fight among yourselves, and thus don't shame our homeland.

In truth, Moscow was still not a town but remained a large village. Wealthier residents surrounded their plots with high fences, inside which stood their cottages, barns and other farmyard constructions. The smell of faeces and the cries of livestock filled the air. Being accustomed to the delights of Rome, Sophia and her foreign entourage did not find the Moscow of this time agreeable. She and her entourage told the Prince about the splendour of European cities: he soon began to crave architectural changes.

The Assumption Cathedral in the Kremlin, built back in Kalita's day, was so run down by now that it could have collapsed at any moment. It was decided to build a new cathedral. Russian craftsmen, invited from far and wide, laid the foundations and erected one wall of the new cathedral, but when they raised it to the height of the dome, it collapsed. One can only imagine the Prince's fury and the number of heads that flew.

Ivan III ordered his ambassador in Rome to find an architect there who knew how to build churches. Italy never suffered from a lack of architects, but who would be keen on travelling to a distant unknown land? After a long search, an architect from Bologna, Rudolfo Fiorovanti, who in addition knew how to cast cannon and bells, and to mint coins, agreed to go for a salary of ten roubles a month (generous for those times). He was nicknamed Aristotle for his intelligence and great knowledge. Fiorovanti was the first Italian architect to arrive in Russia, paving the way for the many European craftsmen who were to follow.

In 1479, after the consecration of Fiorovanti's Assumption Cathedral, where all subsequent coronations of Russian Czars took place, construction began in earnest at the Kremlin. In 1489, the new Annunciation Cathedral was erected, fulfilling the role of Ivan's family church. The Kremlin was surrounded by a new stone wall, with magnificent gates and towers. In place of an old dilapidated church, the new Archangel's Cathedral arose as the burial place of royal personages. A new stone palace was built for the Great Prince and, finally, another masterpiece of the Kremlin: the Granavitaya Chamber, which stands to this day, a place for illustrious gatherings and for receiving foreign dignitaries.

On Ivan III's orders, not only architects but also healers, jewellers, siege engineers, mining engineers, masters of casting and engraving bells, artillery-makers and many others were invited to Moscow. In 1482, the Italian Debosis cast the famous CzarCannon which, although it has never been fired, still amazes visitors to the Kremlin with its massive size. (The Russian expression 'another Czar-Cannon', incidentally, denotes something expensive but useless.)

Unfortunately, the lives of foreign specialists in Moscow were not very enviable. Having arrived of their own free will to work for wages, they often found themselves in the position of prisoners, risking their heads. For instance, Ivan III's eldest son fell ill but Léon, the healer from Venice, was unable to save him. Although Léon had told the Prince as much, on the fortieth day after his son's death, Ivan ordered the healer to be beheaded. Another healer, a German called Anton, who long enjoyed the favour of the Great Prince, was unable to heal a Tatar prince staying in Moscow and was 'handed over with his head' to the prince's son. The son tortured the poor healer, took a large ransom for him and was then prepared to let him go, but Ivan insisted that the Tatar should kill him. According to the chronicles, fulfilling the wishes of the Great Prince, the Tatar took the healer under the bridge on to the ice of the Moscow River and slaughtered him there with a knife, like a sheep.

Such events could not help but scare Fiorovanti, who asked permission to return home to Italy. The furious Ivan, who considered every resident to be his slave, ordered the architect stripped of all he had earned and thrown into prison. After a time, Fiorovanti was released in order to continue captive service in Russia. There are unsupported stories that in the end he was killed after all.

Ivan III's despotism, and his unceremonious treatment of foreigners, did not help to attract educated people to Moscow. After the fall of Byzantium, many Greeks settled throughout Europe, bringing with them their ancient culture, which played a pre-eminent role in the process of the European Renaissance. Relatively few educated Greeks settled in Russia, which aspired to be heir to Byzantium, where the Greek faith was practised and the ruler's wife was Greek; their influence on Russian culture was markedly less than it would have been reasonable to expect.

Sophia died in 1503. The time had come for Vasily, her son by Ivan, to marry. On the advice of a Greek courtier, the choice of bride was made in the

Byzantine tradition. One thousand five hundred of the prettiest girls were brought to the palace. The first elimination round was conducted by the old boyars and their wives. Then came the turn of the midwives, scrutinising the girls in terms of good childbearing characteristics. Thus, only the best and worthiest were finally paraded before the groom. Vasily chose the splendid Solomonia Saburova, daughter of a little-known courtier.

The marriage of Vasily III and Solomonia Saburova was not successful – the Princess was barren. After twenty years of marriage, Vasily ordered his wife's head shaved and that she be sent to a nunnery. He then married Helena Glinskaya, daughter of a Lithuanian courtier. Beautiful, caring but at the same time headstrong, Helena charmed and even subordinated Vasily, who, to please her, shaved his beard, an act that, in the Russia of the time, bordered on the revolutionary.

The marriage promised to be happy, but five long years passed and still there was no heir. It seemed that the nun's habit also awaited the 50-year-old Vasily's second wife. Then, the heavens smiled on her. Bells tolled across Russia, and happy news swept the land – the Princess was pregnant. On 25 August 1530, Russia received its long-awaited heir. Of course, no one could possibly have imagined that he would go down in history under the name of Ivan the Terrible.

2 | WILD MOTIFS OF DISTANT TIMES

THE FIGURE OF CZAR IVAN IV, known for his cruelty as Ivan the Terrible, is one of the greatest riddles of Russian history, which generations of historians have sought to unravel. Some consider Ivan a progressive individual for his times, even a genius, doubling Russia's landholdings and imposing firm sovereign rule over Slavic lands for the first time in history. Others consider him a madman, a degenerate whose savagery outstripped that of Nero or Caligula, and who destroyed his people's budding love of freedom, a passion so inherent among Europeans that it threw Russia back many centuries in its social development – a regression that is still being felt to this day. The fearsome shadow of Ivan the Terrible has pursued this much-suffering country for centuries, providing 'inspiration' to subsequent tyrants. Four hundred years later, history repeated itself in almost exact detail in the form of Joseph Stalin, for whom Ivan was an exemplar and teacher.

According to his contemporaries, Czar Ivan was 'of great height, had a fearsome and intelligent face, a mind cunning and great, very partial to lasciviousness, and in cruelty and bloodthirstiness, indefatigable'. He was a master of the pen, aspiring to be the greatest writer of his day, and even composed music. Recently, among some ancient manuscripts, works of church music, written by the Czar himself, were found. Some hold the opinion that they are 'senseless mooing, a concert for the axe and the block', others detect a wild beauty in those distant motifs.

Legend has it that, on the day of Ivan IV's birth, peals of thunder were heard across the whole land. Let legends remain legends, while we concern ourselves with the facts. Three years after his son's birth, Vasily III died. Although the official heir to the throne was the young Ivan, the reins of power were in fact assumed by his energetic and ambitious mother. For a woman to rule, in the Russia of that time, was not only unusual but also an insult, so it should come as no great surprise that several years hence, according to one historical version, Helena was poisoned by her courtiers. The eight-year-old Ivan was left an orphan. A vicious struggle for power ensued among the boyars in the Kremlin. Within days of the death of his mother, Ivan's favourite guardian was murdered before his eyes. This was followed shortly afterwards by the murder of the nursemaid who had replaced Ivan's mother. Only the fierce antagonism between foes thirsty for power, and their vicious mutual destruction, saved the life of Ivan himself. All this inevitably influenced the character of the already impressionable youth. Throughout his life, Ivan's fear and hatred of the boyars persisted, and as a result would cost Russia a great deal of blood.

The future despot-Czar grew up in the atmosphere of this violent struggle to be vengeful, nervous and cruel. Already, in games and pastimes with friends, Ivan demonstrated the inhumanity which prevailed in the environment that surrounded him. One of his favourite sports was to hurl cats and dogs off the high Kremlin towers and to watch their death throes. His courtiers not only failed to prevent such pursuits, but even condoned them, not understanding that soon, very soon, it would be the turn of people as well. Indeed, the pastimes gradually altered. When he was fourteen, the future Czar, together with boys of his age, would gallop through the streets and marketplaces, knocking down people and assaulting women who crossed his path. Long before Louis XVI, Ivan was already proclaiming, 'I am the State!'

In late 1546, at the age of sixteen, Ivan announced that he intended to marry and assume the throne. Furthermore, he did not intend to take the title Great Prince of Moscow, as his grandfather and father had done, but that of Czar.

It needs explaining at this stage that such a change in title had immense significance. In Slavic church manuscripts, it had long since been hinted that the Kremlin rulers were the direct descendants of the rulers of the Roman Empire and of Byzantium. This idea was especially strengthened after the marriage of Ivan the Terrible's grandfather, Ivan III, to the last Byzantine princess, Sophia Palaeologus. So, in an underhanded way, the notion was being engendered that, after the fall of the great Roman Empire and subsequently of Byzantium (which was known as the Second Rome), the centre of world Christianity was destined to move to Moscow – the Third Rome. This proud dream had long been fostered in the Slavic world, taking root in popular consciousness.

The conversion of Moscow into the Third Rome was prevented only by the fact that the rulers of the Kremlin were not emperors. It was with this in mind that Ivan IV took upon himself the title of the first Russian Czar. Since, in the Slavic language, the terms 'Czar' (from Caesar) and 'Emperor' are synonymous, it seemed that the historic dream was becoming a reality. Hence, in the eyes of Orthodox Christians, the young Czar appeared in a halo of glory and majesty such as none of his predecessors had known. As one proud

Russian monk announced: 'Two Romes fell, the Third stands, and there will not be a Fourth.'

In January 1547, Ivan was officially crowned Czar; immediately afterwards his wedding was lavishly celebrated in the Kremlin. As with his father before him, more than a thousand girls were brought to the Kremlin: beautiful, noble and to the Czar's liking (on the plump side). Ivan chose the pretty and gentle Anastasia Zaharina, who had just turned fifteen, to be his bride. According to Ivan's own memoirs, of all his seven or eight wives, Anastasia was his favourite, having had at least some influence on him. It seemed for a while that this angel of a wife might be the one to restrain the Czar's bursts of anger and bring peace to his subjects. Unfortunately, this was not to be. The marriage did not change Ivan's character. If he did soften, it was not for long.

The youngsters' honeymoon was abruptly interrupted by a terrible fire that raged through the Kremlin. Everything that could burn was consumed. Rumours spread across Moscow that sorcerers among the boyars were to blame; they had allegedly removed the hearts from corpses, soaked them in water, and sprinkled this water over the Kremlin's buildings, thus starting the blaze.

Surrounding the temporary residence to which the royal family then moved, the enraged mob began to threaten the Czar, demanding harsh punishment for those responsible for the fire. Like all his contemporaries, Ivan was a superstitious man, and possibly believed the rumours about the fire. It is far more likely, however, that this was simply a good excuse for him to engage in bloody slaughter among the boyars, whom he had loathed and feared since childhood. Without doubt, such a slaughter would have occurred even without the demands of the menacing mob, but the fiery young Czar saw these as an encroachment on his powers, the enforcement of another's will on his own. This Ivan would not tolerate, deciding to display his true character. As one chronicler wrote: 'The tyrant the people already knew becomes the sovereign they will now recognise.' In front of the Kremlin, Red Square was littered with severed heads. For the time being, these were the heads of the mob.

This event reinforced Ivan's decision to be rid of the guardianship of the boyars and to surround himself with commoners whom he himself would raise from the dust, and who would be loyal to him. It is worth remembering that the traditions of Moscow's government were immeasurably more ossified than those of any European country. The Czar could do whatever he wanted with individuals, but to raise a hand against entrenched custom was not easy, even for a tyrant such as Ivan the Terrible. Soon, however, another event nudged him towards making his move.

A few years after these events, Ivan fell ill. It is hard to say just how threatening his illness was, but knowing his love of theatricality, it is safe to assume that he dramatised the situation. Playing up the possibility of his imminent death, he decided to appoint his first-born baby son as heir and demanded that the boyars swear fealty to him. The inheritance of the throne by the eldest child was a fairly recent institution in Russia and not yet established custom, so the boyars wavered, especially considering that the Czar's cousin was also contending for the throne. When, in his very presence, the majority of boyars took his cousin's side, Ivan fell into a rage.

Eventually Ivan recovered, but apparently this was the last straw for his vulnerable pride. As soon as he was well again, he travelled in the heart of winter to a distant monastery to pray, thereby fulfilling a pledge he had made when ill. While Ivan was on this journey, his new-born son caught cold and died, and several years later his beloved wife also died. Infuriated, Ivan accused the boyars – wrongly – of poisoning the Czarina; he vowed to avenge her, brutally. From this moment on, the 'work of the axe and block' policy commenced; it would continue without respite until the end of his life.

On 3 December 1564, amazed Muscovites were witness to a strange, even mysterious, spectacle. Without warning, the Czar's convoy, numbering several hundred wagons and surrounded by thousands of warriors and servants, rode out of the gates of the Kremlin and headed for an unknown destination. It was not that the Czar was abandoning the Kremlin – such a departure had happened before. But this time he took with him all his goods and chattels, including his treasures – gold, icons, crosses, precious plates. Travelling with the Czar was his new bride, Maria Temrukova, daughter of the Prince of Circassia.* Maria was rumoured to be every bit as fiery, cruel and debauched as Ivan himself.

For a time, no one knew where the Czar had gone or why. Some time after his departure, news reached Moscow that the Czar's convoy had taken up residence some one hundred versts from the capital, not far from the old Russian town of Vladimir, in a small village known as Alexander's Settlement. This news did nothing to unravel the mystery. Finally, the Czar's messenger arrived in Moscow with a letter for the Archbishop. In it the Czar wrote at length of all the ills inflicted on him by the boyars and higher clergy; he also announced

* A nationality from the Northern Caucasus.

that he was casting all his subjects, without exception, into disgrace. Such a pronouncement meant to be removed from the Czar's favour as having incurred his wrath. In effect, any such person lost all the rights of a citizen and was defenceless against another's tyranny. In conclusion, the Czar announced, he was abandoning his country, abdicating his throne, and would settle 'where God wills it'.

Russians were ever partial to theatricality, so the Muscovites understood what had to be done. The Czar was obviously enraged at certain individuals and was preparing something dastardly against them, but for now, he was setting the scene. Moscow decided to support this base comedy. The boyars lapsed into confusion, the populace became agitated. The Archbishop was urged to persuade the Czar to replace rage with mercy, and to 'take back his country'. A delegation was sent to Alexander's Settlement. The Czar magnanimously allowed himself to be persuaded, but announced that he would behead all his enemies, and would only return to the Kremlin when he organised his *oprichnina*.

There is no simple translation for the word *oprichnina*; it is not even comprehensible to modern Russians. It denotes something along the lines of a hand-picked punishment squad gathered from the most bloodthirsty cutthroats, who have limitless powers and answer only to the Czar. Those who joined the *oprichnina* had to take an oath renouncing their father and mother, their duty being to root out and destroy the foes of the Czar. Their uniform was a black caftan, and they rode black horses decked with black breastplates. Tied to their saddles was a broom and a dog's skull, symbolising the resolve of the *oprichniki* to sweep treason from Russia's lands and, like faithful dogs, to bite the Czar's foes. The Czar would not listen to any complaints against the *oprichniki*, on pain of harsh punishment. Crossing an *oprichnik* was a crime that carried lethal consequences.

Exploiting their complete immunity, the *oprichniki* abused the people to an extent not even experienced under the Mongol-Tatar occupation. For loyal service, the Czar rewarded them with lands and holdings they had taken from their previous owners. And should the *oprichnik* show the slightest sign of mercy to anyone, he faced a life in prison, even death. Although, according to official history, the *oprichnina* flouished in Russia for no more than ten years, in fact, once instituted by Ivan the Terrible, it never again disappeared from Russian society.

Count Alexei K. Tolstoy's novel *Prince Serebrianny*, which recounts the life of Ivan the Terrible in Alexander's Settlement, was very popular among nineteenth-century Russian readers. After a long stay in Lithuania, the hero of the novel, Prince Serebrianny, returns to Russia with his war-band. He is not yet aware of what has occurred at home during his long absence. On the road, he meets a company of armed men who, by their appearance and behaviour, resemble bandits. Before the Prince's very eyes, they rob a village, rape the women and kill the men. The Prince protests at the slaughter, but is soon taken prisoner. The bandits turn out to be the Czar's *oprichniki*, whose outrageous excesses are condoned by the Czar himself. The Prince is brought to Alexander's Settlement, where he witnesses horrific scenes. At the Czar's court people are used as bait for hungry wild bears. Finally, having been spared torture, he finds himself at the Czar's feast. Dressed as monks, each with a knife under his robes, the cut-throat *oprichniki* sit alongside the terrified boyars. The Czar himself, laughing fiendishly, hands some of the boyars chalices filled with poisoned wine. As each man falls dead, the Czar, his face alight with pleasure, repeats the same phrase, over and over: 'The boyar is drunk; take him out!'

The feet of the revellers slither in pools of blood. The air hangs thick with the heavy stench of an abattoir. The din of the happy drunken voices of the *oprichniki* mingles with the cries of victims being tortured in the next room. It is like a scene from hell. The Czar orders one of the boyars, who refuses to consent to being dressed in jester's garb, to be killed at the very table. He forces another elderly boyar to gulp down a huge jug of wine; when the latter is unable to do so, Ivan sends him to the cellar to be strangled, crying, 'So that is how you show your goodwill to your Lord! You didn't want to drink? Then off to the cellar with you. There are many different drinks down there. There you shall drink your fill to my health!'

Tolstoy did not invent these scenes but based them on authentic historical facts. Indeed, in the preface to the book, he wrote that to spare the feelings of the reader and in the interests of art, he had toned down the horrors documented in the chronicles.

The appearance of the *oprichnina* introduced the bloodiest period of Ivan the Terrible's rule. According to an English diplomat who visited the Russian court at that time, Ivan was the exemplar of a wily, grasping despot. He was so hot-tempered that the slightest irritation would cause him to become 'covered in foam like a horse'. Pity or mercy were completely alien to him, and in the arts of torture and murder he was an unsurpassed virtuoso. The chronicles have preserved a number of examples of the bloodthirsty deeds he perpetrated on his own people. The following is an edited example of one of Ivan's many acts of reprisal carried out in Red Square before the Kremlin.

There were around three hundred victims. Yet to the amazement of the Czar, when he rode out of the Kremlin's gates, the square was empty. Ordinary folk were no longer attracted by the braziers, nor the red-hot tongs, nor the iron claws and needles, nor the ropes with which the bodies of the tortured were ripped apart, nor the cauldrons filled with boiling water and tar. Of late, this spectacle had been repeated too often; now the terrified people went into hiding. The Czar sent criers through the town, shouting, 'Come out! Don't be afraid! No one will be harmed!' From cellars and attics, the indispensable spectators began to appear.

One of the victims, a deacon of Moscow, was hung by his feet and dismembered like an animal corpse. A young boyar, accused of treason, was impaled. While he suffered for fifteen hours, the Czar's soldiers raped his mother to death before his eyes. Another victim, a sixty-year-old prince, was tied to a tree between two fires and burnt. The chronicles insist that Ivan himself heaped flaming coals closer to the body of the victim with his royal sceptre. Yet another old voivode (a high-ranking warlord) was destined to die along with his son, a seventeen-year-old youth. Both walked to their place of execution calmly, without fear, each holding the other's hand. The son did not want to see his father executed and placed his head beneath the blade first. The father moved him away from the block, imploring, 'Don't let me see you dead!' The youth allowed him to go first, took the severed head of his father, kissed it, glanced up at the sky and prepared himself joyfully for execution.

The royal physician, who had been unable to cure one of the Czar's courtiers, was burnt to death on a huge, specially made frying pan. The son of a former friend of the Czar was commanded to behead his own father. Ivan took an infant into his arms, kissed and fondled it, then slaughtered it with a blow of his knife and threw the body beneath the hooves of his horse. A former treasurer was drenched alternately with boiling and ice-cold water until his skin slipped off him like that of an eel. Even this did not seem enough. On Ivan's orders, the treasurer's young wife was taken and, before the eyes of her fifteen-year-old daughter, was seated naked across a rope tied between two poles and dragged repeated along the rope from one end of the square to the other. When the orgy was over, people were forbidden to remove the victims' bodies from Red Square for several days; there they lay, ravaged by dogs.

The cardinal rule of any form of terror is progression. The instigator can maintain a high level of motivation, coupled with utter insensitivity, by means of ever more violent and terrible acts. In this respect, Ivan surpassed not only all his predecessors, but also the semi-barbaric Khans, famed for their ferocity.

Shortly after the events described, Ivan and his *oprichniki* committed an even more terrible crime, this time on the citizens of the old Russian city of Novgorod. The citizens, hundreds at a time, were herded together and tortured by burning on a low flame. Almost all were then sentenced to death and taken away to be drowned. The bloodstained victims were tied by the head to sleighs and driven to the banks of the Volkhov River at a point where the water did not freeze in winter. Whole families were thrown together down a steep slope into the icy water; infants were drowned tied to their mothers. The Czar's soldiers, armed with spears, boat-hooks and hatchets, patrolled the river in boats; anyone who surfaced was cut to pieces.

The slaughter lasted many weeks. Every day more than a thousand people were sent to meet their maker. In one version of this tale, over sixty thousand people were put to death. The figure is horrifying, the entire Russian population at the time numbered only nine or ten million.

According to the chronicles, when he ran out of people to kill, Ivan vented his fury upon animals. Thus 'an elephant, a gift from the Persian Shah, did not wish to kneel before the Czar, and was slaughtered on the Czar's orders'.

What did it all indicate? Pathology, insanity – or sheer historical necessity? Arguments on the subject have hardly abated in Russia for well-nigh four centuries. A number of historians have come to the conclusion that this period was decisive for resolving a most important issue for Russia – whether history would lead her along the path of democracy and self-rule, or that of slavery and harsh absolutism. One writer gives a frightening analysis of how Ivan the Terrible's bloody rule affected future generations of Russians: 'The terror touched the future with a baneful hand. The cloud of informants and slanderers, like a swarm of hungry insects disappearing, left behind an evil seed in the people.'

This seed did not die; rather, it bore poisonous fruit.

❖   ❖   ❖   ❖   ❖

Half a century ago, the world-famous film director, Sergei Eisenstein, made the film *Ivan the Terrible* at Stalin's request. Try as he and his team might to soften the figure of Ivan in order to please Stalin, their hero inevitably ended up looking like a dangerous animal. This almost cost the director his head, since, as the years passed, Stalin came to admire Ivan more and more, seeing in him the ideal of a firm ruler, and rebuking him only for 'not cutting off enough heads'.

The great Italian psychiatrist Cesare Lombroso (1836–1909) once said that the thirst for blood and sensual love often merge, arousing carnal desire. Violent scenes are often followed by the most furious of sexual perversions. Lombroso's idea is characterised perfectly in the actions of Ivan the Terrible. His bloodthirsty orgies were accompanied by equally cruel perversions. According to one set of chronicles, women were snatched from their homes and taken to the Kremlin to fulfil the desires of the Czar and his henchmen. They were then strangled and returned to their homes where, for weeks on end, they hung above the tables at which their husbands and relatives were required to dine.

In fairness, it must be said that Ivan's cruelty was not unique to those times. Russia, backward and uncultured, was not alone; leading European powers were equally guilty. It is enough to remember the fires of the Inquisition in Spain, St Bartholomew's Day in France, the casemates and scaffolds of Henry VIII's England.

Many such examples can be given. So, taking into consideration the difference between European and Russian levels of culture, Ivan's behaviour is not necessarily untypical of the age. The difference was that Europeans often found the will to dispose of their high-handed rulers at the critical moment, whereas the Russian people viewed their monarchs with different eyes. For them, he was God's representative on earth; any of his actions were beyond reproach.

It was evidently at around this time that the expression 'Only God and the Czar know about that' began to be used when talking about something dubious. What is even more astonishing is that the simple folk not only put up with Ivan, but they actually loved him. In folksongs and folklore, Czar Ivan is never endowed with negative traits. On the contrary, he appears stern but fair, even magnanimous. In the preface to *Prince Serebrianny,* Alexei Tolstoy wrote: 'While reading the chronicles, the books would on occasion fall from my hands, and I would throw my quill in agitation, not so much from the thought that there could have existed such an animal as Ivan IV, but more so because there could have existed such a society that could have looked upon him without indignation.'

Sadism, punctuated by bouts of self-flagellation, is not an uncommon practice. Ivan's bloody orgies were often followed by pious, God-fearing humility. Wearing a monk's tattered robes and kneeling for five or six hours on end, torturing himself to exhaustion, the Czar, along with his henchmen, would prostrate himself before God, begging forgiveness for his sins. Ivan prayed so fervently that his forehead would become covered with bruises and scratches from hitting the floor. At these moments he would wail and weep, call himself 'a foul dog', and 'an animal gorging on human meat'. Then, without respite, he would head for his courtyard of torture to revel at the sight of suffering, or even participate personally in crushing the bones or flaying the flesh of yet another victim. At such times, his scowling features relaxed, and his joyous peals of laughter mingled with the cries of his victims. Ivan always returned from the courtyard in a good mood, cracking jokes as he sat down to dinner, after which he would retire to his bedroom. There, three psaltery players would sing and recite morally uplifting Bible stories. Eventually he would sleep the sleep of the righteous.

At first glance it might seem that a person who spills rivers of blood and does not value the lives of others should at least possess a degree of personal courage. Actually, this is not so. Ivan the Terrible, like his faithful follower Joseph Stalin, was a pathological coward.

Here is how the ancient chronicles describe Czar Ivan's behaviour in the battle for the city of Kazan between the Russians and the Tatars:

One of the Russian princes rode up breathlessly to Ivan, who was at that moment praying. 'Lord, it's time to ride. Your men are moving to engage the Tatars. Your battalions await you.' Ivan did not respond; he continued to pray. After some time, a new messenger arrived. 'Lord, our troops are weakening, the Tatars are getting the upper hand. Your presence is imperative to lift morale.' Ivan let out a heavy sigh, tears flowed from his eyes, and he began to implore the heavens to spare his life. In the end, the prince was obliged – almost forcibly – to seat the Czar on his horse, take the reins, and lead him to the place of battle.

◆　◆　◆　◆　◆

In the sixteenth century, the Kremlin was a small town within which, distributed over a relatively small area, stood almost twenty churches, jostled by scores of monasteries, courtiers' estates, market stalls and workshops. Compared to the splendour of European capitals, the Kremlin, to a foreigner's eyes, looked more god-forsaken than magnificent. However, this impression changed drastically when the visitor crossed the threshold of the Czar's court. In terms of luxury and its army of servants, the court of Ivan the Terrible surpassed anything the stranger might have seen in other lands. A multitude of courtiers, adorned with gold and precious stones, thronged the chambers and passages, filling the palace. In the words of the English writer and diplomat, Giles Fletcher, who visited the Kremlin of that period, Ivan the Terrible was 'the very rich Czar of a very poor country'. Fletcher could not believe his eyes when he saw Ivan's treasures. Piles of emeralds and rubies, mountains of golden plates, hundreds of golden chalices set with precious stones. All these riches were kept in special treasuries from which they were removed only on rare occasions to stupefy the imaginations of foreign dignitaries.

Under normal circumstances, however, the Czar's pattern of life was primitive and squalid. Even beds were a luxury in his chambers: his retinue usually slept on wooden benches crudely hammered together. The semi-transparent windows were covered with mica. Temperatures inside the palace went down to freezing point; water froze in mugs at the very dinner table. In contrast to the expensive, gold-embroidered garments which the Czar and his courtiers donned for official functions, within their private chambers they wore old, even patched, clothing.

Seating at the festive tables was arranged in order of seniority: 'by birth and by rank'. Fierce as Ivan was, no matter how feared by his guests, it was rare for a feast to pass without a squabble over seating. The pecking order corresponded to a boyar's ranking in the court, so neither disgrace nor the possibility of torture and death could force him to sit in a place he considered unfitting. Loss of a place at the table signified loss of rank, not only for himself, but for his relatives and descendants. If the Czar judged his objections unfounded, the boyar departed from the feast. If, however, he was brought back by force, he would crawl under the table. This is how Alexei Tolstoy described the start of a feast:

> Finally the trumpets sounded, the palace bells rang, and Czar Ivan himself entered at a slow pace ... He was tall, fit and wide of shoulder ...
> A large engraved cross hung about his neck on a golden chain. The high heels of his red Moroccan boots were bound in silver crampons. The classical face was still magnificent, but the features were more harshly defined, the hooked nose had somehow become more angled, the eyes burned with a dark fire and creases, which had not been there earlier, appeared on the brow. Ivan was thirty-five years old, but he looked well over forty. So a building changes after a fire: the chambers still stand, but the decorations have fallen, the dark windows look out balefully, and something unpleasant has taken up residence in the empty rooms.

The feast was served by two to three hundred men dressed in gold and silver brocade. Regardless of this grandeur, there were many discomforts here for a European. There were no plates or set cutlery, let alone napkins. The Russians used the knives and spoons that each wore constantly at their belts: there were no forks. The guests used their fingers to help themselves to pre-cut pieces from the platters. Each dish was served to guests in order of seniority; those sitting higher could dishonour those sitting lower by refusing to allow them to share a piece from their own dish.

A feast lasted six to eight hours, and consisted of one hundred or more dishes: fried swans on golden platters, peacocks with their tails displayed, their beaks sparkling with emeralds, rabbits, boar, smoked bear and deer, larks, quail, and many others. But the choicest items on the menu were the gigantic fish caught in the North Sea and transported live, in giant barrels, especially for the occasion. The fish were prepared and placed on the golden platters in such a way that they resembled winged serpents with gaping jaws. They were so large that each had to be carried by five or six men. For dessert, sugar cakes, each in the shape of the Kremlin and weighing around 100 kilos, were served. The walls of the citadel and every one of its towers were carved in meticulous detail, as were mounted and pedestrian figures. Surrounding these massive cakes were trees made of sugar, their branches adorned with muffins and sweetcakes. Beneath the trees were sugar figures of bears, lions, eagles and other animals.

From time to time, Ivan would order one of the guests to be served a piece of food or a chalice of wine from the Czar's table. The name of the recipient was announced loudly by a servant, who recited all the recipient's titles. The guest had to stand and bow, first to the Czar, then to his companions. After this, all present would stand and bow, first to the Czar, then to the guest. Fletcher reported that on one occasion he was obliged to stand and bow ninety-six times during the evening.

The necessity to sit at table for six to eight hours, and to drink and eat from all the dishes and chalices the Czar sent around, drove even the most resilient guest into a frenzy. It was also traditional to send the most honoured guests home with food as well. One diplomat recorded that he left one such feast with the following gifts from the Czar: eight dishes of roast swan, as many of roast crane, several platters of cockerel, roast boneless chicken, capercaillie, hazel-grouse in sauce, duck with pickled cucumbers, geese with rice, rabbit with noodles, deer brains, meat pies, nuts in sugar, jelly, and a hundred chalices of assorted wine.

Apart from this, it was traditional to force foreign diplomats to drink themselves into oblivion. On the one hand, it implied doing him an honour; on the other, it was an opportunity to belittle and laugh at him. In short, getting a foreign diplomat drunk was for the Czar's amusement. If he passed out from drink, servants would carry him home. If he managed to stay on his feet, he faced the task of finding his horse in the pitch-dark Kremlin night. Then, as soon as he got home, he would be accosted by one of the Czar's representatives bearing food and drink. The envoy would pour two huge chalices, proclaim a toast to the foreigner's sovereign, drain the chalice, and upturn it over his own head, to indicate that it was empty. Since the diplomat's refusal to drink would be disrespectful to his own sovereign, the Czar's man rode away secure in the knowledge that the foreign diplomat had finally drunk himself into senselessness.

These feasts, complete with fearsome gluttony and drunkenness, were among the favourite pastimes of the Czar's court. Further amusement was to be had in hunting, the antics of jesters, the keeping of tame and wild bears, and the playing of cards and chess. Chess was forbidden by the Church; only the Czar dared break this edict. Bear-baiting was completely in keeping with Ivan's character. At times he would release wild bears near an unsuspecting crowd; such entertainment would rarely end without victims.

The role of jester could be just as dangerous; but many paid for their jokes with their lives. Once, for fun, Ivan poured a bowl of hot soup on to the head of his favourite jester, who screamed in pain. Ivan, who was drunk, stabbed him in the throat with a knife – again as a joke — and later grieved the loss of his favourite. A court jester fulfilled a certain social role. With his sharp words, to some extent permitted, he satisfied the need for criticism and satire inherent in any society.

Finally, there was Ivan the Terrible's insatiable passion for women, so intense that some modern historians consider him to have been a sex maniac. The perversions in which he revelled often took extremely violent and repulsive forms. Several days before his death, he tried to rape his own son's wife. Rumour also had it that the Czar quenched his desire not only with women, but also with soldiers from his retinue.

Ivan's private family life was just as strange, just as whimsical, and at times just as monstrous as his public life. His first wife, Anastasia, died in 1560 at the age of twenty-eight, her health destroyed by an early marriage and constant childbearing. She had given birth to six children, only two of whom remained alive – Ivan, the eldest son, and Fyodor, the youngest.

Fyodor was a quiet, backward child, with the face of a simpleton and a weak constitution. As the English diplomat commented: 'He seemed to have little in the way of brains, and most likely none at all.' Growing up amidst blood and debauchery, Fyodor spent all his spare time praying or ringing church bells. Yet it was for Fyodor, completely unequipped as he was to rule, that fate, after the death of his father, prepared a place on the throne.

The eldest son, Ivan, emulated his father physically and morally, rivalling him in cruelty and perversion. He was Ivan's foremost companion in wild exploits and brutal orgies. By the age of thirty, the younger Ivan had already married three times. His latest wife, Yelena Sheremetieva, was pregnant when a tragedy was played out in the palace, a tragedy that would influence the future fate of the Czar and all Russian history.

Once, on entering his son's chambers, Czar Ivan saw his pregnant daughter-in-law, whose outward demeanour he considered to lack decency. Insulted by her inappropriate appearance, the Czar began beating her with his cane with such force that she immediately miscarried. Her husband came running at the sound of his wife's cries and threw himself at his father, trying to stop him. The enraged Czar struck his son a mortal blow on the temple with his cane.

The crime was committed unintentionally, but it exceeded even those bounds to which his contemporaries had grown accustomed. Ivan was in despair. He spent entire nights in tears, weeping in anguish; he even decided to abdicate the throne and enter a monastery. He proposed that the boyars choose a new Czar from among their number, but the boyars were afraid, certain that as soon as Ivan's grief died down, they would find their heads on the chopping block – which was close to the truth. As his contemporaries wrote, of all the events connected to the reign of Ivan the Terrible, the death of his son was what shocked the people's imagination most of all. To drown his grief, the Czar gave himself over to even more unfettered savagery and debauchery.

Despite Ivan's deep love for his first wife, Anastasia, only eight days after her death he courted the Polish Princess Katherine. The courtship was unsuccessful. A year later he married the Circassian, Maria, who was, as already noted, just as wayward and cruel as Ivan himself. In 1569 Maria died. Ivan imagined she had been poisoned by his enemies. Fear gripped him. He saw conspiracy and treachery everywhere. This was the period when he wrote his letter asking the English Queen Elizabeth for asylum in England, since in Russia he was being stalked by murderers. The Queen replied that the Czar of Moscow could come to England and live there as long as he pleased, 'all on his own means'.

Instead of fleeing to England, Ivan assembled two thousand young women in the Kremlin for the third time and chose from among them a merchant's daughter, the beautiful Martha Sobakina. Two weeks after the wedding, the young bride died. Ivan insisted that she too had been poisoned, and what is more, poisoned before the marriage had been consummated; he alleged she had died a virgin. (In this way the Czar could carry out his intent to marry a fourth time, which was forbidden by the Church.) Rumour had it that Martha pined away, or committed suicide, because she loved another.

On the Czar's orders, Martha was buried in secret inside the Kremlin, without honours. Centuries passed. It was not until the late twentieth century that, during excavation on Kremlin ground, a group of archaeologists discovered some steps leading down to a door. As it swung open, they saw – only for a moment – the face of a beautiful young woman who appeared to be alive. In an instant, the apparition disappeared; the face crumbled to dust. The scientists had no camera to hand, fresh air rushed into the chamber which had been sealed for four centuries, and the image was gone forever.

According to the laws of the Church, the Czar was not permitted to enter into a fourth marriage, but it was not in Ivan's character to submit to anyone else's rules. The Church was obliged to back down, but it did place an ecclesiastical order forbidding him to cross the threshold of a holy shrine. This was harsh punishment, since, according to tradition, the Czar had to begin and end each day in church. Breaking with this tradition would deprive him of the possibility of bliss in the afterlife. Ivan evaded this restriction rather cunningly. He ordered the construction of a staircase leading directly from the street to the cathedral balcony. In this way, he could attend the service without crossing the threshold.

Anna Koltovskaya became Ivan's fourth wife, but this marriage was also short-lived. After a year, Anna already bored her husband; she was incarcerated in a nunnery where she spent the remainder of her days. After her departure, Ivan took two concubines simultaneously, Anna Vasilchikova and Vasilisa Melentieva. Many legends about these two women circulated among the people, and their fate inspired poets and novelists. In the end, Anna Vasilchikova was killed on the Czar's orders; he parted from her with the words, 'You've lost weight. I don't like skinny ones.'

Yet another wife, Maria Dolgorukaya, appeared in the Czar's chambers. After the first night the enraged Ivan left her, claiming she was not a virgin.

On his orders, she was placed in a carriage pulled by wild horses and, together with the vehicle, was drowned in a pond. As the English diplomat John Gorsei noted:

> This pond was a true Gehenna, a vale of death, akin to a place of human sacrifice; many victims were drowned in this pond, the fish within it ate of an abundance of human flesh and were found to be exceptionally tasty and suitable for the Czar's table.

While Ivan rearranged his love life, the Polish King Stephen Bathory was capturing city after city from him. Ivan sent an emissary to Poland to ask that Bathory halt his military activities during yet another of the Czar's weddings. In response, Bathory wrote to Ivan:

> You are not the Lord of your people, but their executioner. You have grown accustomed to treating your subjects like cattle, not like people. The greatest wisdom is to know yourself and so that you might better know yourself I am sending you books written about you across the whole world ... Do you think that rule everywhere is the same as it is in Moscow? Every Christian King, upon being anointed, must swear that he will rule, not without reason ...

Having swallowed this bitter pill, Ivan once again gathered young ladies together in the Kremlin and chose Maria Nagoy for his wife. She gave birth to Czarevich Dimitri, who was younger than his brothers by thirty years. The tragic fate of Dimitri, which will be discussed in a later chapter, influenced the history of Russia in a crucial way.

Yet even this was not the end of the Czar's love affairs. According to English sources, towards the end of his life, Ivan asked Queen Elizabeth of England to send him her niece, the grey-eyed beauty Mary Hastings, as his wife. At this time he was still technically married, but he was ready to send his wife to a nunnery or to the next life at the drop of a hat. Elizabeth did not refuse the Czar outright, but in deference to her niece, did not hurry to answer.

The Byzantine method of choosing a wife from the 'herd', begun by Ivan's father Vasily III and continued by his son, facilitated the enslavement of Russian women, which, on the whole, had not been their fate in the past. Earlier lords and rulers married their equals, and in choosing a bride took into account not only her outward appearance but also her breeding; now a potential bride was looked upon as no better than a heifer, obliged to produce heirs. There was no further discussion of marriages of equals. No matter what her family background, the wife of a monarch was compelled to sever all ties with her loved ones. Her father did not have the right to call her daughter, her brothers could not call her sister. She belonged only to her lord, both as his wife and his subject, which enslaved her twice over. Her husband chose her on a whim, and could cast her out just as frivolously. There was no one to stand up for her. Yet, although she was a slave, she was also the Czarina. There was no one with whom she could communicate as an equal, and she remained the lonely, unhappy prisoner of her situation. Moreover, since the fashions and morals of the monarch's court were invariably adopted by his subjects, the domestic enslavement of women quickly spread across Russia.

With the years, Ivan became more and more neurotic and suspicious. He no longer even trusted his loyal hounds, the *oprichniki*. By the 1580s, he had changed his entire court retinue five or six times, for the most part by executing them. Now, his new trusted servant was the clever and cunning boyar Boris Godunov, whose sister Irene Godunov was married to the heir to the throne, Ivan's weak-minded son Fyodor. Knowing Ivan's character well, Godunov understood that his influence on the Czar, like that of his predecessors, would be short-lived, and that his life was in danger. According to one historical version, Godunov decided to act, all the more since, from early 1584, the Czar was beginning to manifest symptoms of a serious illness. His body was bloated and he began to give out an intolerable stench. The doctors determined that he had a blood disorder.

According to the English diplomat John Gorsei, Boris Godunov ordered the court astrologers to foretell the date of the Czar's death. What is more, he warned them that if their prediction did not come to pass, they would be burnt alive. This ploy was equivalent to offering a reward for the Czar's murder. The astrologers informed Ivan that he would die on 18 March 1584 at the age of fifty-four. News of the prophecy spread across Moscow. Ivan both believed and disbelieved the prediction; nevertheless, he prepared for death.

Gorsei described the unusual scene that he witnessed. The dying Czar, who invited Gorsei to accompany him and his royal doctor, ordered himself to be carried to his treasure room, where all the valuables he would now be obliged to part with were stored. Taking several pieces of turquoise in his hands, he turned to Gorsei. 'See how it changes colour, how it grows pale? That means I have been poisoned. This is an omen of my death.'

The Czar ordered a sceptre made of rhinoceros horn, thought to have healing properties, to be handed to him. Taking this bone, the royal doctor drew a circle on a table with it. Several spiders were placed within the circle: they instantly died. 'Too late,' said Ivan. 'Now even the rhinoceros cannot save me.' He turned to his jewels and instructed Gorsei: 'Look at this diamond. This is the best and most valuable of all the stones in the East. Diamond quenches anger and drives away voluptuousness … It gives a man power over himself and virtue … I never valued it for its true worth … things are ill for me.'

The chronicles insist that before he died, Ivan showed uncharacteristic kindness to those around him. He advised his son Fyodor to rule virtuously and with love for the people, and to free captives and prisoners. However, the same chronicles relate that Ivan's vicious nature was undiminished to the very end. A few days before his death, he tried to rape his daughter-in-law, Fyodor's wife Irene Godunov.

The day the astrologers had predicted arrived, but Ivan felt quite well, so he took a bath and began to poke fun at the unfortunate soothsayers, promising to boil them in a cauldron for their foolish, unfulfilled prophesies. To which the soothsayers replied, 'The day has only begun, and it will only end at sunset.'

After his bath, before the multitude gathered in the great hall, the half-dressed Ivan began to set up the pieces for a game of chess. He invited Boris Godunov to play him at a game – and suddenly collapsed. According to one historical version, boyars hand-picked in advance by Godunov, rushed forward, quickly suffocated the unconscious Czar with pillows. Then they summoned a priest and, as Ivan had instructed, shaved the supposedly dying, but in truth already dead, Czar in preparation for monkhood.

Thus, a public version of the incident was ready to hand: the astrologers' prediction had come to pass. Death had occurred before many witnesses, the Czar's will had been fulfilled – before death he took monastic vows – so now he could appear before God. Yet in truth, as some historians claim, the royal doctor, on Godunov's orders, had that morning slipped Ivan a slow-acting poison. Such was the end of the first Czar of all Russia.

❖   ❖   ❖   ❖   ❖

The epilogue to this history is the opening of Ivan the Terrible's sepulchre by the famous Soviet anthropologist Mikhail Gerasimov, which took place within the Kremlin Archangel Cathedral in 1963. Using what was left of Ivan's skull and bones, Gerasimov was able to restore the likeness of the Czar with reasonable accuracy. He was a tall man with a flabby, puffy face, looking considerably older than his fifty-four years. The Czar's bones were covered with a thick layer of salt deposits, which must have hampered his movements and certainly influenced his moods.

In his work on Czar Ivan, Gerasimov was confronted by two riddles. The first was the presence of a large amount of mercury in the Czar's body. This may have been remnants of ancient healing methods, or it could have been traces of the poison fed him by the royal doctor. The second, which amazed everyone, was the position of Ivan's right arm. It was raised up, as if crying out to God. How this could have happened is unclear, since in those days the arms of the deceased were always crossed over the chest, in which position the body was wrapped and tied with twine. This fact led to the suggestion that in the commotion at the time of his death, Ivan had been buried alive: he must have tossed about in his grave, trying to get out.

Having examined the Czar's remains, the scientists returned Ivan's bones to his sarcophagus, placing inside a sealed capsule containing a written account of their findings. Thus, after four centuries of sleep, and a brief reappearance before his descendants, Ivan the Terrible once again returned to his eternal rest.

3 | THE FALSE KINGS

ON THE DEATH OF IVAN THE TERRIBLE, who had murdered his eldest son Ivan, the legal heir to the throne was the latter's younger brother, the kindly but simple-minded Fyodor. The marks of degeneration could be clearly seen on the face of the twenty-seven-year old Czar. His puny body was topped by a disproportionately small head, with a face that wore a perpetually senseless grin, and a hooked nose. His gait was infirm, his speech mumbling. His own father had once called him 'The Bellringer', because the only passion that had ever gripped him was ringing the church bells.

According to foreign diplomats, the Czar had a standard pattern to his day. Fyodor awoke at four in the morning. Having finished dressing, he sent for a priest and proceeded to pray. For a quarter of an hour the Czar would wholeheartedly continue bowing to the very ground. Having completed this first morning prayer, he sent for word of the Czarina's health. Then they both proceeded to the house chapel for morning mass, which would last around an hour. After this, the Czar would proceed to the audience chamber where, sitting in his chair, he would hear the boyars' petitions.

Around ten in the morning, the Czar would proceed to the bell tower and personally ring the bells for lunchtime mass. The lunchtime liturgy would take another two hours. Upon its completion, the Czar would go to lunch, and would then take three hours of mandatory daytime sleep – a practice that no self-respecting Russian noble of the time went without. After sleeping, the Czar would head off to evening mass. The remainder of the time until dinner was devoted to completely earned rest. The Czar and his wife amused themselves, listening to the chatter of jesters and following the tumbling of dwarfs. After dinner the Czar once again prayed with his priest, and receiving his blessing, would then retire to bed.

Such was the new master of the Kremlin. The people called this kind of person 'blessed', that is, a quiet unassuming creature whom God made bereft of reason, and hence took under his wing. Such a Czar could not govern the country on his own, so his father, while he still lived, assigned guardian advisors to him, one of whom was the thirty-two-year-old Boris Godunov, whose sister Irene was married to the young Fyodor.

Irene was an attractive woman, with a clear mind and firm character. She was the same age as Fyodor, had spent her childhood in the palace with him, and married him long before he became Czar. After years of living together, she wielded unlimited power over her weak-minded husband. Although they rarely shared common quarters due to Fyodor's poor health, in matters of state she was his first and foremost advisor.

The Czarina loved her elder brother dearly. With her help – after Fyodor assumed the throne – Boris Godunov quickly distanced the guardians and became the most important figure next to the Czar, practically the ruler of Russia. The only dark cloud hanging over the royal pair was the absence of children. All of Irene's pregnancies ended in misfortune. While the young Ivan was still alive, Fyodor's childlessness did not greatly concern Ivan the Terrible; indeed, it worked in favour of the state, since it freed the throne from future pretenders, and from possible civil wars. However, with the death of the eldest son, the situation changed dramatically. Now, with Fyodor as heir, Irene's barrenness threatened the Czar's dynasty with complete extinction.

Ivan the Terrible decided to separate Fyodor from his wife, but the weak-willed Czarevich put up resistance; he did not want to hear of divorce. Had this rebellion occurred before the death of the eldest son, we can only imagine the anger that the fiery Czar would have heaped upon Fyodor. Now, however, broken by sorrow, he decided not to deal harshly with his youngest son and conceded.

With Fyodor's ascent to the throne, the problem of childlessness became even more acute. The discarded guardians understood that one of the ways to remove Godunov from power was through the Czar's divorce from Irene Godunov. But if fear of his father's wrath failed to persuade Fyodor to separate from Irene, Godunov's enemies had even less chance. The quiet Fyodor was so angered by those who had urged him towards a divorce that some of them paid with their heads. It was then that one of the Czar's guardians – Godunov's main foe – came up with a different move.

Fyodor was the son of Ivan the Terrible from his first marriage. His younger brother Dimitri also lived in the Kremlin with his mother Maria Nagoy, Ivan's last wife. Godunov's enemies, relying on the mental ineptitude of Fyodor, and his inability to rule the country, concocted a plan to put the young Dimitri forward as a rival to the Czar. This was no simple plan, since the Russian Orthodox Church only recognised the first three marriages as legal; all the others were considered illegal, and it was doubtful that the offspring of such marriages could become pretenders to the throne. The situation was delicate, one that, in the appropriate circumstances, could lead to a palace revolt.

Under the influence of Boris and Irene, Fyodor dealt swiftly and decisively with the conspirators. Several of the former guardians were sent into distant exile, while Dimitri and his mother were compelled to leave the Kremlin and move 200 versts from Moscow to the ancient Russian town of Uglich, which had been bequeathed to Dimitri by his late father. All things considered, the gentle Fyodor did not harbour ill will towards his younger brother and his mother. He sent them expensive gifts to Uglich from time to time, and they in turn sent cakes and sweets to the Kremlin. Obviously, no one could foresee that fate had decreed young Dimitri to be the main character in one of Russia's great national dramas, which would go down in history as the 'Troubled Times'.

Although the palace revolt was unsuccessful, Boris Godunov clearly understood that his career depended wholly upon the position of his sister. The absence of an heir and the weak health of Fyodor, who had been promised a short life, hung over Boris like the sword of Damocles. The question of Dimitri's rights to the throne could resurface at any moment, especially considering that during the first year of his reign Fyodor was taken seriously ill and nearly died. To rely on Irene keeping the throne after the death of her husband was unthinkable. In such a situation Dimitri, despite the illegitimacy of his birth, was the only direct descendant of Ivan the Terrible.

Boris searched feverishly for a way out of this situation. He secretly offered Vienna a chance to discuss the question of marriage between Irene and an Austrian prince, with the subsequent accession of the prince to the Kremlin throne. Simultaneously, he sent an agent to London, requesting that a midwife be sent to Moscow in the hope that she would help Irene finally to give birth to an heir. Boris believed that such an event would remove the question of Dimitri as successor and strengthen his own position in the court.

Soon enough, all these secret negotiations became public knowledge and spilled over into a huge scandal. News that Godunov had turned to nonbelievers and heretics caused a storm in the Kremlin. The attempts to find a match for Irene, while her husband was alive, offended Fyodor, now recovered, to the depths of his soul. Relations between Fyodor and Boris, until then cloudless, darkened; the meek Czar was quick to take up cudgels to teach his brother-in-law a lesson.

The story goes that one prisoner, sent to Siberia back in 1591, has survived to this very day. According to the laws of the time, prisoners were mutilated: their nostrils were torn, their ears were cut off and their tongues often torn out. This was a method of marking their criminal past for the rest of their lives, as well as removing all hope of escape. The prisoner in question did not escape this punishment; his ears were broken, and his tongue was torn out. By birth, he was from the ancient Russian town of Uglich and his crime was that on 15 May 1591 he informed the citizens, with a loud clamour, of the death of the seven-year-old Czarevich Dimitri. The prisoner in question was a bell.

Uglich, where the young Dimitri and his mother Maria Nagoy were exiled, was the centre of the anti-Godunov opposition. Maria's relatives understood that after the death of the childless Fyodor, Dimitri would have a strong chance of assuming the throne at the Kremlin, and prepared him for this day. They stoked his hatred for all those close to Fyodor, first and foremost Boris Godunov, whom they considered – with good reason – to be the main obstacle on their way to the throne.

These seeds were sown in fertile ground, since Dimitri – even though still a child – totally replicated the character traits of his late father. He was fiery, vengeful and cruel. His favourite pastime was tearing the heads off chickens. During the winter, while playing with his friends, he would create human figures out of snow and name them after those associated with his older brother – not forgetting, of course, Boris Godunov himself. Then he would slash at these figures with his sabre, yelling, 'Here's what you'll get when I become Czar!'

All this, of course, caused little pleasure to those at the Kremlin, not least Boris. According to reports from Uglich, Boris Godunov had already tried to poison this dangerous rival more than once, and the relatives of the Czarevich were on their guard. Then, on 15 May 1591, news spread across Russia that Czarevich Dimitri had died in mysterious circumstances. Either he had accidentally fallen on a knife or he had been murdered. People reflected, 'Who needed to do this and who benefited?' Certainly it was to the advantage of Boris Godunov.

The death of Dimitri was such an important event in the history of Russia, with such a great influence on her further development, that it merits examination in more detail.

There are several versions of the death of the Czarevich. One, the official account, written in the report of the investigation conducted on the orders of Boris Godunov, claims that it was an accident. While playing with his friends, the Czarevich had an attack of epilepsy, from which it was known he suffered. As he fell, the child stabbed himself in the neck with a knife he was holding. The wound proved fatal. According to the second version, widespread among the people, the Czarevich was killed by Godunov's men. While playing in the garden, he was approached by one of the hired killers, who asked to see the necklace around the Dmitri's neck. The child turned up his head to show the necklace, at which moment the killer sank a knife into his throat.

Subsequent events unfolded with gathering momentum. With loud cries, the Czarevich's nursemaid and companions, who were also in the garden, rushed towards the stricken child. The Czarevich was still alive, although he had lost consciousness. His mother ran outside, startled by women's cries. Now something strange happened. It would be reasonable to expect that a mother would rush to help her child; instead she grabbed a log and, in a frenzy, started to beat the nursemaid. The latter's son, who had been playing with Dimitri, tried to defend his mother. The Czarina then hurled herself at the boy, yelling that he was her son's killer.

This was all witnessed by a church guard who happened to see the whole scene from the bell tower and immediately sounded the alarm. A crowd gathered, including two of the Czarina's brothers, one of whom was dead drunk. Among the assembly were some of Godunov's people, long-standing enemies of the Czarina and her relatives. One of her brothers pointed them out, shouting that they had killed the Czarevich on Godunov's orders. The enraged mob attacked them. The nursemaid's son, who was trying to hide in the church, was killed at the altar – a most heinous crime, according to the laws of the time. In all, about fifteen people were killed.

What became of the Czarevich amidst this turmoil and bloodshed? According to the chronicles, 'He still shuddered a long time' in the arms of his nurse. When did he die? It is not known. Who verified his death? Also unknown. His body was taken to the church and buried in haste. A rider was sent to Moscow to explain what had happened.

The Kremlin wasted no time. A commission arrived in Uglich, on Godunov's orders. Its findings were unanimous – an accident. Even so, the bloody slaughter was met with no less bloody retribution. The Czarina was sent to a nunnery where she took the veil.

Two hundred citizens of Uglich died under interrogation. Others had their tongues cut out and were sent to Siberia. This was also the detination of the unfortunate church bell, whose crime was that it rang untimely.

Fifteen years later, after Godunov's death, the church named Dimitri a saint. His grave in Uglich was opened, and his body was moved to the Kremlin. Dimitri lay in his grave, 'as if alive', in the words of one chronicler. In one hand he held a handkerchief, in the other some hazelnuts covered in blood.

Or perhaps a doll lay in the grave? As for the bloodstained hazelnuts, it is hard to believe that these would survive lying in the ground for fifteen years, let alone be still visibly covered with blood. And where did these nuts, which seemed to support the version of murder, come from anyway? More than likely, they were painted hazelnuts, slipped into the grave after it was opened. But who needed to do this, and why?

Considering that Godunov was already dead by this time, and that the Kremlin was occupied by people who bitterly hated the former ruler and wished to sully his name in any way they could, including, for example, reinforcement of the theory of the Czarevich's murder, then everything falls into place. According to the laws of the Church, even an accidental suicide could not be granted sainthood: hence the hazelnuts slipped into the grave, as if to say that there was no suicide, but there was a murder. The 'blood' on the nuts gave the added impression of a death marked by suffering.

There is another, third possibility, mentioned by Nikolai Kostomarov, although only a few historians support it. The gist of this version is that the Czarevich did not die at all. He was spirited away and hidden by his relatives, while another child was buried in his place. This whole deception was organised by Dimitri's relatives in order to save him from what they considered to be the encroaching menace of the all-powerful Godunov, and simultaneously to slander their foe in front of the people. If we accept this version, then many of the events to follow will become much clearer.

World history has produced figures who, down the ages, have acquired the status of archetypes of good or evil, integrity or villainy. They present us with moral dilemmas which we try to solve in the context of the intellect or of art. Mozart and Salieri are such archetypal figures. The example of their relationship has confronted historians for two centuries now with the question: are genius and villainy compatible characteristics? Boris Godunov comes into the same category. His life has intrigued not only historians but also Russia's great writers, poets, painters and composers.

On 6 January 1598, in the forty-first year of his life, Czar Fyodor died, leaving behind no legitimate heir. With his death, the line of Ivan the Terrible ceased to exist. The country where the will of the ruler was akin to the will of God was left without a master. Boris Godunov used this opportunity to organise several processions to the Kremlin. The people begged him to become Czar and save the country. Twice Boris refused the throne – to good effect; on the third occasion, he agreed. The new Czar, forty-seven years old, gave a solemn vow: he would not spill blood for five years.

According to contemporaries, Boris Godunov was an outstanding orator, a gift enhanced not only by his keen wits and clear voice, but also by his general demeanour, his handsome face and friendly air. Although he gave the impression of being quite meek, even sentimental, he possessed an indomitable will. He was ready to do good if it did not hinder his personal plans, but would not shrink from evil if he considered it useful. Was he a liar? No more and no less than the whole of Moscow society, who had always seen hypocrisy as a political instrument, magnified tenfold during the reign of Ivan the Terrible – the liar incarnate.

Godunov's contemporaries were likewise impressed with the constancy of his family life, his devotion to his children, and – uncharacteristically for a Russian – his aversion to drunkenness.

Despite these good points, contemporaries attributed many evil deeds to Boris Godunov – from poisoning Ivan the Terrible to the murder of Czarevich Dimitri. Even when a daughter born to Czar Fyodor and Czarina Irene died a few months after the birth, rumour had it that Godunov was responsible for the baby's death. However, many modern historians consider these accusations to be fabricated. In their opinion, Boris Godunov was a man with an outstanding intellect for government. His management of the country's foreign policies was competent; and had fortune favoured him he could have introduced Russia to the benefits of European civilisation a hundred years before Peter the Great. Boris Godunov might have been acclaimed one of the world's most successful rulers had the blood of a Czar, rather than that of a minor boyar, flowed through his veins, giving him the right, according to the laws of the time, to be considered God's representative on earth, and granting him limitless powers over the lives of his people.

Yet Boris, as an 'unnatural' Czar, had no such rights in the eyes of the people. The thousands of executions perpetrated by Ivan the Terrible did not arouse the smallest fraction of popular indignation that was stirred up by Boris's individual reprisals. In the midst of a terrible famine, Boris tried to help the population by distributing wheat: the people murmured that their hunger was sent by heaven because a murderer sat on the throne – an unlawful Czar. Whatever good Czar Boris did, the people always suspected him of duplicity and trickery. The mob immediately attributed any death to his evil will.

What can be said about all this? People seemed to be slaves to a peculiar form of morality. They forgave the lawful Czar – the Czar by blood – any evil deeds, since they saw him as the executor of God's will. The unlawful Czar was forgiven nothing; moreover he was held responsible for all the evils of the world. This relationship which sprang up between and Czar Boris and his people has fascinated Russia's finest minds: Pushkin, Tolstoy, Dostoyevsky, Mussorgsky and many others. Generations of theatre directors have tried to express this conundrum on the stage, not merely in the context of Russian history, but also as encapsulating the eternal theme of good and evil: whether the ends justify the means, blood versus prosperity, the price of progress. Russian literature and art accepted the version that Boris was responsible for the death of Czarevich Dimitri and, leading on from this, that he was also responsible for all the misfortunes that befell his reign.

In Mussorgsky's opera *Boris Godunov*, based on the play of the same name by Pushkin, the renowned Russian bass Fyodor Chaliapin, in the part of Boris, sang:

> Like a hammer, the reproach beats in my ears, And everything feels still, my head is spinning, And blood-drenched boys rise before my eyes.

A firm, thoughtful ruler such as Boris Godunov was not frightened by vicious rumours, but he was weighed down by remorse. For thirteen years on end he dreamt of the dead boy. The torments of his conscience were unbearable. Herein lay the great tragedy of Boris Godunov. Against the enormous power that he wielded rose a spectre, the spectre of a murdered child.

Rumours started to spread across the country that Czarevich Dimitri was not dead. A miracle had saved him. Now, more than ten years after his supposed death, he moved on the Kremlin with a Polish army, to take his rightful place.

The story of the False Dimitri ranks among the most dramatic episodes of its time. Who was this new pretender to the Kremlin throne? To this day this question lacks a conclusive answer. According to a version spread by Boris Godunov's supporters, he was an outlaw monk. Not surprisingly, the opponents of Boris endorsed the account of the miraculous escape of Czarevich Dimitri. Whatever the facts, a person calling himself Czarevich Dimitri, who went down in history as the False Dimitri, appeared in Poland.

He was a well-built young man with a dark complexion and an aristocratic air. Apart from the interest aroused in his mysterious past and potential future, he possessed courage and grace. In Poland, the pretender quickly found himself patrons who were ready to take advantage of the situation.

One such was an influential Polish noble, with whose daughter, Marina Mnishek, the pretender fell in love.

Marina was considered a beauty, although the portraits that have survived show her as rather plain, with a predatory nose, sharp chin, thin mouth, and tightly pressed lips hardly conducive to kissing. Only the beautiful almond-shaped eyes and the elegantly curved eyebrows somewhat soften the dry, prim face. What was immediately obvious was her inordinate ambition. Yes, she was ready to give her hand to this dubious Russian, but first let him become Czar.

And so, with two thousand warriors gathered from among free Polish knights and adventure-seekers, the False Dimitri crossed the Russian border. The first rumours of the pretender's appearance did not trouble Boris Godunov. Similar tales had circulated before, especially at the time of the Czar's illness, a bad harvest or during general unrest. Boris had seemingly made his peace with the fact that the shadow of Czarevich Dimitri was his lot, a fate from which he might never be free. Even he could not swear with complete conviction that Dimitri was dead. The small army of this pretender could not present a serious threat. On Boris's orders, a messenger was sent to Poland with a letter, making it clear that this individual was nothing more than an outlaw monk, convicted of theft by the courts. But as time showed, the enemy turned out to be far more dangerous than those in the Kremlin suspected.

A three-year famine, brought on by bad harvests, preceded these events. The likes of it could not be remembered by grandfathers or great-grandfathers. It drove whole regions to cannibalism, and cast the country into a state of apathy. This terrible harvest was once again attributed to the fact that an unlawful Czar – a regicide – sat on the throne. Thus, rumours of the miraculous escape of Czarevich Dimitri fell upon fertile ground: the people were expecting a miracle. There were further reports of all manner of omens. In one place, a hurricane demolished a church's bell tower, in another the birds disappeared. Women and farm animals gave birth to freaks, someone saw two suns in the sky, and finally, in the summer of 1604, a comet appeared in the heavens (one event that did, in fact, occur).

Volunteers to join the pretender's small army poured in from all sides, cities opened their gates and battalions sent against him defected to his side. The situation was becoming very serious, and Boris Godunov understood this. On his orders an attempt was made to poison the pretender, but the monks who were entrusted to the task were caught and the attempt was foiled.

Godunov next commanded that Maria Nagoy, Czarevich Dimitri's mother, be brought to the Kremlin from her distant nunnery. If she were to appear before the people and proclaim that her son had died in her arms thirteen years ago, this would check the pretender in his tracks. This was what Boris asked of her; but Maria would answer only that she did not know if her son was alive or not. Her silence was tantamount to an endorsement of the pretender. At one such interrogation, so the chronicles tell, Godunov's enraged wife threw herself at the widow of Ivan the Terrible in an attempt to burn her eyes with a candle flame; whereupon the latter allegedly cried out, 'He's alive!'

News that Dimitri's mother had proclaimed the pretender her own son spread quickly across Moscow. Commoners in their homes openly drank to Dimitri's health. The situation was compounded by the fact that Czar Boris was gripped by inertia. Assailed by illness, his physical and spiritual strength were waning, and he rarely left the palace. On 13 April 1605, he felt better and climbed up to the bell tower, from where he often looked over Moscow; but he quickly went back down, complaining that he felt unwell again. The doctor was sent for, but it was too late. Boris lost consciousness, bled from his ears and nose, and died a few hours later. It took a whole day for the court to announce his death to the people, and rumours immediately spread that, fearing the arrival of Dimitri, Boris Godunov had poisoned himself in a bout of depression.

To this day, the puzzle remains. How much of this was truth and how much fabrication? Was the death of Boris, at a time so critical for Russia, a simple coincidence or murder? Or was it suicide?

Boris Godunov left two children: the sixteen-year-old Fyodor and a daughter named Xenia. Fyodor was an interesting, intelligent and capable young man, having received an excellent education by the standards of the time. His father had engaged foreign tutors for him, and started to introduce him to the workings of power from an early age. Xenia, famed for her beauty, was equally well educated. Immediately after Boris's death, the Kremlin throne passed to Fyodor. Muscovites swore loyalty to him without a murmur, but whispered among themselves that the children of Godunov would not rule for long. When Czar Dimitri arrives … And they were right: Fyodor remained Czar for one month.

◆　◆　◆　◆　◆

In the meantime, the False Dimitri slowly advanced on Moscow, sending messengers ahead with letters to the citizens of the capital. Moscow buzzed like a hive, awaiting the legitimate Czar, the true son of Ivan the Terrible. Fyodor Godunov, his mother, and those of the boyars who still remained loyal to him 'shut themselves in the Kremlin, half-dead with fright'. If any among the people still had doubts, these were brought to an end when a former guardian of Czarevich Dimitri swore publicly that Boris had tried to have the Czarevich killed, but had failed. He himself had personally saved the son of Ivan the Terrible. 'Down with the Godunovs!' the mob bellowed. 'Root them all out! Why show them mercy when Boris didn't show mercy to the rightful heir?'

On 6 June 1605, the walls of the Kremlin bore witness to yet another tragedy. The mob, under the leadership of boyars who had gone over to the pretender's side, poured into the Kremlin. Czar Fyodor sat on the throne in the Granavitaya Chamber. Next to him, holding icons, stood his mother and sister. The brave young Czar stubbornly fought for his life, but in the end his head was shattered with a club and he was suffocated with pillows. Boris Godunov's widow was killed along with her son. Xenia took poison, but was given the antidote in time – condemning her to a more gruesome fate. She was spared 'for the amusement of the ruler'. As the chronicler tells, Xenia was a true Russian beauty: white skin, a bright blush, ruby lips, and long hair that fell across her shoulders in plaits. 'Her body was like cream,' exclaims the chronicler, 'and her eyebrows came together in an arch.' The False Dimitri had long since been informed of her attractions; now the trophy awaited him in the Kremlin.

The body of Boris Godunov was exhumed from the Archangel's Cathedral, where he had been buried two months earlier, and together with the bodies of the rest of the family, was interred in a far-flung village cemetery. Thus the reign of another Russian Czar came to its ignominious end.

It is curious that Pushkin first finished his play *Boris Godunov* with the words, 'Long live Czar Dimitri!', compelling the people to hail the new Czar. However, just before handing the manuscript to the publisher, the great poet changed the end of the play. Instead of the final exclamation, he inserted a phrase which became very familiar in Russian culture and society. In the rewritten version, the play ends with the stage directions: 'The people stand silent.'

The crowd falls still, and in these seconds an important moral event occurs. A moment ago they were reviling the former ruler, actively supporting the new Czar. Now, blood has been spilt, and the new power has treated the young son of Godunov just as harshly as Godunov once dealt with the young Dimitri. In so doing, the victor has begun to dig his own grave.

On 20 June 1605, Muscovites, dressed in their best clothes, clambered up trees and thronged the roofs of houses. The bells were rung. Everyone await-

ed the new Czar's arrival in the capital. 'We bow our head before our beautiful sunshine!' rang out from all sides. 'God give you health!' The 'sunshine'
approached in splendour and might. His face was not handsome – a wide
nose, red hair – but he was wonderfully well-built, and below his magnificent
forehead shone a pair of intelligent eyes. He wore a coat of woven gold and
a lavish necklace around his throat, and was mounted on a splendid horse
that was bridled with a valuable harness.

Before the eyes of all Russia, and all Europe, an event occurred which
exceeded the plot of any adventure novel. Accompanied by the triumphant
cries of the crowd, the pretender entered the Kremlin. His 'mother', Czarina
Nagoy – half blind and half mad – was led before him. Flattered, implored
and eventually convinced, she finally proclaimed recognition of her long-dead
son in the young mail-clad knight before her. The knight himself, dismount-
ing his horse, walked on foot beside the carriage, kissing his mother's hands.
Both were crying. The people also wept tears of tenderness. In the Archangel's
Cathedral of the Kremlin, falling upon the grave of Ivan the Terrible, the pretender cried such bitter tears that no one any longer doubted his being the
rightful heir.

The coronation of the new Czar surpassed in splendour anything the
Kremlin had yet seen. 'I shall not be your Czar, I shall be your father,' the
False Dimitri promised. 'The past is forgotten. The ages will not tell that you
served Boris and his children. I shall love you, I shall live for the benefit and
happiness of my beloved subjects.'

Unlike previous Russian Czars, who had been indifferent towards everyday comforts, the new Czar ordered his chambers in the Kremlin to be fur-
nished with unprecedented luxury. The walls were covered with expensive
tapestries, nails and chains were coated in gold, and fireplace grates were cast
from silver. The daily, lengthy attendance of church services ceased. The
ancient tradition of the after-lunch nap – without which Muscovites could not
imagine the life of an important nobleman – came to an end. Whereas in previous times bearing arms in the palace had been an insult to the Czar, now
swords started to be worn in the Czar's chambers, as in the West. And finally, notwithstanding popular surprise and disapproval, forty musicians were
invited from Poland: an orchestra began to play in the Kremlin.

The Polish beauty Marina Mnishek – bride of the Czar and future mistress
of all this splendour – arrived separately at the Kremlin. Accompanied by a
two-thousand-strong Polish entourage, she rode in a red carriage with gold-
painted wheels. She sat on a cushion embroidered with pearls, and wore a

white satin dress liberally adorned with jewels. Bells rang, cannons fired. Yet amid all the glamour of her arrival, there was some disquiet. Here, at the gates of an Asian capital, two opposing cultures clashed. The tumultuous welcoming clarions of Moscow's trumpeters were a painful assault to genteel Polish ears. In their turn, the melodies of Polish popular music, which thundered out from the Polish orchestra, and which was echoed by the Czarina's entourage, did not exactly warm the hearts of the Muscovites.

A series of colour etchings shows details of the Czar's wedding in the Assumption Cathedral of the Kremlin. While the future Czarina reclined upon a golden chair set with six hundred diamonds, six hundred emeralds and six hundred rubies (the chair has survived to this very day), her Polish entourage, lounging on the floor of the cathedral, openly expressed their disdain for Russian customs and sacraments. Even Marina failed to conceal her chilly attitude towards the old-fashioned Russian rituals. When the icons were presented, the uninitiated Catholics kissed the images of the saints on the lips, thereby shocking the Orthodox.

Muscovites had never seen such a Czar. Feasts and games did not prevent him performing his duties. All were astounded by his intelligence, his wit, and the speed with which he solved the most complex of issues. He doubled the salaries of the military, and decreed that landowners would lose power over their serfs if they did not feed them during a famine. He also forbade the trial of bondsmen for escape if more than five years had elapsed in the meantime. Without exception, every subject was given the right to trade and practise his craft freely.

The Czar also ordered harsh penalties for bribes, and returned all those boyars whom Godunov had sent into exile, granting them new titles and holdings. Twice a week, he gave the people an audience in the Kremlin forecourt, where any pauper could come to him with their grievance. Any citizen could travel freely beyond the borders of the country, and return again. The new Czar would not tolerate informants. If someone spoke harshly of Godunov in his presence, he immediately interrupted him: 'You bowed before him while he was alive, and now that he is dead you curse him.' (Such tolerance, however, did not extend to surviving members of Boris's family. The unfortunate Xenia, shorn of her beautiful hair, disappeared behind the walls of a nunnery where she soon gave birth to a son.) Yet as one English diplomat wrote, this was the first monarch in Europe to grant such freedom to his subjects.

The people were equally impressed by the habits of the young Czar. He did not pray before lunch, and did not sleep after it. He went for walks along the streets, peeping into trading booths and craft shops, and talked with passers-by. When mounting a horse, he would reject the proffered footstool, grab the mane and leap into the saddle; and whereas previous Czars had trotted slowly and majestically on quiet, tame horses, this one would choose a wild, unbroken animal and gallop away for all he was worth. During the city games, the new Czar did not sit upon a däis, as was usual, watching the contests between Moscow's brave lads and hungry wild bears, but instead grabbed a boar spear and took on the animals himself.

The new Czar earned general approval – except that he had taken a Catholic wife, and had apparently forgotten the traditions of his ancestors while abroad. The people disliked his fondness for foreigners, particularly resenting the Poles who had arrived with the Czarina and were quartered in private houses, often getting drunk and behaving outrageously towards Russian women. One day, to the horror of Muscovites, a masterpiece of European mechanics appeared alongside the Czar's new chambers: a huge, brass, three-headed dog, Cerberus, with snapping jaws, bared metallic fangs and fearsome claws. Nor was that all. A number of women appeared in the Kremlin. They did not cover their faces, nor conceal their figures, and they sat down to dine with the men. These were scandalous transgressions against the age-old patriarchal traditions. The people murmured; rumours began to spread. The question was asked: 'Is he really the Czar's son?'

Dissent flamed still more fiercely when Muscovites learned that as part of the wedding celebrations, a masquerade was being planned for the Kremlin. According to Russian concepts of the time, to wear a mask – to change your face – was to serve the Devil. This was permissible least of all to an Orthodox Czar. A plot was hatched among the boyars. Urged on by them, the tumult among the people grew even greater. Informed of this, Dimitri declared: 'I don't want to hear of it. I cannot abide informers. It is they whom I shall punish.' The next day, several foreign diplomats brought him the same news, but Dimitri cut them off sharply: 'All this is foolishness.'

On the night of 17 May 1606, while the Czar was throwing yet another ball where forty Polish musicians played, the Kremlin bells rang out. People started to gather in Red Square. A mob surrounded the Czar's palace. Conspirators spread the rumour that the Poles wanted to rob the Kremlin and kill Dimitri. The enraged mob, led by the conspirators, burst into the palace, crushing the small number of guards. The group of conspirators broke through first. The Czar, showing inordinate physical strength and agility, leapt up to defend himself, crying, 'I'm not your Boris!' The forces, however, were not evenly matched and he tried to save himself by flight, judging correctly that if he could get through to the people – who loved him – and tell them the truth, they would save him. Unfortunately, the 20-foot drop from the window down to the cobblestones proved too much. As the Czar, his leg broken, lay unconscious, the conspirators finished him off, informing the mob that on his deathbed he had confessed to the deception: he was not the son of Ivan the Terrible.

The bloodsoaked body of the man who only recently had been hailed Russia's 'sunshine' was dragged along the embankment of the Kremlin by a rope and thrown on to the place of execution in the centre of Red Square. The corpse was then obscenely desecrated. The face was covered with a clown's mask, and a flute was hung about the neck – no longer a Czar, but a despised jester. Maria Nagoy was once again led to the scene of the crime, where she was asked, 'Is this your son?' It is alleged that, mad with grief, she shouted, 'Why didn't you ask me this before? Now he surely isn't mine!'

For several days the body was left in the square, then it was burned, the ashes loaded into a cannon and fired westward, in the direction of Poland, back to where he came from. Thus ended the eleven-months' reign of the pretender, who came to be known in Russian history as the False Dimitri.

So, was he false or not? Again, a mystery remains unanswered. According to Nikolai Kostomarov, there was a ledger found in a monastery. It contained the signature of that same outlaw monk who, according to the official Boris Godunov version, was hiding under the name of Dimitri. This signature is nothing like that of the False Dimitri. If Dimitri had been a poor, common monk without family, it is improbable that he could have managed – within a mere two years of arriving in Poland (the length of his stay, according to the official chronicles) – to master so brilliantly the skills of the Polish aristocracy: ballroom dancing, sitting comfortably in the saddle, using weapons, showing a comprehensive knowledge of the Polish language, and even speaking in Russian with a Polish accent. Some people had also noticed that on the day of his arrival in Moscow, while kissing the icons, Dimitri did it clumsily, not in the accepted Russian way. A monk could not have made such an error.

There was one final point against the conclusion that the monk and Dimitri were one and the same person. If we accept that Czarevich Dimitri was rescued by his family, it is hard to believe they would have allowed him to spend his childhood and youth in poverty, wandering from monastery to monastery and, most importantly, living in constant danger of being recognised and killed. More than likely they would speedily have taken him somewhere abroad, far from Godunov – perhaps to Poland.

Based on such arguments, many consider him to have been not an outlaw monk but a native of Poland. Whatever happened and whoever he was, he represented a new breed. It is possible, had he reigned longer, that Russia would have embarked on her reforms long before the advent of Peter the Great.

◆ ◆ ◆ ◆ ◆

Pretenders. They have been known in many ages and in many different countries: the False Nero in Rome, several false emperors in Byzantium, the false kings of Portugal. Yet, not in all these countries combined did so many pretenders emerge as in seventeenth to eighteenth-century Russia.

How can this be explained? Why had a hundred pretenders or so called themselves Czar Dimitri, Czar Peter, Czar Konstantin? Was it merely to deceive? Why did writers such as Pushkin, Tolstoy and Dostoyevsky express so much interest in these individuals? Outright deception alone would have been unlikely to capture their imagination.

Here we come face to face with the most contemporary of problems stemming from auto-suggestion and mass hypnosis. Surviving chronicles suggest that many pretenders, during the early stages, considered themselves divinely blessed (similarly to the spirit voices of Joan of Arc). By repeating 'I am Czar Dimitri', 'I am Czar Peter', they began genuinely to believe that the Czar's spirit had descended into them. In Pushkin's *Boris Godunov,* the pretender announces: 'The shadow of Ivan the Terrible has adopted me.' Such self-belief was even transmitted to the sceptics. 'God knows, he obviously isn't the son of Ivan the Terrible, but there is something in him nevertheless.'

Many modern historians still debate the problem. Resolving it might throw new light on that mystery which has long been known as 'The Riddle of the Russian Soul'. Although, according to one classic source, perhaps the greatest secret of nature lies in the fact that there is no secret at all.

After the death of the False Dimitri, rumours once again started to spread that he had not died. The people wanted to believe that the man who had died was not the true Czar, and that the real one, the true son of Ivan the Terrible, had been spared. Already, in one corner of Russia, an army headed by the False Dimitri II was raised, bent on conquering the Kremlin. Elsewhere the False Dimitri III appeared. The ambitious Marina Mnishek, having survived – thanks to her diminutive height – the nocturnal slaughter in the Kremlin by hiding under the wide skirts of a maid, suddenly announced that her husband was not dead. She acknowledged the False Dimitri II as her husband, lived with him, and gave birth to his heir. However, this 'Czar' soon died in battle, without having taken the Kremlin. Marina searched for other patrons who would help her recapture the Kremlin's throne. They were easily found. Marina was passed from hand to hand until she was finally locked in a nunnery where she lived for many years with her unfortunate son until, according to one version, she died there of hunger.

In the meantime, several rulers briefly took over in the Kremlin, until finally a Polish garrison locked itself in there. The disintegration of Russia appeared to be unavoidable, the country fragmented into innumerable centres of rebellion. People spoke of divine vengeance upon the land for the barbarism of Ivan the Terrible, for the murder of Czarevich Dimitri, for the lies, for the pretenders ...

◆　◆　◆　◆　◆

A monument to two Russian heroes stands in Red Square, not far from the Kremlin. One of the figures is standing, urging the second to battle; the second is seated, because of his wounds. These are the merchant Minin and Prince Pozharsky: two men who played a role in Russian history similar to that of Joan of Arc in France.

Russia was in ruins, the Kremlin was occupied by Poles, and there was no Czar. Suddenly, in this difficult and troubled time, the Russian merchant Minin sacrificed his fortune to free his country. With passionate words he first inspired the citizens of his home town, Nizhny Novgorod, where he was an elder councillor, and subsequently of other Russian towns. Everyone was required to give one-fifth of their possessions for the needs of the motherland; those who had nothing were to become the servants of those willing to pay for them. This money was to go towards the formation of a voluntary Russian army.

The volunteer battalions, headed by Prince Pozharsky, moved towards the Kremlin, and the Polish garrison prepared for a hard siege. After a few months, a terrible pestilence broke out inside the palace. The defenders, driven mad by hunger, even cooked the starch out of the parchment of Greek manuscripts. In the end, the Poles were forced to open the gates of the Kremlin.

Just as Joan of Arc presented France to Charles VII, so Minin and Pozharsky offered Russia a new dynasty of Czars in the person of sixteen-year-old Mikhail Romanov.

4 | THE TRAGIC DYNASTY

THE RUSSIAN PEOPLE, who had suffered greatly during the Time of Troubles, demanded peace and order. The question of choosing a new Czar was discussed at a number of meetings in and around the city. It is even said that prayers were spoken throughout the lands of Moscow, asking that the election be made not according to the laws of human intrigue, but according to the Will of God.

There was no lack of candidates for the Kremlin throne, from foreign dynasties to famous local boyar families. However, all were rejected. The people had suffered too much over the last decade. They wanted to see someone on the throne who had himself been wronged by the previous rulers, and who thus understood their suffering. According to the people, the Romanovs were just such a wronged and yet worthy family.

The founder of the Romanov line was a native of Prussia, Andrei Kobila. The first and favourite wife of Ivan the Terrible, the Czarina Anastasia – famous for her gentle nature and her willingness to intercede on behalf of ordinary people – also belonged to this line. Her brother Nikita Romanov left a similar favourable impression, having saved a great number of people from the chopping block. The father of the future Czar, Fyodor Romanov, was the fourth generation of the line.

Fyodor Romanov was intelligent and able, always courteous, well-educated – he was fluent in Latin – and with an enquiring mind. According to his contemporaries, he was a very paragon: there was no better dressed man, nor a more handsome devil, nor a better rider in the whole of Moscow than he. If a Moscow tailor was making a set of clothes for someone, or wanted to boast about his work, he would usually say: 'Now you'll be just like Fyodor Romanov.'

During Boris Godunov's reign Fyodor Romanov was forced to retire to a monastery and was renamed Filaret. When the False Dimitri ascended to the throne, Filaret was restored to the Czar's favour and was raised to the title of Metropolitan.

Not just commoners, but also the boyars and important people looked favourably upon the selection of a Czar from the Romanov line. They remembered the bloody rule of Ivan the Terrible, and they did not want to repeat the experience. They demanded guarantees that the new Czar would not send them to the chopping block on a whim, without trial or investigation, and that he would not rule as a dictator, without seeking their counsel. To ensure this, they thought the Czar should come from a modest, not particularly wealthy line, so that he would have nowhere to expect aid from and would thus be compelled to rely upon them in matters of government.

The Romanovs fitted these requirements perfectly. As far as the boyars could see, the sixteen-year-old Mikhail Romanov, who was put forward as a candidate, did not demonstrate any remarkable capabilities or any sign that he would be able to dispense with their advice.

And so the boyars, the elected representatives from Russian cities and regions, and a great crowd of Muscovites gathered in Red Square before the Kremlin. The high clergy mounted the Place of Execution to ask the electors for their final choice of Czar. Before the electors could answer, the whole crowd in Red Square began shouting: 'We want Mikhail Romanov!!! We want Mikhail Romanov!!!'

Thus began the three hundred year rule of the Romanov dynasty. It was fated to end with the murder of the last Russian Czar Nicholas II and his family by the Bolsheviks, in a cellar in the distant Ural town Ekaterinburg (now Sverdlovsk). But this tragedy of Russia was still far in the future, for now the people shouted 'We want Mikhail Romanov!!!'

The sixteen-year-old adolescent Mikhail Romanov who, from 11 July 1613 was the crowned Czar of all Russia, was by nature soft-hearted, gentle and even melancholic. He did not possess any extraordinary capabilities, and had received hardly any education; at the time of his ascension to the Kremlin throne, he could barely read. But, he wasn't stupid.

It was a hard time for Russia. Bands of brigands roamed the countryside, robbing, raping and burning. Hunger ravaged many regions, driving people to cannibalism. The fields lay fallow. Unburied corpses lay in empty cottages. Towns once bustling with life now numbered only a few hundred souls. The treasury was empty. But perhaps the greatest tragedy was, as the mother of the Czar noted, that the people had become 'small of spirit'. They had lost their moral values. Gone were concepts such as honour, conscience, respect for the law, patriotism and self-sacrifice. Everything was for sale, even justice. Theft, extortion, embezzlement and bribery had become the norm. Everyone who was entrusted with governing the country robbed it. The sixteen-year-old Czar was surrounded by people who did not excel in intellect and energy, but rather in falsehood and self-interest. The Dutchman Massa, who observed Russian life at the time, wrote:

'... I trust that God will open the eyes of the young Czar, as he did with the previous Czar Ivan [the Terrible]; since it is that kind of Czar that Russia needs, otherwise she will perish. The people of the country flourish only under the heavy hand of a master, and only in slavery are they prosperous and happy ...'

It is not important how profound the analysis of the foreigner was, made almost four centuries ago, nor what percentage of truth it contains. What is shameful and disappointing is that it should contain any element of truth at all, as it undoubtedly does.

'The preceding sorrowful history of Russian society was bearing bitter fruit ...' wrote Kostomarov. '... The torture of Ivan the Terrible, the insidious rule of Boris Godunov, and finally the Troubles and the complete disintegration of the entire fabric of government, created a piteous and petty generation, a generation of dull and narrow-minded people, incapable of rising above their everyday self-interests ...'

Having passed through the 20th century, looking back and reading these thoughts written over a hundred years ago by a famous Russian historian, one is overcome with sorrow. How our history repeats itself. How little we learn from the mistakes of the past ...

In 1616 Czar Mikhail turned twenty. It was decided that he should marry, so by tradition a horde of girls was gathered at the Kremlin. The Czar's eye was caught by Maria Hlopov, the daughter of a not too wealthy noble. She was 'raised upon high', in other words she was announced as the Czar's fiancée and was moved to the palace.

The whole country was preparing for the wedding when palace intrigues interfered. One of the influential boyar families close to the throne, fearing that the new relatives of the Czar would remove them from power, took it upon themselves to break up the wedding. Their plan was facilitated by the fact that the bride was taken ill at the time, although the examining doctors concluded that the illness was not serious and would soon pass. It was most likely brought about by overindulgence in sweets, and would not have affected her ability to have children.

The Czar and his mother, however, were told something quite different. They were informed that the illness was dangerous and incurable, and that the girl would not be able to bear the Czar's heirs. Mikhail's mother demanded that her son call off the wedding and send Maria away. With his father the Metropolitan Filaret a prisoner of the Poles, Mikhail's grim mother had a huge influence on the meek and obedient Czar. He did not dare disobey her. Maria and her relatives were exiled to their distant estates.

The Metropolitan Filaret did not return to Moscow from captivity until July 1619, six years after Mikhail's coronation. The son met his father on the outskirts of the city, bowed deeply at his feet, and Filaret in turn bowed to his son the Czar. They both lay upon the ground, embracing and crying. Ten days later, Filaret received the title of Patriarch of Moscow.

Filaret had an authoritative, even imperious appearance. If Mikhail's rule had previously been marked by meekness, soft-heartedness and even lack of will, and in no way by autocracy, now, with Filaret's appearance, the actions of the young Czar became firm and decisive. It was clear that the strong-willed figure of the father now stood at his shoulder. No decree now was signed by the Czar's quill without the blessing of Filaret. He was a strict spiritual pastor, trying to restore the shaken morals of Russian society.

In September of 1624 the Czar, against his will and once again upon the insistence of his mother, married Maria Dolgoruky, the daughter of a count. The marriage did not last long. The very day after the wedding the Czarina was taken ill, and within months she was dead. A year after her death the Czar married a second time, this time Yevdakiya Streshnov, the daughter of a little-known noble and the future mother of Czar Alexei.

◆　◆　◆　◆　◆

Ravaged by the Troubles, the country demanded stability and peace. The main concerns of the new government were to fill the treasury and to quell the rampant bandits. The death penalty was introduced for murder and brigandry. For a first and second theft, the culprit lost a hand, for the third he lost his life.

Many methods was adopted to help fill the treasury, some of which are still valid today. For instance, systematically turning the people into drunkards. The government instituted a monopoly on winemaking and the sale of wine, and did everything possible to ensure that the people drank more. Drinking houses were built everywhere, springing up like mushrooms. This served two purposes: filling the treasury, and distracting people from the real troubles of their lives.

In the spring of 1642 Czar Mikhail sent an ambassador to Denmark, intending to betroth his daughter Irena to the Danish Prince Valdemar. The ambassador was instructed not to show Valdemar a 'likeness' or portrait of the Czarina, but instead to praise the bride verbally, pointing out such positive traits as her 'modesty and cleverness in all things and that she has not been drunk a single time in her whole life'.

At the time Europe viewed Russia as a wild and fearsome land, and most Europeans were unwilling to venture there. However, the Danish king decided to accept the proposal. First, he secured several conditions: the Prince would not be compelled to change his faith; he would be beholden only to the Czar and to no one else, and was to receive a generous land grant which would become hereditary. The Russian Czar accepted these conditions, offering his future son-in-law several ancient Russian towns. So the Prince Valdemar headed for Moscow.

Moscow welcomed him grandly and warmly. The Czar threw a feast in his honour. The Czarina sent him several dozen towels, which had symbolic value as a traditional wedding gift. Everything was proceeding smoothly, when suddenly the Czar told the Prince that there was one small formality that must be performed before the wedding – conversion to the Orthodox faith. Valdemar refused, pointing out the prior agreement. When the Czar insisted, the Prince then demanded to return to Denmark, but was refused. Losing his patience, Valdemar tried to leave Russia secretly, killing one of his guards and being viciously beaten himself.

Valdemar then found himself a prisoner of the Czar. He was treated with politeness and respect, was entertained and taken on royal hunts, but his every move was watched. 'Well-wishers' who were assigned to him whispered both sweet and terrifying things, that he could end his life in Siberia if he remained stubborn and that his bride was wonderful. However, the Prince remained firm in his conviction. He was ready to part with his life, but not with the faith of his fathers.

It is hard to say how this dishonourable story would have ended if Czar Mikhail had not died in July 1645. His son Alexei ascended to the throne, and allowed Valdemar to return to his homeland.

The reign of the first Romanov cannot be numbered among the shining epochs of Russian history, and he himself is remembered by history as a rather colourless figure.

◆　◆　◆　◆　◆

Alexei Romanov was nicknamed 'the Quietest' by ordinary people. Historians maintain that he was the kindest of all the Russian Czars. Outwardly he was a portly but attractive man; tall, sporting a beautiful full beard. He was strong, had a welcoming, good-natured gaze and a joyful disposition. He believed that God wanted people to be happy, and that if a person is sorrowful they were offending God.

Not even his enemies could accuse him of being dishonourable. He was a wonderful family man, drank in moderation, had a good heart and a poetic soul. He was extremely pious; his favourite reading material was church manuscripts and he observed religious fasts meticulously. On Mondays, Wednesdays and Fridays he ate only black rye-bread bread and water. On Palm Sundays the Czar personally led the Patriarch's horse by the reins, symbolizing the entrance of Jesus into Jerusalem. For this service he received one hundred ducats from the Patriarch which he put aside for his funeral, as money earned by his own sweat.

Before significant holidays the Czar would visit prisons and almshouses, when he would pardon criminals, buy out debtors and give generously to the poor. Sometimes he would invite down-and-outs into the palace and sit down to dinner with them, even serving them the food himself.

It must be noted here that dabbling with good works for the poor is a very common phenomenon throughout the ages. It is human nature for people to show off their wealth and importance, and the poor are a kind of contrast to their significance. Also, by the unwritten laws of the church, the poor enjoy a form of ritual respect, asking God to forgive the rich man's wealth in return for a modest amount of alms.

Czar Alexei's kindness and humanity have entered folklore. The chronicles tell of a hospital that the Czar visited, where the stench was so overpowering that those accompanying him became physically ill. The Czar however patiently moved from cot to cot, asked the sick about their lives and kissed them upon the lips. Another time the Czar refused to confirm the death sentence on an army deserter, announcing: 'God doesn't give courage to everyone.'

All these good works of 'the Quietest' Czar need to be considered in the context of the times. In spite of all his kindness, Czar Alexei didn't balk at beating a boyar who had enraged him, or pulling him around by the beard, or even tearing a part of his beard clean out and sending him scurrying with a boot up the backside. The Czar's anger did not last long however, and the abused usually received generous gifts as a peace offering.

The Czar's entertainments were traditional: chess, hawking, the tales of frail old men about days gone by, midget jesters, and during winter – especially during the holidays – fights between hunters and wild bears. The hunter entered a walled-off circle armed with a boar-spear, and was soon joined by a hungry and wild bear. There was nowhere to run, so they had to fight. The bear would roar fiercely, stand up on his hind legs, and advance upon the hunter with bared teeth. The hunters were a brave bunch however, so the bear did not always win. When it did, the man was torn to pieces.

Chess became a major part of the everyday life of the Russian court. There was even a special workshop in the Kremlin to make and repair chess pieces. The aged storytellers were similarly important. Some of them claimed to be a hundred years old or more. They were specially housed close to the court and during the long winter evenings, the Czar would invite them to his chambers where his whole family gathered and the greybeards would tell of distant lands which they had visited, about foreign customs, and about ancient Russia. Towards the end of his life the Czar Alexei became interested in dramatic theatre – that new western fad which was beginning to make headway into Russia.

Another passion gripped the Russian monarch: a passion for pomp and ceremony. All foreigners visiting Moscow during that period were awed by the magnificence of the court and the slave-like obeisance shown to the Czar. The street was swept before his carriage, and riders heading in the opposite direction would dismount and prostrate themselves. It was forbidden not only to approach the palace doors, but even the palace itself on horseback. People of lower rank would have to dismount far from the palace and continue on foot, regardless of the weather. Common folk would doff their hats and walk bareheaded if they even spied the Kremlin from afar. In other words, the Czar became the personification of the nation.

Czar Alexei's court presented a very exotic picture. The Kremlin had always been an amalgam of buildings haphazardly thrown together: towers and churches of different epochs connected to each other by indoor or outdoor walkways, galleries and underground passages. And the older it got the more sprawling it became. Women's wings did not fall under the concept of the Czar's court, it was a purely male phenomenon. All courtiers living in Moscow – who numbered in the thousands – had to present themselves in the Kremlin every day, as if to place themselves at the Czar's disposal. Thus the court was extraordinarily overcrowded. Fights would often erupt, although no one could bare steel since it was forbidden to enter wearing weapons. Duelling in its western form was as yet unknown, so arguments were decided with fists and bloody noses, or if a combatant was particularly enraged, with a brick to the head.

In 1647 Alexei decided to marry. Once more a legion of young women was gathered in the Kremlin, out of which the Czar chose the daughter of a low-ranked courtier. Everything was proceeding smoothly until the bride was first dressed in the clothes which the Czar had presented her with. The overzealous attending women tightened the corset so much that the poor girl fainted in front of her prospective 'groom. This was taken as a sign of 'falling sickness' (epilepsy) and the marriage was called off. Since she was supposed to have 'hidden her sickness' she and her family were sent into exile in Siberia.

The event had such an effect on the young Czar that he refused food for several days. His guardian, the boyar Boris Morozov, was compelled to distract him with banquets and hunting. The people however, who always knew everything, whispered that the incident with the bride was no accident, but was orchestrated by Morozov himself. To strengthen his position, Morozov hatched a plan to marry the Czar to one of the daughters of a subordinate, while he himself would marry the other girl and thus become related to the Czar.

One day, while accompanying the Czar during prayers in the Assumption Cathedral in the Kremlin, Morozov pointed out these two sisters to the Czar. The Czar liked one of them, and he declared her his fiancée. On 16 January 1648 Alexei Romanov was joined in marriage to Maria Miloslavsky.

The marriage was a happy one. It gifted the Czar with eight daughters and five sons. The fate of Morozov however, did not go according to his imagined plan. He married the other Miloslavsky sister, even though there was a large age difference between them, and the couple 'gave birth not to children but to jealousy', as the people say. So the young wife had to endure more than a few lashes administered by the jealous husband.

After the Czar's marriage, Morozov began to move the relatives of the young Czarina – who were now his relatives as well – into key positions. They were all greedy people, eager to increase their holdings. There was one clear path to quick riches: bribes. Two of the relatives made their living not only from bribes, but also from extortion. Their henchmen would accuse innocent people of imaginary crimes. The accused would then be arrested and bribes tortured out of them to secure their release. No complaints ever reached the Czar; everything was decided by Morozov himself.

Unrest stirred among the people. A mob decided to look for an opportunity to forcibly confront the Czar in public and demand that he punish the extortionists. They found their chance in May 1648, when the Czar was returning from a monastery. Frightened but gentle, Alexei promised that he himself would get to the bottom of the affair and punish the guilty. At this, the crowd might have dispersed and the incident might have ended, had not Morozov's henchmen attacked the crowd as soon as the Czar's party departed.

As a result, an angry mob ran to the Kremlin, demanding that the two extortionists be handed over to it for punishment. Trying to calm them, Morozov himself went out to the people, only to be met with stones and shouts of 'We want you as well!' The frightened Morozov hid in the Kremlin while the mob threw itself upon his estate and began to demolish it. Morozov's young wife was only spared because she was the Czarina's sister, but the mob looted and destroyed everything. People were wading through the wine cellars waist-deep in wine, and some got so drunk that they drowned in it.

After the riot, the enraged mob returned to the Kremlin and repeated its demands for the two extortionists. The situation was becoming critical. The Kremlin decided to sacrifice these two, and gave them to the crowd. They were immediately beaten to death with sticks, but the crowd did not disperse, demanding that Morozov himself now be handed over. It is hard to say how this all would have ended, but suddenly a fire sprang up in the city, distracting the attention of the mob. An inn and the surrounding bars were burning. The mob threw itself at the bars, breaking the barrels of vodka and scooping it up in handfuls and in their hats.

All these events frightened the young Czar. His good-nature remained, but he became more cautious and less trusting. It is said that out of fright he once killed an innocent petitioner who had approached the Czar's carriage, and then bitterly regretted his action. It was these and similar events which prompted Alexei to form the Department of Secret Business, a secret police organisation which was a reflection in history of Ivan the Terrible's *oprichnina*.

In October 1649 Alexei also created the *Ulozdeniye*. This was a collection of written laws, formalising the crimes and punishments which were usually enforced by custom, tradition or the will of the powerful. In modern language, this was a step in the direction of a law-abiding government.

For intentional murder the *Ulozdeniye* carried a punishment of six weeks' imprisonment and torture, followed by beheading. For a first theft, two years' imprisonment and the removal of one ear. A second theft meant prison in exile and the removal of the second ear. A wife who poisoned or killed her husband was buried in the ground up to her neck and left until she died.

These harsh penalties were in keeping with the customs of the time, but what the *Ulozdeniye* did was enshrine them in the form of law, thus attempting to curb arbitrary punishments or vengeance. Everyone now knew what awaited them for committing this or that crime.

The *Ulozdeniye* also made legal in Russia a barbarous law known as 'The Czar's word and deed'. Something similar was already in effect in a number of European countries. Under this law, everyone was required to report any behaviour or language which might be thought to show evil intent towards the Czar, irrespective of the wealth, honours and rank of the suspect. A beggar in the street could point to a notable boyar and yell the phrase 'The Czar's word and deed!', meaning that he wanted to make a serious accusation against the other. Both would be seized and taken to be investigated. If the accused did not admit to his guilt, he was subjected to torture. If he denied the accusation under torture as well, then the accuser was subjected to the same torture. If the accuser could not stand the torture and admitted his accusations to be fraudulent, then he was executed. However, if he could withstand the torture three times, then the accusation was considered proven.

In both Russia and much of Europe, the 'ethics of jurisprudence' of the times meant that a person was not usually executed until he had confessed, if necessary under torture.

The punishment for not reporting someone was equally harsh. Wives reported husbands and children reported fathers to avoid being executed themselves. Naturally, if anyone heard anything suspicious, they hurried to report it so that they themselves would not be punished. Spies and informants spread across the whole country. They were at weddings and at funerals, at parties and friendly gatherings.

The reign of Alexei Romanov is a vivid example of how enormous power, placed in the hands of dishonest and dull-witted bureaucrats, can turn the rule of even such a soft-hearted man as Alexei into a living hell.

◆　◆　◆　◆　◆

1669 was a tragic year for the Czar's family. The Czarina died in childbirth, and several months later, one after the other, two of the Czar's sons also died. This was a series of fearsome blows for the impressionable soul of the Czar. However, towards the end of the year he had recovered, and began to think of a second wife. On 23 January 1671, Alexei Romanov married Natalia Narishkin, and on 30 May 1672 she gave birth to Czareivitch Peter – the future Emperor of Russia.

Czarina Natalia was a woman of the world, holding progressive views for the time. While the Czar's first wife Maria Miloslavsky followed ancient tradition and went to church from the palace via special corridors so she would not accidentally be defiled by a stranger's glance, Natalia rode in an open carriage and showed herself to the people.

With her involvement, a theatre was started in the Kremlin and a wandering troupe of German actors was invited. Later, a special building was constructed, a 'comedy hall' which had a half-circle stage, scenery, drop curtains, a special place for the orchestra and a box for the Czar. In other words, a real theatre. At first only plays on biblical themes were performed, but gradually they moved to more modern plays. Although the theatre of Molière was flourishing in France at the time, and Shakespeare's *Hamlet* and *King Lear* were already over half a century old, for Russia the theatre was an almost revolutionary event. It was not very many years since the False Dimitri lost not only his throne but also his life for holding a masquerade in the Kremlin

Innovations even began to seep into the inner chambers of the palace. The furniture consisted of the usual benches and trunks, while the windows were made of mica, but here and there between the benches one might glimpse a rare newcomer from Europe: silver or gold enamelled stools and armchairs, covered in velvet. Paintings appeared on the walls, mostly depicting biblical themes, and in the most inaccessible places, shyly hiding behind curtains, there hung mirrors – a very ambiguous novelty according to Russian morals of the time. And finally, to top off everything, bright parrots from across the seas squawked in their cages.

Despite his imposing appearance, Czar Alexei Romanov was a man of fragile health, and his corpulence also undermined his health. In his late forties, his strength started to wane. On 28 January 1676 he bequeathed the throne to his oldest son Fyodor and issued some final orders. Prisoners were released from the dungeons, people in debt to the government were forgiven and private debtors were bought out. Finally, Alexei received the Eucharist, and on the morning of 29 January quietly went to the next world at the age of forty-seven. Thus ended the rule of the kindest of all Russian Czars.

5 | THE GREAT SKIPPER

IT MIGHT SEEM FAIR TO ASSUME that the fourteenth child of Alexei Romanov would stand no chance whasoever to inherit the throne; yet this particular fourteenth child turned out to be none other than Peter the Great.

At the time of Peter's birth, the Kremlin more resembled a fortified camp than a Czar's palace. Narrow rooms with low domed ceilings, dark hallways, candelabras flashing in the darkness, iron grilles on the windows, armed men at the doors ... Groups of soldiers and monks were everywhere. The Czar's palace was flanked by a cathedral on one side and a monastery on the other, and differed little from either of them. Faint sounds could be heard from behind the thick walls of all three buildings, flowing together into an overall hum: the monotonous repetition of prayers, the songs of women locked away in towers, the echoes of orgies secretly taking place in some corner of the palace, the loud cries of prisoners being tortured in the dungeons. Yet the overall impression was of silence; people spoke in whispers, ate guardedly, warily watched one another. It was, in its various guises, a crypt, a harem and a prison. All of Russia was distilled here, and although many centuries had passed, the country remained unworldly, completely isolated from neighbouring Europe, which ignored her.

Peter was born in such an environment, the youngest of eight sons and six daughters of Alexei Romanov. Both physically and spiritually he differed markedly from his sickly and weak brothers and sisters. Unlike them Peter was unusually tall (well over 6 feet), powerfully built and brimming with health – in striking contrast, too, to his sick father. Rumour already circulated around the Kremlin on this point. According to one story, a German doctor working at the court switched his son for the daughter born to the Czar and his young wife. Another told how Peter himself once asked a courtier of massive build: 'Whose son am I? Not yours perhaps? Don't be frightened, speak, or I'll strangle you.' 'My Lord ...' answered the courtier in confusion, 'I don't know what to say ... I wasn't alone ...'

Alexei Romanov died, leaving the throne to his eldest son, the fourteen-year-old Fyodor, who was intelligent, educated, but sickly from birth. He could only walk with the aid of a stick, and his hat had to be removed by servants. Naturally, the power in his hands was only nominal.

In the summer of 1680, Fyodor saw a girl he very much liked during the Easter celebrations. She was the daughter of a little-known courtier of Polish origin, Agafia Grushetski. True to tradition, Fyodor ordered that girls be gathered in the Kremlin, and chose Agafia from among them. On 18 July 1680 they were married. With the arrival of the young Czarina, Polish customs and language began to infiltrate the Kremlin. The Czar himself spoke Polish quite well and read Polish books. It was all short-lived: in July 1681 the Czarina and her newborn baby died in childbirth.

The Czar in the meantime was deteriorating. To bolster his will to live, his counsellors recommended him to take another wife. In January 1682, Fyodor married a second time, wedding Marfa Apraxin. But within two months, on 27 April 1682, Czar Fyodor, not yet twenty-one, died.

After Fyodor's death the throne was due to pass to Alexei Romanov's next son Ivan, who by then had turned fifteen. Ivan, however, was almost blind and, though harmless, mentally ill. The boyars were therefore unanimous in their approval that the throne pass on to the ten-year-old Peter.

Apart from eight sons, Alexei Romanov also had six daughters, but only the name of one – Sophia – entered history. Sophia was Ivan's sister (by the same mother), and was twenty-six years old at the time. Here is how a French diplomat described her: 'A hideous body of inordinate thickness, a head as wide as a kettle, a face covered with hair and lumps on her legs.' A Russian historian, trying to soften the picture wrote: 'Unpleasant to the eyes of foreigners, Sophia could seem attractive to the Muscovites of the time, who did not consider stoutness a failing.' On one matter, however, all chroniclers agreed: 'Although her body was short, wide and ungainly, her political mind was sharp and developed.'

Before 1682, Sophia's life in the Kremlin was like that of any other Russian girl of the time. The daughters of the Czar lived like prisoners in their towers. Apart from close relatives, no one could visit them, and they could certainly not appear anywhere in public. Even the doctor was only admitted in the case of very serious illness. The curtains were drawn when he entered, and he could feel the patient's pulse only through a cloth. Secret passages led from the towers to the churches, where the Czarina and her daughters were hidden from the curiosity of the other churchgoers behind red curtains.

The fear of sin, blasphemy, temptation, the evil eye – all this required that the young Czarinas be held in captivity. Lacking the right of marrying a mere mortal due to their lofty birth, and not permitted to marry a foreign prince since he would be of another faith, they were cursed with loneliness, without love, marriage and motherhood. Such was the law.

Sophia broke the rules by falling in love with a courtier. Since a woman could not assume the throne in Russia, her secret wish was to marry her beloved, raise him to the throne, and thus become the Czarina. Obviously such a plan could be realised only if the mentally ill Ivan were to be Czar rather than Peter. The sick brother would be in need of his older sister's advice, and this would open her path to the throne.

A month after Peter was proclaimed Czar, Sophia organised a rebellion among those sections of the royal army known as *streltzi* (infantry). Rumours spread among them that relatives of Natalia – Peter's mother – wanted to poison the Czarevich Ivan. On 15 May 1682, the *streltzi* broke into the palace, instigating a bloody slaughter that lasted three days, during which time almost all of Peter's relatives on his mother's side were killed. As the ten-year-old boy looked on, the *streltzi* cut his loved ones to pieces, feeding the body parts to the dogs, hurling people out of the palace windows on to the spears of those standing below, and revelling in torture. These terrifying three days were to be forever etched into Peter's memory, propelling him towards a no less bloody revenge. In the end, following the demands of the *streltzi*, Ivan and Peter were declared joint Czars, Ivan being the senior, and Sophia was named Regent until the brothers came of age.

Peter was naturally terrified by the events taking place before his eyes. Together with his mother, he abandoned the Kremlin and moved to a village outside Moscow. This exile represented joyous freedom from the conservative life of the Kremlin, and changed the entire inner world of Russia's future reformer.

After that appalling butchery Peter felt only hatred for the Kremlin, going there only when absolutely necessary, when the young Czars needed to preside over some official ceremony. For this purpose, a special throne was brought from Holland, and the young brothers would sit side by side while Sophia stood behind them, telling them what to say. Thus her dreams were realized. She and her lover had reached the pinnacle of power as Russia's true rulers. In her free time away from government matters, Sophia amused herself by writing plays for the Kremlin theatre, of which she played the leading part. The feeble-minded Ivan could not prevent her exercising power, while the young Peter was virtually an exile in a village where he spent an isolated boyhood.

History has a habit of colouring the biographies of great people. It was said of Peter, for example, that at twelve years old he was already voicing original thoughts on the art of war. This is mere fabrication. Quite the contrary: the boy developed very slowly, both physically and mentally. At the age of three he still had a wet-nurse, and he could not yet read or write at eleven.

Even at sixteen years of age he had barely mastered the written language and only two laws of arithmetic. His education was in no sense systematic, so in effect he was self-taught, although possessing a heightened sense of childish curiosity.

Living in a village, far from the notoriety of the Kremlin, the young Czar acquired friends from among the servants. They were the children of stablemen, cooks, cleaners and washerwomen. Left to himself, he spent all his time with them, playing soldiers, instinctively assuming command, building earthen fortifications to attack. Thus, in the form of a game, the foundation was laid for what would later be known as the 'Toy Army'.

On one occasion Peter came across an old English boat rotting in a cellar. It was repaired and set afloat. From then on, trips on the water became the young Czar's passion. He had never seen the sea and began to dream of it. A historian would later say: 'Peter gave Russia a fleet, before he gave her the sea.'

It was not only the future army and fleet that were created in these boisterous games of fiery youth. In due course he would promote his brash friends, raised in kitchens and stables, to the level of counts and field-marshals. The members of this new gentry exhibited all the vices of Russian society of the day, but they could never be accused of incompetence and laziness. The feeling of good fellowship derived from those early days with common folk marked Czar Peter for life; he always remained their good comrade and drinking partner, but he also retained their rough manners and cynical high spirits.

Time passed, and the war games of the young Czar began to take on a very imposing scale. Toys become weapons. A fortress was built on the river-bank near the village, from which cannons roared, while real naval battles were played out on the water. Such pastimes troubled the Czarina Natalia. Her son was slipping completely out of her control, not to mention the fact that he repeatedly exposed himself to serious danger as accidents occurred. Once, an exploding hand-grenade burned his face. To put an end to this, the mother resorted to a tried and tested method; she decided to marry off her seventeen-year-old son.

On 27 January 1689, Peter entered into his first marriage to Evdakia Lapuhina, who was to bear his eldest son Alexei. Although the marriage only lasted three months, it was nevertheless crucial to the power-loving aspirations of Sophia, since according to Russian tradition, a married man was considered to have come of age. Consequently, Peter now had the right to free himself publicly from the Regency of his elder sister.

All this was clearly understood by Sophia, whose lust of power and the throne now reached its zenith. She decided to meet fate head-on. During the night of 7 August 1689, Peter was suddenly awoken by informers who had come from the Kremlin to warn him that Sophia had gathered the *streltzi*, intending to attack the village and kill him.

Peter fled. Barefoot, in his nightshirt, he ran into the stables, mounted an unharnessed horse and hid in a nearby forest. Soon several stablehands arrived with his clothes, followed by other friends. They all galloped to the Monastery of the Trinity outside Moscow, a traditional refuge for the Czar's family. Next day, they were joined by loyal guardsmen from the 'Toy Army', by now a formidable force.

Sophia's game was lost. On Peter's orders, she was stripped of her power and sent to a monastery. The simple-minded Ivan had no way of hindering his younger brother, and in 1696 he quietly moved on to the next world. Sophia's downfall signalled the beginning of Peter's unchallenged rule and ushered in a new period in the history of Russia.

A punctilious German observer noted in his diary that, on 21 August 1698 Czar Peter returned to Moscow incognito from Europe. Not wishing to stay in the Kremlin, he secluded himself in his village, where he happily spent time among the troops. This was an extraordinary break with tradition. No previous Russian Czar had ever travelled to Europe, let alone under an assumed name. Yet this Czar had spent more than a year there, posing as an officer named Peter Mikhailov. In Holland he learned shipbuilding, working as a simple carpenter on the wharf, spending his evenings in bars, bellowing songs with local sailors. To this day, Peter's house at Saardam still stands, carrying the inscription: 'For a great man, there are no small tasks.'

In Germany the Russian monarch was shown a preserved human embryo in a museum, and was so moved that he grabbed it from out of the jar and kissed it. Sitting at table, this 'gentle savage' did not know what to do with his napkin, which he had never used in his life, and dancing with a lady, mistook her corset for her natural body – marvelling at how hard the backs of German women were. In Denmark he discussed with the King how much a street harlot should cost, establishing that the price should be no more than one kopeck for three embraces. In France, at Rochelle's grave, this strange Russian officer exclaimed: 'Oh, great Cardinal! I would give you half my kingdom, if you would but teach me to rule the other half.' In the country of sailors – England – this fanatical lover of the sea exclaimed: 'I would prefer the title of an English Admiral to that of a Russian Czar.' Eventually the disguised monarch found his way to Venice, where a lavish reception awaited him, but then bad news from home forced him to drop everything and return to Moscow immediately. Precisely because of this, the Czar bypassed the Kremlin and headed straight for his village, into the protection of his beloved 'Toy Army'.

The problem was that while Peter was travelling, the hated *streltzi* – incited by Sophia – once again tried to overthrow the Czar and return his elder sister to power. However, regiments of guards loyal to Peter defeated and captured the *streltzi*, and now the Czar himself had returned for trial and retribution.

The day after his arrival he invited guests to his village and organised a great feast, where rivers of vodka flowed. The Czar kissed many of the invited boyars, and immediately cut off their beards personally with a pair of scissors, ordering them henceforth to adopt a European appearance and wear shorter clothes. This was a grave insult to their piety. Nowadays, it is difficult to imagine what it was like for the Orthodox boyars to be left without beards – to 'bare their faces'. A man without a beard lost his likeness to God. The boyars held their tongues, however, fearing the angry Czar and his favourite officers – 'the chicks in Peter's nest', ready to carry out any order he gave.

These 'chicks', raised by Peter from the commonest ranks, were now high-ranking army officers. For instance, the former servant of a pie-maker – Alexashka – was now Alexander Menshikov, Peter's chief minister, the second man in the government. He was completely illiterate, signing with a mark, but clever, cunning and energetic. With the help of competent secretaries he controlled cities and armies. He was the only illiterate man to become a member of Britain's Royal Society. Isaac Newton himself signed his diploma, for which the impoverished genius received a precious ring from the fabulously wealthy Menshikov.

At this very feast, in which the boyars were humbled, the drunken Czar, noting that his first minister was defying European convention by dancing without unhitching his sword, hit him so hard that the minister's nose gushed blood. Still apparently under the influence of drink, and responding to renewed rumours of a *streltzi* conspiracy, Peter then rode to the Kremlin at night to see his eight-year-old son Alexei, whom the *streltzi* were allegedly threatening to murder by suffocation. Twenty years later the Czar himself would condemn his son to death, while his mother – Peter's first wife – was to end her life in a rat-infested prison cell. But for the time being, kissing his son and riding away from the Kremlin, the enraged Czar vowed a swift and gruesome vengeance on the *streltzi*.

Retribution began within a month. Some two thousand *streltzi* were rounded up in Moscow prisons. Interrogations took place in the Czar's village. The accused were first whipped, then placed on hot coals. According to the chronicles, up to thirty fires were lit every day, over which the rebels were 'roasted'. Finally, on the morning of 30 September, a huge crowd gathered to see the *streltzi* taken away for execution. Long columns of carts rolled from the village to the Kremlin, where scaffolds were already standing in the Red Square. Two of the condemned sat in each cart, holding lit candles in their hands. Following the cart with heart-rending wails ran their wives and children. They were duly hung in the square, their arms and legs were broken, their bodies hacked with swords and axes. The Czar himself is said to have cut off personally the heads of five victims, ordering that those close by do the same, showing anger when they did so half-heartedly and clumsily. The bodies of the executed were hung upon the spiked walls of the Kremlin. As a warning to enemies of the Czar, they remained there, pecked to pieces by crows, for the entire cold winter until spring, when it was finally permitted to bury them.

The great Russian painter Surikov recorded the event in one of his finest works – *The Morning the Streltzi Were Executed*. During the period of Stalin's harshest terror, the famous Russian poetess Anna Ahmatov wrote in her *Requiem*: ' ... like the wives of the Streltzi, I shall wail at the Kremlin walls ...'

On Peter's orders, Sophia was this time forcibly shaved and locked in a monastery, while several *streltzi* were even hung above on the shutters of her cell, so close she could even touch them if she wished. She suffered here until her death in 1704.

It seemed that in his rage Peter was avenging himself not only on the rebels, but also on the hated Kremlin, Moscow and the entire old world. The French ambassador wrote of him at the age of twenty-six: 'His facial features are rather handsome, one can even glimpse goodness in him sometimes. Looking at him it is hard to believe that he personally cuts off the heads of subjects who have incurred his displeasure.'

Peter always stood out from the crowd by reason of his height, and his strength was further developed by his constant work with the hammer and axe: he could roll a metal plate into a tube with his fingers. In time, however, his handsome face became marred by a nervous tic, tremors and head-shaking, seemingly brought on by the nervous traumas of his childhood years, compounded by late-night drinking. The uncontrollable anger expressed in his face not only aroused general fear but was even known to cause ladies to faint. He moved with resolution, waving his right hand expansively, so that his companions often had to run to keep up. As a rule, he was averse to staying in one place, and seemed almost pathologically driven to be always on the move.

Peter's style of dress, however, was completely out of character. One of the richest monarchs of Europe, he walked around in thick patched woollen stockings and very grubby, worn shoes. This was complemented by a similarly shabby overcoat, which often had little to distinguish it from that of a peasant, and he received visitors in a torn robe. He travelled in a run-down carriage, pulled by an old nag, and only borrowed a smarter vehicle in exceptional circumstances.

Nor was his home any more worthy of a Czar. By ancient tradition he disliked like low ceilings and the rooms built for him were cell-like. Only once did Peter allow himself to be persuaded to wear a ceremonial costume stitched with silver. This was at the coronation of his second wife Catherine. But even on this occasion he still wore his favourite grubby boots.

In fact, in every aspect of behaviour, the Czar more resembled a regular at a dockside bar than the owner of a palace. The representative of the Polish king, who knew Peter well, once wrote in his diary that while dining with the Czar in Berlin, as the guest of the Crown Prince, he was pleasantly surprised that on this occasion time Peter behaved almost respectably: 'He didn't burp at the table, didn't fart, and didn't pick his teeth ...'

Apart from work, revelry was Peter's main passion. 'He didn't miss a single day without getting drunk,' wrote one contemporary. Getting up very early, usually at five in the morning, the Czar would begin his day by drinking a whole glass of vodka. In the company of women, to whom he was never averse, the Czar delighted above all in vulgar debauchery. He got pleasure from seeing them drunk. Well-bred young girls were compelled on order to drink Grenadier-like portions of vodka. The future Empress Catherine herself – 'A first-rate drunk', according to a contemporary – won the Czar's favour to some measure due to this particular trait. Peter's favourite drinking companions were ship captains, Dutch merchants or even palace lackeys. Glass in hand, he would often sit long past midnight with them, mixing dirty anecdotes with jokes and explosions of anger. He had the habit, too, of inciting brawls among them; but anyone who incurred the Czar's wrath was punished by having to drain a huge schooner of vodka, after which he would usually slide under the table. To the end of his days Peter did not modify his simple tastes, not did he lose his natural wildness.

Was the Czar a cruel barbarian? His contemporaries considered him such, arguing that it was impossible to explain many of Peter's actions without conceding that the pain and suffering he caused gave him gratification. He was often present during torture, and not only as a spectator. Voltaire describes an incident related to him by Frederick the Great, which allegedly took place during a dinner Peter had with the Prussian ambassador. According to the latter, the Czar amused himself during dinner by cutting the heads off twenty *streltzi* and drinking as many glasses of vodka, offering his guest the chance to do the same. More than likely this is an exaggeration, but it illustrates the wealth of rumours that surrounded the Russian Czar. Another contemporary recounts how the Czar bludgeoned a servant to death before his eyes, simply because the man did not remove his hat quickly enough in the royal presence. Clearly, much depended upon mood. The story is told of a fanatic who tried to kill the Czar while he slept. He shot twice, but both times the pistol misfired. Gripped by terror, the murderer woke the Czar. 'It seems God sent me to give my Lord a sign that he watches over you,' he said. Now kill me, my Lord.' 'You don't kill messengers,' Peter replied calmly, and turned over on to his other side.

The Czar was completely devoid of sentimentality. He could enter a prison cell containing a former favourite and calmly announce that, regrettably, he was obliged to have the man hung tomorrow. Before executing an ex-mistress, he kissed her on the steps of the scaffold, then took her severed head and proceeded to explain its anatomical construction to those around him. Despite all this, it was Peter who gave Russia the foundations of a legal system, writing in his proclamation: 'It is better to pardon ten guilty criminals, than condemn one innocent to death.' For those harsh times, this was quite an extraordinary step.

Peter remained active throughout his life. He was apparently versed in fourteen professional trades; considered the best shipwright in Russia, capable of constructing a ship from start to finish, he worked alongside his carpenters. His curiosity was as boundless as it was lacking in a sense of restraint. When his elder brother Fyodor's second wife died, he decided to check the rumours that although the sickly Fyodor was sexually impotent, his wife was never unfaithful to him, even after his death. To this end the Czar himself performed the autopsy and evidently satisfied himself as to his sister-in-law's chastity.

Hospital personnel were ordered to inform the Czar of any interesting patients who needed an operation. Peter not only attended the operations, but often took up the surgical knife himself. In fairness it must be said that his operations rarely ended well. Upon falling sick, those close to the Czar would be terrified that Peter would find out and turn up offering his services. After returning from Holland, Peter always carried a set of dental instruments on his person, and missed no opportunity to put them to use. In the St Petersburg museum, a batch of teeth ripped out by the Czar has survived to this day. Rumour had it that he would often pull good teeth out along with the infected ones.

In Copenhagen the Czar was very impressed by a mummy exhibited in the museum, and became determined to acquire it. The curator of the museum passed this on to his king, who politely declined, explaining that 'this mummy is of exceptional beauty ... there is no other like it ...' Peter, enraged, went back to the museum, grabbed the mummy, tore off its nose, disfigured it in various ways and left with the words: 'Now you can keep it!'

Many tales circulated about Peter's workaholic tendencies. It is said that the Prussian ambassador was obliged to climb to the top of a mast to give the Czar his credentials, since the monarch was busy tightening the rigging at the time and refused to cut short his work and return to the deck. This is most probably a legend, but it was attested that after a drunken nocturnal orgy, when many glasses of vodka were already consumed, the Czar, hearing the sound of fire alarm bells, would leap on to his horse and gallop to the other end of the city, labouring there many hours on end as a simple fireman. The citizens knew this for certain. Once, while visiting a factory, Peter vanished among the workers and worked beside them for several hours on end with a hammer in his hands. Afterwards, he demanded payment for his labour from the owner. After scrupulous calculation it turned out that the Czar had earned fifty-four kopecks. Accepting them, Peter showed his satisfaction, declaring that he would spend them on new shoes, since his old ones had completely fallen apart.

Peter was also much diverted by the operations of his secret police force. Having a whole army of detectives and spies at his command, the Czar nevertheless liked to engage in this activity himself, wandering among the tables at feasts and eavesdropping on the babblings of drunken tongues. It was said that he would even take late walks in the evening or at night to listen under people's windows. Almost every prominent courtier had a secret informer assigned to him, either in the form of a secretary or a servant. Under pain of harsh punishment, citizens were ordered to inform on each other. It was enough to shout the key phrase, 'The Czar's word and deed!' to indicate that such an individual had information worthy of the Czar's ear: it might be that someone spoke slightingly of the Czar or his family, had concealed valuables from the treasury, or had simply mouthed an incautious word against the government.

The arrest of a suspect invariably resulted in the detention of dozens if not hundreds of others. More often than not, they were completely unrelated people whom the accused had named, under torture, as his co-conspirators. Sometimes the arrested man was led through the streets, where he had to 'recognise his accomplices'. In such cases the street quickly emptied, people scattering with cries of 'A tongue! A tongue!' This was the name given to the accused, who had now become a deadly threat to any passer-by, since he could single any of them out.

Thus Peter raised the new Russia on the twin pillars of enlightenment and barbarity. Axes were employed both to chop off heads and to cut down forests to build St Petersburg, a new capital on the Baltic Sea, or as people said, to 'cut a window into Europe'. The question was, and still remains: what will gain the upper hand in Russian life, enlightenment without barbarity, or barbarity without enlightenment?

As mentioned, Peter was very fond of women, but was not very selective. In Copenhagen, for instance, he summoned to his presence a dockside prostitute. It is recorded, too, that Peter once fought with a gardener, who was obliged to use a rake to ward off the drunken Czar from a peasant woman working in the fields. Another episode at the Czar's table involved a somewhat unattractive woman called Barbara. Peter told her, 'I don't think that anyone would want you, my poor Barbara. You're far too ugly. But I won't let you die without experiencing love.' With these words, in front of everyone present, he threw her on to a couch and fulfilled his promise.

History asserts that the number of Peter's illegitimate progeny rivalled that of Louis XIV. Almost all of the four hundred unmarried women in the palace who worked as cooks, servants and washerwomen, carried richly dressed youngsters in their arms; in reply to the query as to whose child it was, they would politely answer, 'The Czar honoured me ...'

But these were all 'simple pranks' compared to what happened on 2 May 1712. On this day the Czar celebrated his marriage to his second wife Catherine, a former pastor's servant and 'soldier's girl'. The story of Catherine's rise to the Russian throne is a story out of *The Thousand and One*

Nights become reality. Catherine was born in the outskirts of Riga, in a simple peasant family. At the age of twelve she became an orphan and was taken in by the local pastor, who ran a hostel, where she began to work. According to the recollections of the residents, Catherine was thrifty and made very small sandwiches; but in another respect she proved very generous. At the age of sixteen she gave birth to a daughter, who died within a few months.

History does not mention how she first fell in with the Russian army and began to entertain the soldiers. A junior officer snatched her away from the lower ranks and she then became the lover of the army commander himself. After that she ended up in the home of the first minister, Alexander Menshikov, who employed her to 'wash shirts', and it was on a visit there that Peter first saw her. He was apparently amazed at the cleanliness of the house, whereupon Menshikov laughed and opened a door to a neighbouring room, where the Czar saw a girl with bare legs, wearing an apron, who dashed from chair to chair, singing and cleaning windows. It is said that for the first night spent with Catherine, Peter gave her one ducat.

The story goes that the Czar determined to marry Catherine in the course of a military campaign, during which she showed considerable calmness and bravery at critical moments. Between 1704 and 1723 she bore her lover, later her husband, eleven children, most of whom died at an early age. The frequent pregnancies did not prevent her from accompanying the Czar in all his travels. She was a true 'campaign' officer's wife, rivalling Peter in endurance, living in a tent and joining him in lengthy marches on horseback. Although she could in no way be considered beautiful, Peter was clearly captivated. According to one unflattering contemporary: 'She was of modest stature, solid, with a very dark complexion, and did not distinguish herself with beauty or grace. Seeing her was enough to recognise her lowly origins. In her strange attire, she could be taken for an actress in a provincial theatre, or a servant in a German hotel.'

She possessed another quality, however, that apparently played an important role in this marriage. From early childhood, Peter was subject to frequent attacks of 'strong brain seizures', accompanied by shocking headaches. These afflicted him for hours at a time, during which he could tolerate the company neither of strangers or friends. At such times he seemed to verge almost upon madness, and everyone kept their distance. Only Catherine approached him with no fear, spoke to him lovingly but firmly, and calmed him down. She would take his head and gently stroke it, running her hands down his long shoulder-length hair. Soon the Czar fall asleep, his head on her breast. She would sit that way motionless for hours, until he awoke, fresh and lively, and boundlessly grateful to his 'doctor'.

Despite his attachment to Catherine, and despite the immense power that he wielded – by that time not simply Czar but Emperor of Russia – Peter's marriage to a former 'soldier's girl', who could not even sign her own name, was publicly unacceptable, and could have unforeseen consequences both for Russia and Europe. Peter had to make a decision, especially since their two illegitimate daughters were already growing up. So he took the absolutely unprecedented step of ensuring Catherine's power in the event of his death and assuring the future of his daughters. In the Kremlin's Assumption Cathedral he pronounced her the first Russian Empress, personally placing the crown upon her head. Kneeling before the altar, Catherine wept, embracing her husband.

Not six months after the coronation, however, a dramatic event in the palace threatened to destroy the happiness of the imperial couple. Returning from a trip, Peter learned that a suspicious friendship had developed between Catherine and a courtier. The enraged Emperor set an ambush, and caught his wife with her lover in a pergola. Inevitably the courtier was executed, and his head, on Peter's orders, placed in a jar of spirits and displayed in the Empress's bedchamber. Catherine maintained her composure, which enraged Peter all the more. Evidently he smashed a magnificent Venetian mirror in her presence, yelling: 'The same will happen to you!' to which she calmly objected: 'You have destroyed one of the finest ornaments in your palace; has it become better for it?'

Everyone feared that Catherine was doomed, that Peter would exact terrible vengeance. The star of fortune, however, did not desert her. Within a month Peter was gone, dying suddenly in St Petersburg, on 8 February 1725, of simple pneumonia.

Throughout twenty years of life with Peter, the Empress had suppressed her natural tendencies and instincts. Now, at the hour of her husband's death, they were released. At one time she had earnestly guarded Peter from night-time orgies, but now she gave herself over to unabated drunkenness and debauchery, with a new lover every night. This debauchery continued for almost all of her short reign, as she outlived her husband for precisely sixteen months.

◆　◆　◆　◆　◆

In Soviet, especially Stalinist, times the figure of Peter the Great, like that of Ivan the Terrible, acquired a kind of idol-like aura. This was understandable, for Stalin emulated many of the actions and deeds of these two former Czars, often imitating them step for step. No historian can deny the importance to Russia of Peter the Great. But no objective historian can remain silent on the wilder excesses of his despotic rule. What was for the benefit of Russia translated in real life into pain and suffering for the people. Achieving a worthy goal at any price is the traditional road of many tyrants.

Peter's reign proved exceptionally hard for Russia. Bent on expanding the borders of the country, he waged many wars, which bankrupted an already poor nation. As a blind admirer of Europe, Peter aimed, with a single leap, to bridge the centuries-old gulf that separated Russia from the West. Moreover, he did so in characteristic fashion – brusquely, unceremoniously and mercilessly. Even a rigorous leader such as Lenin was to admit that Peter's reforms were conducted by barbaric methods, in a barbaric country.

Take, for example, the building of St Petersburg, an achievement comparable to the construction of the Egyptian pyramids. Peter literally mobilised the whole country for this operation, demanding not only resources from the poverty-stricken country, but also lives. The city sprang up where there was no soil, no rocks, no forest – only swamps. They were buried under earth carried in the folded hems of the labourers' shirts. Whole islands were poured out in this way. On the Czar's orders, everyone, regardless of rank and title, was obliged to participate. Disobedience was severely punished. There were even written standards, how much a pedestrian should carry, how much for a rider, how much on a cart. Hundreds and thousands of male peasants were herded into the construction site from all corners of Russia. They were escorted under convoy like prisoners.

Relatives said their farewells to those who were taken away, like condemned prisoners, forever. To prevent people from running away, a barbaric new law was passed. If anyone tried to escape, the whole work brigade would pay with their heads. With swamps all around and hunger rife, food had to be delivered by carts and by river from immense distances. Both in summer and winter, the labourers lived in huts. If the weather turned bad, the huts became graves. People died continuously and indifferently – death was preferable to life. Peter built his new capital literally on the bones of the people. According to contemporary accounts, during the laying of the foundations for the Fort of Peter and Paul alone, some one hundred thousand people died.

Peter put everyone to work. The city's main thoroughfare, Nevsky Avenue, was laid out by Swedish prisoners of war, and one alley was constructed by foreign guests, under the personal supervision of the Czar. The city, once built, had to be populated. But who would want to move for choice from a settled place such as Moscow to a swamp? The Czar issued a new decree: people of good moral character should be transferred there from all corners of Russia. Once again, a list was drawn up: so many courtiers, so many merchants, so many trades-people and workshops ... Failure to comply resulted in harsh punishment and bankruptcy. For the inhabitants, those who incited disorder or polluted the city were subject to a stiff penalties. Those who threw litter in the river Neva were sentenced to hard labour, the poor and homeless were sent to gaol, coachmen were lashed for a first careless driving offence and sent for hard labour after a subsequent one. Thus did the Venice of the North arise from a swamp.

Peter considered adherents of the old faith – 'Old Believers' – to be among his most deadly foes, bent on preventing reform. The prisons overflowed with them. To escape being hunted and tortured, they fled into the deep forest, founding secret settlements there. Even here, however, the law would catch up with them. Often, to avoid falling into the hands of the Czar, the Old Believers would stage large-scale suicides in which up to a thousand people would voluntarily walk into flames, 'for the faith'. A far greater number fled the motherland for foreign parts. In 1714 an order was given to take a census of all Old Believers and, to distinguish them from the rest of the population, to compel them to wear a 'symbol of yellow material'.

It hardly needs saying that the Czar earned countless enemies. The Orthodox called him the Anti-Christ. One wild story circulated to the effect that the Russian Czar Peter had never returned from Europe; he had been stuffed in a barrel by the Germans and thrown into the sea, and his place had been taken by a foreign look-alike.

Even leading figures of the time, who appreciated the benefits of Peter's reforms, denied him their support, considering that he had acted too abruptly and too harshly. The Czarevich Alexei, Peter's eldest son, became the focus for the discontented. His succession would point the way to the resumption of old ways and customs. Although Alexei, because of his nature, could not possibly prove a leader, he was known to be opposed to his father's reforms, so his name could still be used to rally the disaffected.

Peter showed no mercy to his opponents. Alexei himself died under torture, and his supporters were executed. Peter then issued a decree whereby the throne was not to be automatically inherited by the eldest son; rather the heir must be endorsed by the Czar himself.

Peter the Great died unexpectedly, failing to carry out his own decree, having no time to endorse an heir to the throne. But back in 1712, a long time before his death, he transferred the capital of Russia from the hated city of Moscow to distant St Petersburg. The focal point of Russian history thus shifted from the Kremlin to the shores of the Baltic sea for more than two centuries. Fate determined that the centre of power would eventually return to the Kremlin, but even during the interval, Russian history would once more focus briefly upon the Kremlin.

6 | 'MOSCOW ISN'T THE HOME OF THE CZAR. MOSCOW IS THE HOME OF RUSSIA HERSELF!'

FOR THE FIRST TIME IN SIX CENTURIES, the Kremlin was not the centre of government power, and Moscow was not the capital. Commenting on the Russian situation, the French philosopher Denis Diderot (1713–84) remarked that the heart of an organism cannot be located in the tip of its finger. Nevertheless, it happened.

However, when the throne changed hands, coronations still took place in Moscow, not in St Petersburg. Fireworks blazed in the sky, military salutes thundered, fountains of wine bubbled forth on Red Square, and tables covered with cakes and snacks stretched for hundreds of metres. A huge, noisy crowd filled Moscow. Here is how William Howard Russell, a reporter from London, describes the coronation of Alexander II in 1856:

> The celebration was grand and stunning in every respect. The riches of the huge kingdom were out on show, with an Eastern extravagance that was this time coupled with the tastes of the educated West. Instead of cramped theatre stage, the spectacle was played out in the ancient capital of the hugest kingdom that has ever existed in the world. Instead of trumpery and trinkets, shone real gold, silver and precious stones ... It is doubtful that any of the foreigners had seen something similar ... The magnificence of the carriages and uniforms, the livery and harnesses on the horses, was worthy of the Roman Caesars, or the most famous Eastern overlords.

After the coronation the Emperor, accompanied by his entourage, would proceed to the Archangel's Cathedral in the Kremlin where he would pay homage to the graves of his ancestors. Then he would continue alone to the Annunciation Cathedral, from where he would ascend to the Red Porch to greet the gathering. A feast was then organised in the Granavitaya Chamber for the clergy and high nobility.

The coronation celebrations lasted from several days to several months. During this time a visiting foreigner could see many strange and unusual sights. One visitor reported on a curious and possibly unique death statistic: 'During the coronation in Moscow, eight thousand roubles worth of serfs were crushed to death!'

Eventually the celebrations would end, the guests would travel north and Moscow would once again become a province that would hear about government events, new fashions, and the achievements of science only through rumours and after a long delay.

The great city did not, however, collapse. To the chime of the Kremlin's bells, trade was noisily conducted from benches, tents and huts in Red Square. The square bubbled like a human anthill. 'A row of shops selling wine stretch out in one place ...' a writer of the period, A. Kazivetter described. '... glasses chime and the buyers snack on almonds and raisins ... In another, hundreds of sturgeon and sterlet are laid out ready for sale ... Further on, wares are displayed on sleighs that are squeezed together so tight, that it is impossible to get through and one must constantly climb over horses' harnesses. Beyond is the bird market, and further on the furriers, cobblers, saddlers, pie-makers ... A "comedy tent" towers in the centre of the square. People are jostling at the entrance ... The play begins, German or Russian, and the stage begins to almost emulate the noise and bustle which until a moment earlier, had permeated the audience hall ...'

An incredible variety of faces and clothes gathered in Red Square. Different centuries and even epochs seemed to have come together. Next to people in long, old-fashioned peasant garb, wearing shoes made out of bark and with bushy Russian beards, walked those who seemed to belong to a completely different era, with French wigs, kaftans, décolleté dresses. No other country could boast such a wild variation. Ancient Russian speech could be heard side-by-side with the language of the noble-born – at first German, and then French ...

Although Moscow was turned into a mere province, not only the Russian people but also their enemies sensed that the heart of Russia remained there. During the war between France and Russia in 1812 Napoleon didn't advance on St Petersburg, but on Moscow, certain that it was in the Kremlin that the fate of the war would be decided. 'Moscow isn't the home of the Czar, Moscow is the home of Russia herself!' Russia's greatest poet, Alexander Pushkin, would later exclaim.

The main battle between the Russian and French armies occurred outside Moscow on the Borodino Field. In our day and age we are used to enormous casualties in war, but this must have been a fearsome battle if, without tanks, aeroplanes and machine-guns, the Russian army lost 47,000 men and the French 57,000. The Russians retreated, surrendering Moscow. The soldiers wept, and heavily wounded General Bagration, hearing that the French were in the Kremlin, leapt up, tore away his bandages, and died of loss of blood. Those who only saw the Kremlin as a 'military object' understood nothing about Russia. Edifices such as the Kremlin accumulate the energy of many generations, and only in moments of danger does it become clear how important and indispensable they are to the nation. Half a century later, Leo Tolstoy described this in his classic novel *War and Peace*.

On 15 September Napoleon entered the Kremlin. The huge, almost desolate city greeted the French with a huge fire, ignited by Muscovites themselves. At first, Napoleon ignored the fire, but a day later the wind picked up and the flames spread. The sea of flame washed over the centre of the city near the Kremlin. On the morning of the 17th Napoleon inspected the fortress. What he saw from the Kremlin walls shocked him. According to the tales of the officers who accompanied him, the Emperor grew pale and silently watched the flames for a long time before finally saying: 'What a fearful sight! They did this themselves ... What decisiveness! What a people! They are Scythians!'

Meanwhile the fire began to threaten the Kremlin itself. It was already impossible to leave through some gates. Although Napoleon's officers pleaded with him to abandon the burning fortress, he hesitated. For a time he even personally participated in the battle against the flames, but soon this attempt had to be abandoned. When Napoleon and his entourage finally left the Kremlin, it was becoming hard to breathe and sparks showered them like rain. 'We walked upon a fiery earth, under a fiery sky, between walls of flame,' one of his officers later recounted.

Not long before his death on the island of St Helena, the French Emperor wrote: 'All the poets who ever described the fabled fire of Troy, could never have imagined anything akin to the fire of Moscow. An ocean of fire, mountains of flame ... This was the most incredible, stunning and yet terrifying spectacle that I had ever seen.' Napoleon had seen quite a few things in his days, so his words are worth a great deal.

During the French occupation, the Emperor's commissaries not only defiled the Kremlin by setting up stables in its palaces, but also looted it. Retreating, they didn't even have time to wipe their calculations from the walls of the Assumption Cathedral: '*Gathered, 288 kilograms of gold, and 5200 kilograms of silver.*' On the Emperor's orders the golden cross was removed from the highest bell-tower in the Kremlin – the tower of Ivan the Great – and sent to Paris to decorate l'Hôtel des Invalides.

According to the memoirs of French soldiers who took part in the Russian campaign, Napoleon experienced some of the most difficult days of his life in

Moscow. He was either gripped by rage or for long hours he would maintain total silence, deep in thought. Nothing in this wild country played by the rules. The Kremlin was taken, Moscow was burning, victory was at hand, but now they had to retreat.

After a month in the desolate, burning Moscow, Napoleon began to pull out his troops. The Emperor once said: 'I never do pointless things.' But perhaps the malevolent silence in the Kremlin had irritated the French, and they wanted revenge against it, for Napoleon now gave an order that was not only pointless, but also barbaric: to blow up the Kremlin.

Sappers placed explosives under the walls and towers. The fuses were lit, and the French departed. But fate once again smiled upon this ancient Russian relic. Rain began to fall. The fuses were soaked. The flames went out ...

It would be a long century before the Kremlin once again gained power, and then its might would be malevolent.

PART II

7 | LEADER IN AN ACCURSED TIME

IT WAS MORE THAN TWO CENTURIES later that the Kremlin once again became the centre of power in Russia. On 11 March 1918 the new Bolshevik* government, headed by Vladimir Lenin, who had seized control in Russia a year previously, travelled from St Petersburg to Moscow.

This transfer of central power into the ancient residence of the Russian Czars set the intelligentsia guessing and debating. Why did the Bolsheviks need this? There were a number of reasons. St Petersburg, which offered easier access to Western philosophy and democratic ideas, had become a far more educated city over the past two centuries than patriarchal Moscow, and offered the Bolsheviks strong resistance. By building it, Peter the Great had tried to forge 'a window into Europe', and the new leadership – foreseeing a lengthy confrontation with the West – would now try to close this 'window'. Moreover, in the consciousness of the Russian people – especially the many millions of peasants – the Kremlin had always played a special holy cum patriotic role, symbolising rightful rule in Russia. Considering the national feeling, the Bolsheviks used this move to try to induce a sense of legitimacy to their rule among the people, to portray it as an inheritance, and to show themselves as being free of the foreign influence exemplified by St Petersburg.

Vladimir Lenin became the new master of the Kremlin. It is still difficult to paint an accurate portrait of this man. This is not only because many details of his life are only now beginning to appear from the depths of secret archives, but also because, for three-quarters of a century of Bolshevik rule, the image of the man was constantly being transformed so that it is hard to establish which aspects are true and which are lies. The Soviet era created a harsh stereotype of Lenin's image, from which Russians of the older generations are still gradually and painfully trying to rid themselves.

According to this iconic image, here was a man completely out of the ordinary: impossible even to imagine that he ate and drank like anyone else, that he could argue with his wife or stare at the legs of a pretty woman, let alone that he could ever intrigue or lie.

Had anyone dared whisper the suggestion that Lenin suffered from syphilis, either inherited or acquired abroad, the penalty would have been ten

* The majority – the ruling party.

years if not the firing squad. Yet, inevitably, rumours abounded. In the memoirs of the son of the German doctor Ferster, who was invited to treat Lenin late in his life, there is an anecdote concerning an Italian diplomat, a close friend of Vorovsky, the Soviet ambassador to Italy. At a party the diplomat asked Vorovsky: 'So what is your leader really like?' To which the somewhat tipsy ambassador answered with a wry laugh: 'Actually he is a provincial school teacher of German, whom syphilis granted a grain of genius before finally killing him.'

For a long time even Lenin's mother's maiden name, Blanc, was a top government secret. It would have indicated that the leader's heritage was not purely Russian, a fact that was quite impermissible. The fact that Lenin had Swedish and German roots on his mother's side is known by few in Russia to this day. Another secret recently revealed was the story of the last years of the leader's life. What disease did he have and how did he die? Is it true that Stalin precipitated his death? And finally, the last but perhaps most important question: what was the role of this first Bolshevik master of the Kremlin in all the subsequent bloody history of Soviet Russia?

In seeking a brief answer to these questions, responsibility for possible errors must lie with the authorities who hid and destroyed original documents about the life of this remarkable man who had such an impact on twentieth-century history.

Vladimir Ulyanov, better known under the pseudonym Lenin, was born in the small provincial town of Simbirsk, on the river Volga, on 10 April 1870. The Simbirsk of those days was a sleepy river harbour, smelling of fish, grain, wool and saltpetre, with a population of thirty or forty thousand people. There were many Chuvash, Mordvinians* and other 'heathens' who worked as dockhands or as barge-haulers. The town had one foot on the lower Asiatic bank of the Volga, and the other on the European shore. There is a certain symbolism here in Lenin's Eurasian beginnings.

To this day the origins of the name 'Lenin' are unclear. According to one version, in his student years Vladimir Ulyanov was infatuated with a fellow student called Lena, according to another the name is derived from that of the Siberian river Lena, although what connection he might have had with this Siberian river is a mystery.**

---

* Local nationalities.
** A document has recently been uncovered to the effect that, during one of his illegal trips overseas, Vladimir Ulyanov used the passport of a dead landowner from the Yaroslavl region whose surname was Lenin. This, allegedly, is where the pseudonym originated.

His father, Ilya Nikolayevich Ulyanov (1831–86) hailed from a line of Russian serfs. His paternal grandfather gained his freedom, and moved to the town of Astrakhan at the mouth of the Volga where he became a tailor. His paternal grandmother was a Kalmyk, which would explain Lenin's pronounced Asiatic features. Ilya Ulyanov was promoted within his profession to regional school inspector, a position which gave him a civilian title equivalent to that of a general in the army.

Lenin's mother, Maria Alexandrovna Blanc (1835–1916) was the daughter of a baptised Jew, a police doctor named Alexander Blanc and Anna Grosskopf, whose line originated with a Swedish jeweller Karl Frederic Estedt, who had moved to St Petersburg in the eighteenth century. In Russia this many-branched Swedish-German family worked in jewellery design, millinery and general commerce. Although official Soviet historians never acknowledged Lenin's Swedish roots, he must surely have been aware of it since Swedish and German were both spoken in his mother's home. Lenin's own grandmother, Anna Grosskopf, never learned to speak Russian fluently and maintained her Lutheran beliefs.

As Professor Volkogonov writes: 'The voice of Russian fate can be heard in Lenin's origins: a Slav beginning and wide Asiatic spaces, the Jewish element of national intellect and German western culture. This cannot be escaped, and indeed need not be. Russia is in its essence a Eurasian country, and thanks to chance or perhaps God's design, Vladimir Ulyanov expressed in his personal destiny all the complexity and national contradiction of one of the last great empires of our planet.'

Of the eight children of the Ulyanov family (two died at an early age), Vladimir was the fourth by birth. Their father was a man of hard peasant upbringing and in any case was very busy, travelling around the region a great deal as an inspector. Hence all the upbringing of the children fell upon the shoulders of the mother, a deeply religious woman, who spoke foreign languages and loved music, and who stemmed from a more educated environment than the father. Due to the complex nature of the latter, with his insistence on strict discipline for his children, and behaviour that often led to conflict with the authorities, the family's private life was apparently not as cloudless as the official historians described. Vladimir Ulyanov inherited many of his father's internal and external traits. Both had high foreheads, bald pates, red beards, short legs, a strikingly similar dry laugh and an inability to pronounce the letter 'r'. Father and son were very conscientious workers, possessed inexhaustible energy, and were bad at personal relationships. Both died at approximately the same age, from similar diseases, the father from a blood clot on the brain, the son from sclerosis of the brain.

It is difficult to say what particular talents Vladimir possessed during his school years, but one thing is certain: he was a child with strong will-power, accustomed to discipline and hard work. His heightened sense of ambition, sharp tongue and love of cruel jokes did not make him popular among his peers, so that he lacked close friends apart from his family during his school years.

In 1886 Vladimir left school with high distinction, and prepared to enter the University of Khazan. Here, however, two successive family misfortunes occurred. In January 1887, at the age of fifty-four, his father died suddenly from a brain haemorrhage. This was apparently due to some inherited condition, since years later at the same age and with similar symptoms, Lenin himself was to die, followed by his younger sister Maria. The family had not had time to come to terms with this first tragedy when it was struck another blow. In May 1887, at the age of twenty-one, Lenin's elder brother Alexander, a student of St Petersburg University, was hanged for conspiring to assassinate Czar Alexander III.

Of all the family, only the oldest sister Anna knew of Alexander's association with a terrorist organisation. She too was arrested over this incident, but was later released due to lack of evidence. For all the other members of the family, the event was a bolt from the blue. 'My Lord!' wrote the mother of the accused in her plea to the Czar. 'I beg you to spare my children. Return my children to me. If my son's reason and feeling were accidentally clouded, if criminal thoughts crept into his soul, my Lord, I will set him right. I will again resurrect the best of human feelings and intentions in his soul, by which he lived until so recently. I beg my Lord mercy, mercy.'

The Czar was ready to forgive Alexander Ulyanov, and his mother was so informed: all her son had to do was sign a request for clemency, but he refused. As the lawyer present at the last meeting of mother and son recalled, Alexander said: 'Imagine mother, two people face each other in a duel. One has already shot at his opponent, while the other has not. The one who has already shot then appeals to his opponent not to shoot. No, I cannot act this way.' Misguided Alexander Ulyanov may have been, but he showed himself to be brave and honourable. His last request to his mother was to bring him a volume of poems by Heinrich Heine.

Alexander and Vladimir had never been close. They differed in outward appearance, in character and in ethical principles. In fact, Alexander did not much like his younger brother. Asked by his sister why, Alexander answered evasively, 'I just don't.'

In the second half of 1887 Vladimir Ulyanov entered the law faculty of the University of Khazan, but studied there only a few months. At this time a wave of student unrest swept across Russia, engulfing Khazan as well. The cause of the dissent was the introduction by the government of certain harsh measures connected with the recent attempt on the Czar's life, which had involved students, including Alexander Ulyanov, almost exclusively.

A turbulent meeting was held at the start of December in the university's conference hall, as a result of which forty students were arrested and expelled, Vladimir Ulyanov among them. After two days under arrest he was sent twenty-five miles outside Khazan, to the farm of his grandfather Alexander Blanc, where he was to live for a year. Less than a year later, his punishment was rescinded. He returned to Khazan, but was unable to reinstate himself at the university. He was permitted, however, to sit the law faculty examinations externally, after which he took a job as a lawyer's assistant.

In 1893 Vladimir moved to St Petersburg where his 'revolutionary activity' began. He became a member of Marxist societies, and in 1894, at one such group, he met his future wife, Nadezhda Krupskaya, a Sunday school teacher. To be precise, he met Nadezhda and her friend Apollinariya Yakubov. The latter made a greater impression on him, and after a while he proposed marriage, but received a categorical refusal. The attractive girl was apparently put off by his appearance. Alexander Potresov, who knew him very well wrote: 'Vladimir Ulyanov, who had then not yet turned twenty-five ... was young only in his passport. To look at, you could give him no less than thirty-five or perhaps forty years. A pallid face, almost completely bald except for some sorry tufts left on his temples, a thin red beard, shifty and slightly sunken eyes squinting at his interlocutor, a hoarse not-young voice ... As far as I can remember the young Lenin had no youth ... He was nicknamed 'Old Man' and we often joked that Lenin even as a child was apparently just as old and bald ...'

Having been rejected by Apollinariya, Vladimir switched his attention to Nadezhda, who was a year older than him. Her nickname among her friends was 'Lamprey', due to her slightly bulging eyes. Nadezhda was the only daughter of a retired colonel of the Czar's army, Constantine Krupsky (the masculine version of the surname), and Elizabeth Tistrov, an orphan who had graduated from finishing school and who worked as a governess in a rich family. The first four years of marriage for the father and mother went happily, and nothing would have changed had Constantine not become interested in revolutionary ideas. This interest did not pass unnoticed by the authorities, and he was discharged from the army. With unemployment came destitution; yet making personal sacrifices, her parents sent her to one of the best girls' schools in St Petersburg. While not having inherited her mother's beauty, Nadezhda grew up to be kind and contented, not envious of her companions' romantic successes, though not finding love herself. Her father's revolutionary friends began to shape her political awareness. Once she read an appeal in a newspaper by Count Leo Tolstoy to the intelligentsia, to help educate people by adapting difficult classics for common readership. Nadezhda wrote Tolstoy a letter and received her first 'Party' assignment from him, to adapt Alexander Dumas's novel, *The Count of Monte Cristo*.

At a party thrown by friends, Nadezhda met a 'strange man from the Volga'. There was much talk during the evening about how to help the people. The majority agreed that one must begin from 'small actions'. Then Krupskaya remembered hearing the cruel dry laugh of the newcomer: 'If someone wants to try to save the fatherland with a literacy committee, well we won't protest ...'

Next time they ran into each other coming out of the library and went for a walk. Her new acquaintance then started to visit her family on Sundays. They studied together and read Marxist literature while Nadezhda's mother, glancing suspiciously at the prematurely bald suitor, silently brought them tea. Of course he could be taller and more handsome, but what could you do, her daughter was no beauty either. Her friends recalled that to the end of her days Elizabeth was an open critic of her son-in-law who in her opinion did not have a 'real job'.

Several years later, already in exile, Lenin wrote Nadezhda a letter in which he asked her to become his wife. 'Well, if a wife then a wife,' Nadezhda replied laconically. This 'well' was not to be taken as indifference, but as acceptance to accompany him through life in any capacity: as wife, girl-friend or comrade.

In 1895, after getting over an illness, Lenin travelled abroad to Switzerland for several months to recuperate. His new foreign friends asked him to carry some illegal newspapers and books back into Russia. Being a very cautious man, Lenin wavered, but his friends insisted. The literature was placed in a suitcase with a false bottom. Usually the lax customs officials almost never checked passengers' bags, but the brother of an executed terrorist was, after all, a notorious figure, so his suitcase was thoroughly searched and examined. The customs officers apparently discovered that it had a false bottom and informed the police of this, but the passenger was for some reason not detained. Evidently the police wished to trace the further movements of the illegal literature.

After this Lenin was placed under surveillance and on 9 December 1895 he was arrested. The formal reason for the arrest was his membership of the illegal organisation that comprised the various the Marxist groups of St Petersburg and published anti-govemment leaflets, which Lenin edited.

Official Soviet history always described the revolutionary activities of Lenin and his comrades-in-arms as an unbroken chain of heroic exploits. They skilfully tricked the Czarist police, risked their lives daily, stoically endured suffering in prison and exile, and engineered daring escapes from confinement. In reality, however, this is all far from the truth. Following the history of the Bolshevik movement in Russia, one is more likely to be amazed not by the 'heroism' of the revolutionaries, but at the stunning liberalism and even laxity of the Czarist regime in relation to them. This is especially evident today, with the distance of time, when the Russian people have personally endured Lenin and Stalin's KGB and other instruments of the Soviet law-enforcement system. Compared to them, the Czar's police force bore more resemblance to a lazy uncle than a terrifying law-enforcement machine. In comparison to that of Stalin, its prisons and places of exile were 'rest homes' where the self-education of the revolutionaries took place.

The following is an account of Lenin's life in prison, according to his sister Anna Ulyanov and his fiancée, Nadezhda Krupskaya.

Lenin was placed in a temporary detention wing. Contact was allowed twice a week, one privately and one publicly. With a few simple tricks it was possible to talk about absolutely anything at these meetings. Food could be brought three times a week, books twice a week — as many as were wanted – and subjected only to perfunctory examination. The prisoner could even receive weekly magazines. In this way, the severance from daily life, which is perhaps one of the hardest aspects of incarceration, was practically non-existent. Apart from this, the prison boasted a rich library, so many of the prisoners – especially among the workers – seriously supplemented their education here. As Lenin's older sister recalled, his mother prepared special dietetic meals for Vladimir and brought them to prison three times a week, as recommended by doctors. He also had special meals that he paid for, as well as milk. Thus even his stomach, not completely healthy, about which he had gone abroad to see famous Swiss doctors, was in significantly better condition after a year in prison than it had been when he was free.

Lenin managed to arrange his life in prison so that his whole day was filled with correspondence with his comrades and work on his own writing. For the sake of secrecy he wrote in milk. When the milk dried on paper it became invisible, but if a little water was applied to the page it would show through again. He made his inkwells out of bread and filled them with milk, so as soon as the lock to his cell clicked open, he would eat the entire inkwell. 'I ate six inkwells today ...' he wrote to his family. He worked on one of his central works in that cell. When they released him he even joked: 'A pity they let me out early. I needed to work on the book a little more ...'

This was the 'draconian' regime of the Czarist prisons. Years later, many of Lenin's comrades would find themselves in Stalin's prisons. Beaten, hungry and half-alive, having lost even the appearance of humanity, they would remember the Czar's prisons as 'heaven-on-earth'.

Lenin spent about a year in prison, after which he was to be sent into exile to eastern Siberia for three years. His mother deluged the authorities with letters and requests that, 'in light of the poor health' of her son, they allow him to travel into exile not under escort like everyone else but voluntarily at his own expense, and to permit him to stop in St Petersburg for a few weeks and then in Moscow: also, that they exile him not to the harsh northern areas of Siberia, but to milder, more southern ones, and so forth. What is perhaps most amazing is that all her requests were granted.

The Czarist government provided exiles with a salary of eight roubles a month. In those times, that amount was more than enough. As Nadezhda Krupskaya remembered, on this stipend Lenin rented himself a room with full board with the family of a local peasant, including laundry and the mending of clothes – and he was considered to be paying a lot. The house was clean, the floors covered with hand-woven rugs, the walls white-washed and decorated with fresh-smelling fir. Nadezhda went on to complain that lunch and dinner were a bit simple. One week they bought the tenant a lamb and fed him lamb day-in day-out, another week they would buy a bullock and feed him chops. There was an abundance of milk and vegetables. In short, there was more than enough food both for Lenin and for his hunting dog.

A year later Nadezhda arrived with her mother who exclaimed on seeing her daughter's amply fed husband-to-be: 'Well, you've filled out!' Now, renting a more spacious dwelling and hiring some staff they started to live as a family. A couple of months later the pair were officially married, which according to the mother-in-law's firm insistence, took place in a church, 'like regular people'. From that day forward Nadezhda Krupskaya became 'Lenin's shadow', his most faithful lifelong partner.

The image of Krupskaya presented to my generation meant that we were barely aware she was a woman. Thanks partly to Soviet propaganda's depiction of the couple's married life, with its emphasis on arm-in-arm revolutionary struggle and dedication to duty, and partly to the unflattering official portraits of a sexless creature with a tired, puffy face, messy hair and no make-up, Nadezhda hardly conforms to an ideal of femininity. Comrade, fellow-warrior, friend, but not first and foremost a woman. Surely for this couple there was no question of the simple pleasures of life, let alone sex. The Leader was above such things!

Undoubtedly this was no ordinary husband and wife. Their bond was affirmed primarily by a deep ideological affinity, but not by this alone! It was in exile, after her marriage, that Nadezhda's womanhood came into full flower. According to Larissa Vasilieva: 'A powerful and passionate woman awoke in her, and although a little late she nevertheless enjoyed everything at once: nature, love, and spiritual communion with her idol ... This is when she became a real beauty. Her cheeks burned. Her thin figure and modest St Petersburg dresses drew amazed glances from the local village girls. She let her long flowing locks flow out of female coyness, so that everyone might see how sweet she was, how lovely, how young, although thirty years old ... All praised her magnificence in one voice. Everyone fell in love with her ...' Moreover, she even enticed and was attracted to another exile, but only in a platonic sense. Vladimir had no need not worry.

Krupskaya recollected that Lenin was a keen hunter. He bought himself a pair of leather trousers, and tramped around the swamps with his dog and rifle, tracking game. Sometimes he and his friends would travel out to the islands, where rabbits were as thick as flies. There was nowhere for them to leave the island, so they would run around in circles like sheep. Vladimir would usually come home after such a trip with a boat-load of dead rabbits.

They would often go to visit other exiled friends in nearby villages or receive guests at home. Such journeys were allowed by the police: seeing in the New Year, celebrating weddings and birthdays or, in the case of poor health, to see a doctor. Time during these trips, as Lenin wrote, would pass 'very merrily'. During the summer they walked, swam or hunted. In the winter they would ice-skate on the frozen river, play chess, discuss political questions …

On long winter evenings Vladimir would usually read books on philosophy: Hegel, Kant, French materialists. When he was tired he would turn to Pushkin, Goethe's *Faust* in German and Hiene's poetry. All in all, life in the quiet village provided a very conducive environment for study and self-education. There were no distractions. The mail arrived twice a week. They received books, newspapers and letters. The correspondence was voluminous, both with friends in Russia and from abroad. They would often get parcels from home. The family would send whatever Vladimir asked for: a new suit, fresh shirts, a straw hat, even kid-skin gloves. Once he thought of asking for a hunting dog, but then changed his mind and bought one locally. In short, as Krupskaya concluded, exile went rather well. They were years of serious study …

Compare this with the realities of exile during the Soviet era. Any reader familiar with Alexander Solzhenitsyn's *Gulag Archipelago* will need neither clarification nor commentary. Lenin himself could not then have imagined the abyss into which he would push this long-suffering nation in seventeen years.

After his release from exile in January 1901, Lenin, followed a year later by Krupskaya, moved abroad and lived until 1917, with a few short breaks, in Munich, London, Paris, Zurich, Geneva and Cracow. Meanwhile he continued to write, publishing the newspaper *Iskra* (Spark) which was slipped into Russia via illegal channels. Lenin's theories and revolutionary activities lie outside the scope of this book. We are interested in Lenin as a character, the man himself without the mask. To do this we shall turn to the people who had close contact with him during this period of his life.

One such person was the then young Bolshevik (not an opponent of Lenin but his supporter) Nikolai Valentinov, who lived in Geneva at the time and was in touch with Lenin for almost a year. 'Usually around four o'clock (five minutes to four, Lenin was extremely punctual!) he would go out for a walk and we would stroll for half an hour or more.' Valentinov recalled: 'It can't be said that we spoke. Only Lenin himself spoke. I only listened … He paid almost no attention to other people's views … Lenin was a passionate and prejudiced person. His speeches during our walks were mean and derogatory with regard to his opponents. He wasn't ashamed to express himself, literally oozing bile … In a more normal state, Lenin was partial to a calm and ordered life, with exactly established hours for eating, sleeping, work and rest. He didn't smoke, couldn't abide alcohol, worried about his health for the benefit of which he exercised every morning ... Every morning, before starting to read the papers, write and work, Lenin, duster in hand, would set about cleaning his writing table. He would reattach a loose button on his jacket or trousers himself. He would immediately try to extract any stain on his suit with benzene. He kept his bicycle so clean it might have been a surgical instrument ...'

But this 'normal' state persisted only as long as it took to set out on another 'campaign' – the campaign for the ideological annihilation of his enemies, the campaign to ensure Russia's defeat in the First World War, the campaign to seize power ... At such moments 'Lenin, like a revving motor, would develop an amazing amount of energy... Squinting his little eyes even further, he would spew fierce hate upon his ideological adversaries, he wanted to smack them in the face, to insult them, to trample them, to spit on them ... There was but one idea before him, one goal, like a closed door against which he stubbornly beat himself in order to open it or break it down ...'

Wishing to find out a little more about Lenin, Valentinov planned to start a conversation with him about literature. He shared his intentions with one of his colleagues, a man by the name of Vorovsky whom we have already mentioned, who was living in Geneva at that time. 'So, you want to investigate Lenin, do you?' Vorovsky asked humorously. 'Well why not, I invite you to try. He investigates all of us, why shouldn't we try to probe him ... But I warn you, Lenin often likes to 'play dumb'. I once wanted to find out if he had read Shakespeare, Byron, Molière or Schiller. I got neither a yes nor a no in response, but I nevertheless understood that he had read none of them and had in fact not gone beyond what he had learned in school. He only read Goethe's *Faust* in the original, and even memorised a few of Mephistopheles' tirades. You haven't been here long; once you spend some time here you are bound to hear Lenin fire an arrow from that bow while in discussion with someone. Apart from *Faust*, however, he has not read anything else by Goethe. He divides literature into the necessary and unnecessary, but what criteria he uses to decide are unclear to me. He apparently has time to read popular science-digest compilations, but ignores Dostoyevsky, saying, 'I don't have time for that shit.'

Such selectiveness in Lenin's interests is indirectly supported by Krupskaya, who told of how it was hard to drag him into even the best museums of London or Paris. If nevertheless she managed to get him in, he couldn't spend more than ten minutes inside without getting bored. Lenin never went to exhibitions and concerts, and he couldn't stand Modernism. When he became head of the government, he slashed the budget of the Bolshoi Theatre, announcing that it was 'a pure slice of bourgeois culture'. The only exception was perhaps the museum of the French Revolution in Paris.

One of Lenin's close female friends remembered how once in Italy they climbed a high hill. The ascent was very difficult, they scrabbled along, grasping at the shrubbery, breathing heavily and soaking in sweat. From the summit, however, a breathtaking vista of Italy opened up before them. The friend was cast into a lyrical mood, preparing to read some poetry, when suddenly Lenin exclaimed distractedly: 'Damn, those Social-Democrats are certainly messing things up for us ...'

One of a multitude of Lenin's secrets, about which Soviet history maintains an embarrassed silence, was the mystery of his income. To travel freely around Europe, live in luxury, publish a newspaper and hold the reins of his comrades who were all wholly dependent financially upon him, required substantial amounts of money. In those days it is doubtful that Valentinov could have known that Lenin's income stemmed from the 'Party coffers', which he personally controlled. These 'coffers' were filled in various ways. One was by robbing Russian and foreign banks, post offices, railway ticket offices, trains and ships. These thefts were carried out by specially prepared groups of guerrillas, one of whom was Joseph Stalin. In the Bolshevik lexicon the word 'robbery' was replaced by the more sophisticated 'expropriation', which later developed into the slogan 'Steal the stolen!'

One of the most famous 'expropriations', replete with gunfights and murder, rumoured to be organised by Stalin himself, took place on 26 June 1907 in Tiflis, the capital of Georgia, on one of the central squares of the city. As soon as the two carriages containing the money appeared in the square, a man in an officer's uniform who happened to be strolling around with a bored expression suddenly gave a signal and, as if out of nowhere, a group of 'expropriators' appeared. Bombs started to fly. Three soldiers from among the guards were killed, many were injured. The attack lasted three minutes. Over three hundred and forty thousand roubles were stolen, a massive sum for those days. Unfortunately for the robbers, all the bank notes turned out to be in large five-hundred rouble denominations, and they were difficult to exchange since the banks knew their serial numbers. Several people trying to exchange them were arrested, and the rest of the notes had to be burnt in order to avoid capture. This story became widely known in its aftermath, and would bring the Bolsheviks many problems. In Stalin's time, merely to mention the affair was tantamount to suicide.

Apart from robbery, the 'Party coffers' were also topped up with donations. Ridiculous as it might seem today, such millionaire donors nevertheless existed, as for instance the head of an enormously wealthy Russian merchant dynasty, Savva Morozov, and his brother Ivan. The Bolsheviks did not balk at fraud either. After the death of the Russian textile magnate Nikolai Smidt, Savva Morozov's nephew, his estate was inherited by his two sisters. It was then that Lenin and his comrades hatched a somewhat simple plot. Two comrades were given instructions by the Party to marry the sisters, gain control of the money and hand it over to the 'coffers'. The operation went ahead without a hitch, although one of the husbands, having become a millionaire, refused to deliver the money. He was eventually forced to hand over at least part of it. All in all, the 'coffers' profited by another two hundred and eighty thousand gold roubles.

Finally it is worth remembering that Ulyanov's widow also had a decent income, and regularly provided her son with money. 'Lenin urged Russia towards violent revolution from a marvellous and safely distant Europe,' writes his American biographer Louis Fischer. 'But he accepted golden roubles from his mother, whose source was the Czar's pension, and the income from his grandfather's estate ...' In short, 'the warrior for the working class' did not live a poor life overseas, and was able to stay at the most expensive resorts.

In 1910, in Paris, Lenin met an attractive Frenchwoman named Inessa Armand. He was forty at the time, she was thirty-five. Inessa was born in Paris, into the family of the famous opera singer Théodore Stephan. Her half-French, half-Scottish mother Natalie was a singing teacher, but died early in her daughter's life. Inessa was educated in Moscow, where she ended up with her grandmother and aunt, a teacher of music and French. Inessa spoke fluent French, Russian and English, played the pianoforte brilliantly, and inherited much of her father's good looks. At the age of nineteen she married Alexander Armand, the son of a wealthy Russian merchant who loved her dearly. They lived outside Moscow, in the village of Pushkino. During the eight years of their happy marriage they had four children. Everything seemed cloudless and eternal, but suddenly the unexpected happened. Inessa fell in love with her husband's younger brother and went to live with him. This romantic marriage did not last long, however.

Her second husband died of tuberculosis in Switzerland, leaving Inessa with yet another child.

At the time of her meeting with Lenin, Inessa was already the mother of five children. Her friends recall her as a brave and strong woman, a tireless rebel inclined towards terrorism. In her private life she was a fierce supporter of 'free love'. Her most hated literary character was Natasha Rostov from Tolstoy's *War and Peace*, whom Inessa described as a heifer, capable only of bearing children. Lenin was passionately infatuated with her, although he did not share her views about 'free love'. Despite his radical politics, on questions of relations between men and women he was extremely conservative. After politics, it seems that his love for Inessa was the greatest passion of his life.

For the next ten years their destinies were inseparable. Inessa followed Lenin everywhere, immersing herself in the Russian Revolution. At some point, however, just before the revolution, doubts started to creep into her mind about the validity of the path chosen by her idol. Larissa Vasilieva recounts a story told by Ivan Popov, who knew both Inessa and Lenin very well, and who was experiencing similar doubts which he shared with Armand. 'Walk away Ivan, walk away and don't look back,' she told him. 'You are young, somewhat weak-willed, idealistic. This kind of life isn't for you. Write books and love life, if you are able. I don't have anywhere else to go. I am under his spell forever. I cannot be otherwise. If I walk away, then all my sacrifices have been in vain, and my life has been for nothing.'

After the Bolsheviks took power, Inessa and her children moved to Russia. The tragic conclusion was played out in 1920. The revolution exhausted her, and she wanted to return to Paris at least for a while, to rest and recover. Lenin, however, persuaded her to go and rest in the Caucasus. And then the fearful telegram arrived, whose import he refused to understand: 'Top priority. Moscow. To Lenin. Unable to save comrade Inessa Armand from cholera. Stop. She expired on 24 September. Stop. The body is being sent to Moscow.'

'When Inessa died in 1920, Lenin was unrecognisable,' wrote Alexandra Kollontai, a prominent Bolshevik. 'I had never seen him in such a state before. He walked behind the coffin, his eyes closed, it seemed as if he would fall over at any moment ... he could not get over Inessa. Her death hastened his illness, which became cancerous ...' 'I glanced across at Lenin ...' continued Angélique Balobanov, another participant of the procession. 'He appeared to have fallen into despair. His cap was pulled down over his eyes.

Never of a great height, if seemed that he had withered and become even smaller. He looked pitiful and fallen in spirit ... This was more than the loss of a good friend. I got the impression that he had lost something valuable and very close to him.'

This long-term relationship was no secret to Nadezhda Krupskaya. She must be given her due, she made no family scenes and treated Inessa as a friend, although she herself was very ill at the time, suffering from a progressive goitre, accompanied by the weakening of her nervous system. From time to time Krupskaya would express her intention of leaving Lenin, but he would stop her and she would obey. At this time he was no longer merely her husband but rather her political idol. Staying with him meant serving the revolution, which was her greatest passion.

It was not just that Krupskaya needed him as a political soul-mate; he also needed her as his most reliable, loyal and deeply sympathetic friend, as an ally ready to do anything for him. In some ways she was a mother to him. It can be said with a great degree of certainty that without her Lenin would not so easily have achieved the goals that he set for himself.

The relationship between Lenin and Krupskaya during this period is another little-known aspect of his biography. According to people close to them, 'They lived together, but as two comrades.' In this vein the following curious detail is relevant: none of Lenin's many apartment-museums contains a proper double bed. They all have two separate bedrooms, his and hers, with narrow, almost military-style beds. As the first commandant of the Kremlin recalled, when setting up Lenin's apartments in the Kremlin he was ordered to arrange 'two simple metallic beds for Lenin and Krupskaya'. And another detail. Once, many years after Lenin's death, while Stalin was angry at Krupskaya over something, he told her: 'If you don't obey, we'll simply announce that you weren't Lenin's wife at all, and we'll give him another wife.' In answer to Krupskaya's amazed expression, he added: 'Yes, yes, don't be so shocked. The Party can do anything.'

In February 1917 the Russian Revolution caught Lenin in Switzerland. Nicholas II abdicated the throne. Freely elected by the people, a temporary government came to power which survived for eight months before the Bolshevik coup. Lenin found out about the revolution in February from the newspapers. He immediately set off for Russia. But how could he get there? Russia was at war with Germany. For a Russian immigrant to travel through German territory and across the German front was completely unthinkable. Lenin began to concoct far-fetched plans: to fly across the front lines in a balloon, to get his hands on the passport of some foreigner from a neutral coun-try and paste in his photograph, and other 'ravings' as Krupskaya put it. It paved the way for another of Lenin's secrets.

On 27 March 1917, Lenin and thirty other Bolsheviks crossed Germany in a specially provided train carriage with all amenities and a good cook. They were not allowed to leave the carriage, which is why Trotsky referred to it as 'sealed' in his memoirs. Krupskaya wrote: 'No one asked to see our pass-ports. No one checked our luggage.' Moreover, at one junction the train of the Crown Prince was delayed for two hours in order to give way to the train containing Lenin and his team. How did this skilfully executed operation come about? And why did Germany let the Bolsheviks cross her territory?

Time passed, and the secret found an explanation. The press reported that an agreement had been reached between Lenin and the German government, an agreement in which the Bolsheviks undertook to sabotage the battle-readi-ness of the Russian army, to persuade Russian soldiers to end the war, to prac-tise the 'politics of defeat'. In return the forces of the Kaiser not only allowed Lenin to cross their territory, but practically began to fund the revolution, set-ting aside for this purpose the then massive sum of fifty million German marks. This was seen as a case of openly aiding the enemy, falling under the jurisdiction of a military tribunal.

The rumours were first published by the German Social-Democrat Edward Bernstein. Later, at the end of the Second World War, when the American army captured the archives of the German Ministry of Foreign Affairs, they were backed up by documented evidence. After Bernstein pub-lished this secret material Lenin violently denied it, accusing Bernstein of libel. Bernstein then publicly invited the Bolsheviks to take him to court, after which the storm died down. The Bolsheviks did not demand a trial or an investigation, which spoke for itself.

Leon Trotsky writes: 'Reports began to appear in the paper, quoting doc-uments from the Justice Department, that Lenin and his people were simply agents of the German High-Command ... The authorities issued an order for Lenin's arrest.' There were arguments among the Bolsheviks: should Lenin go on trial 'to challenge these rumours' or should he go into hiding? Many, who seemed to know nothing of Lenin's secret arrangement with the Kaiser's Germany, demanded that he go on trial to 'clear the Party of these lies'. Lenin, however, had other ideas, and went into hiding in Finland.

On 6 November 1917 a Bolshevik uprising took place in St Petersburg. The temporary government was arrested. At a quarter to eleven that same evening, wearing a disguise and a wig, Lenin returned from Finland. The Bolsheviks assumed power.

Why did Lenin not co-ordinate the uprising himself, but instead, hiding in Finland, leave this task to Trotsky? Was it possible that in all this chaos and confusion, when there was not even any real authority, there was a realistic possibility of his being arrested? Why, when the uprising was virtually over, did he feel the need to appear in disguise? It is appropriate here to quote Tatiana Alexinsky, who in 1906 had been present at a rally outside St Petersburg where Lenin made a speech: 'When someone shouted "Cossacks!" [the mounted police], Lenin was the first to break and run. I watched him go. He jumped the barrier, and his bowler fell from his head ... With the fall of this ungainly bowler, Lenin himself fell in my eyes. Why? I don't know ... His flight, leaving behind his fallen bowler, somehow didn't gel with his image as the harbinger of the revolution ... The other participants of the meeting didn't follow Lenin's lead. Standing their ground they started a dialogue with the Cossacks, as was the usual practice in such situations. The only one who ran was Lenin.'

And now let us return to the beginning of our tale. On 11 March 1918, a special train transported Lenin and his government from St Petersburg to Moscow. Once again Moscow was to become the capital of Russia, and the Kremlin restored as the centre of power.

Shaken by the revolution, with its normal pattern of life interrupted, Moscow was filled with confusion and worry. Shops, kiosks and restaurants were closed. People milled around Red Square in a daze. Things were being bought and sold from hand to hand, pickpockets prowled among the crowd. The lawless elements of society were rising to the surface.

The Kremlin, which had been open to the public from the day it was founded, buzzed like a hive of troubled bees. It was the home of monks, church servants, workers from the many government offices and their families, museum caretakers, artists, guards, servants. They had all lived here since time immemorial. This was their home, and none could have guessed that they would soon have to leave it.

One of Lenin's first decrees upon his arrival in the Kremlin was an order 'to check whether everyone has a reason and the right to live here'. The churches were closed, the monks and church servants evicted, and soon all the other 'undesirable elements' were compelled to leave the Kremlin. On Lenin's orders, the ancient Russian icons mounted on the walls of the towers and churches of the Kremlin were removed, and monuments connected with the rule of the Czars were toppled. The commandant of Moscow's Kremlin remembers with pride how Lenin once personally oversaw the removal of an imperial monument from its pedestal, 'jovially' throwing a noose around its neck.

A strong guard of soldiers appeared at the gates of the Kremlin, and passes were now required for entry. Thus the Kremlin gradually began to transform into the secret citadel whose mighty walls were to protect the new government from the people for many decades. Some time later, the majestic eagles atop the Kremlin's towers which were the age-old symbols of Russia would be thrown down and replaced by huge red stars, the emblem of the new regime.

On 30 August 1918 an event took place which resounded across the whole country. On this day, late in the evening, Lenin was wounded by two gunshots during a speech he was making at one of Moscow's factories. According to the official version, the perpetrator of this act was one Fanny Caplan.

For many decades this story was a cherished subject in official Soviet literature, telling of the 'heroic life of the leader'. Fanny Caplan was presented as a vengeful terrorist, sent by the enemies of the revolution. At the same time rumours were spread about 'Lenin's supreme humanitarianism', forbidding the execution of the would-be assassin because she acted out of political conviction. Only recently, publications have appeared which shed the light of truth on this story.

Fanny Caplan was born in 1887 in a small town called Bobruisk in Belorussia, to the family of a provincial schoolteacher. At the age of sixteen she had already joined a band of revolutionaries fighting against the monarchy. During an attempted terrorist attack, the bomb went off ahead of schedule and Fanny herself was badly injured. She was arrested and sentenced to death, but due to her youth the sentence was commuted to life in a hard-labour camp. Suffering from a bad eye condition from childhood, Caplan went completely blind in the camp. Several years later, however, her sight returned partially. After the February revolution, having spent more then ten years in the camp, Fanny was set free. The methods by which the Bolshevik uprising was accomplished, and the subsequent repressions of political opponents, awoke her anger and misgivings. She attached herself to a party of social-revolutionaries, intent on expressing their protests via terrorist acts. The extent to which the conspirators were naïve and unprofessional can at the very least be judged by the mere fact that they seriously considered sending Lenin a woman who would 'give him a dangerous disease'.

At the time of the shooting on 30 August Caplan was indeed near the scene, but there is not a single piece of evidence to indicate that it was she who shot at Lenin. 'Fanny was standing with an umbrella under a tree, in the evening twilight, which is how she aroused suspicion in those who grabbed her. They grabbed her on class instinct ... In any case, could the almost blind Fanny Caplan have made several aimed shots late in the evening?'

At her interrogation this thin, sickly-looking woman with a long, slim neck and sad eyes, conducted herself with dignity, as her many years at a labour camp had taught her. According to several modern investigators, Caplan did not shoot at Lenin, nor even try to hide, consciously assuming the tragic role of 'patsy' and taking the guilt of the actual gunman upon herself, so as to throw pursuit off the scent of like-minded comrades. As Professor Litvinov asserts, Lenin was shot by an operative of the Party secret police (the future KGB), one Protopopov, who was also apprehended and immediately executed. Caplan was not aware of this, however, and continued to play out her tragic role to the end.

A mere three days after the attack, Fanny Caplan was killed without trial or investigation by a gunshot to the back of the head in a cellar of the Kremlin (directly under the apartment of Lenin's deputy Jacob Sverdlov). The gunshot was muffled by the roar of car engines, which were being revved precisely for that purpose. As the executioner himself proudly announced: 'On 3 September the sentence was carried out, and the executioner was I, a Communist, a sailor of the Baltic Fleet, the Commandant of the Moscow Kremlin, Pavel Malkov.'

Is there any need to comment on this 'heroic' boasting of an executioner who managed to shoot a lonely, blind woman in the back of the head? A woman who had spent most of her short and difficult life in prisons and labour-camps. The only witness of this brutal revenge was the Bolshevik poet Dimyan Bedni, who had asked to 'have a look'. By order of that same deputy, Jacob Sverdlov ('Destroy the remains without a trace') the body of Fanny Caplan was stuffed into a barrel of black oil and burnt.

Although Soviet literature has dramatised the attempt on his life, announcing that 'a fearsome struggle with death ensued, a struggle for Lenin's life', in reality the wound was not dangerous. Lenin walked up the stairs to his third-floor Kremlin flat by himself, and two weeks later was already back at work.

This was the best known, but not the only attempt, on Lenin's life. The first occurred in Petrograd (the renamed St Petersburg) on 1 January 1918, when the leader's car was shot at in broad daylight in the centre of the city. The comrade sitting next to him managed to push Lenin's head down, and himself was wounded. Lenin faced another predicament exactly one year later, this time in Moscow. In truth this was not a political act, but simply a criminal attack. As investigators later established, it was carried out by three Moscow criminals – 'Jacob-Wallet', 'Driver-Rabbit' and 'Leon-Bootmaker'. Most likely they themselves did not know whom they were robbing. They stopped Lenin's car, the driver assuming they were a patrol. In response to Lenin's demand to show him their documents, one of the bandits quickly pressed the muzzle of a revolver to his forehead. They then evicted the passenger, cleaned out his pockets, took his money, weapons and even his Kremlin pass, jumped into his car and drove away. After this incident Lenin's trips outside the Kremlin were dramatically curtailed, although he rarely left the fortress anyway. He never went to the front lines, or visited the provinces. Once, he was getting ready to go to Genoa to an international conference, but the secret service informed him that the Poles might be planning an attempt on his life, so the trip was cancelled.

In revenge for Fanny Caplan's attempt on Lenin's life, the Bolshevik government issued a decree beginning with the words: 'Everyone, Everyone, Everyone!' It announced 'merciless mass-terror for all enemies of the revolution'. This was the beginning of the 'Great Red Terror', which bathed Russia in blood.

Educated Russians have for many decades discussed the question, formerly in whispers, now in open argument: who was the real architect of the system which governed Russia for almost three-quarters of a century? This system, which destroyed tens of millions of Russian citizens, drowned the country in blood, and subjected the people to a measure of slavery not experienced even under Ivan the Terrible. Some think that this architect was Stalin. It was he and only he who brought the country into a terrifying Dark Age, perverting the path which Lenin had planned for his gigantic experiment. Others believe that Stalin was merely the pedantic executor of Lenin's experiment, bringing his theories to their logical conclusion. None other than Lenin, they say, uttered the following words at the Third Party Congress: 'We do not believe in eternal morality, and will expose the lies behind various moral fairy-tales.' Dora Shturman, an investigator of Lenin's philosophy, explains that Lenin's ethics 'fit into Hitler's fatal formula: "I will free you from the chimaera of conscience."'

So who was the main architect of this terrifying programme of violence, Stalin or Lenin? Here is a direct accusation of Lenin by Victor Chernov, one of the leaders of the revolutionary movement in Russia, who knew him well. After the Bolsheviks fired into a peaceful demonstration of workers on 5 January 1918, protesting against the unlawful seizure of power, Chernov wrote an open letter to Lenin:

> ... I, being your ideological adversary, have nevertheless sometimes praised your personal qualities. More than once, in those difficult times for you, when your trip across Germany raised the most foul of suspicions against you, I considered it my debt of honour to defend you before the workers ... Then, I considered it my duty to show restraint. Now you are at the pinnacle of power Now I am morally free from restraint ... and I deny you the right to call yourself an honest man ...
>
> Oh no, you are not a thief in the vulgar sense of that word. You would not steal another's wallet. But if you need to steal another's trust, and especially the trust of the people, you won't stop at any lies ... There is no political machination before which you would balk ... In your private life you love children, kittens and all living things. But with one stroke of your pen ... you will spill as much and whoever's blood is necessary, with a heartlessness that would be the envy of any degenerate of the criminal world ... You are an amoral person to the most central core of your being. You allowed yourself to step through all barriers known to the human conscience ...
>
> To clear your way to power you committed the dirtiest of deeds: you shot down a peaceful street-protest of workers ... Murder coupled with lies and betrayal mixes blood with dirt, and this fearful compound can never be removed ...

In modern parlance, this was the first instance of Lenin being accused of 'Stalinism'. If during the period of Gorbachev's *perestroika* the question of responsibility in Soviet history could still be raised and argued over, today it is quite unequivocal. Today, it can be questioned only by those who are unwilling or afraid to see the truth.

On 6 September 1991 the Russian parliament agreed to allow access to Lenin's secret archives. 'The massive, heavy metal door opened with difficulty, and we entered a spacious lobby. Beyond was another door, similarly reinforced, leading to the communist relics, Lenin's original documents: manuscripts, articles, speeches, notes ... On special shelves, in special boxes, all the written evidence is gathered of the man whom some still speak of as a genius, while others deride as the curse of the epoch. Here had been gathered and hidden for decades 3,724 of Lenin's documents which had never been published previously.' (D. Volkogonov)

Why? The Party had always asserted that every one of Lenin's words was 'worth its weight in gold'. Why did it hide this 'treasure trove' from the people for so many decades? Let us familiarise ourselves with a few excerpts from these documents:

To the city of Penza. 11 August 1918. Hang, specifically hang so that the people can see, no less than a hundred wealthy villagers, kulaks,* parasites ... Publish their names in the local newspapers ... Take away all their grain ... Make it so that for hundreds of miles around the people see, worry, know, shout ...

Execute the conspirators and those who are wavering, not asking anyone's permission and not allowing any idiotic bureaucratic delays ... (A letter to the town of Saratov, 22 August 1918)

Take hostages from the local peasants with a view to executing them if the snow is not cleared ... (From a decree by the Defence Committee, under the chairmanship of Lenin, 15 February 1919)

'Regarding the foreigners, I suggest we not rush the deportation. Would it not be better to send them to concentration camps, in order to exchange them later?' (To Stalin, 3 June 1919)

Is it possible to mobilise another 20,000 workers, plus another 10,000 bourgeois, mount machine guns at their rear, shoot a few hundred and thus effect a real, powerful advance against General Yudenich ... (To Trotsky, 22 October 1919)

We need to mobilise our whole cheka (secret police) to execute anyone who doesn't show up for work because of 'Nikolai' (the day of St

* Wealthy peasants.

Nicholas, 19 December). (From a letter to a representative of the Defence Committee, 28 February 1920)

Put together a manifest to the people, to the effect that we will cut all their throats if they burn or damage the oil refineries, and conversely, that we will spare everyone's lives if the cities of Maykop and especially Grozni are handed over whole. (To the Revolutionary Committee of the Caucus front, 28 February, 1920)

We need to punish Latvia and Estonia in a military fashion. For instance, cross the border somewhere going about a mile or so deep, and hang 100–1,000 of their bureaucrats and wealthy folk there ... Offer a bounty of 100,000 roubles for each one hung. (To the vice chairman of the Defence Committee, August 1920)

Is there any need to go on? Even here Stalin loses out to Lenin in terms of innovation. To reiterate, to date there are 3,724 such documents known to exist, hidden for over half a century in the Party's 'nuclear bunker'. And almost all of them are preceded by notes made by the leader himself: Secret. Top Secret. Arch-Secret ... He was perfectly aware of the moral value of these papers.

Only recently, it would have been unthinkable to ask the question which now seems to be formulating. How mentally stable was a man who could link such concepts as execution, hanging and the cutting of throats, with problems such as peasants clearing snow, people who were merely wavering as to whether to accept his ideology or people who took a day off work on their religious holiday?

The famous Italian psychiatrist and criminologist Professor Lobrozo has written a work entitled *Genius and Madness*. This title speaks for itself. So was it possible? 'Having observed some of Lenin's reactions over the course of several years, as a doctor I came to the conclusion that Lenin sometimes experienced psychotic episodes, with distinct symptoms of madness,' wrote Bogdanov, Lenin's close comrade-in-arms and friend of many years. This suspicion began to occur also to Lenin's brother-in-law, the husband of his elder sister. G. Solomon, author of the book *Lenin and His Family*, who knew his protagonist very well, also noticed this. Describing one of his conversations with Lenin, he concluded thus: 'And his eyes lit up with an evil, a fanatically evil light. In his words and stare I felt and understood a clear threat from a half-deranged person ... Some kind of madness was brooding inside him.' While such moments as '... he fell into a rage ...' were noted by many of his friends.

In 1922 Lenin began to show symptoms of a serious illness. They caused him sometimes to collapse and lose consciousness. During such attacks, part of his body was gripped by paralysis and subsequently he would lose his power of speech for some time, his reason seemed clouded and it became difficult for him to express his thoughts.

At first the attacks occurred no more frequently than once a week, and lasted twenty to thirty minutes, after which Lenin would again return to normal. Russian and foreign doctors were invited to see him, but at the time they did not yet observe symptoms of irregular brain function. Things continued this way until December, at which point they took a sharp turn for the worse. The right side of his body was completely paralysed, and from March 1923 the paralysis also affected his speech and comprehension. As Professor Osipov, the doctor treating him, noted: 'Lenin only had a few words at his disposal that he could use ... He also couldn't completely understand what was said around him ... His condition at the time was so bad that the question of how long he can hang on was even raised.' Considering that analogous symptoms had led to the death of his father, a group of doctors travelled to the homeland of Lenin's ancestors near the town of Astrakhan, to study the leader's genealogy. They wanted to find out if there was any hereditary syphilis in his bloodline, which was not a rare occurrence in Kalmyk families.

However, the patient's healthy nature, the care with which he was being attended, and the excellent treatment he was receiving all did their work. Lenin started to improve, although the fierce headaches, hallucinations and bouts of rage, which would reduce his family to terror, were still with him. He only calmed down when he was taken for a ride around the room in his wheelchair. He was soon able to understand what was said around him, and was even able to repeat some words himself. His wife started to work on speech exercises with him. 'His ability to read gradually returned ... He could already recognise letters, and read some words. He would be shown a picture and by glancing at it, he could name the item depicted on it.' The illness was gradually receding. Although Lenin remained paralysed, he was feeling so much better at this time that he was even taken for car rides.

This continued until October 1923, at which point a catastrophic turn for the worse took place. 'People who saw Lenin during this period experienced complex emotions,' wrote Professor Volkogonov. 'The man sitting before them had, only a year and a half ago personified the heart and mind of the revolution. Now he was a creature with a pitiful half-smile and sad, sick-looking eyes which shone with madness.' Lenin's brain was slowly but irrevocably dimming. Later, when an autopsy was conducted, experts would be amazed at how Lenin could have remained alive so long. Arteriosclerosis in the blood vessels of the brain was so severe that they literally ossified, and when tapped with tweezers they emitted a sound similar to stone. After observing Lenin's preserved brain, the artist Yuri Annenkov wrote that one of the hemispheres of his brain 'was shrunken and shrivelled, no bigger than a walnut'.

There was an event in the last period of Lenin's life which for decades remained yet another of the Kremlin's secrets. Many of those who knew about it ended their lives in Stalin's concentration camps. It was the conflict between Lenin and Stalin, and a version that claims Stalin hastened Lenin's death. When talking about the 'last period of Lenin's life' we are referring to the period between December 1922 and March 1923, when Lenin could still speak and dictate, when he was still trying to escape from the deep well of his muteness and clouding reason.

When Lenin experienced his first attack in May 1922, the doctors began to insist that he temporarily cease active duty. Although he was moved to a dacha* outside Moscow, he nevertheless continued to take part in political life, dictating memoranda to his secretaries, talking to colleagues. Due to his illness, genuinely concerned about his health, the Bolshevik hierarchy proposed isolating him 'both from personal contact and from correspondence'. Personal responsibility for carrying out this resolution fell upon Stalin, who at the time was the Party's General Secretary.

It must be noted that in Lenin's time the post of General Secretary of the Party did not have the same meaning as it would acquire later. Lenin was the head of the government, the accepted leader, while the post of General Secretary which Stalin occupied was merely an administrative position, although a high-placed one. Having at one time agreed to Stalin's appointment to this post, Lenin naturally could not have imagined that this poorly educated but cunning Caucasian would concentrate enormous power into his hands in the near future. By the time of his illness however, it seems that Lenin was already sensing Stalin's hidden agenda. Their relations become more and

* A summer house.

more strained. Even then, apparently, Lenin was thinking about moving Stalin from that post, as would be outlined by him in a few months in his political 'Will'.

Stalin of course sensed Lenin's changed attitude towards him, and understood that a threat was looming over his political career. Hence, being made personally responsible for Lenin's isolation came as a gift from heaven. From now on, he had the ability to control Lenin's every move, every line of his correspondence. To this end he had his informants, among them one of Lenin's private secretaries and one of his attendant doctors.

In December 1922 Lenin dictated his political 'Will', which was not destined to see the light of day for another half-century. In it, he demanded that Stalin be removed from the post of General Secretary. Although this document was considered Top Secret, and at Lenin's request the envelope with the 'Will' was only to be opened and read at the forthcoming Party Congress, Stalin nevertheless soon received a copy of the document through his informants. In Leon Trotsky's words: 'When Stalin first read the text of the "Will" he cursed Lenin soundly ... He spoke of the "Will" as a document written by a madman under the influence of "heifers"' (referring to Nadezhda Krupskaya and Lenin's sister Maria Ulyanov, who resolutely remained at the sick man's side).

Another incident occurred at this time, which marked the final break between Lenin and Stalin. With Krupskaya's help, Lenin dictated a short note addressed to Trotsky. Stalin found out about this and fell into a rage at the thought that one of Lenin's notes had slipped past his control. He phoned Krupskaya and insulted her in the most vulgar language imaginable. As Maria Ulyanov wrote in her notes: 'This conversation upset Krupskaya a great deal. She was acting completely unlike herself, sobbing, thrashing about on the floor and so forth ...'

Not wishing to upset her sick husband, Krupskaya did not tell him about the incident. He only found out about it some time later, and dictated an angry letter to Stalin: 'You were callous enough to call my wife on the phone and insult her. Although she expressed a willingness to forget what was said I do not intend to forget what has been done against me so lightly ... and what is done against my wife I consider to be done against me. Hence, I ask you to consider if you are willing to take back what was said and apologise, or do you intend to break off relations between us completely.' This was Lenin's last letter.

Although Stalin offered limp apologies, as Trotsky writes: 'He could no longer be in any doubt that Lenin's return to active duty would signal his political death. Only Lenin's death could clear him a path to power.'

Now we enter the realm of supposition and guesswork, first expressed by Leon Trotsky. Before the last incident with Krupskaya, Stalin told a select circle of his Party colleagues that Lenin had summoned him to his side, and asked him to acquire some poison. 'The old man is suffering. He says he wants to have poison at hand. He will use it if he becomes convinced that his situation is hopeless.'

Why did he turn to Stalin with this secret request? In his circle there were people far closer to him. Trotsky thought it was because no one in Lenin's entourage apart from Stalin would agree to carry out such a request. Trotsky believed that Stalin told his colleagues about this in order to deflect suspicion away from himself, in the event that poison was discovered in Lenin's body. 'I don't know if Stalin brought Lenin poison,' Trotsky wrote, 'but I know for a fact, that Stalin could not sit idle while the fate of his struggle for power hung by a thread, and the outcome depended on a slight, ever so slight, movement of his hand.'

On Friday 21 January 1924 Lenin died. At ten to seven in the evening blood suddenly rushed to his face, which quickly turned a deep burgundy colour, he sighed deeply and death followed swiftly thereafter.

Lenin's death caught Trotsky on his way to a holiday in the Caucasus. He immediately got in touch with the Kremlin: 'I consider it imperative to return to Moscow. When is the funeral?' An hour later he got a reply: 'The funeral will take place on Saturday. You won't make it back in time ... Stalin.' Actually, the funeral took place on Sunday. Trotsky thinks that Stalin lied because he was afraid of Trotsky's presence at the funeral. He was afraid that, remembering the conversation about poison, he might begin to suspect something and demand a more thorough medical examination. Stalin wanted to keep him at a distance, until the routine autopsy was over, the internal organs cremated, and the shell of the body treated for preservation. After that it would be very difficult to determine anything.

Trotsky wrote about all this in the mid-1930s. In December 1989, the afore-mentioned notes of Lenin's sister Maria Ulyanov were published, in which she confirmed that Lenin really did request Stalin to bring him poison. In short, 'We do not know if Lenin was poisoned by Stalin, and will probably never know,' writes Professor Ioffe, 'but, that Stalin created an environment which contributed to his death can hardly be brought into doubt.'

Immediately after Lenin's death, the afore-mentioned Victor Chernov wrote something resembling an obituary, a fine complement to his previously quoted open letter:

> Lenin possessed a powerful but cold intellect – an ironic, sarcastic, cynical intellect. Lenin was often accused of not being and not wanting to be an 'honourable foe'. But for him the concept of an 'honourable foe' was itself an absurdity ... To trick your foe, to knowingly spread rumours about him, to blacken his name, Lenin considered all of these activities to be perfectly normal options ... As a man who had 'truth in his pocket', he didn't value the creative efforts of others, didn't respect other people's opinions. The awestruck love of freedom, which is a quality of the creative soul, was foreign to him ... Lenin's will exceeded his intellect, and the latter always functioned as the servant of the former ... He was very fond of an expression of Napoleon's: 'Let's get stuck in first, and then we'll see' ... Thus he invariably became a charlatan, an experimenter, a gambler ... Even passive resistance to the ideas of his party constituted enough of a basis for him to execute hundreds of people, without even a hint of doubt. But despite all this, he genuinely loved to play with children, dogs and kittens. He died. His party is now led by people whom he, over the course of many years, moulded to his image and essence.

Thirty years on, as if finishing the portrait of Lenin which Chernov started, an extremely talented Soviet writer named Vasili Grossman wrote:

> 'Traitor ... lackey ... toady ... hireling ... Judas' – Lenin often used such words to describe his opponents. In an argument Lenin didn't search for the truth, he sought victory, and for victory any means will do. Lenin's impatience, his unwavering rush towards his goal, his hatred of freedom, his barbaric behaviour to those of an unlike mind, and his capacity to unblinkingly wipe off the face of the earth not only fortresses but even whole regions who dared challenge his orthodox authority, all these traits did not arise in Lenin after the Revolution. These traits were already possessed by Vladimir Ulyanov. These traits have deep roots. All his capabilities, his will, his passion, were subservient to one goal: to seize power ... For him, the Russian

Revolution wasn't about Russian freedom. The power that he sought with such determination was necessary to him personally. In order to thirst for power with such passion one must be extremely politically ambitious, one must love power very much. If we imagine Lenin the man as a personal equivalent of Lenin the politician, then we are confronted with a primitive and harsh character: impudent, domineering, merciless, rabidly ambitious, dogmatically argumentative. If we extrapolate these traits into everyday life, if we see how they might interact with a wife, a mother, children, or a neighbour, we are left with a feeling of loathing.

January 1924 was fiercely cold. Red Square was dotted with campfires around which people were keeping warm. The people were seeing their leader off to his final journey – some with unmitigated grief, others secretly joyous. Despite the fact that Lenin's relatives, his sisters, brother and Nadezhda Krupskaya most of all, considered it imperative that he be buried in the ground, next to his mother's grave, the Party had other ideas. Stalin disposed of his foe in an old, foolproof fashion: he turned him into a harmless icon. He needed the dead Lenin in order to put his embalmed body in a massive granite tomb, so that he himself could ascend to the top of that tomb. He needed the granite-like unity of the Party.

The old caretaker of the Mausoleum told how once, as if sensing her imminent demise, Krupskaya entered the place for the final time. She stood alone by the sarcophagus, uttered a deep sigh and quietly said: 'He's still the same, and I am getting older.' In a few days, on 26 February 1939, she celebrated her seventieth birthday. Her old friends gathered in a Party sanitarium in the outskirts of Moscow. They drank tea, and ate a cake that Stalin sent. The next morning she died in hospital, from some kind of stomach complaint. More foul play? Another poisoning? I do not think so. She was not the only one who ate this 'cake from Stalin'. Did it even exist? More likely than not it was a legend. In any case, Stalin personally carried the urn containing her ashes to the walls of the Kremlin, although this does not tell us anything either. The day after the funeral, Stalin's secret police searched her flat in the Kremlin and her dacha. They did not leave a stone unturned.

Many decades have passed. The founder of Bolshevism lies there to this day, in a grave of cold granite, his spirit restless, not given over to the earth as is the custom, haunted by doubts. And in the shadow of this tomb, entombed in the wall of the Kremlin, lie the ashes of the two women who were closest to him – Nadezhda Krupskaya and Inessa Armand.

The revenge of history is more fearsome than any human revenge ...

Postscript: Many years passed. The Western public did not believe that it was the real Lenin who lay under the glass of the sarcophagus, but a wax dummy. So journalists were invited into the Mausoleum, Professor Zbarsky lifted the glass lid of the grave, grabbed the mummy by the nose, twisted its head slightly to the left, slightly to the right. It was indeed Lenin.

8 | THE COUNTRY AND THE DESPOT

A NEW FIGURE ASCENDS to the top of the Kremlin hierarchy. About him the world, and even the Russian people, so far know very little. Almost thirty years of Kremlin history are linked to the name Stalin. Here, beyond the Kremlin walls, legends of the Living God were forged, and here also, the secrets of his real life were concealed. If the Kremlin is observed at night, from the direction of the Red Square, a window can be seen where the light never goes out. Perhaps it was some sort of service closet or guard room, it does not matter; but this never-extinguished light was one of the many methods with which the legend was upheld among the people, that day and night, without respite, Stalin was working for them. 'Whoever you might be,' wrote André Borbius, gushing with adoration, 'the best part of your fate lies in the hands of a man who remains vigilant for and labours for us all, a man with the brains of a scientist, the face of a worker, and wearing the clothes of a simple soldier.' Rumours circulated that that permanently lit window was in fact Stalin's study. As Nikita Khrushchev accurately mentioned in his memoirs, the whole country knew that Stalin worked at night, but only a narrow circle of people knew that he slept most of the day.

Hundreds of thousands of pages have been written about Stalin, many thousands of feet of film have been shot, but the secret of this man's soul, who is inscribed in history as one of its most bloodthirsty tyrants, has never fully been revealed.

For decades, a mighty man looked down upon the Russian people from massive portraits, a veritable giant; in life, however, small benches were placed on stage for him, to make him appear taller. On the enlightened face of the leader's portraits, there was never a wrinkle nor a shadow of doubt, but in life, his always poorly shaven face was riddled with smallpox scars and two yellowish tiger-like eyes shone out from below a low forehead. He was called the 'genius of mankind', creating and disproving scientific truths, yet in real life he was a school drop-out. Lenin, the leader of the Russian Revolution, whose every word was law for the Bolsheviks, rejected him from the party leadership, but he became the master of a gigantic country. A coward by nature, never having seen a real battle with his own eyes, he ended up victorious over the mightiest army in the world, and bestowed upon himself the mantle of Generalissimo. The greatest of politicians looked upon him as an equal, and it took decades for them to come to their senses. 'Roosevelt thought a gentleman sat in the Kremlin, when in fact there sat a bandit from the Caucasus' – was Winston Churchill's later judgement on him.

Soso was what his mother tenderly called him in childhood. Koba was the pseudonym he chose for himself, based on a legend about a famous Caucasus bandit. Stalin was the name under which the whole world came to know him.

The Persians have a belief that children born on 21 December – in the longest night of the year – are children of evil. Joseph Dzhugashvili (Stalin) was born on 21 December 1879, in the picturesque Georgian town of Gori, some one hundred kilometres from the Georgian capital Tiflis. Although at the time of his birth his mother had barely turned twenty, he was already the fourth child. The first three had died in infancy.

Crooked streets, haphazardly placed houses and fruit orchards all made Gori seem more a village than a town. No more than six thousand people lived there at the time. Stalin's family occupied an old clay-walled cottage, the sandstone roof of which had long since admitted the wind and rain. Their room was no more than ten square metres, with a brick floor and a tiny window that stingily let in light. The living environment consisted of a table, a stool and a wide ottoman. A sewing machine was later added.

During Stalin's rule his past was a dangerous, untouchable topic, so naturally it spawned countless of rumours and speculations. Some of them were apparently concocted by his enemies, in order to accuse him of a 'bourgeois upbringing', considered almost a crime in those days. Other stories, however, were spread by his supporters, possibly even on Stalin's direct orders, somehow to enhance his biography, since a lumpen-proletariat upbringing in no way augmented authority.

Thus, according to one version, he was the illegitimate son of a local Georgian nobleman, Jacob Ignatashvili, in whose household Stalin's mother worked as a servant. To conceal his maid's pregnancy, the noble gave her away to be married to a cobbler, Visarion Dzhugashvili, from the village of Didi-Lilo. Evidence was put forward in support of this version, that whereas he had destroyed almost all witnesses of his childhood, Stalin had not touched the relatives of this nobleman. Indeed, the latter's two sons – Stalin's alleged half-brothers – were even made members of the Georgian parliament which, considering their backgrounds and the mood of the times, would have been quite impossible without direct support from the top.

All this, however, is nothing more than legend. In fact, Stalin's parents were Katherine Geladze and Visarion Dzhugashvili, people of peasant stock who did not know how to read or write. His mother was a Georgian, his father, it seems, was an Osset. They never mastered the Russian language in their lifetime. As Stalin's daughter, Svetlana Alliluyeva, remembers, when she and her brother first met their grandmother in 1934, the only method of communication was by gesture since she did not speak Russian and they did not know Georgian. 'We were taken to her, and she impulsively hugged us with thin knotted arms ... Her eyes were bright in a pale face, covered with freckles. Her head was covered with a scarf, but I knew – since father had told me – that in her youth she was a redhead, which was considered beautiful in Georgia.'

After moving from their home village of Didi-Lilo to the town of Gori, Stalin's father took up shoemaking while his mother worked at various jobs – washing floors, doing laundry, sewing. Life was poor and hard. Katherine was a deeply religious woman. Her difficult life was an endless service to God, her husband, and her only son whom she loved dearly and dreamed of making into a priest. Decades were to pass, and on a visit to her now all-powerful son, she would sigh and say, 'A pity that you didn't become a priest after all.'

Joseph's father, Visarion Dzhugashvili, was a person of harsh temperament and a terrible drunkard. He drank away most of his meagre earnings, so all the financial burden of the house fell upon the mother's shoulders. The father wanted to make a cobbler out of his son, but did not have the time. He died from a knife wound in a drunken brawl, when Joseph was eleven years old.

As mentioned, Stalin did not like to be reminded of his childhood, when he and his mother had often to endure vicious beatings from his drunken father. Once he even threw himself at his father with a knife, to defend his mother, after which he had to hide with the neighbours for several days. Before going to sleep, the father would always try to cuff his son, who plainly did not love him. The mother watched on in pain as, by his actions towards his son, her husband 'chased love for God and people out of his heart'. The father's early death did not grieve the boy; he merely felt himself liberated. As his childhood friend remembers, from an early age, Joseph began to transfer his secret animosity towards his father, and his desire for revenge on to anyone who had, or could exert any manner of power over him. In youth, the realisation of his vengeful fantasies became his goal, to which he devoted all his being.

At the age of seven Joseph nearly died, suffering from smallpox, the scars of which remained on his face for his whole life. Doctors consider that the reason for his withered left arm was the alcoholic heritage of his father, although another suggestion is that the twelve-year-old Joseph was run over by a carriage and injured his left arm, which in time became shorter and weaker than the right. Whatever the truth, Stalin carefully concealed this defect throughout his life, trying not to undress in front of people and rarely visiting doctors. He did not like to bathe and never learned to swim, and during his holidays on the Black Sea he usually walked along the shore without removing his clothes.

Short of stature and physically weak, he could not count on victory in childhood fights, and always feared being beaten. As a result, he was to take a dislike to tall and physically athletic people, maliciously punishing them for this fancied form of humiliation.

In 1890, soon after the death of his father, Soso attended the local theological school and finished it with distinction after five years. Thanks to his excellent results, Joseph Dzhugashvili was accepted into the Tiflis Theological Seminary. As his peers remember, during the first courses of the seminary Joseph was a good pupil. He possessed an exceptional memory, and remembered lessons from the teacher's words, without needing to go over them.

Life seemed predestined. A few years would pass, and a Georgian village would welcome a young, short-statured Orthodox priest. The Caucasus mountains would shelter him from the whole world, and his everyday affairs would entail worrying over his small parish, his flock, and a horde of his own children, which every Georgian family raised as a matter of tradition. Life would carry on placidly and uneventfully.

Unfortunately, for his many million future victims, his life did not flow along this path. Joseph Dzhugashvili not only failed to become a priest, as his mother dreamed, but did not even manage to complete his diploma, abandoning the seminary a year before graduation. According to one version he was expelled for some kind of hooligan-like prank; according to another, he began to be interested in revolutionary matters, cooled towards his studies and was expelled from the seminary for poor academic performance. He was twenty years old at the time, which for quickly maturing Georgians is a completely adult age. Nine years of religious studies could not have failed to leave a deep mark upon his character, and upon the form of his thoughts.

Soon after leaving the seminary, Joseph began work as the book-keeper of the Tiflis observatory. Despite the measly pay, he enjoyed the work since it left him a lot of free time for his personal business – revolutionary activity. He even acquired the typical outward appearance of a provincial revolutionary. According to the recollections of an acquaintance, 'Koba wore a black Russian shirt, a red tie, and a Russian peaked cap on his head ... It was impossible to see him in anything other than a dirty shirt and scuffed boots.' This colourful ensemble was completed by a mass of shaggy, unkempt hair.

In 1901 police began to take an interest in the young Dzhugashvili, and he moved on to adopt an illicit lifestyle, becoming a professional revolutionary. From then on, he no longer had a name – only an underworld nickname. The police, for their part, also gave him a nickname of their own: 'Pitted', from the smallpox scars on his face.

Joseph Dzhugashvili understood early on that he could not count on anyone in life except himself. He had to forge his own path. His comrades in the revolutionary struggle told him more than once that he had a strong will. This praise went to his head, and he decided to strengthen this aspect of his character with an appropriately revolutionary pseudonym. That is how 'Stalin' evolved, from the word 'steel'.

It must be said that this was not empty praise. He really was a man of rare self control, mental endurance and level-headedness. His nature was wary, unforgiving and vengeful. His face seldom expressed the slightest emotion, maintaining a cold and sarcastic attitude to events around him. 'Compassion for people or animals was alien to him,' wrote a childhood friend, Joseph Iremashvili: 'I never saw him cry.' Life with a drunkard father had taught him brutality, while study in a theological seminary had fostered cunning and evasion. The traits of introspection and inner coldness, which people noticed at an early age, were in time transformed into callousness and absence of mercy. When he became a dictator he learned to wear the mask of a calm and, in public, even a personable man.

In 1903 Joseph Dzhugashvili married Katherine Svanidze, a pretty, presentable young woman, born in the same village as his father. The marriage was an auspicious one. His wife saw him as almost a demi-god, since as a Georgian she had been raised in traditions that compelled a wife to serve her husband. 'This truly Georgian woman,' wrote the same childhood friend, 'worried about the fate of her husband with all her heart, spending many a night in fervent prayer awaiting her Soso, when he took part in secret gatherings. She prayed that Koba would turn away from his heretical ideas for the sake of quiet family life.'

Unfortunately this marriage, which to some extent softened Stalin's callous heart, did not last long. In 1909 Kato, as she was known at home, died from typhoid, leaving Joseph with a six-month-old son called Jacob. As

Iremashvili went on to say: 'Joseph was shaken by the death. His spiritual turmoil was very powerful and long lasting. He was not even capable of hiding it from people. When the modest procession reached the graveyard, Koba squeezed my hand tightly, pointed at the coffin and said: 'This creature softened my stone heart. She died, and with her the last of my warmth towards fellow men died also.'

As mentioned in the previous chapter, the Party, in acute need of money, tasked Stalin with the robbery of banks, postal carriages and shipping in order to fill its coffers. This was the period that coincided with Stalin's detention in prison and exile. All in all he spent about eight years in detention, alternating periods of incarceration with escapes and legal release.

Exile at that time was, according to the revolutionaries, 'a sieve' from which only the lazy did not escape. It sufficed simply to reach the nearest railway station, get on a train and ride away. Even capture as an escapee did not carry any special threat as they were merely returned to sit out their term. Subsequently, Stalin himself was amazed at how ineptly the czarist regime struggled against its enemies. Perhaps it was at that point that he came to the conclusion that strong rule needs a harsh penal system.

People who knew Stalin from exile say he was a difficult and unpleasant cellmate. In one of his last places of exile, in eastern Siberia, Stalin lived with Lenin's future deputy Jacob Sverdlov, and in his memoirs, Nikita Khrushchev passed on Stalin's stories about this exile (attempting to reproduce his turn of phrase):

> Jacob Sverdlov and I lived together, prepared our meals. There really wasn't much to do there, we didn't work, living on the means the government handed out. Our main pastime was catching fish ... going hunting. I had a dog, called it Jacob (to annoy Sverdlov). Sometimes after supper, when it was Sverdlov's turn to wash the dishes, he'd wash the plates and spoon, but I never wasted my time on things like that when it was my turn I would finish eating, leave my plate on the floor, and the dog would lick everything clean ...

A very curious episode from Stalin's life in exile is recounted by Professor Boris Illizarov, who was allowed to examine the documents presented to Khrushchev by agents of the KGB after the leader's death.

It was 1914. Stalin was then in exile in the far north, in the tiny settlement of Kureika, which contained a mere 38 men and 29 women. Here is what

Ivan Serov, the KGB minister at the time – whose people conducted the investigation – writes to Khrushchev:

> According to citizen ... [the name of the woman was then kept secret], it was established that while in Kureika I. V. Stalin seduced her at the age of fourteen and began to cohabit with her. In connection with this, I. V. Stalin was summoned before police-officer Laletin to be charged with cohabiting with a minor. I. V. Stalin gave Laletin his word that he would marry ... when she came of age. As ... told, she bore (Stalin) a child which died. She later bore another who was named Alexander. When his exile was over I. V. Stalin departed (1916), and she was forced to marry a local peasant who adopted the young boy Alexander. During his whole life I. V. Stalin never helped her in any way. At the present time (established by the KGB – c.1953) Alexander is serving in the Soviet Army and holds the rank of Major.
>
> > Chairman of the Committee for National Security (KGB) of the USSR I. Serov*

According to a generally accepted rule among the revolutionaries, political prisoners would try not to have any contact with criminal inmates. Stalin, on the other hand, could always be spotted in the company of swindlers and robbers. He felt at ease among equals then, and was always impressed by people of 'realistic' professions. The company of people with more intellectual pursuits wore him down.

'There were some great lads among the criminals in exile,' Stalin remembers, as retold by Khrushchev. 'Times would be, we'd walk into the tavern, check out who had a rouble or three. Stick the money on to a window-pane and keep ordering until we drunk through it all. I'd pay one day, someone else would pay another, we took it in turns. There were some great lads among the criminals. The politicals on the other hand, there were some real scum among those. What did they arrange? They arranged a tribunal of comrades and tried me for drinking with the criminals.' Stalin certainly knew how to drink. 'When I was still in my crib, my father would sometimes walk up, dip his finger in a glass of wine and give it to me to suck. He taught me when I was still in the cradle.'

---

* I am personally aquainted with another of Stalin's extra-marital children. This is a former employee of Moscow Television, Constantine Kuzakov. Joseph Dzugashvili was a boarder in Kuzakov's mother's apartment, again during his Siberian exile. Father and son are of very similar appearance.

It was here in exile that the first stage of the Russian Revolution and the Czar's abdication from the throne would overtake Stalin. In March 1917 Stalin returned to Petrograd directly from exile. In the future, in all of Stalin's falsified biographies, it would be underscored that he not only seemingly took an active part in the Bolshevik uprising, but that he was in fact its actual head. This is completely divergent from the truth. Returning from exile, Stalin manifested such incredible passivity that some Western historians would later call him 'the man who missed the revolution'.

At this time, another important event took place in Stalin's private life. He became aquainted with Nadezhda Alliluyeva, his future second wife, who had then just turned sixteen. More precisely, they had already known each other for a long time in the Caucasus, where the Alliluyeva family lived. According to family legend, in 1903 Joseph Dzhugashvili saved a two-year-old girl who had fallen off a promenade into the sea. This girl was Nadya (the short version of her name, Nadezhda) Alliluyeva, and it seems that this incident remained in the child's memory to acquire a romantic shade with the passing of years. Nadya was younger than her husband by twenty-two years.

Nadezhda Alliluyeva was born in the Caucasus, in the family of a Russian worker, a railway engineer. She was a striking brunette with eastern facial features and most assumed her to be a pure-blooded Georgian. This inheritance came from her mother, who had both Georgian and gypsy blood. Stalin was drawn to this pure, naïve semi-child, and from that time on he often visited the Alliluyeva household. Nadya for her part also took an interest in this 'old revolutionary', as he called himself.

Everyone who knew Nadya Alliluyeva would maintain that she was the exact opposite of her future husband: gentle, personable, always kind. Even as the wife of an all-powerful dictator, she tried as best she could not to take advantage of her position. In the Industrial Academy in Moscow, where she studied along with Nikita Khrushchev, few people knew that she was Stalin's wife. Her life, as we shall later see, was to be an unhappy one, ending in tragedy.

In 1921 an event took place which marked the start of Stalin's journey to power. At the time, it did not attract undue attention, but it later became crucial to the future history of the country. In March 1921, Stalin became General Secretary of the Bolshevik Party. How could this have happened? How could a man considered so thoroughly mediocre by all who knew him assume such an important post? To understand this phenomenon, we must delve more deeply into the political intrigues which were occurring at the pinnacle of power.

The unquestioned leader of the Party was Lenin. Beside him stood men of a slightly lesser order, like Trotsky, Zinoviev and Kamenev. Between Trotsky on the one hand, and Zinoviev and Kamenev on the other, a continuing struggle was going on to determine who would become Lenin's right hand – his heir. When it became necessary to choose a General Secretary for the Party, neither side wanted to give the post to the other, preferring to plant a dull mediocrity in the position, who would be easy to control and not become a hindrance. Zinoviev and Kamenev recommended Stalin for the post. Kamenev already knew Stalin from the Caucasus and later when they both spent time together in exile. It was generally assumed that Stalin not only would pose no threat but would, moreover, be an obedient figurehead in the battle with Trotsky. Naturally, none of those supporting him could begin to imagine that by pushing him to the top they were signing their own death warrants.

It must be said that Lenin was not impressed with this new candidate, and uttered his prophetic statement: 'I don't recommend it. This cook will only prepare spicy dishes.' However, he did not actively oppose Stalin since, as mentioned earlier, the post of General Secretary was not as important at the time as it would become in the future, essentially that of a servant, without any real power.

At the end of 1921 Lenin was struck down by a serious illness, and in May 1922 he was already paralysed and bedridden. It became clear that his days were numbered. The situation changed drastically. Now the battle was waged not over who would become Lenin's right hand, but rather who would scoop up the falling sceptre of power. By the powers of blind fate, Stalin found himself between two warring factions, both of whom continued to look upon him as a harmless figure and tried to use him in their battle with each other. Today, with the distance of time, it is difficult even to imagine that these far from foolish people did not comprehend Stalin's primitive cunning. Rather than they manipulating him, it was he, exploiting their mutual rivalry, who wound his way through them and headed towards power. When they finally understood this it was already too late, the situation had become irreversible. At first, with the help of Zinoviev and Kamenev, Stalin levered Trotsky away from power – sending him into exile, and then overseas. In time, too, Stalin would send his 'faithful friends' Zinoviev and Kamenev to be shot in the cellars of the KGB.

It is worth mentioning here the methods of battle which Stalin was already employing in the first stages of his rise to power. Boris Bozhanov, Stalin's former personal secretary, remembered how he once entered Stalin's Kremlin office without knocking and caught his boss sitting at his desk and talking on the phone. More accurately, Stalin was not speaking, but simply holding the telephone receiver and listening. Bozhanov paused, anticipating the end of the conversation. After some time he noted with astonishment that the receivers of all four phones standing on the desk were lying in their cradles, and that Stalin was holding some other receiver in his hand, the cord of which disappeared into a desk drawer. It was then Bozhanov realised that it was not a receiver for conversation, but rather for surveillance.

Earlier, the entire Kremlin net passed through a switchboard, where girls would make the various connections manually. Such a system was certainly undesirable, since it did not facilitate the secrecy of conversations. Then a special foreign specialist was conscripted from overseas – a Czech communist – who assembled an automatic switchboard for the Kremlin capable of handling 60–80 numbers. It was considered that it would now be impossible to eavesdrop on conversation. However, during the installation of the switchboard, a special secret line was laid into Stalin's office on his own orders, enabling him to listen in on all the telephone conversations of the Kremlin net. It goes without saying that the Czech engineer was liquidated immediately upon the completion of this work, so apart from Stalin, this secret was known only to his two closest aides. Now his private secretary had unexpectedly discovered it.

'Stalin raises his head and looks me in the eyes with a heavy unflinching stare,' writes Bozhanov. 'Do I understand what I have discovered? Certainly I understand, and Stalin sees this … His glare asks me, do I understand what the consequences of this discovery are for me personally? Of course I understand. In the matter of Stalin's struggle for power, this secret is one of the most important … It is clear, that for the slightest careless word about this secret Stalin will destroy me instantly. I also look Stalin straight in the eyes. We don't say a thing, but everything is clear without words. Finally, I pretend that I don't want to disturb him and take my leave. Perhaps Stalin decided that I would keep the secret …'

Later Trotsky wrote that the first stage of Stalin's rise was unexpected, even unbelievable, even for Stalin himself. If dictators such as Hitler and Mussolini needed to travel a certain road on their way to power – form their own parties, raise the masses, engender their ideas – then Stalin experienced nothing similar. The bureaucratic machine of the Party apparatus automatically headed for power. Stalin was mounted on this machine, and he had to simply hang on, it would raise him to the top itself. 'The grey figure', Trotsky wrote, 'unexpectedly separated itself from the Kremlin wall and the world first glimpsed Stalin as a ready-made dictator.' It was an historical lottery, in which Russia drew the losing ticket.

We cannot understand Stalin and his future successes without understanding the basic elements of his nature: a love for power and an active, constant jealousy of anyone more capable, stronger and greater than himself. A burning desire to lord it over others was the driving force of his personality. Having obtained power, Stalin, as Trotsky accurately put it, 'seemingly first tasted blood'. His next task was the annihilation of anyone who presented even the slightest competition for him, or at least simply knew his true worth.

Some peoples of the Caucasus have a tradition of blood vengeance. Stalin translated this tradition from individual to nation. He never forgot anything and formulated his long-term plans for the destruction of people who displeased him. To incur Stalin's displeasure it was not necessary to be his political enemy; it was sufficient simply to earn his envy in some way, by intelligence, appearance, physical strength ... For example, one of the staff of the Ministry of Foreign Affairs was secretly executed merely for enjoying success with women, since once, as his friend wrote: 'This matter happened to pique the interest of the General Secretary, who forgot and forgave nothing.' Once, in a rare moment of sincerity, Stalin told a small select circle that more than anything in life he loved 'to select a victim, get everything prepared, mercilessly move against them, and then have a glass of nice wine and go to bed'.

There is no doubt that apart from anything else, Stalin's character also contained an element of primitive, pathological sadism. As an all-powerful dictator, he amused himself at his dacha by pouring oil over anthills and setting them alight, watching the dying insects writhe in the flames. Once, while seeing in a new year, a drunken Stalin rolled little cylinders out of pieces of paper, placed them over his secretary's fingers and lit them like candles. The secretary squirmed with pain but did not dare remove them. Stalin guffawed.

After the destruction of a victim whom Stalin knew personally, he liked to hear the executioners describe how the victim died. The more a person lost his human dignity in the face of death, the more Stalin was pleased. A tale has survived from a high-ranking member of the Cheka (the former KGB), about how at a certain party, when all present had already drunk a solid amount, the head of Stalin's guard presented him with an improvised performance depicting how Zinoviev and Kamenev had acted before their executions. It must be borne in mind that the victims were not only his revolutionary colleagues of many years, but also the men who had brought him from nothing to the pinnacle of power. The head of the guard played Zinoviev, who was being led into the basement to be shot, and two people present played the guards. 'Zinoviev' clung helplessly to the shoulders of the guards, and whined pitifully, dragging his feet and fearfully rolling his eyes. In the middle of the room he fell to his knees, hugging the boot of one of the 'guards' and wailing in terror, 'Please, for God's sake ... Call Comrade Stalin!' Stalin followed the performance with peals of laughter. Those present, seeing how much he enjoyed the scene, demanded that it be repeated. This time Stalin laughed so uncontrollably that he doubled over, clutching his stomach. Then a new element was introduced into the improvisation, and now, instead of falling to his knees 'Zinoviev' threw his arms up towards the ceiling and shouted, 'Hear me Israel! Our God is one God!' Stalin could no longer bear it and, choking with laughter, made motions with his hand to stop the performance.

Incidentally, not long before their arrest and execution, after Stalin had already manoeuvred Zinoviev and Kamenev away from power, Kamenev tried to remind Stalin who had brought him to power. 'Does Comrade Stalin know what gratitude is?' he asked. Stalin took his pipe out of his mouth and replied with a smirk: 'Why certainly, I know, I know it very well. It's a kind of disease dogs get.'

On 21 December 1929, Stalin widely celebrated his fiftieth birthday. Presents and congratulations flooded in from all corners of the country. The largest city on the Volga – Tsaritsin – was renamed Stalingrad. An unprecedented political mythology began to evolve, the creation of the image of a 'genius-leader', which continued for the remainder of Stalin's life. He was accredited with characteristics he did not possess, qualities he did not have, feats of heroism he did not accomplish. To anyone unfamiliar with the Soviet reality, it is hard even even to imagine the methods used to create Stalin's new 'biography'. Every moderately important accomplishment of the old revolutionaries was now attributed to one person. If someone's heroic deed needed to be assimilated, and the perpetrator of the deed was still alive and did not want to bend the facts, then he was simply destroyed. The widows of old revolutionaries were forced to write memoirs discrediting their husbands and acknowledging their accomplishments to Stalin. Those who did not comply, took a trip to the KGB basements. Even Lenin's younger sister, Maria Ulyanov, being mentally and psychologically handicapped, but endlessly devoted to her brother, nevertheless succumbed to the lie, creating the myth of a close friendship between Lenin and Stalin. Only Lenin's wife, Nadezhda

Krupskaya, did not lend herself to this confusion, but her silence was itself a concession brought about by fear for her life. Stalin could not stand her, and only Lenin's name saved her from physical harm. As soon as she died in 1939, the press was forbidden even to mention her name, and everything she wrote was removed from libraries.

Gradually, Stalin's vanity assumed global proportions and took on Asiatic forms. The press and radio circulated his name, which could no longer appear without the epithets 'Mighty', 'Genius', 'Father of the People' ... Millions of examples of his portraits and sculptures filled the country. Poetry, usually sheer doggerel, praised him:

You are the bright sun of the people,
The unsetting sun of the modern age,
And more than the sun, for in the sun there is no reason ...

Finally, an explosion in the centre of Moscow tore down the greatest church in Russia, her pride, the Church of Christ the Saviour, built over the course of fifty years, so as to erect in its place the biggest monument to Stalinism – the Palace of the Soviets. This monster was supposed to leave both the Colisseum of Rome and the Pyramids of Egypt far behind. Its height was planned to be 400 metres, and on top of it was to be placed another 100-metre statue of Lenin. The main hall was designed to seat 21,000 and could house the entire Vatican Cathedral of St Peter under its roof. Stalin let it be known in no uncertain terms that it would not simply be a palace, but a palace celebrating him, the leader, for all ages. Fortunately, like all similar utopias, this project was not destined to become a reality.

And so, Stalin became God, filling the whole Universe with himself ...

On the night of 8 November 1932, a tragedy is played out in Stalin's Kremlin apartments. Nadezhda Alliluyeva ended her life with a pistol shot. As Stalin's daughter Svetlana tells, the final straw in the difficult life of her mother was a fight with her father during a party commemorating the fifteenth anniversary of the Revolution. Stalin, who had already been drinking heavily, had just finished yet another toast when he noticed his wife was not drinking. 'Hey you, drink!' he shouted at her angrily and harshly. 'I'm not your "hey"!' she exploded, leaving the table. Rumours added that apart from the yelling, he also threw a burning cigarette butt in her face. Whatever happened, when Nadezhda was discovered in bed the next morning she was already dead.

Khrushchev, who knew Nadezhda Alliluyeva well, offered a different version, related to him by the head of Stalin's personal guard. According to this version, Nadezhda was not even at the party. After the celebration Stalin did not go home, but to his dacha instead, bringing along the very attractive wife of one of the military chiefs. Late at night, looking for her husband, Alliluyeva called the dacha. The guard on duty replied that Comrade Stalin was there. 'Who is he with?' she asked. The guard named the woman. In the morning, when Stalin returned home to the Kremlin, Nadezhda Alliluyeva was found to have died.

A third version also exists, according to which Stalin himself shot Nadezhda Alliluyeva in a fit of rage, furious at the determination of his strong-minded wife. It was only later that rumours were circulated about her suicide due to jealousy, or some petty family squabble.

Stalin's daughter Svetlana supports only the first version. Whatever the case may be, these were merely the closing notes of a tragedy, which had itself started long ago. As Stalin's former personal secretary Boris Bozhanov wrote: 'Nadia was nothing at all like Stalin. She was a very good, fair and honest person. She was not pretty, but her face was kind, open and striking. She didn't have any girlfriends at this stage, and male company was afraid to go near her. If Stalin were to suspect that anyone was courting his wife, he would make that person's life a living hell. I got the clear impression that the dictator's wife was in need of the most basic of human interaction. Her home life was difficult. At home, Stalin was a tyrant. Forced to control himself all day long in his official dealings, at home he didn't stand on ceremony. Nadia told me more than once "He hasn't said a word for three days. He doesn't talk to anyone and doesn't respond when someone speaks to him. An unusually difficult man."'

Often, in response to Nadia's accusation that 'You are not interested in family and children', Stalin interrupted her with low vulgarity. The couple fought. Nadia left her husband twice, taking the children and going to stay with her parents in Leningrad. But time would pass, the hurt would die down and everything would begin again.

Stalin's difficult character and his wife's unhappy life could not be a secret in the narrow world of the 'Kremlin residents'. 'He walks around the Kremlin scowling like Ivan the Terrible', the Kremlin servants would mutter. The widow of Jacob Sverdlov, seeing Nadia's often tear-stained eyes, would clap her hand to her mouth and murmur: '... Poor, poor woman ...'

'Mother had her own ideas about life, which she defended,' Svetlana Alliluyeva wrote. 'Father was once mother's ideal example of a new kind of man. In the eyes of a young high school girl, he was an "unconquerable revolutionary", a friend of her parents, recently returned from Siberia. She saw him that way for a long time, but not for ever. In the end, she was overcome by frightening, draining disappointment ...'

Svetlana continued: 'Father was shaken by mother's death. From time to time he would be overcome by some manner of evil ferocity. This is partially due to the fact that mother left him a note. It was terrible. It was full of recriminations and accusations. The letter was in some part also political. Father was angered and saddened by this, so much so, that when he came to pay his respects at the civil funeral, after approaching the coffin he suddenly pushed it away, strode off and left. He did not visit her grave even once ... He considered mother to have departed as his personal enemy.'

Of all Nadezhda Alliluyeva's relatives, Stalin only spared her parents. All the others, including her own sister, were to suffer prison and exile, many would be executed. The same fate would also befall the relatives of Stalin's first wife. People who for many years had eaten and drunk at the same table as he, slept under the same roof, were to die in the basements of the KGB. Once, in reply to his daughter's question as to what had been the crime of her aunts and uncles, Stalin grumbled, 'They blabbed too much, knew too much ...' and after a few moments of silence added, 'You also have a tendency towards anti-Soviet declarations.' Was he perhaps preparing to send even her to a detention cell?

After the death of Nadezhda Alliluyeva, Stalin lived alone until the end of his days, his daily routine entrusted to a housekeeper, 'a young, snub-nosed Valentina, whose mouth never shut all day long from merry laughter'. Valentina Estomin lived in Stalin's house for eighteen years, until the end of his life. She accompanied the master on all his trips, and when he died, 'She collapsed on to her knees beside the couch, threw her head upon the chest of the deceased, and howled in grief – like in a village. She could not stop herself for a long time, and no one disturbed her. ' Evidently he was closer and dearer to her than to all his former brothers-in-arms. Khrushchev maintained it was no business what their relationship was. In the end, even great people live with their housekeepers. Karl Marx himself had an illegitimate son with his maid, Helen Demunt.

After the death of his wife, Stalin was left with three children. The eldest son Jacob from the first marriage, was only seven years younger than his step-mother, while eleven-year-old Vasili and six-year-old Svetlana were from the second. The fates of all the children turned out tragically.

Jacob Dzhugashvili spent his early childhood in Tiflis, with relatives of Stalin's first wife, and moved to Moscow when his father was already living in the Kremlin. The relationship between father and son did not work out. Stalin did not like Jacob, considering him a weakling, in which, as time was to show, he was mistaken. Everyone who knew Jacob remembered him as a decent, honest and shy person. Trotsky, whose Kremlin apartment was located next to Stalin's, remembered how Jacob was subjected to frequent and harsh punishment from his father, because he, like all boys at that time, smoked. The father, who himself seldom let his pipe out of his mouth, punished this boyish sin with the ferocity of a backwater despot, seemingly re-creating the child-raising methods of his drunken father. Jacob would frequently be forced to spend the night in the street, as his father refused to let him into the house. 'With burning eyes and a pale cast to his cheeks,' Trotsky wrote, 'Jacob often sought sanctuary in our Kremlin apartment. "My father is crazy," he would mutter, in a strong Georgian accent.'

Jacob finished university, became an engineer and married his classmate, the daughter of a priest, but the first marriage did not bring him happiness. Stalin was strongly opposed to the union, acted the petty tyrant and drove his son into attempting suicide by shooting himself in the chest. Fortunately, the bullet passed through cleanly and he remained alive. Finding out about it, Stalin mockingly quipped at his son, 'Ha, you missed?' After this, Jacob abandoned his father's house and went to live with the parents of his stepmother, the Alliluyevas, in Leningrad. It is here he met his next wife to be.

This marriage, however, did not last long and soon fell apart. Upon his father's insistence, Jacob quit his engineering career and went to study at the Gunnery Academy. At this time he met a very pretty dancer called Yulia Meltzer and married her. Yulia was Jewish, and this once again raised his father's fury, although at this time he did not yet display aggressive anti-Semitism. This trait was to flare up later.

On this occasion Jacob displayed firmness of character, and no amount of paternal displeasure would compel him to leave his darling wife and newborn daughter Galya, whom he adored. His father did not help his son in any way, and the latter lived apart with his family, like any ordinary individual.

The day after Hitler's attack on the USSR Jacob went to the front line, and a month later ended up a prisoner of war. According to the official version, the whole battery that he was commanding was encircled, but other sources claim he was kidnapped from the front lines by German Intelligence. The Germans naturally tried to turn this into good propaganda material, dropping leaflets with photographs of Stalin's captured son, and with a letter, allegedly written by him: 'Dear Father, I am a prisoner, healthy and will soon be sent to a prison camp for officers in Germany. I am being treated well. I wish you good health, my regards to everyone. Jacob.'

Enraged, Stalin ordered the arrest of Jacob's wife Yulia according to a draconian law that punished the relatives of those taken prisoner. As was well known, Stalin's doctrine decreed that there were no prisoners of war in the Red Army, only traitors to the motherland.

Jacob spent more than two years as a prisoner. When the German High Command offered Stalin to trade his son for Field Marshal Paulus, taken prisoner at Stalingrad, according to one version Stalin replied, 'I have no son', and according to another remarked, 'We don't trade Generals for soldiers.'

Many eyewitness accounts have survived from people who were imprisoned together with Jacob. According to their stories he behaved bravely, like a patriot. There are several versions of Jacob's death. One widespread report was that, driven to despair, he threw himself at the barbed wire fence surrounding the internment camp and was shot by the guards. Recently, however, another version has appeared, put together on the basis of foreign and archive material researched by Alexander Kalesnik.

The last place where Jacob found himself, was a camp called Sachsenhausen, near the town of Oranienburg. A number of officers from different countries were housed in one of the barracks of this camp, including several Englishmen. The Englishmen obediently carried out the orders of the camp administration – stood to attention in the presence of German officers and generally behaved in a disciplined fashion. The Russians were quite the opposite, considering it dishonourable to submit to the enemy, for which the whole barracks would often be punished. On this basis, not even considering everyone's frayed nerves, friction would often occur. An argument ensued one day that was transformed into a confrontation. One of the Englishmen, named Cushings, leapt at Jacob and struck him in the face. The overall tension, on top of this incident, proved the culminating point that the proud Georgian character could no longer bear. In the evening, Jacob refused to return to the barracks and demanded a meeting with the camp Commandant. When he was turned down, he threw himself at the barbed wire, and was shot by the guards. This happened on 14 April 1943; he was then thirty-five years old. Documents relating to the incident later fell into the hands of the Western Allies. At first, they wanted to pass them on to the Soviet side, but since their countrymen played an unworthy role in the affair they refrained, so as not to 'aggravate Stalin'. The papers were only declassified in 1968.

The life of Stalin's second son Vasili turned out quite differently, although no less tragically. An atmosphere of flattery and indulgence made him weak-willed and capricious. Not without the help of his father, who would pour him a glass of wine at dinner from an early age, he soon gave himself up to alcohol. After the death of his mother, his main role model became a general of the KGB, the head of Stalin's personal guard. Teachers were afraid of their hot-tempered, highly placed pupil, since he could insult them in front of the whole class without a second thought.

Vasili's career headed rapidly upward. At the age of twenty, soon after graduating from the Air Force Academy in 1940, he was awarded the rank of colonel. He took part in the war, flew twenty-seven battle sorties and shot down one enemy plane. Truth be told, though, after the capture of Jacob Dzhugashvili by the Germans, Vasili's battle missions were limited and in the course of them he was closely guarded. At the age of twenty-seven he was already a major-general of the Air Force, and at twenty-nine he became a lieutenant general, commanding the airborne forces of Moscow's military district, although by this time he already drank so much that he could no longer fly a plane himself. As his sister Svetlana describes:

> A spirit of drunken revelry entered the house. Guests came to see Vasili. Sportsmen, actors, his pilot friends, abundant revels were arranged constantly, the radiogram blared loudly. They were celebrating as if there was no war ... Various dark individuals jostled around him, inciting him into numerous shady transactions ... He did not care about the treasury. He was given the right to control enormous amounts of money. He allowed himself everything, removing inconvenient people who got in his way, some of which he sent to prison.

The kind of 'commander' may be judged by the simple fact that in the end his own father was compelled to remove him from this position, 'for actions unbecoming the occupied post'. The word 'actions' concealed drunken binges, orgies and beatings, and not only involving those in under command. For example, receiving a reproof from a higher-ranked commander after a flight, Vasili proceeded to slap the man right there on the airfield. At the first moment of his arrival at the air-detachment where he was sent to serve, he informed the commander, 'You are going to do as I say.' He was no less aggressive in everyday life. He thought nothing, for instance, of stopping a passing car, which he considered did not make way for him quickly enough, and viciously beating up the driver. He drank, and step by step became a chronic alcoholic. Once, he even appeared drunk at a commemorative banquet at his father's, where the top military staff of the country were gathered. His father's reaction was instantaneous: 'Get out of here!'

He also brought a fair share of grief to his four wives. Some he left, others left him themselves. A mere twenty-one days after the death of his father, the thirty-three-year-old Lieutenant General Vasili Stalin was cashiered from the army without the right to wear a military uniform. After this, he hit the bottle even harder. 'He sat at his dacha and drank,' writes Svetlana. 'Like all alcoholics, he did not need a to drink a lot. Downing a glass of vodka, he would collapse on the couch and go to sleep ... He lost all touch with the real world, of his place in it, he felt himself to be the Crown Prince.'

Two months after the death of his father, Vasili was arrested and sentenced by military court to eight years' imprisonment. Formally, this was a sentence for former crimes: embezzlement of state money, the beating of underlings, intrigue at the highest level as a result of which several people went to prison and several others died ... This was the formal reason for his isolation, but in reality he was simply too loose-lipped. He spent all the time after his father's death in the restaurants of Moscow, drank with anyone and anywhere, and yelled from every street corner how his father had been 'killed', 'poisoned' or simply 'driven to death'. He was warned that this could end badly, but he scorned everyone, forgetting that he was no longer the figure he used to be. In the end, those at the top got tired of it and he was simply put out of the way. His daughter Nadezhda Stalin remembers these days:

Once, returning from school, I discovered everyone gone, father had already been taken away and the house was being searched ... In prison father was kept under the surname of Vasiliev. Mother and I visited him every week ... Often, while we were waiting for him, we could see how he was being led through the open door in the corridor. Wearing a quilted jacket, a cap with earflaps and tarpaulin boots, he walked with a slight limp, his hands behind his back ... Incidentally, after father's arrest I went to school as usual. The director of the school, however, met me at the cloakroom. Tearing my coat from the rack and throwing it into my face, she yelled, 'Get lost, back to your father and grandfather!' I was so stunned that I involuntarily blurted out, 'I have nowhere to go. Father is in prison and grandfather is in the ground' … I was in seventh grade at the time …

What can justify such viciousness from a teacher towards a child? Life is a boomerang. Was it not Stalin's system itself that gave rise to it? How much does a person have to survive and suffer in order to become so callous?

Vasili spent seven years in prison. He wrote letters endlessly to all members of the government, pleading, begging, threatening. He was even preparing to ask the Chinese for help. In the end he was brought before Khrushchev. Vasili threw himself at his feet, begged forgiveness and promised to be a different person. According to Vasili, Khrushchev received him as would his own father. They hugged and kissed, both cried, remembering times gone by. Vasili was released from prison. All his titles and privileges were returned to him, but this did not last long. His former friends began to gather around once more. The revels and fights started all over again. There were especially many Georgians among his entourage, who worshipped his father and tried to convince the son to move to Georgia, where they promised him the luxurious life of a prince.

A month after his release from prison, Vasili was involved in a serious car accident while drunk. Khrushchev was enraged, swearing profusely and saying, 'What shall we do? If we put him in prison he'll die. If we don't he'll die anyway.' They offered to change Vasili's prominent surname, but he refused. In the end he was sent into exile, to the city of Khazan. He was given a one-bedroom flat there, where he lived with his latest wife. But vodka, debauchery and prison had turned him into a full-blown invalid. During yet another drinking binge, Vasili died, never having managed to sober up.* He was forty-two years old at the time. He left behind seven children, four of his own and three adopted. The grave of the 'prince' is adorned merely with a laconic inscription, made by his last wife: 'To my only one, from M. Dzhugashvili'. There was once also a photograph, but it was broken, torn off and defaced.

Vasili's life was unremarkable, yet it vividly illuminates that 'dead zone' in which Stalin's closest entourage existed. Some of them died in the basements of the KGB, others died by their own hand, still others were compelled to be obediently silent while the leader sent their wives, brothers and sisters into those basements, thus testing the 'loyalty' of his comrades. Stalin understood that if a man endured the arrest of his wife, father or friend, he was no longer

---

* According to another version, which Sergo Beria put forward in his memoirs, Vasili was stabbed to death in a drunken brawl, dying in exactly the same way as his grandfather the cobbler.

an individual but a crushed, snivelling nobody who would never raise his hand against his master. Finally, Stalin himself became a prisoner of the 'dead zone' he had created.

The youngest in the family was Svetlana. She had turned six when her mother died. It seems that when she was a schoolgirl, her father loved her more than his sons. If any softer intonations can be found anywhere in his life, it can only be in early letters to his daughter, whom he tenderly called 'mistress'. She had apparently inherited a lot from her mother and grew up a pleasant, respectable girl, doing nothing in particular to dissatisfy her father.

A change in their relationship occurred when Svetlana was in her final year of school, and like all girls of her age experienced an attraction to men for the first time. The man in question was the famous journalist and scriptwriter Alexander Kapler. He was thirty-six years old, she was seventeen. As Svetlana remembers, they met at the end of 1942 at the dacha, where her brother Vasili had brought Kapler. There was some sort of party, everyone was dancing and Alexei asked Svetlana to dance: 'I felt some sort of unusual trust towards this fat, good-natured person. I got a sudden urge to place my head on his chest and close my eyes ... We were uncontrollably attracted to one another.' With a hulking bodyguard accompanying their every step, they spent several days in a row together, going to the cinema, the theatre, art galleries and once even kissing. That essentially was the whole romance, which ended with Svetlana breaking with her father, and with somewhat more dire consequences for her suitor. A few days later Kapler was arrested. Svetlana was to write:

I had never seen father this way. He was was choking with rage. 'I know everything! All your telephone conversations ... Your Kapler is an English spy, he has been arrested!' 'I love him,' I finally said, recovering the power of speech. 'Love him?' my father screamed with indescribable fury at the very word, and slapped me twice across the face for the first time in my life. 'Just think nanny, what she has come to!' He could no longer control himself. 'There is such a bloody war on, and she is running around ...' and here he uttered a number of profanities. 'She couldn't even find herself a Russian ...' The fact that Kapler was Jewish seemed to irritate him more than anything. From this day forward, my father and I were strangers for a long time.

Kapler was exiled for five years to the far north, to the town of Varkuta, where he worked in the theatre. After this time was up, however, he was arrested for a second time, and this time sent to a hard-labour camp, to work in the mines. He was released only after Stalin's death, paying for his infatuation with ten years' loss of freedom.

Two years after meeting Kapler, while a student at Moscow University, Svetlana married a young fellow student named Gregory Moroz. He was Jewish, which once again did not suit her father. This time, however, he did not resort to extreme measures, giving his consent and waving the matter aside. The only condition he made was that her husband never set foot in his house. That is how it was: they never met.

The marriage lasted three years then fell apart. Svetlana writes that it failed due to personal reasons. Khrushchev, however, insisted that it collapsed under pressure from her father, whose anti-Semitism was beginning to come into sharp focus at the time. Whatever the truth, the black soul of the leader could not resist sending the father of his daughter's husband into the basements of the KGB.

After the marriage Svetlana was left with a son, Joseph, named in honour of his mighty grandfather. Joseph was a beautiful boy, with dark Semitic eyes and long lashes. Svetlana remembers that when the grandfather first saw his grandson, he melted ... 'What thoughtful eyes,' he said tenderly, '... such a clever boy.' Despite Joseph's half-Jewish descent, Stalin loved him more than all his other grandchildren, of whom he had eight. Many of them he had not even expressed a desire to see during his whole life.

Svetlana's second marriage took place not only with her father's blessing, but also at his insistence. Her husband was Yuri Zhdanov, the son of Stalin's closest henchman, one of the bloodiest figures in the entire circle, who at one time was even touted as the leader's political successor. The marriage was loveless and fell apart immediately after Stalin's death, leaving Svetlana with a daughter, Katya.

There followed difficult years of coming to terms with the past. Svetlana rejected her father's surname and began to use her mother's maiden name, Alliluyeva. In 1962 Stalin's daughter was baptised and became a believer. Further events of her life are widely known. In 1967 her fourth husband, an Indian journalist accredited in Moscow, Radj Bridj Singh, died. Svetlana accompanied his body to India for burial. After the funeral, she approached the Soviet ambassador requesting permission to stay with her husband's relatives for a few more months. The ambassador categorically refused, demanding she return home immediately. As Khrushchev wrote: 'If a Soviet ambassador advises a citizen of the Soviet Union to return home immediately, this quickly puts them on their guard, especially considering that she knew all the protocols that we used in such matters.'

Upon receiving the refusal, Svetlana turned to the government of the United States, asking to be granted political asylum. She travelled from India to Europe, and then on to the USA. This was already the era of Brezhnev, a return of the 'long winter' after Khrushchev's brief 'thaw'. Svetlana's failure to return home became a large political event, creating a storm in the party élite. Figures such as Nobel Prize-winning writer Mikhail Sholokhov labelled her a renegade, a traitor to the motherland. As Svetlana later remarked, if her father had been alive, he would have had her shot.

After her arrival in the United States, Svetlana Alliluyeva accepted an invitation to stay with the widow of the famous architect Frank Lloyd Wright, who had Slavic roots herself. In that house she met the architect William Peters and married him. She gave birth to her daughter Olga, wrote her memoirs, but did not find happiness in this either. After two years the marriage ended. She moved to England and in 1984, having received permission from the Soviet government, returned to Moscow. After a brief stay in Moscow she went to live in her father's homeland of Georgia, hoping to find some spiritual balance there. Unfortunately, this was not to be. Her son and daughter, whom she left in Russia and had not seen for seventeen years, were almost strangers to her. The attempts of her son, who had by this time become a famous doctor, to establish warm relations with his mother were not rewarded with success, while her daughter simply refused to meet her.

After a short stay in Russia, Svetlana Alliluyeva left once again and returned to the West. 'I no longer comfort myself with the illusion that I can ever be free from the yoke of "Stalin's daughter",' she says. 'There is something predestined in my life ... Sometimes, I regret that my mother did not marry a carpenter.' One Western journalist remarked that this woman, like Antigone, cannot escape the curse hanging over her line. She was and will remain Stalin's eternal captive.

Such are the sad fates of the children of a man who possessed the lives of millions, but did not possess happiness.

◆　◆　◆　◆　◆

Let us return, however, to the 1930s. On 1 December 1934, an event occurred which is commonly held to herald the beginning of the 'Great Terror'. On this day in Leningrad, Sergei Kirov, the leader of the Leningrad Bolsheviks, was shot dead from point-blank range at the door to his office.

Kirov was not only one of Stalin's closest people, but also his personal friend, a part of the family. In Stalin's life this man may well have been the only one of his colleagues to whom he showed seemingly genuine goodwill. A book given to Kirov by him was signed 'To my friend and favourite brother, from the author. Stalin.' It is unlikely that he ever expressed such words to anyone else.

The murder occurred when Kirov was at the height of his popularity. A little earlier, during a Party congress, a group of delegates, who were dissatisfied with Stalin's growing autocracy, had a private conversation with Kirov in which they offered to put forward his candidacy as head of the Party instead of Stalin. It is said that Kirov was so frightened by the conversation that he immediately went to Stalin and told him about it. Stalin allegedly replied, 'Thank you. I won't ever forget you did this.' These words can be interpreted in two ways. In any case, when recounting the tale at home upon his return to Leningrad, Kirov threw in the phrase, 'Well, now my head is on the block.'

The murderer was a thirty-year-old communist called Nikolaiev, recently excluded from the Party for some misdemeanour and allegedly hating Kirov because of this. Several days before the attack Nikolaiev had already been detained by officers of the KGB, near the building where Kirov's office was located. His attaché case contained a gun and a map, plotting out the route Kirov usually took. Despite such clues, however, the local KGB officials demonstrated completely uncharacteristic liberalism and released the future murderer, even returning his gun.

Two hours after Kirov's murder, Stalin left Moscow on a special train bound for Leningrad. He was accompanied by his closest people, including the head of the USSR's KGB, Henrich Yagoda. Arriving in Leningrad the next morning, Stalin greeted everyone meeting him on the platform with extreme profanities and slapped the head of Leningrad's KGB across the face. Afterwards, he personally conducted the interrogation of Kirov's murderer. Rumor has it, that when Nikolaiev was brought into the room for interrogation he fell at Stalin's feet and yelled, 'I did this on Party orders!' And when a bloody and unconscious Nikolaiev was carried from the room, Stalin allegedly turned to Henrich Yagoda and threateningly growled ,'Moron!' This comment has been interpreted as: 'Idiot. Couldn't you tie up the loose ends?'

The head of the Leningrad KGB, who got slapped by Stalin, was arrested and sent to Siberia, although he went there in unusual comfort, even managing to take his family with him. His colleagues from Moscow still sent him his favourite wines and new records, which he collected, for a long time to come. The simple fact that high-placed friends from the KGB still continued to communicate with the arrested man, which had been completely impossible during Stalin's period, shows that this was not a real arrest. Nevertheless, in a moment of honesty while in hospital, the phoney victim told a doctor that he was doomed anyway; he would be destroyed because he knew too much. He turned out to be right. A few years later he was secretly executed. As one high-placed KGB official told his friend: 'This matter is so dangerous, that the less you know the better.'

Many years later, after Stalin's death, Nikita Khrushchev would form a special commission charged with unravelling this mysterious murder. Later still, when Khrushchev had familiarised himself with the results of the investigation, he would hide them away in a safe with the words, 'While Imperialism exists in the world, we cannot publish these documents.' What he was in fact saying was that they could not admit in front of the whole world that a common criminal had stood at the helm of the government. The findings of this commission have not been published to this day, but from what became known it can be concluded that Stalin himself organised the murder. With this he not only freed himself of a dangerous competitor, but could also use his death to take care of any inconvenient political opponent, accusing him of participating in a conspiracy against Kirov.

The train that Stalin took back to Moscow also carried Kirov's body. It was laid out in state, in one of the biggest halls of the capital. The papers wrote that Stalin, while standing honour guard over Kirov's body, experienced such a wave of grief and love towards his dead friend that he approached the coffin and kissed the deceased. *

---

* The version of Kirov's death offered above has already existed for many years. Recently, however, the memoirs of Russia's main 'saboteur and terrorist', Lieutenant General Pavel Sudoplatov, the organiser of Leon Trotsky's murder and many other 'wet' operations, were published. Being the head of a top-secret department, General Sudoplatov certainly knew many of the KGB's secrets, so his words deserve careful consideration. He maintains that Stalin did not in fact organise Kirov's murder, but made maximum use of the opportunity presenting itself to him to fabricate a 'conspiracy' and unleash a bloody terror in the country. According to the general, the lone gunman was Nikolaiev, who committed the act out of jealousy. His pretty young wife, Milda Draule, worked as a waitress in Leningrad Party Headquarters and was Kirov's lover. As General Sudoplatov writes, Kirov was a very lecherous man and had many mistresses from the ranks of the ballerinas of the Bolshoi Theatre, and Leningrad's theatre, opera and ballet crowd. After Kirov's death, they were all interrogated by the KGB. The powers that be were silent about this aspect of Kirov's life for decades, in order not to contravene 'the golden rule of the party, never to lift the curtains of the private lives of Politburo members'. Fearing that the private motives for the murder might become common knowledge, Stalin even ordered secret surveillance of Kirov's widow. This surveillance continued until the end of her life. Two or three months after the attack, Milda Draule and her mother were executed without cause. They were exonerated only in December of 1990. That is General Sudoplatov's version.

In the days following Kirov's murder, a wave of arrests swept the country. Law enforcement organs were ordered to simplify all types of investigation, keeping procedure down to a minimum. Torture was officially sanctioned ('physical methods of coercion'). Death sentences were required to be carried out immediately after sentencing, since there would be no re-evaluation of cases. (Remember Lenin's words: 'Execute ... not allowing any idiotic bureaucratic delays ...') According to new laws children as young as twelve years could stand trial; what is more the death penalty would extend to them as well.

This was the beginning of the 'Great Terror'.

A new era began in the life of the Kremlin, the era of Stalin's ascent to a level of absolute power enjoyed perhaps only by the pharaohs of ancient Egypt. A few months after Kirov's murder, in Leningrad alone over 40,000 people had been arrested, and across the whole country that figure was approaching a million. The radio and press endlessly exhorted citizens to watch and betray one another. All independent thinkers were targeted. Fear gripped the people. The country turned into a huge concentration camp.

Moloch kept eating his children, eventually getting to himself. Forty thousand high-ranking army officers met their maker in the basements of the KGB, along with tens of thousands of Party members. Fear of imprisonment triggered an epidemic of suicide even in the highest echelons of power, and even within Stalin's own circle. Those undesirables who did not resolve their problem in this way ended up dying under mysterious circumstances, the writer Maxim Gorky being an example. It came to the point that even the wife of Mikhail Kalinin, the formal head of state, was sent to a gulag for seven years, where she was found 'privileged' work: washing and picking lice out of the prisoners' rags. Her husband, in the meantime, continued to perform the role of a toy president in the shadow of an all-powerful dictator.

The execution papers of high-ranking figures were signed by Stalin himself every evening, after which he usually retired to watch a film. (Remember Ivan the Terrible who, upon returning from the torture chamber, would blissfully go to sleep listening to the biblical tales of the storytellers.) The daily average for these execution lists would often exceed three thousand people. As the old Georgian revolutionary, Buda Mdivani, who knew Stalin very well from a young age, told his interrogator not long before his execution: 'He won't be satisfied until he slaughters everyone, starting from his illegitimate infant, all the way to his half-blind great grandmother. That's the way it's going to be. I've known Stalin thirty years.'

Finally, the pinnacle of this bloody orgy became the Great Show Trials, where the 'cream of Lenin's old guard', the creators of the Revolution, stood accused in the docks. These were the last of those who knew Stalin's true worth. For this alone they needed to be destroyed.

The whole world watched in bemusement as former underground revolutionaries, who once could not have been accused in lacking firmness of will or fanatical devotion to their ideals, now obediently confessed to all manner of conceivable and inconceivable crimes: espionage, terrorism and sabotage. The Western press put forward dozens of theories, perhaps they testified against themselves under hypnosis, or perhaps it was not them in the courtroom, but rather their doubles, and so forth. In reality, however, everything was a great deal simpler. Interrogation and torture drove them to such a state that it was easier to die than to live on. The bestial interrogators not only beat but also mutilated the prisoners – they put out their eyes, tore out their nails, crushed their genitals with heavy boots, urinated in their faces, and raped under-age daughters in front of their fathers. Stalin personally promised to spare the lives of some high-ranking prisoners if they played out this final performance for him, one 'necessary for the Party'. If they refused, a terrible fate awaited their wives, children and close friends. They performed not only because it was the last ray of hope, but also because they were intimately aquainted with the nature of the power structure that they themselves had created. While at the helm of power, they employed exactly the same methods. Hamlet's question 'To be, or not to be' was not an issue for them.

Rumour has it that Stalin personally attended some trials, concealing himself behind a screen on the balcony, from where a small flame occasionally flared as he lit his pipe. Considering that he liked to quiz his executioners about how his former brothers-in-arms behaved before they died, these rumours can be believed. It is doubtful that the leader would deny himself the pleasure of relishing the final agonies of his victims.

In one such trial, those in the dock included Henrich Yagoda, the former head of the KGB and Stalin's loyal 'dog', with whose hands the leader disposed of many of his opponents. Stalin sacrificed him in order to dump the murder of Kirov on him. Of all people, Yagoda knew his master's habits well. Standing up in the dock during one of the trial proceedings, Yagoda spoke over the heads of those sitting in the hall and appealed directly to the 'screen on the balcony', asking his life to be spared. Rumour has it that only the quiet puffing of a pipe could be heard from that direction over the complete silence of the court. Earlier, in an interrogation cell, Yagoda told an interrogator who came to see him: 'When you write your report to Stalin, you can tell him that God exists after all. From Stalin, I have deserved nothing except gratitude for faithful service, but from God I should have earned the harshest of punishments for breaking His commandments thousands of times. Now look at where I find myself and judge for yourself, whether God exists or not.'

It would be fair to mention that in his closing statement Yagoda was braver than any of his colleagues in misfortune. In response to the prosecutor's question as to whether he regretted his criminal acts, Yagoda replied, 'I regret very much ... I regret very much that when I had the opportunity I did not execute the lot of you.' It was easier for him to be brave than for the others, since he had no illusions about the final outcome of the 'trial'. He himself had orchestrated similar procedures more than once, on the leader's orders.

According to the very approximate estimates of historians, between the murder of Kirov in 1934 and the beginning of the war with Germany in 1941, Stalin managed to send nineteen million of his fellow citizens to prisons and camps, of whom a minimum of seven million were executed. If the count is started from Stalin's magnificent fiftieth birthday, then the number of deaths needs to be increased by a further ten million. Stalin, however, had his own arithmetic on that score. Pacing in silent, stealthy strides across the carpet of his office, he once muttered to no one in particular, 'In ten or twenty years, who will remember all these bastards? No one. Who remembers the names of the boyars that Ivan the Terrible killed? No one.'

Stalin was never known for his courage, but in former times he did not fear to freely roam the precincts of the Kremlin, sometimes appearing on the streets of Moscow and even dropping in to visit the 'proletarian poet' Dimyan Bedni. Now, however, he himself apparently started to believe his own myths about conspiracies and terrorists. While Lenin was once guarded by three or four bodyguards, around Stalin there were now several hundred. He was even wary of travelling without an escort around the precincts of the Kremlin, even though the Kremlin itself was guarded by the Internal Security forces, and by hundreds of secret agents.

The thirty-five kilometre road from the Kremlin to Stalin's dacha was guarded by an army of the KGB in three shifts, each shift numbering 1,200 men. In other words, armed men stood within thirty metres of each other along the whole road, twenty-four hours a day, regardless of whether the leader was using it or not. He was driven in a special limousine, which was commonly referred to as a 'comfortable truck'. This was a machine made entirely out of steel. The total weight of this monstrosity approached ten tons. Thirty such cars were made. Twenty of them were in Moscow and in the surrounding dachas of the leader, two in Leningrad and the rest in the Crimea and the Caucasus, where the leader went on holiday. Before passing into service with Stalin, each of these 'peacetime armoured personnel carriers' was field tested with heavy machine guns. After the tests the cars underwent bodywork to iron out the dents. Stalin usually occupied a place on the back seat, flanked by a pair of sturdy guards who, on top of everything else, protected him with their own bodies.

On Stalin's orders, Muscovites who lived in the buildings past which the leader usually drove on his way to the dacha were rehoused. These buildings were occupied by proven members of the KGB. Snipers sat in the attics and on the top floors, ready to neutralise any suspicious target.

Stalin's dachas were surrounded by several layers of high fences, equipped with special alarms. Guards with dogs were posted between the fences, and units of anti-aircraft batteries were stationed around the outside, in case of attack from the air. Each of the dachas had many bedrooms, and the domestics were obliged to prepare all of them every evening, since no one knew in which of them the leader would sleep each night. This was another method of confusing potential terrorists. On Stalin's orders, the trees around the dachas were thinned-out in such a way as to provide clear line of sight to every metre of the grounds. Curtains at the windows were trimmed a metre from the floor, so no one could hide behind them. As Svetlana Alliluyeva writes, even she found it hard not only to reach, but even to get through to her father on the phone:

> The system was complicated. You first had to phone the guard on duty, who would inform you if there 'is movement' or 'is no movement'. That meant that father was either asleep or reading in a room, and not moving through the house. When there was no movement, then there was no point calling. Father could sleep during the day at any time, his regimen was completely disrupted.

On his way south for a holiday, Stalin undertook the preparation of a special train for himself in Moscow, and simultaneously, a ship on the Volga. No one knew ahead of time which one he would finally choose. Both the ship and train had to stand in readiness for days and weeks, ready to depart at any moment. Stalin only announced which option he had chosen, an hour or two before departure.

Ahead and behind his armoured train travelled two vehicles, full of guards. Thousands of secret agents were deployed along the whole distance of the journey, taking the entire transport service under their control, from dispatchers to signalmen. People were removed from every station and adjacent area through which the train would pass. The guards were ordered to fire, without warning, at any figure who unexpectedly appeared.

Stalin's train was equipped and supplied well enough to withstand a two-week-long siege. If the alarm sounded, its windows were automatically covered by armoured shutters. The author of this book was able to visit one of the leader's carriages, which weighed eighty-three tons. The first compartment was the kitchen, the second was occupied by the guards and the third was the master bedroom. The fourth and fifth were joined into a study. The entire second half of the carriage was equipped as a conference hall.

Stalin almost never used aeroplanes, mistrusting and fearing this mode of transport. The one and only time in his life he entered a plane was in 1943, when he was obliged to fly to Teheran to meet Roosevelt and Churchill. An airborne armada of fifty planes took to the air. No one knew which of them carried Stalin: it was a secret.

Khrushchev told how one time, while walking in the dacha grounds, to Khrushchev's amazement and fright the leader spoke to no one in particular: 'I am a doomed man. I don't believe anyone, I don't believe myself …' This was the fear of paranoia. Having turned a huge country into a concentration camp, he himself became a prisoner of the gaol he had made.

The massive guard around Stalin was organised by a man named Pauker. He was a Hungarian who came to Russia during the First World War and remained there. Before the war he had been a hairdresser in a ballet and opera hall in Budapest. In Russia Pauker joined the Communist Party, and after the Revolution went to work in the law-enforcement agencies. Finally, he arrived at the post of head of the Kremlin guard.

The figure of Pauker himself is of little interest, but is worth mentioning since it reflects the tastes and predilections of Stalin himself. As Alexander Orlov, a former KGB general who knew Pauker well, tells in his memoirs, this was a man gifted with the qualities of both servant and clown. He was a brilliant teller of anecdotes, and anticipated the slightest wish of his masters. Stalin valued such people, and soon brought Pauker into favour, thus making him a noticeable figure in the Kremlin.

Pauker provided all of the needs of Stalin and his closest circle, including food, clothes, cars, dachas and other worldly goods. He not only satisfied all their desires, but also inflamed them. Noticing that Stalin liked vulgar jokes and anecdotes, Pauker immediately started to collect them, so as to always have a fresh one at hand. If Orlov is to be believed, Pauker even ordered albums containing pornographic pictures for Stalin from overseas. As mentioned earlier, in the improvised scene of Zinoviev's mock execution, the main role was performed by Pauker himself.

Pauker observed that Stalin, despite widespread stories to the contrary, was not indifferent to his outward appearance and would even preen before a mirror. Moreover, being a short man, the leader preferred shoes with high heels. Here Pauker excelled himself. He personally invented boots of a specific design for Stalin, with unusually high heels that added several centimetres to the leader's height. Stalin was exceedingly delighted by this, going even further and ordering that when standing on a podium a wooden block or small bench be placed under his feet. This gave him the appearance of being a man of average height.

Due to the smallpox scars on his face Stalin always looked badly shaved. Pauker, as a former hairdresser, offered Stalin his services. This was unheard of audacity, since no one had ever been able to come close to Stalin's throat with a razor in his hand. Pauker, however, had succeeded in attaining an unprecedented level of closeness and trust.

For fifteen years Pauker guarded his master and fulfilled all his everyday needs, until Stalin had him executed. Why? No reason, it was simply time to change the staff.

* * * * *

The shortest night of the year descended on Moscow on 22 June 1941. It was three in the morning. Accompanied by the cars of his guards, Stalin's armoured limousine moved along the deserted streets heading for the dacha. Stalin watched the city at night, not suspecting that at that moment Hitler's air force was already taxiing for take-off and his tanks were taking up battle formation.

Arriving at the dacha, Stalin himself made the bed prepared for him in one of the many bedrooms and was already falling asleep when there was a soft knock at the door. The leader was startled; it was unheard of for him to be woken without permission. The general on duty poked his head through the doorway ...

Stalin did not succumb to shock in the first hours of the war. He did not yet comprehend the magnitude of the catastrophe. But it hit him a little later, when he realised the deadly threat that hung over him personally, and the true scale of the crisis finally dawned on him. It was during these days that he said tearfully, 'Lenin created our country, and we shat it away.'

The leader was prostrate. For several days he did not leave his dacha and did not take part in any of the events. His name disappeared from the pages of newspapers. Khrushchev recollected 'that he was completely paralysed in his thoughts and actions, and even muttered about his refusal to lead the country'. For the first days of the war the country was without a leader.

According to Anastas Mikoyan, a member of Stalin's government, the situation was desperate. Something had to be done. Six people from Stalin's closest circle decided to visit him at the dacha. They found him sitting in an armchair. He looked strange, his eyes wandered. 'Why are you here?' he asked darkly.

It may be supposed that seeing his closest people suddenly appearing at the dacha, Stalin thought they had come to replace or even arrest him. It was so convenient, all misfortunes could be blamed on him. He himself would have acted in exactly that fashion. But their fear of Stalin was still so great that such a thought could not even enter their heads.

That aside, the catastrophe itself really was unimaginable. In the first few days of the war the Soviet Union had already lost more than a million soldiers, vast territory and almost the entire air force. There was nothing to fight with. Khrushchev remembered calling Moscow from Kiev asking that they be sent rifles, but received the reply that none were available. A number of antique specimens from the previous century were sent for the defence of Leningrad. Moscow recommended to Khrushchev that they forge their own spears and swords ...

Stalin did not doubt that the war was already lost. During those days he discussed the question of surrender among a very small group of colleagues. In exchange for a cessation of hostilities he intended to offer Hitler all the Baltic states, the larger parts of the Ukraine and Byelorussia as well as a part of Russia. To this end, contact was made with the Bulgarian ambassador in Moscow, Stamenov, through whom it was decided to contact Hitler. The Führer, however, sure of a quick and easy victory, did not even respond to this proposal. It is interesting to note that the Bulgarian ambassador, the ambassador of a country that had virtually sided with the enemy, had a higher opinion of Russia and her people than Stalin and his government. Finding out what was afoot, the ambassador said, 'Hitler will never beat the Russians; tell Stalin not to worry.'

During these days a train was already prepared and ready at a station outside Moscow for the evacuation of Stalin and his family. A plane with warmed-up engines was waiting at the airport for the same reason. The household items were loaded in carriages, and everyone merely awaited Stalin's word. Only a half-hour before the time scheduled for departure, Stalin suddenly called the head of his guard and announced: 'We aren't going. We are staying.' The family left without him.

Once the initial shock wore off, Stalin's astute mind began to look for scapegoats. A group of generals were executed on his orders. Soldiers and officers who were captured were labelled traitors to the motherland and those of them who managed to escape German captivity were greeted with concentration camps in their homeland. Stalin lacked rifles, but he had more than enough people, and he was not squeamish about using them.

On 7 November 1941, while German forces were a long-range artillery shot away from Moscow, a military parade was held on Red Square in honour of the anniversary of the Bolshevik Revolution. The forces marched double-time straight from the parade to front lines, to defend Moscow. This parade was entered into Stalin's biography as yet another of his heroic feats.

Certainly, in that situation, when Nazi bombs could have fallen at any moment, when German mastery of the sky was absolute, when Stalin was a surpassingly tempting target for Hitler's planes, the staging of such a parade and standing up on the Mausoleum itself was indeed a brave action. But did it really happen? Yes, a figure in a long overcoat with a raised hand could be seen up there. Yes, Stalin's voice did make a farewell speech. But was it Stalin, or his double? Was it a live speech or a pre-recorded tape? There are no clear-cut answers to these questions. In the film archive material where Stalin is making the speech and he is shown in close-up, there is no breath emerging from his mouth. It was after all a cold November day. In that same archive footage steam can be seen coming out of the breathing mouths of people standing up on the Mausoleum, but nothing from Stalin. How can this be explained? Perhaps these close-ups of the leader were filmed later, inside? Taking into account his timidity and fear for his own life, this is entirely possible.

The atmosphere in the Kremlin at the time is well conveyed in a book by a Polish publicist named Prushinski, entitled *Night in the Kremlin*. This book was published in New York in 1944, with a tiny circulation and was comparatively unknown until the present day. In it, the author tells how he visited the Kremlin in December 1941 as part of a Polish delegation headed by General Sikorski. This was for Russia the difficult starting period of the war. Distant reports of artillery fire could be heard in the Kremlin and Leningrad was already besieged by the blockade and facing starvation. Life in the Kremlin, however, continued as usual, plenty at the dinner tables, false smiles and sycophantic toasts. The following is an excerpt from the book:

The guards checked our passes. A powerful torchlight searched the cabin of the car, slowly and carefully examining every corner ... When we moved on, the roar of motors accompanied us, belonging to an escort of motorcyclists, indistinguishable in the darkness, which attached themselves to us on the territory of the Kremlin, akin to a demonic honour-guard. The cars stopped ... Huge doors opened before us. A blaze of blinding light cut through the darkness. In the bright glare we saw a huge tall staircase ... On either side of the staircase, agents of the KGB froze silently. We found ourselves in the vestibule of the Great Kremlin Palace. As we moved forward, the palace grew in majesty. The revolution had never penetrated these walls. Ancient furniture, faded canvases of Dutch masters, slightly dim Venetian mirrors in golden frames ... The immobile figures of KGB operatives appeared in ever-greater numbers ... We finally stopped under a wide dome full of gold and light. Huge chandeliers sparkled with crystal. I noticed a group of men. They were approaching us through a suite of rooms on the other side of the banquet hall. They walked bunched together, from a distance reminiscent of a group of workers arriving for their shift. The majority wore dark clothing, so the figure of the thickset man in a light-coloured suit buttoned up to the very neck, looked especially striking. I observed Stalin. He spoke little and calmly. Listened carefully. From time to time, leaving the conversation he would step aside to smoke by himself. No one would decide to interrupt his silence ...

Finally we were invited to the table ... In the centre of the table stood ancient crystal decanters and massive silver jugs of exquisite craftsmanship. [They used to be displayed at banquets for show by Ivan the Terrible.] The waiters wore white overcoats. Some of them spoke in French ... After the soups came the meat dishes, wild game, fish, all in a wide selection. The first bottles were exchanged for the next, glasses were refilled again and again. Of course, the culmination of the evening was an address by Stalin. 'I raise a toast in honour of the magnificent Polish army...'

Naturally the author of these notes could not have then known that the man who just raised a toast in honour of the Polish army had only recently given the order to execute twenty thousand Polish officers in the Katyn Forest.*

By Russian tradition, dessert was served in another room, outfitted in the style of Louis Philippe ... The attendants offered cigars, coffee and sweets. Stalin and Sikorski were discussing something, looking over a white sheet of card. It wasn't a map of military movements, nor an international treaty, rather the movie schedule. The lights went out and we saw excerpts of film reels up on the screen, episodes of the recent November parade in Moscow and Stalin's speech ... Midnight approached. To sign the Soviet-Polish declaration we needed to go to another Kremlin palace, where Stalin's personal study was located. It was pleasant to walk through the Kremlin courtyards, deep and dark like canyons, between churches, chapels and cathedrals. There was something threatening and foreboding in this centre of religion, bound into silence. Stalin met us in his study. He did not walk with us from the Great Kremlin Palace, but despite this got there ahead of us. How? A secret. Secrets are a tradition of the Kremlin, a tradition of Russia ... The night in the Kremlin drew to a close. I felt like a spectator, getting up from his seat after a wonderful performance, masterfully acted and presented.

Stalin was masterful at staging such shows. Everything was planned to the last detail. Every motion of the leader had to look like a ritualistic movement. As Stalin's biographer Professor Volkogonov recounts, often in the tensest moments of the war, during some important military briefing made in his study by a high-ranking general and in front of the entire government, Stalin would suddenly interrupt the meeting, call his secretary and demand a cup of tea. Then, all those present had to observe the leader's solemn ceremony.

* In 1940 in the forest of Katyn outside Smolensk, 20,000 Polish officers were executed on secret orders from Stalin, a fact which the Soviet government long denied. In 1943, when Smolensk was occupied by the German army, these mass graves were discovered. In Khrushchev's time, the Soviets officially admitted this crime.

Unhurried, he would squeeze a lemon into the cup, then would walk to the sitting room located behind the writing desk and open a door, which could not be distinguished from the wall, bringing back a bottle of cognac. In the general silence, he would pour two or three spoons of cognac into the tea, carefully carry the bottle back to the cache, sit back down at the table and, stirring the tea with a little spoon, would instruct the general, 'Continue.' Even this simple cup of tea, which incidentally was very rarely offered to those present, was turned into a ritual embodying some form of higher meaning, known only to Stalin himself.

The terrible war raged on. Europe was turned upside-down. People were displaced wholesale. A grim Churchill, stick in hand and cigar in mouth, ignoring the dangers, climbed across the smoking bombed ruins of London and crossed the ocean repeatedly. Even the half-paralysed Roosevelt travelled to distant places on cruisers and aeroplanes. Only the world of Joseph Stalin was as always limited to the walls of the Kremlin study and the dacha. Twenty paces in one direction, from the writing desk to the globe, from the globe to the writing desk. He stood in silence, smoking. There were rumours that the 'armchair general' directed the battles by pointing the mouthpiece of his pipe around the globe. Nonsense of course, but it was born in military circles and reflects the military staff's opinion of the leader's strategic talents. The objection may be made that after all he won. Yes, but at what cost, and was it in fact he who triumphed?

Stalin believed that from the silence of his study, as from the summit of the Caucasus range, he could see the entire world. He did not need any realistic contact with life. He felt the 'breath of war' by watching film reels in the comfortable Kremlin cinema. The orders he issued under the influence of these films were to lead to massive loss of life and have catastrophic consequences.

During the whole war Stalin only travelled by air once, flying to Teheran to meet Roosevelt and Churchill. It was the first and last flight of his life, which he never forgot. Somewhere above the mountains, the plane was hit by turbulence. His face twisted in fear, gripping the arms of the seat, the leader took some time to regain his composure, glancing around to see if those around him had noticed his agitation. He undertook another trip to Yalta at the end of the war and this time by train, to meet those same leaders of the 'Big Three'. Finally, the last journey of his life that took him beyond his 'living space' was to the conference in Potsdam.

The journey to Potsdam was apparently prepared no less carefully than the advance on Berlin. Stalin did not even want to hear about flying, despite the fact that the KGB Minister Lavrenti Beria completely guaranteed his safety. The mere memory of the flight to Teheran struck him with terror; he decided to travel by train. The 'operation' was prepared with remarkable caution. It involved tens of thousands of people. Stalin was regularly and personally briefed on the progress of the preparations, sometimes several times a day. He quizzed the minister of the KGB even about such details as the thickness of the armoured plate that would protect his carriage of the train. The scale of this 'operation' is best described by the following document:

To Comrade Stalin

The KGB of the USSR reports ... Sixty-two villas (overall area of 10,000 square metres) have been prepared in the region of Potsdam, as well as one two-storey town-house for Comrade Stalin: fifteen rooms, an open veranda, an attic, 400 square metres. The town-house is fully outfitted. There is communications equipment, supplies of game and other meats, groceries and other products and drinks. Three farms have been created within seven kilometres of Potsdam with domestic animals, poultry and vegetables. Two bakeries are functioning. All the employees are from Moscow. Two special airports have been prepared. The guards consist of seven divisions of KGB, and 1,500 special service people. The guards are organised into three rings. A special train has been prepared. The distance of the journey is 1,923 kilometres (1,095 kilometres across the USSR, 594 kilometres across Poland, and 234 across Germany). The length of the journey is guarded by 17,000 KGB troops and 1,515 special service people. From six to fifteen guards are located over every kilometre of the track. Eight armoured KGB trains will patrol the length of the journey.

2 July, 1945, L. Beria

Sitting in the comfortable saloon of an armoured train, looking melancholically out of the window where soldiers of the guard stood beside the tracks, flashing by as facelessly as telegraph poles, it is doubtful that the leader remembered that Russian soldiers had marched this whole distance from Moscow to Berlin on foot, under a withering hail of enemy fire, securing victory at the expense of hecatombs of their own corpses.

Meeting with Truman in Potsdam Stalin would say, 'My apologies for being a day late. I was delayed by talks with the Chinese. I wanted to fly but the doctors forbade it.'

With an eye towards history, Stalin did make two attempts to get closer to the front. The first time was in October 1941. In the middle of the night, a procession of armoured cars under heavy guard drove to the outskirts of Moscow from where, for a period of several dozen minutes, the leader gloomily observed the distant flashes of artillery fifteen kilometres away. They say that Stalin wanted to get even nearer to the front, but his limousine got mired in the mud and, transferring to the accompanying car of the KGB Minister, the leader turned around, having decided not to tempt fate further.

Stalin made his second attempt to justify his future title of Generalissimo in the eyes of history in August of 1943, travelling some 250 kilometres in the direction of the front. An old locomotive was adopted as a disguise, complete with half-destroyed carriages and even a platform full of logs. He was accompanied yet again by the minister of the KGB and a large contingent of guards in disguise. Having heard the report of the army general staff, and spending the night in a peasant's cottage from which the owners and all their belongings had earlier been removed, the leader turned around, not wishing to travel out to the troops and meet the soldiers and officers. The return journey was made by car and was uneventful, while the cottage where the leader spent the night apparently carries a memorial plaque to this day as a reminder of his heroic feat.

In this way the debt of history was paid and in his communiqués with the Allies Stalin could now write with veiled pride: 'It becomes necessary to personally visit various parts of the front more often ...' (to Roosevelt, 8 August 1943), 'I am obliged to visit the troops of one or more areas of the front more often than usual ...' (to Churchill, 9 August 1943).

Stalin understood mass psychology well, and knew that close contact with the people was not at all necessary to maintain a leader's authority; quite the contrary, it could even be harmful. Some time after the war, on his way south for a holiday, Stalin allowed himself to make several stops along the way and 'walk with the people'. One did not have to be overly intuitive to get the feeling that meeting him not only created a great deal of curiosity in people, but also an inner disillusionment. They were expecting a genius, a leader, a Generalissimo, great in every way. Instead, a small scarred man stood before them, with a disproportionately small body, a low forehead, and a round belly poking out from under his coat, a mat of sparse thinning hair on his head, and yellow, nicotine-stained teeth. An image somewhat at variance with the notion of 'heroic', conjuring up a silent question in people's eyes: could

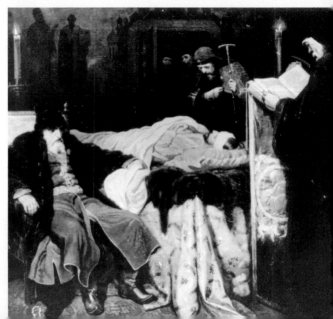

The feeble-minded Fyodor, Ivan the Terible's son.　　　　　Czar Boris Godunov.

Below left and right: The False Dimitri and his bride, the Polish aristocrat Marina.

ove: Peter the Great
d (top right) the
lpture of the Czar by
strelli, displayed in
Hermitage museum,
Petersburg.

ht: The palace
side Moscow where
er the Great was
n.

ow right: The
dding of Peter and
therine in 1712,
nted by A. Zubov.

Above: 1812. In a Moscow set ablaze by its
inhabitants, Napoleon abandons the fire-threatened
Kremlin.

Below: An 1830s view of what would later become
known as Red Square.

Vladimir Lenin in 1914 and two of his women – Nadezhda Krupskaya (left) in her student years when Lenin first saw her, and Inessa Armand (right), the Frenchwoman who was the love of his life.

Above: Lenin in 1897 with members of a Marxist circle in St Petersburg and (above right) with t[
writer Maxim Gorky in St Petersburg.

Below: Speaking from the Place of Execution in Red Square, Lenin strains to make his point to t[
crowds. Below right: Lenin and his wife in their dacha outside Moscow. She is clearly concerned [
her ill husband.

Joseph Dzugashvili, the young Stalin, in 1913.

Below: Lenin's wife (far left) and Stalin (third from her left at the table). 'If you don't obey, we'll simply announce that you were not Lenin's wife at all, and we'll give him another wife ... yes, yes, don't be shocked, the Party can do anything ...'

Bottom: Stalin with Nadezhda Alliluyeva on a picnic.

Right: Probably a forged photograph, created at a later date to suggest the two men enjoyed a close relationship, this image purports to show Lenin and Stalin together at a dacha outside Moscow in autumn 1922.

Left and below: Stalin and his daughter, Svetlana.

Right: Nikita Krushchev in the 1920s.

Below: Many of the Kremlin leaders have been avid hunters, and Krushchev was no exception.

Bottom: Khrushchev enjoys the attention of a large crowd in Cairo as he visits President Nasser in Egypt.

Above: Khruschev with Cuban leader Fidel Castro. Below: In retirement, with dogs and his grandchildren.

Left: The Brezhnev family. Leonid's fat[her] is sitting in the mid[dle] and his mother on [the] far right, holding h[is] granddaughter Gal[ina]. Leonid and his wife Victoria are on the [left] standing.

Left: Seen here in th[e] Ukraine in 1933, Leonid Brezhnev (le[ft]) was already the hea[d] Party representative [at] the Metallurgical Institute.

Left: Brezhnev (on t[he] right) in discussion with colleagues at a government dacha outside Moscow.

Left: Galina Brezhnev with her police general husband (left) and the Minister of Internal Affairs (right), who committed suicide soon after this photo was taken.

Below left: After making a speech in Berlin, Brezhnev, now in poor health, has to be led off the stage by East German President Erich Honecker and a bodyguard.

Below right: Yuri Andropov.

Bottom: Konstantine Chernenko meets Margaret Thatcher. Already an ill man, he would have to resort to his large-print briefing notes as soon as he had shaken hands with a visiting politician.

Left: Mikhail Gorbachev as a 20-year old student at Moscow University.

Below: Raisa Gorbachev with her husband as they meet American President Reagan. The couple were a shock to the Western world and its leaders.

Bottom: The Black Sea residence of the Gorbachevs where he was effectively imprisoned for several days during the coup o August 1991.

ove: A tense exchange between Gorbachev and Yeltsin.

ow left: Boris Yeltsin with his parents in the 1930s.

ow right: The victor and the vanquished – Gorbachev has just unenthusiastically congratulated
 new President.

Above: March 1991. Boris Yelstin 'plays to the gallery'.

Right: Boris Yelstin as he often appeared when he was not aware he was being filmed.

Below: A sombre Yeltsin views the body of the writer and academic, Andrei Sakharov.

this really be Stalin? One woman even tried to touch his sleeve, to convince herself the figure was real.

In any event, Stalin did not allow himself any more of that kind of frivolity. More than once he expressed to Khrushchev his contempt for people in the mass, referring to them as 'manure'. The best way to communicate with them was from the podium of the Mausoleum, through images on film or via portraits and busts. The more mystery, the more legends and myths. It is no accident that he showered the film director Mikhail Chaureli with awards for his films *The Unforgettable 1919* and *The Fall of Berlin*. In the former, a young black-moustached Stalin appears before the people on the steps of an armoured train, the saviour of the Soviet Republic delivering her from the enemies of the Revolution. In the second, the wise Generalissimo at the pinnacle of his glory and majesty stands in the middle of a conquered Berlin, surrounded by people jubilant to see him. That is he, the real Stalin, the rest does not concern them …*

While the war raged on and the true enemy was clearly defined, the leader's energy was concentrated in that direction, and his killer-instinct went into hibernation. That does not mean that the arrests and executions stopped, they were merely drowned out by the roar of battle. But the war ended, and the instinct was again aroused. New victims had to be found. As one member of Stalin's government remarked, 'You'd go to see Stalin for a friendly dinner, and you'd never know if you would go home afterwards, or straight to prison.'

How did Stalin live in the years after the war? What did he do? What did he think about? Khrushchev paints a striking picture of Stalin's way of life in his memoirs. Even today, when we know a great deal about Stalin and his circle, it is nevertheless hard to comprehend that such men oversaw the fates of millions and ruled a mighty country. In Khrushchev's words:

> He usually woke at seven or eight in the evening, arrived at the Kremlin and summoned us to the Kremlin cinema. He'd call and tell us to be at the theatre at a certain time, so we'd all turn up. He chose the films himself. The pictures were war souvenirs for the most part. There were a lot of American pictures. Cowboy films. He liked them. He

---

* People recount the following episode: Stalin was once upbraiding his son Vasili for behaving badly in school. 'Do you think that you are Stalin?' he tells Vasili. 'Or do you think that I am Stalin? There, there is Stalin …' He points at his grandiose portrait on the wall …

mocked and correctly evaluated them, but would immediately order new ones. The films were not translated, and were 'dubbed' by the minister of cinematography ... He 'translated' from all languages, although he didn't know any. He was told the plot beforehand, tried to remember it and thus 'translated'. In some scenes he would say something completely amiss, or just explained, 'There he goes, that way.' Beria would jump in and 'help'. 'See, he's running, he's running ...' Usually when the viewing was over Stalin would offer 'Well, shall we go eat or what?' We didn't want to go, it was usually one or two in the morning, we needed rest, we had work the next day. Stalin didn't work, however, and didn't take us into consideration. Everyone readily agreed that they were hungry. The lying reflex was already well developed. We'd drive to Stalin's. There we sat down to dinner ... We would go to Stalin's almost every evening. We only missed it when Stalin was not feeling well; there were no other reasons since Stalin didn't know what to do with himself ...'

The dinners usually lasted until sunrise and spilled over into heavy drinking sessions. 'Stalin literally made drunkards of people,' Khrushchev says, 'and the worse a person's hangover, the more enjoyment Stalin got.' It was impossible to refuse a drink, that could earn the leader's fury. Most government matters, and indeed the fates of millions of people, were decided at these drunken parties.

Only men were usually present at these dinners. Perhaps age was the reason, or the Georgian custom of endless male gatherings. Apart from drinking, they found amusement in singing and dancing to the accompaniment of a harmonica played by Voroshilov, and listening to Beria's obscene witticisms and Stalin's inebriated bluster. A horrible scene if one were to imagine it, fat, drunken, old men dancing with each other. Khrushchev recollected one such night:

We ate, snacked, drank ... Stalin was in a good mood, so he drank a lot himself and encouraged others to do the same. An extraordinary amount was already drunk. Stalin wandered up to the radiogram and began to play records – Russian and Georgian songs. Then we put some dance music on and started dancing. I dance like a cow on ice, but I danced all the same. Stalin danced as well, shuffling his feet and putting up his arms ... Then Svetlana turned up. She arrived and found herself among a pack of not so young people, to put it mildly. Stalin forced her to dance immediately. She was tired, I could see she was barely able to dance … She stopped and leaned her shoulder against a wall. Stalin walked up to her and I approached as well. Stalin swayed on his feet. He said, 'Well Svetlana, dance mistress, dance'; she replied, 'I've already danced daddy, I'm tired.' He grabbed her by the hair and jerked her. As I watched, her face flushed with colour and tears formed in her eyes … That was a father's expression of love for his daughter.'

It was not only impossible to refuse to drink, but also to dance. As Khrushchev noted: 'When Stalin says dance, every sensible person dances.'

Similar parties for the amusement of the bored leader were often also staged in the Kremlin, but there they were called banquets. If the revels at the dachas hosted half a dozen to a dozen close comrades, then the Kremlin banquets attracted several hundred. The cream of Moscow society was invited, artists, writers, directors, singers, famous sportsmen. These banquets were described to the author of this book by one of their regular participants, the famous film actor Boris Andreiev. Andreiev was a very large man, massive, with a low bass voice, a typical Russian face, and appeared in films in the role of a 'Russian Epic Hero'. Stalin liked him, and always invited him to the Kremlin revels.

These usually started after midnight and lasted until morning. The actors in attendance normally arrived after an evening performance, with barely enough time to remove their make-up. Times were lean then, and here the tables were loaded with every delicacy imaginable. It was hard to pass up such an enticement, and dangerous as well; heaven forbid Stalin should notice that you ignored his invitation. It was not rare to observe the following scene. An actor arrives, hungry as a dog. He has breakfasted in the morning, then spent all day in the theatre, from rehearsal to performance, not having eaten. Naturally, finding himself at such a magnificent spread, he grabs, say, a chicken drumstick, a second and a third. He follows it up with two or three shots of vodka and feels happy, satiated. Suddenly, a quiet, gentle voice sounds behind him. 'Why have you stopped, my friend? Eat, please, eat.' He turns around, and there stands Stalin. Naturally he says thank you and, to be polite and not offend the host, he takes another drumstick. He eats it, but Stalin is still there. 'Eat, eat, don't be shy.' Well, you can't say no to Stalin, he takes another … In such a taunting manner he could drive a person to the brink of unconsciousness from gluttony.

Sometimes drinking competitions were organised for Stalin's amusement. They usually featured heavy drinkers. Once, two actors, both of whom played Stalin in films, were matched. In one of the more sadistic examples of such drinking contests, two identical fruit bowls were filled to the brim with vodka, and the vodka was set alight. The idea was to drink and simultaneously blow back the flames so as not to get burned. The loser was the first one to collapse out of his seat. Stalin would be very pleased. Andreiev recalls:

> One time, I'm sitting at a banquet in honour of Stalin's seventieth birthday. Suddenly a guard approaches me and quietly whispers in my ear, 'Comrade Stalin asks that you step into his study.' I stand up and go in. Entering the study I greet everyone. Stalin is sitting there with Mao Tse-tung – who has come for Stalin's jubilee – and a translator. They are surrounded by glasses, bottles and appetisers. Stalin pours me a large wine-glass of vodka – about two hundred grammes – and offers it to me. 'Please, Comrade Andreiev.' He does not offer me a seat. Well, I know what he needs; he needs a theatrical performance. I take the glass and drain it. 'Have a snack,' says Stalin, motioning towards the food. I reply, 'Thank you Comrade Stalin, but I don't snack after the first.' Stalin smirks and pours me a second wine-glass. I empty it again and put it back on the table. 'Well, now have a snack,' says Stalin. I reply again, 'Thank you Comrade Stalin, but I don't snack after the second either.' Stalin smiles with satisfaction and turns to Mao Tse-tung, saying, 'That's what a real Russian soldier is!'

It must be said that outwardly, Boris Andreiev was a simple and uncomplicated-looking man. But that was only outward appearance. In fact, he was full of insights. He had unravelled the truth about Stalin long before many philosophers and thinkers. Andreiev came from a simple family, knew full well how hard life was for the common folk, and hated the leader with a burning passion: 'Sometimes you stood in front of him ... squeezing a two-bit clown out of yourself, while your head is thinking – oh to strangle you, you scum ...'

Belittling people was one of Stalin's favourite pastimes. So for instance, during summer at the dacha, being in a good mood, he might order one of the attendants to put a large juicy tomato under the cover of an armchair that a guest was supposed to sit in, especially if the guest wore a light-coloured suit, laughing loudly when the confused and uncomfortable person got up out of the chair in wet trousers. Or, taking a walk through the park after a solid meal and a good drink, he might, in jest of course, push one of his companions into a shallow pond. It goes without saying that the victim also had to laugh jovially at this joke.

In fact, there was a sadistic element in all of Stalin's humour, which was based upon fear. A clear example of Stalin's humour is the following anecdote. Among the soldiers guarding the door to Stalin's study there was a certain Captain Ivanov. Walking past, Stalin would often joke, 'How are things going, Comrade Ivanov? Haven't they executed you yet?' At which Captain Ivanov paled, shuddered and snapped back, 'No sir, Comrade Stalin!' Time went by, Ivanov became a colonel, but as usual remained among Stalin's guards. And walking past, Stalin would still joke, 'How are things going, Comrade Ivanov? Haven't they executed you yet?', whereupon Colonel Ivanov paled, snapped to attention and replied, 'No sir, Comrade Stalin!' The war came to an end and Victory Day arrived. Stalin made a speech at one of the banquets in honour of the victory ... 'Our people were victorious because, even in the hardest days of the war, we were able to enjoy a good joke ...' Stalin swept the hall with his gaze and paused at the general sitting in the first row. 'Isn't that right?' Stalin asked him. 'That is correct, Comrade Stalin!' replied General Ivanov, paling and leaping to his feet.

Stalin was becoming decrepit. His nocturnal lifestyle and lack of physical activity speeded up the process. It was especially noticeable in his failing memory. He was not only mixing up surnames, but the names of cities, countries and events. No one thing could hold his attention and he jumped from topic to topic. Sometimes, sitting at his desk, he could stare a long time at a person he had known for decades and met almost every day and suddenly ask, 'What is your surname?'

All this annoyed and scared Stalin. He was angered at his helplessness before the process of life, not under his control. In times past, he had firmly believed the legends of Caucasus longevity, and comforted himself that way – especially since the legends were vastly inflated by the Soviet press, to please the leader. Now even this faith abandoned him. He could no longer hide his emotions as previously, and in his wrath would often break telephone receivers against the wall or berate those around him with base obscenities.

His seventieth birthday approached. The night of 21 December was celebrated by 'the appearance of Christ before the masses'. High above the Kremlin, at the focal point of dozens of projectors against the clouds, a gigantic image of Stalin appeared. The leader appeared to the world in all his majesty and divine magnificence. At the same time, the 'living-god' himself was on the stage of the Bolshoi Theatre – filled to capacity – where he was greeted by a continuous half-hour of applause. Many hours of speeches about him had already been delivered – 'the brilliant strategist', 'father and teacher', 'the genius of all ears and peoples', 'the leader of the world's proletariat', 'the saviour of mankind' ... If the Egyptian pharaohs had five or six titles, then Stalin had almost thirty. The Bulgarian delegation presented him with a letter of gratitude, signed by over five million people – the entire adult population of his nation – which elicited lively commotion in the hall. The writer Leonid Leonov went even further, proposing that a new count of years should begin, starting with the leader's birth. Yet only Mao Tse-tung called him merely 'great', which put Stalin on his guard. Was there any plotting here?

Today, reading of such events, our mind accepts them but cannot easily comprehend that this really occurred. Thousands and thousands of adult people shouted these words in some kind of primitive ecstasy of fear or stupidity, trying to concentrate all human wisdom within a single brain case with a rather low forehead. Perhaps Stalin was right after all, when standing on the Mausoleum and observing the columns of approaching marchers carrying thousands of his images, he muttered in irritation, 'Here come the sheep ...'

Many weeks after the jubilee, the papers, magazines, radio and newsreels were full of articles of praise, oaths of loyalty, outpourings of love and gratitude to the 'greatest of the great'. The birthday gifts numbereded tens of thousands and were displayed in museums. It seemed that the very flow of life was unthinkable without him. Millions of pygmies grovelled at his feet, thanking him for their existence. The humiliation of a mighty people reached an apogee. Stalin could congratulate himself: the process of creating a new religion was complete.

As Stalin himself admitted, none of this improved the health. After the festivities, the leader started to age even faster. He appeared in the Kremlin more rarely, staying longer at the dacha, sitting for hours in front of the fireplace watching the destructive work of the fire with tear-filled eyes. What did he think about? What did he remember? After all, there is no soul in creation that does not feel so much as a twinge of conscience.

After his death, several notes he had kept were found in his writing desk. These were from people who were once close to him and whom he had destroyed. One of them came from Nikolai Bukharin, and began with the words: 'Koba, why do you need my death?' Perhaps now, staring into the fire, he remembered their rowdy parties and playful wrestling, when Nikolai would often pin him down – yet another thing he was incapable of forgiving.

Or perhaps he was remembering Alioshka Svanidze, the brother of his first wife, with whom he liked to play billiards. Alioshka was a fine player, but so as not to prick the easily injured pride of his friend, would often let him win, in punishment for which Stalin would playfully chase him under the table. He really should not have had him shot, but he did send a message to the prison that if Alioshka repented he would be forgiven, and Alioshka refused, saying he did not know what to repent about. How proud Alioshka turned out to be; was it that hard to repent? Perhaps he even remembered the cold Siberian train, as he journeyed from exile. He was feverish and Kamenev, whom he later had shot, removed and gave him his last pair of woollen socks. Or maybe this is all just fantasy, and nothing stirred in that black soul ...

Stalin might have remembered how he had recently played host to his former friend, with whom he had studied together in the theological seminary. Now he was a grey, imposing old man with the title of bishop. Visiting the Kremlin he apparently took a long time to make up his mind what to wear. If he wore his robes Soso might get angry, if he wore a plain suit God would be wrathful. In the end he wore a plain suit. Seeing him, Stalin smirked and raising his arms on high, chuckled: 'Ha! You're not afraid of God, but you're afraid of me.'

Dread and loneliness preyed on the tyrant in old age. His daughter wrote that her father was tormented by fear, turning into a full-blown paranoia over the last few years. He now saw terrorists and poisoners everywhere, even among his close circle – incidentally, not without a degree of credibility.

'Now Stalin would not eat or drink at the table until someone else had something from that specific plate or bottle,' Khrushchev wrote. 'When someone else tried some and nothing happened to them, then he'd have a drink as well ... "Here is some goose pâté, Nikita, have you not tried it yet?" "Ah well, I forgot," I say, seeing that he wants some but is afraid. So every dish had its own taster, who determined whether it was poisoned or not while Stalin watched and waited ...'

Recently his personal doctor had told him that his health was not the best and that he had to take care of himself, especially since he had had several fainting spells, falling down in his study. He must work as little as possible. This drove Stalin into a frenzy. He no longer trusted doctors and would not let any of them near him. In truth, this is how the famous 'doctors' plot' started. Knowing his anti-Semitism, someone bent on advancement concocted this 'plot' in which the main protagonists were Jews. These were elderly men, respected doctors each of whom had saved many lives in their day. Now they were accused of knowingly mistreating members of the government, in order to drive them to early graves.

Stalin liked this 'plot' immediately. It had scope, public interest and an on-going plot – an international Zionist conspiracy, whose trail led even to the highest echelons of power. The people would easily understand and support the accusation. A series of show trials could be organised, as in the pre-war years. It was high time for a reminder, lest people forgot their place. Sergei Eisenstein for example, had shot the second part of *Ivan the Terrible* in which he portrayed Ivan as a bloody despot, half-mad, and his personal guard as nothing more than a band of cut-throats. That was not right, it was an insult to Russian history. Ivan was a wise and progressive Czar. He did the right thing, cutting off the boyars' heads. Strong government needs a strong leader. Ivan's only mistake was that he did not chop off enough heads, and the mistakes of history should not be repeated. Obsessed with the Jewish doctors, Stalin yelled down the telephone at his Minister of Internal Security: 'Beat them! Beat them and put them in manacles until they confess!'

Truth to tell, this was not his first 'Jewish plot'. After the war he was approached by members of the Jewish Anti-Fascist Committee, who collected funds for the Soviet Union during the war among the Jewish groups of America. They included some of the most famous people in the country, such as the actor Solomon Mikhoels, the former Minister of Foreign Affairs Maxim Litvinov, the publicist Solomon Lazovski and even the wife of Vyacheslav Molotov, Polina Zhemchuzhina. They asked Stalin to consider the question of establishing a Soviet-Jewish autonomous region in the Crimea. Their argument was that the Jewish people had suffered more than any other during the war. Scattered and diffused across the Soviet Union, the community was losing its national culture and it would be an act of justice and humanism of the highest order if it were to be offered 'its home' in Russia.

'Stalin literally went into a frenzy,' remembered Khrushchev. 'The arrests started some time later. Lazovski was arrested, and some time later so was Zhemchuzhina. The question of the existence of the Jewish nation itself and its place in our Soviet country was raised ... Not only sanctions in the form of arrest, but other methods were also employed. Stalin once again began to order secret killings ...'

Mikhoels, for instance, was brutally murdered in Minsk by agents of the KGB on New Year's Eve with a crowbar-blow to the head (poisoned in another version), after which his body was stuffed under a lorry, implying an accident. Stalin even arranged a lavish funeral for him, while secretly awarding medals to his murderers. A similar fate was prepared for former Foreign Minister Maxim Litvinov, but he 'tricked' everyone, dying peacefully in his own bed of natural causes, sadly and mysteriously whispering in parting to his English wife, 'English lady, go back home.'

Of the many dozens of people accused of this 'plot' only Polina Zhemchuzhina survived, living many years in camps and exile. She was only freed after Stalin's death. Beria had her brought to his office and personally 'delivered' her to Molotov, half dead.

Now Stalin was preparing to bring the 'Jewish question' to a conclusion. The plan was deviously simple. 'Zionists in white coats' were destroying the best people in the country. The people were naturally agitated, and Jewish pogroms might flare up at any moment. A group of 'progressive Jewish public figures' had appealed to Stalin via a letter in which they asked him to save their people. Stalin naturally would heed their call and, governed by the highest principles of humanitarianism, would save the Jews from the 'people's just anger', deporting them to the Far East. Spare railway lines outside Moscow were said already to be filled with hundreds of trains for this very purpose.

The only thing the leader did not foresee was that the hourglass of his life was already empty. It is not known whether he was ever told the final words of his former KGB Minister Henrich Yagoda: 'Tell Stalin that God exists after all ...' These words would now have been most appropriate.

The guards began to worry at ten o'clock at night. No movement had been observed in the House from the previous night. The master had not called for tea, nor checked the post. To go find out what was wrong was dangerous, Stalin could become angry over the violation of the established order. At eleven o'clock they nevertheless decided to reconnoitre. One of the guards, taking the post as an excuse, moved towards the House. He moved from room to room, turning the lights on as he went, until he reached the Small Dining Room. Stalin was lying on the floor in his nightshirt, his eyes open and filled with terror. He moved his hand, beckoning the newcomer to assist him. Croaking sounds were escaping from his throat.

He was moved to the couch and people started ringing the KGB in search of Beria. The problem was that, according to orders, no doctor could be summoned to Stalin without the permission of the KGB Minister Lavrenti Beria. The master of a huge country, one of the most powerful people in the world, found himself trapped by his own system.

Beria was not located quickly; he was somewhere in a country villa in the company of another new lady. He arrived very tipsy. The other members of

Stalin's entourage were called at the same time. They filed into the room where Stalin lay, one of them just in his socks, having tucked his new shoes under his arm so they would not squeak.

Stalin lay on the couch, emitting either croaks or snores. Beria started to berate the attendants in a whisper for starting a panic and disturbing the leader's sleep. 'Get out of here ...' he hissed at the guards, 'can't you see that Comrade Stalin is sleeping peacefully?' As one of the guards would explain, the impression was that everything was going according to a pre-determined plan.

Everyone went home. At nine in the morning, however, all were once again summoned to the dacha. This time doctors and medical staff were also called in. It was 2 March 1953.

The version outlined above was put together by Professor Volkogonov, from the testimony of one of the guards. Nikita Khrushchev gave a slightly different account of events. He was already asleep when he was called and informed that something was amiss with Stalin. He and several other people from Stalin's close circle immediately drove out to see him. Half an hour later they were already with the head of the guards on duty at the dacha. They did not decide to go to Stalin themselves, sending in instead an old woman who had worked with Stalin as a servant for many years. Returning, she said that Stalin was lying on the floor, sleeping, but that there was a large puddle under him. He had apparently wet himself. Several guards were then sent into the House; they moved Stalin to the couch and retreated. Khrushchev and the others decided not to enter the House, in order not to catch the leader in such an unbecoming situation. It is possible that his comrades-in-arms decided that Stalin had got very drunk and that this was the result. Everyone went home.

A short time later, between one and two in the morning, Khrushchev got another call, saying that something was the matter with Stalin after all. It seemed this was not quite normal sleep. Everyone once again gathered in the head guard's office. This time doctors were summoned and everyone went up to the House. From this point the first and second version coincide.

All the doctors were new, seeing Stalin for the first time. (His regular doctors were sitting in prison.) They touched him fearfully, as if he were red-hot. Beria even angrily snapped at one of the professors, 'You're a doctor, so handle him properly!' Stalin had suffered a brain haemorrhage, paralysing part of his body, his speech, and then his consciousness.

His daughter was summoned directly from her classes and driven straight to the dacha. 'When I met her,' reports Khrushchev, 'I suddenly got very emotional and started crying. I could not help myself, I honestly felt sorry for Stalin ...'

'The great hall where my father lay was thronged with people,' wrote Svetlana Alliluyeva. 'They put leeches on his forehead and neck, took cardiograms and x-rays of his chest. A nurse was constantly making some sort of injections. One of the doctors was ceaselessly charting the progress of the illness in his journal ... The Academy of Medical Science was in emergency session somewhere, trying to decide what further measures to take. Everyone was fussing, trying to save a life that could no longer be saved.'

Yes, everyone was fussing, but not everyone was trying save that life. Beria was elated, he foresaw his finest hour. He held in his hands the mightiest law-enforcement agency that had ever existed in the world. If the master died, who could bar his own road to power? From time to time he would approach the bed and peer into the dying man's face. At one point the dying man suddenly became lucid. 'Beria immediately rushed to Stalin,' Khrushchev writes, 'threw himself on his knees, grabbed the leader's hand and started kissing it. When Stalin lost consciousness once more and closed his eyes, Beria stood up and cursed.' (Most likely this is merely Khrushchev's fancy, since the episode is not verified anywhere else.) 'In the silence of the hall,' writes Svetlana, 'Beria's loud voice (speaking to the servant) could be heard, not hiding his triumph: 'Khrustaleov, the car!' After this he suddenly left the dacha and remained away for several hours. It is quite possible that he went to the Kremlin to clear out Stalin's safe, which may have contained documents that compromised him.

His son Vasili appeared several times in the hall in which the dying man was lying. He was, as always, drunk, and would periodically yell out, 'Murdered! Murderers! The bastards have killed father!' He then went to the guardhouse and got even drunker there. Svetlana recalls the last minutes of her father's life:

The agony was frightening .... It choked the life out of him before everyone's eyes. At one moment, apparently at the very last minute, he suddenly opened his eyes and swept his gaze over everyone who stood around him. It was a ghastly glare, either insane or angry, filled with terror. The gaze swept everyone in less than a minute. Suddenly, with an incomprehensible and frightening gesture which I don't understand to this day but cannot forget, he suddenly lifted up his left arm which was not paralysed and either pointed upwards somewhere or threatened us all with it. The gesture was incomprehensible, but menacing, and it was unclear to whom and to what it indicated. In the next moment, his soul gave a final push and tore free from the body …

It was 9.50 in the morning, on 5 March 1953. The bloodiest tyrant in the history of humanity was dead. 'I suddenly felt so sorry for him …' remembers the nurse who washed Stalin's corpse. 'A swollen little belly, thin arms, thin legs – a little spider …'

What emotions did the people surrounding him feel at this moment? They must have been complex and contradictory. On one hand it was a shock – God had died, who only yesterday seemed immortal. Khrushchev, for instance, honestly wept. On the other hand, there would have been a sense of relief. His closest circle could not help but know that lately, most of their lives had been hanging by the slenderest of threads. In the past few years Stalin had been preparing a new 'Palace Uprising', new show trials, getting ready to send his closest brothers-in-arms down into the KGB basements and replace them with new people. He had already taken the first steps, accusing Molotov of being an American spy. Why? That was the structure of Stalin's power, Lies and Fear, Fear and Lies …

To this day rumours have not been disproved that, fearing for their own lives, the men closest to him hastened the leader's death. It was confirmed at least that not long before the attack Beria persuaded Stalin to have a steam session in a sauna, although the doctors had specifically forbidden it due to high blood pressure. Svetlana Alliluyeva writes that immediately after her father's death, the purge of officers in his guard began, two of whom even shot themselves. It is hard to believe this was from grief for the departed master. Could these ordinary KGB men really have considered themselves the soldiers of the pharaoh, honour-bound to go to the grave with him. Is it not more likely to suppose that being direct participants in the events, they simply knew more about the leader's death than they should have done, and this determined their fates? Finally, why was it necessary to lie to the people in the official announcement, saying that the attack occurred in the leader's Kremlin apartments, when in reality it occurred at the dacha. All this still remains a mystery, but knowing the almost thousand-year customs of the Kremlin court, the version of a hastened death can certainly be entertained.

Bizarre as it seems, with the exception of the occupants of the gulags, the people Stalin had mauled and cowed and whom he referred to as 'manure', honestly grieved at his passing. People could be found on the streets weeping so copiously they might have been putting to rest their own father. Crowds streamed endlessly day and night towards the central hall of the capital, where the coffin containing Stalin's body was laid out for a final farewell. Overflowing trains headed for Moscow, crammed with mourners from the roofs to the carriage steps. Everyone wanted to come to the funeral. Hundreds of thousands filled the squares, streets and lanes, moving towards the centre of Moscow.

A tyrant as a rule does not go to the grave alone, but takes many victims with him. Stalin did not break this tradition. The mindless crowds of people pushed and shoved, crushing those in front against the walls of buildings or the sides of military vehicles barricading the streets, smashing others against lamp posts and pushing them through shop windows. There were screams, groans and cries for help. To save themselves, people climbed up poles, on to the ledges of buildings, only to slip off and fall under the feet of the mindless, ungovernable crowd. There was blood on the walls, on bridges, on vehicles. The sea of people even swept the dead along, not allowing the bodies to fall.

For two days and two nights, the continuous human stream flowed towards the leader's grave. Meanwhile covered trucks drove through the back streets, removing the nameless victims of the great display of mourning. The leader was true to himself; going to the grave, he lured thousands more lives in with him ...

The ancient tradition of embalming and mummifying the leaders was completely appropriate in Stalin's case. He was, after all, an ancient eastern despot in spirit. After the funeral ceremony, the embalmed body of the leader was carried into the Mausoleum and placed in a sarcophagus, next to that of Lenin. This was intended to be its resting place for centuries to come. During those days no one could even imagine that in less than ten years, on an October night of 1961, it was to be removed from there in virtual secrecy. The former commander of the Kremlin division, who was entrusted with the reburial of Stalin remembers:

When it got dark, the place that had been chosen for reburial – behind the Mausoleum near the Kremlin wall – was fenced around. Stalin's body was removed from the sarcophagus and placed in a wooden coffin. The gold buttons on the coat were replaced with lead ones. When the lid went on the coffin, it turned out there were no nails to shut it with ...'

So who was he, Joseph Stalin, one of the most bloodthirsty tyrants of human history? Like Hitler, in his youth he dabbled in the arts. The great Georgian poet Illiya Chavchavadze included his poems from those early years in Georgian literary textbooks:

The Rose blooms, hugging the Violet,
The Lily awakes, bowing before the Zephyr.
Rising into the sky, the songbird sings melodiously,
The swallow gently whistles his song ...

Churchill christened him the Caucasus Bandit. Leon Trotsky called him the great mediocrity. Alexander Solzhenitsyn expressed the belief that if this terrible system of violence that Stalin created did not come about by accident, of its own accord, but was envisaged and pre-planned by him, then he really was a genius – a dark genius of evil.

9 | THE JESTER AND THE KING

IT WAS AN OVERCAST SEPTEMBER MORNING IN 1971. A light drizzle was falling. The ancient Moscow cemetery, located in the grounds of a former women's monastery, was ringed by ranks of soldiers and KGB operatives. Military vehicles were parked bumper to bumper. In the narrow passages between them, people wearing civilian clothes but carrying themselves in military fashion, were checking passes. The orders were specific, no ceremony, no outsiders, only the family and close friends of the deceased.

About sixty people had gathered at the freshly dug grave. The parting words were already spoken, but people continued to stand, as if waiting for something. 'I'll ask you to part with the deceased, only quickly, without lingering,' said a man in civilian clothes. 'Say your farewells and disperse,' he added gravely.

Thus ended the life of one of the most contradictory rulers of the Kremlin, Nikita Khrushchev. The papers carried a tiny announcement about the death of a pensioner of national standing: nothing about who he was, or who he became, only that he died.

In folk tales, poor damsels usually become princesses. In American versions, the children of poor immigrants become automobile tycoons and billionaires. The Soviet system also gives birth to its own miracles: the children of shoemakers and shepherds are transformed into the rulers of a mighty nation. This is no accident, every system chooses heroes appropriate to itself.

Nikita Khrushchev was born on 17 April 1894 in a peasant family, in the village of Kalinovka, outside the city of Kursk, on the border of Russia and the Ukraine. His mother was a deeply religious woman and every corner of the cottage that they lived in was decorated with icons, under which burned oil lamps. Daily life in the family was strict and repetitive. Nikita himself worked as a shepherd's assistant, helping to feed the family itself. ('Sometimes the shepherd would summon me: "Go on Nikita, go and round up the sheep" and I would run and round them up ...')

In 1909 the family moved to the mining town of Usovka, in the Ukraine, where the father found work in the mines. Nikita apprenticed himself to a metal craftsman. Thus, for a very short time, Khrushchev became 'working class', something of which he would be very proud in the future, and was to mention in all of his speeches. Truthfully, he would not call himself a metal craftsman but rather a miner. Apparently work underground seemed more heroic.

From 1914 Nikita Khrushchev began to be interested in revolutionary activities and became a regular reader of the paper *Pravda* (Truth). Also in 1914, he married his first wife, Yefrosinya, a miner's daughter.

In 1921, during the civil war in Russia, while Nikita was at the front, Yefrosinya died of spotted fever leaving him two young children, a five-year-old boy Leonid and a two-year-old daughter. Leonid's later life was tragic. He was to become a pilot and saw action in the Second World War, ending up in hospital. There, while very drunk, he and his friends started playing a none-too-clever game: shooting at bottles. Putting a bottle on the head of one of his friends, he missed, shooting the man in the head and killing him outright. After the court martial, Leonid was sent to the front and died in an aerial battle in March 1943. (In another version he was taken prisoner.) His wife Luba was be arrested and sent into exile for fifteen years, for alleged links with foreigners. Their daughter Yulya – Khrushchev's granddaughter – was brought up in her grandfather's family. Never in his life was Khrushchev to talk to the girl about the fate of her mother. Being a member of Stalin's all-powerful government, he would never gather the courage even to try to defend the wife of his fallen son. Only many years later, at the end of his life, he was to let drop a phrase addressed to his granddaughter: 'Your mother was innocent ...'

Nikita returned to Usovka in 1922, after the Bolshevik victory in the civil war, as an active member of the Party. As a result he immediately assumed a position of command, first as the deputy head, and then the head, of mining operations. He had boundless enthusiasm, but no knowledge whatsoever, so he had to go study at the 'Workers' Faculty', which at the time provided an education equivalent to the younger classes of primary school. Nikita remained a mining manager no more than a year before moving on completely to Party work.

In 1917, while not yet a member of the Bolshevik Party, Khrushchev somehow attended a political meeting where he met Lazar Kaganovich, a future close comrade of Stalin. All in all, it was this chance meeting that determined his rise. Apparently Kaganovich liked this simple-seeming, round-faced young man, not bereft of keen peasant wits and cunning. This outwardly inoffensive and homely impression would faithfully serve Khrushchev throughout his Party life. It was to protect him not only from Stalin's paranoid suspicions, which cost the lives of many in the leader's entourage, but would also blunt the awareness of future dangerous foes.

In 1924 Khrushchev married for the second time, wedding Nina Kuharchuk, who worked in the school for miners where she taught political education. In 1929, with Kaganovich's assistance, Khrushchev was sent to Moscow to study at the Industrial Academy, where Stalin's wife Nadezhda Alliluyeva was also a student at the time. Despite the imposing title of 'academy', these were merely courses where Bolsheviks from working-class and peasant backgrounds, whom the Revolution had moved into positions of industrial and agricultural management, got a basic education. As Khrushchev himself remembered: 'People varied a lot in the academy. Many had only finished village schools and only knew the four laws of arithmetic.'

The fact that Nadezhda Alliluyeva studied together with Khrushchev was to the final touch to Nikita's future career. As Stalin's former secretary Boris Bozhanov wrote:

> During these times Stalin put into action a massive nationwide meat-grinding operation – forced collectivisation* – where millions of peasant families ... were sent to concentration camps for extermination. Those who studied in the academy, people who had come from the provinces, had seen this hideous annihilation of the peasants with their own eyes. Of course, finding out that the new student was Stalin's wife, they firmly shut their mouths. Gradually, however, they came to realise that Nadya was a wonderful person, she could be trusted. Tongues were loosened, and they started to tell her what was really happening in the country ... Nadya was horrified, and proceeded to share this information with Stalin ... Stalin of course insisted that it was all lies and counter-revolutionary propaganda. 'But all the witnesses tell the same stories,' insisted Nadya. 'All?' asked Stalin. 'No,' Nadya replied. 'Only one says that it isn't true, but he is clearly lying and saying so out of cowardice, he's the Party Secretary of the Academy, Nikita Khrushchev.' Stalin remembered that surname. Everyone who trusted Nadya was arrested and executed ... and from this period on, Comrade Khrushchev began his brilliant career.

It was the middle of the 1930s. The time of the 'Great Terror' and the show trials began. It was precisely at this time that Stalin appointed Khrushchev head of the Moscow Bolsheviks. This is unlikely to have been a coincidence, one needed to possess qualities that Stalin valued. Nikita had such qualities: a complete lack of personal opinion, and a boundless adoration of the

---

* The forced joining of individual farming enterprises into collective farms.

leader. Apart from that, Nikita also had an inherent element of charm about him, what is known among the people as 'our own lad'. Stalin saw all of this quite clearly.

In the biographical literature devoted to Khrushchev, one sometimes comes across claims that of all of Stalin's close circle he was the only one not to get his hands dirty participating in the repressions. This is complete balderdash. At the time, not a single even slightly famous individual in Moscow – let alone a Party figure – could be arrested and moreover executed without the sanction of the Party's 'city father'. There were in fact tens of thousands of such repressed individuals in Moscow, and the sanction for their destruction was given by none other than Nikita Khrushchev.

Incidentally, when he later became head of the Ukrainian Bolsheviks (the timing to coincide with the annexation of the western Ukraine by the USSR), in order to please the leader Khrushchev would develop such a brutal process of 'Sovietisation' that even Stalin was obliged roughly to rein him in with the words, 'Calm down, you idiot.'

We can at least agree that unlike most of Stalin's circle Khrushchev was by nature not a born sadist, but he was an obedient facilitator, and that must not be forgotten. The artist Boris Zhutovsky, who had a part in fashioning Khrushchev's tombstone, writes:

> Almost his whole life, Khrushchev was obliged to think about how he might preserve it. He didn't have the opportunity to become educated. He was brought up in a house where a scarred executioner decided who was to live and who was to lose their head. He sang limericks in that house, debased himself, and acted the jester at Dzhugashvili's teat. Yes, he participated in the repressions, but as a person I feel he hated it. He played the role of jester in a bloody court ...

The famous Soviet publicist Ilya Ehrenburg, from whose light pen the period of Khrushchev's rule received the nickname 'The Thaw', called Stalin's time 'The Time of the Great Fear and Silence'. In this vein it is interesting to remember the following episode. After the leader's death, when Khrushchev was giving his famous speech about Stalin's cult of personality, a voice suddenly rang out from the crowd, 'And where were you when this was going on?' In other words, why didn't you speak out against Stalin's depravity? Khrushchev fell silent, swept the hall with his gaze and remarked, 'Would the person who asked that question please stand up.' Naturally, no one stood up

– their fear was still too great. 'That is exactly the same place we were,' Khrushchev said after a long pause.

What has been said above in no way nullifies the positive things Khrushchev accomplished, and perhaps even strengthens them. Almost no one from Stalin's entourage could escape the web of Stalinism, even after the leader's death, but Khrushchev – perhaps not completely but in the most vital way – somehow managed it. A monument now stands at Khrushchev's grave, half made of dark marble, the other half of light marble. It is the Khrushchev that we remember with gratitude that is represented by the light half. But what happened, happened. History is like a song, you can't throw out a word.

Some five hundred years ago, Niccolo Machiavelli coined the phrase, 'Brutus would have become Caesar if he had played the fool.' Khrushchev managed to accomplish this to a point. In telling his story, it is unnecessary to repeat familiar facts covered in the previous chapter. We are primarily interested in the new Khrushchev, a man of his own actions and his own destiny. Before continuing, however, we must pause to consider one other personality of the Kremlin, without whom the new Khrushchev could not have come into being – Lavrenti Beria.

Stalin had not yet exhaled his final breath on his deathbed, when the all-powerful KGB Minister, the light sparkling off his pince-nez, snapped at his adjutant: 'Khrustaleov, the car!' He had nothing further to do at the bed of the dying leader. He was hurrying to the Kremlin to 'take power'. This phrase heralds the beginning of the post-Stalin era.

Nature created Lavrenti Beria as the ideal machine of destruction. Devious, energetic, cunning, born for manipulation and intrigue, aroused by the slightest hint of blood or power. He was a good match for his master, and in some ways even surpassed him. He began his life as a scoundrel back at his school desk. He stole the student evaluation files, thus getting his elderly teacher shamefully dismissed, and by using middlemen sold the contents of the files to his fellow classmates. At the time, this young schoolboy from the southern city Suhumi was fifteen years old.

By 1923 Beria was already on the staff of the Georgian KGB. As the historian Antonov-Ovseenko colourfully writes about him:

He was an inexhaustible source of fabrications, a master of intrigue and imputation. Like no other, he knew the right moment to spread a dirty rumour, in order to split his opponents on the road to power and then defeat them one at a time. Something was always boiling, bubbling and hissing around him. He managed to glance into the boiling pots, adjust the frying pans on the stove without burning his fingers, throw a few logs on the fire, add a pinch of hot pepper, and skim the fatty residue off the top of the boiling cauldron. Despite all this, the young Beria convincingly played the role of 'our own lad'.

In 1924 he met Stalin for the first time. This was truly a pivotal meeting for Russia. Two executioners met, as close in spirit as two brothers. A year later Beria was already the deputy head of the Caucasus KGB. It is not necessary to describe in detail his journey to the summit of power, since it differed little from that of many in Stalin's circle, except perhaps being marked by even more intrigue and blood. Even a butcher like Stalin did not go so far as personally to execute his opponents in his own study, which some sources say Beria did more than once.

Stalin needed someone exactly like that. In the second half of the 1930s Beria moved to Moscow and a short time later was already the absolute master of the KGB's Lubjanka headquarters, and a personal friend of the leader. Stalin's little Svetlana, sitting comfortably on his knee, would fondly refer to him as 'Uncle Lara'.

The capital did not daunt this provincial. Quite the contrary, here his field of activity expanded even further. What does it matter where you murder people? People are people everywhere, they still write neat accusations against each other, betray those close to them, submissively endure slander, die in prisons and venerate the leader. Some sources say that Beria personally executed in his own office the arrested Marshal Bliukher, ordering that he first be beaten so fiercely that the marshal's eye fell out into his own palm. When the widow of an old friend from Georgia dared to announce that Lavrenti Beria had taken upon himself the authorship of a book written by her late husband, Beria killed her in his own office as well.

His personal arsenal of death included poisons as well as bullets. Searching for methods of employing them in clandestine murders, Beria set up a special secret laboratory in which the effects of poisons were tested on prisoners. As Professor Mayranovski, who carried out these secret murders, testified during his subsequent trial:

I was never told why one or another individual needed to be killed ... Meetings with the individual marked for extermination were organised for me at clandestine apartments where, during the eating and drinking, I would mix poisons into the food or drink.

Everything thus far mentioned by no means constitutes a complete inventory of his foul deeds, rather only a few brush-strokes on a portrait. Here is how Antonov-Ovseenko describes the interrogation of a famous Soviet diplomat named Evgeni Gnedin, in Beria's Kremlin study:

> A desk stood at the far wall of the huge chamber. When Gnedin was brought in, Beria was talking about something with (his second) Kabulov. They spoke in Georgian. Beria finally interrupted the conversation and Kabulov officially reported: 'The interrogated, Gnedin, behaved impudently ...' Not waiting for a question, Gnedin declared that he would not admit himself to be guilty. This was rapidly answered by a sharp punch to the jaw. Kabulov was sitting nearby, and in a comfortable position to administer the beating. Gnedin slumped to the right. A blow from Kabulov's aide returned him to his previous position. They beat him a long time, professionally, with a taste for it. Beria sat opposite and observed what was going on with calm curiosity ... Stunned, crushed and broken, Gnedin's courage did not falter. He refused to confess to treason. Beria stood up and commanded Gnedin to lie on the carpet. He first laid on his back. 'Not like that!' the master barked impatiently ... Several more 'specialists' appeared in the study. Beria ordered them to continue working on the uncooperative spy. They stripped Gnedin, flipped him on to his stomach, and proceeded to beat him with rubber coshes. 'Don't leave any marks,' ordered Beria ... They beat him until they were tired themselves ... The beaten and naked diplomat was thrown into a cold cell. A short time later, there was another execution in Beria's study.

If Khrushchev and his colleagues from Stalin's closest circle were mainly grey, faceless and mostly uneducated, then unlike them, Beria was an individual. He was the ideal functionary of death, with the morals, psychology and humour of an executioner. For example, while sending his Party colleagues to the next world, many of whom were close comrades of Lenin in his time, Beria ordered that after cremation – as a joke – their remains be distributed in the form of manure, to the fields of the Lenin Kolkhoz* outside Moscow. This all occurred even before lampshades of human skin started being made in Oswiecim.

* Collective farm.

But Lavrenti Beria's amusements did not stop there. Usually, the black limousines with government licence plates roared around Moscow at great speeds. Some of them, however, with specific numbers belonging to the KGB, moved very slowly, trying for some reason to hug the footpaths closely. From behind a curtained window, passers-by were watched by the attentive eyes of Beria himself – or more often those of his henchmen. They were picking out pretty women and girls for their boss, from twelve years old and up. The procedure was perfected. The victim was brought to a town house outside the city where she was met by the prematurely paunchy and flabby Beria, his lips curved into an obscene smile. Oh no, he did not leap upon his victim like a street thug, tearing off her dress. Quite the contrary, he invited her to the table, to dine with him and drink a glass of wine to Comrade Stalin's health. Refusal was impossible, that would be committing a crime. After the glass of wine, which was mixed with special powders, the victim fell into a deep sleep ...

Sometimes even this was not necessary. As a famous Soviet film actress told the author of this book, when she – then still a young girl – was tricked into being brought to Beria, he said with a crooked smile, 'You are a rational person, and understand that you are in my power. No one will help you, so let's leave out the excesses ...' and politely invited her to bed. According to rumour, this bloodsucker was responsible for the rape of hundreds of women.

Beria celebrated his fiftieth birthday on 29 March 1949, at the height of his power. If he was not yet the equal of Stalin, then he was at least a close second. It was no wonder his nickname was 'Little Father', as opposed to the 'Big Father'. In the last years of his life Stalin was not simply wary of Beria, he was afraid of him. With his finely trained instincts, the leader sensed mortal danger from the direction of his protégé, and began to prepare an operation to destroy his entire entourage. It was, however, already too late ...

In the previous chapter we touched on the question of whether Beria had hastened Stalin's death. It appears that he did. At any rate, those of Stalin's former guards who have survived to this day are certain of it. Thus the retired Major Ribin recalls that Beria gave instructions: 'Tell no one and call no one about Stalin's illness.' The first doctors arrived to see the patient a whole day later. Stalin himself often used such 'medical' methods to remove unwanted figures.

Now, not waiting for the master's final breath, Beria was hurrying to the Kremlin to 'take power'. One can imagine the state Khrushchev and his colleagues were in. Even while Stalin lived, they were terrified of Beria, so what would happen now? Renewed fear for their own lives, and sycophancy, but now before the 'Little Father'. Once more, life either as jester or lackey. And would he even spare their lives?

What to do? Hide in the undergrowth as before, or take action? For the first time in his Party life Khrushchev overcame his perpetual terror and chose to act. Give him his due, this required considerable courage, since any false move in the game would cost him his head.

The first step was to unite Stalin's former cronies. All, however, were pathological cowards, since Stalin did not tolerate any other types. Khrushchev knew that not one of Stalin's henchmen was reliable, so every conversation was a risk. The office-intrigue players, the experienced careerists – they had never trusted one another, keeping a close watch on every move their opponents made. Nothing bound them together. If one of them betrayed the others and informed, then Beria would crush them all. In this instance, however, there was something that this whole cowardly team had in common: fear for their own lives.

Beria's arrest was scheduled for 26 June 1953. There was supposed to be a session of the Politburo on that day. The commandant of the Kremlin, who was loyal to Khrushchev, summoned a battalion from outside Moscow, commanded by his son. Apart from Khrushchev, only a few people knew the whole plan of operations, including the Deputy Minister of Defence, Marshal Zhukov. Two hours before the start of the session, Khrushchev called his wartime friend, now commanding the forces of the Moscow Military District:

Khrushchev: You have people you can trust? The kind you trust like you would yourself?
Commander: Of course.
Khrushchev: Take four people with you, and bring some cigars along.
Commander: What cigars are you talking about?
Khrushchev: You've forgotten what we called them at the front?
(Khrushchev meant handguns.)

An hour later they were already entering the Kremlin in the Defence Minister's car, which the Kremlin guards did not stop. They went up to the second floor. Here it was, Office Number One, where Stalin once worked and where the Politburo now met. There were about fifteen people in the antechamber. They had to give the impression that everything was fine, that nothing was going on, since some of these could be Beria's people.

Khrushchev remembers these as nerve-wracking minutes. Everyone was gathered, but Beria had not yet arrived. What if someone had warned him? Then he would certainly crush them all right there, as in a mousetrap. Finally, the door opened and Beria entered. He absent-mindedly dropped his briefcase on the windowsill and, flopping down heavily on an armchair next to Khrushchev, asked: 'What is on today's agenda?'

'There is only one matter to be resolved,' Khrushchev declared, rising from his seat – the question of Lavrenti Pavlovich Beria.' Khrushchev remembers that Beria shuddered, looked up at him and tugging on his sleeve, asked: 'Nikita, what are you blathering about?' 'You should listen,' Khrushchev replied. 'That is what I am going to talk about.'

About twenty minutes after the start of the session, two long rings sounded in the antechamber where the military men were waiting. This was the agreed signal. The officers, headed by Marshal Zhukov, got to their feet and headed towards the office door. Their path was blocked by the uncomprehending secretary, but moving him aside they entered the office. Beria was sitting with his head bowed, hurriedly writing something on a piece of paper. He was scribbling one word over and over: 'Alarm', 'Alarm', 'Alarm ...'

Khrushchev continues: ' "Hands up!" Zhukov snapped at Beria. The other newcomers drew their weapons. Beria leapt towards his briefcase, lying behind him on the windowsill. I grabbed Beria by the arm, to prevent him getting to his weapon, if he had one in the briefcase ...' (It should be mentioned here that Khrushchev told this story often, in many situations and always differently, so it is safe to assume that a large portion of it is embellishment.)

Under military guard, Beria was taken to a room adjacent to the office, which once served as Stalin's private chamber. They took his pince-nez and crushed it, cut the buttons off his trousers ... He now sat short-sighted and helpless, clutching his trousers to keep them from falling down. The questions now arose, what to do with him next? How to slip him unseen out of the Kremlin, which was crowded with his people? If he managed to get a signal off, the situation would immediately be transformed.

These were dangerous hours, when it was not at all clear how it would all end. Beria was of course nervous, repeatedly asking to go to the toilet, obviously counting on being able to alert his supporters. The generals guarding him, guns at the ready, went with him. The remaining members of the Politburo then went off to the ballet at the Bolshoi Theatre, so as not to raise suspicion and simultaneously not let one another out of their sight, in case of betrayal.

This continued until midnight. Meanwhile, in government cars that would not be searched, a large group of officers entered the Kremlin, taking control of the corridors along which Beria would be conducted. He was taken by the back ways, and placed in the Defence Minister's car. Officers flanked him, pressing the muzzles of their guns into his ribs. Half an hour later he was already in a special underground bunker, outfitted in case of war as the command centre of the Moscow Military District. Additional troops, tanks and armoured cars were summoned to guard the bunker.

The fear of a possible attack by KGB battalions intent on freeing Beria was so great that the investigation and the trial – which lasted six months, according to official sources – were conducted in the very same bunker. Radio contact was established between the bunker and a room in the Kremlin, where Khrushchev and his colleagues – leaning close to the speakers – could listen to Beria's interrogations, in case he made an accusation against one of them. Beria was executed in that same bunker. Antonov-Ovseenko describes the end:

> His shirt was removed, leaving him in a white undergarment, his hands were tied behind him and he was hung up on a hook attached to a wooden shield. The shield would protect those present from possible ricochet. The judge read the sentence.
>
> *Beria*: Allow me to say ...
>
> *Judge*: You've said everything already ... Gag his mouth.
>
> A wildly bulging eye flashed above the gag, Beria closed the other ... The bullet hit him in the middle of the forehead. The body went limp against the ropes ... The doctor was summoned. 'Why examine him?' the doctor noted. 'He's ready. I know him. He rotted away a long time ago. He suffered from syphilis as far back as 1943.'

(According to another version, told by one of the generals participating in the execution, fear of Beria was still so great and the nerves of his accusers stretched so thin that someone snapped and shot him in the back, a few steps away from the room where the execution was supposed to occur.)

Beria was a murderer and a bloodsucker, but his colleagues destroyed him for completely different reasons. The number of crimes Beria committed were sufficient to earn him the death penalty. The court did not need to be manipulated. Nevertheless, as the press of the time reported, the main accusations against Beria were not for the murders of thousands of innocent people, but for 'espionage for Western intelligence agencies' and 'an attempt to restore Capitalism in the USSR'. In other words, that same complete rubbish that Beria's underlings had beaten out of their victims in the basements of the KGB. The question is, why did Khrushchev and his fellow conspirators need these stupid lies? Why did they not, dispensing with needless artifice, try Beria for his real crimes? Evidently because his real crimes were not in fact crimes in their eyes, and if they had been, they would have had to share the responsibility together with Beria. 'We did not have any direct criminal accusations against him,' wrote Khrushchev. The system that raised him and them was one and the same; they did not intend to fight it. This is why, when remembering Khrushchev's courage in his battle with Beria, it would be wise not to forget the motives of that courage.

The aforementioned version of Beria's arrest was mainly told through official sources – the press, Khrushchev's memoirs, and also the accounts of the servicemen who participated in it. However, was this really how things happened? Was there a real trial for Beria? Why hasn't one photo, one frame of film from the trial, survived? Where is Beria's grave? There were rumours that he was simply shot that same day in the Kremlin. What about Khrushchev's account of Beria's capture; isn't it just too theatrical? And what kind of judge can order a man gagged before he is executed? What did they fear Beria would say, deep in an underground bunker? And what kind of doctor would show such cynicism? Once again, yes; Beria was a monster and deserved the sentence he was given, but he was being put on trial by a civilised court, not a gang of bandits, or at least that is how the authorities wanted it to be seen.

A book was published recently by Beria's son Sergo – *My Father Lavrenti Beria*. According to this book, the author's father was the personification of decency and honesty. He dreamed of setting the prisoners free. Without him, the situation in the country would have been even worse than it was. Half a century before Gorbachev he was already prepared to introduce *perestroika*, but was hindered by the bastards who surrounded him. And Khrushchev accused him of 'attempting to restore capitalism in the USSR ...' As for that 'female business', those were just evil-minded rumours. If they had been true, his proud Georgian wife would have fought him tooth and nail.

Of course, a son is a son, and that must be taken into account. Moreover, some of the details he brings up warrant careful attention. He claims, for instance, that there was no arrest and trial of his father – he was treacherously killed in his Moscow flat. This same version is supported by Professor Vedenin, a KGB operative at the time who, by his own admission, personally participated in the action (the newspaper *Nedelya,* No. 22, 1997). Whatever happened, one conclusion can be drawn: the truth about Beria's 'trial' has not been completely revealed and is awaiting its investigator.*

If Beria's removal marked the moment in Khrushchev's life when he was transformed from Stalin's lackey into an independently minded head of government, then his finest hour undoubtedly came with the speech he made about Stalin's 'cult of personality'

It was 1956, the third year after Stalin's death. Although the country had sensed a slight 'thaw', and a small trickle of 'rehabilitated' had even appeared, little had changed overall. Millions of completely innocent people remained languishing in prisons and camps. The KGB still terrorised

---

* New details concerning the 'Beria Affair' were given to Western and Russian journalists (see the Moscow *Izvestiya,* 6 January, 1998) by Major Mikhail Hidznak-Gurevich, a former officer of the Soviet army who fought at Stalingrad and Berlin in the Second World War.

As the Major recalls, in 1953 he took part in the trial and execution of Lavrenti Beria. The day of Beria's arrest, the Major and fifty other officers were ordered to wait at the gates of the Kremlin. A black government limousine containing the prisoner emerged from the gates at midnight. The military personnel in the car forced the former all-powerful minister to lie on the floor, so he would not be noticed by the Kremlin guard. As has already been described, Beria was taken to a heavily fortified bunker in one of the suburbs of Moscow.

The Major was ordered to guard and take care of Beria. Over the next six months, he lived and slept in the cell next to him. He brought food, and carried out his requests. The Major had orders to shoot Beria in the event of the bunker coming under attack. When the prisoner was brought to the bunker '... I offered him food and put a bowl of soup on the table in front of him ...' the Major recounts. 'This angered him. He grabbed the bowl and threw it at me.'

When the trial started the Major escorted Beria daily to the courtroom, which was located in the same bunker. 'Beria knew he would die, but didn't panic,' the Major said. 'He let me know that he wanted me to find his son and tell him everything. He was an intelligent man. He was no coward.'

After Beria was sentenced to death he was dressed in black clothing, the Major fastened handcuffs on to him and took him to a special cell where five officers, led by General Pavel Batitsky, were already waiting. Several minutes went by. The General shot Beria from close range. The Major and the other officers were ordered to also take one shot each. When everything was done the Major was left alone in the cell, having been ordered to wrap the body in a sheet. At that point the officer lost consciousness. He later took the body to the crematorium. After the cremation the ashes were scattered by a powerful fan.

The Major tried to carry out the dead man's wishes and contact Beria's son, but the son did not want to meet him.

Thus, the version put forward in Sergo Beria's book claiming that his father was killed on the day of his arrest on 26 June 1953 can no longer be deemed valid. As we have already said, the 'Beria Affair' still awaits investigation.

the people. The inertia Stalin had created persisted. Truth be told, the camps were not quite the same as before. Their administrators were themselves at a loss, and the prisoners could not help but notice it. Any ill-treatment of them stirred up a storm of protest, which had been unthinkable only a few years ago. Riots and even uprisings began to occur from place to place. Although they were crushed no less ruthlessly than before, nevertheless these were troubling signs of a new time for the Soviet system. This is how the Hungarian doctor Frans Varconi describes an uprising in one of the gulag camps*, in which he himself participated. The prisoners captured the camp precincts. KGB soldiers, tanks and planes were sent in to crush them:

> Rifle shots, screams, the groans of the dying, fill the rocket and fire-lit area of the camp. Drunken KGB soldiers are capturing the scattering prisoners. Screaming and shooting, they finish off the wounded lying on the ground. With a crash, a tank is manoeuvring its way between the barracks. Continuous gunfire is coming from its hatchway ... An elderly Armenian volunteered to go to the soldiers and inform them that the barracks were ready to surrender. This was a very old man, the wind billowing around his long grey beard. 'Listen, lads ...' he began, but a bullet did not let him finish. One of the soldiers cut his head off with a knife and threw it back in the barracks. The women and girls from the second barracks take each other's hands and walk out singing, to meet the tanks. The tanks won't simply cut through rows of women, they hope. But the tanks do. The caterpillar treads crunch over female bodies. The drunken drivers at the helms are in a blood frenzy ...

It was February 1956. The Twentieth Party Congress in the Kremlin was drawing to a close, the first congress after Stalin's death. In practice it differed little from all the previous congresses – the same unanimous raising of hands, the same ringing applause and shouts of 'Hear hear!' The last day of the congress approached. Khrushchev was tormented by the question of what to do, to tell the truth about Stalin or to stay silent. If he remained silent, then what next? Sooner or later people were going to walk out of the camps and tell that truth themselves. And then what? On the other hand, what would happen if

---

* The KGB's forced labor empire was under the authority of the Main Administration of Corrective Labor Colonies, or GULAG.

the truth about Stalin were told? It was not only a matter of casting down the idol, it would mean, in the words of the historian M. Gefter, 'the casting down of the system, laying bare its sacred mechanisms, of which the mechanism of secrecy was no less important than the mechanism of fear'.

According to Khrushchev's recollection, the moment he hinted to his Politburo colleagues that it might be a good idea to tell the truth about Stalin, a storm erupted. The main point against the idea was fear – fear of responsibility, which certainly fell not only on Stalin's shoulders. Many execution orders, after all, also bore their signatures. Khrushchev was practically the only one of them who considered it necessary to tell the truth about those times. It was then, seeing that they would not let him speak as the head of the Party, he announced that he would address the congress personally, as an ordinary delegate. This was not simply a rash move, but a brave one, which would earn him a place in history. In the end it was decided that the speech would be confidential – for the congress delegates only.

The modern reader would find it difficult to imagine the atmosphere of that hall, filled with fifteen hundred of the faithful, raised on the age-old postulations of the Party bible. Shaken and apprehensive, they sat listening to Khrushchev with bated breath. For four hours a deathly silence hung over the huge Kremlin auditorium, only punctuated now and then with gasps of amazement. Khrushchev spoke on. He told of the destroyed lives, of barbarity and torture, of mutilations and executed children, of palace murders reminiscent of the Middle Ages, of the Pyrrhic victories of the Generalissimo. The deathly silence of the hall was disturbed only by the solitary buzzing of a fly. This was a silence that screamed.

Of course, it was naïve to think from the very start that such an event could be kept a secret, nor did Khrushchev himself try to do so. A few days later, a complete transcript of the speech was circulating the Western world. Everyone knew about it, apart from the citizens of the Soviet Union. And then, on orders from above, this 'secret document' began to be 'clandestinely' read across the whole country. Numbered copies of the speech were sent to work-places with clear instructions that after the secret collective readings they were to be returned to Moscow.

As a student at the time, I shall always remember that evening when several hundred of us were crammed into a cramped university auditorium designed for about fifty people. Pressed up against each other, sitting on tables and windowsills, not fidgeting, bathed in sweat, we played back that terrifying documentary film of our lives in our heads …

Khrushchev's speech delivered a knock-out blow to the the country. People looked at each other aimlessly, spoke in whispers, some literally in shock. For decades they had been taught words in praise of the greatness of their system, of the infallibility of their leaders – who had attained an almost godlike purity. In reality, however, they now turned out to be nothing more than a pack of criminals.

I remember that after the reading of the speech we left as quite different people from those who had entered the auditorium – quieter, more contemplative, more adult. We left like 'Khrushchev's people', who would never again take anything on blind faith. This was an awakening, an awakening of an entire nation. For the young it was a revelation, but for those of the older generation, who had devoted their whole conscious lives to this system, it was a heavy, nerve-wracking shock from which they could not recover for a long time. After Khrushchev's speech, society was never the same again. Without intending to do so, Khrushchev had shaken the whole structure of the Bolshevik system.

To steel himself for such an action required more courage than for Beria's arrest. Khrushchev must have understood that the whole system organised by Stalin, and continuing to function according to the scheme Stalin had devised, would collapse upon him.

It is unnecessary to consider in detail all the pros and cons that Khrushchev measured in coming to this decision; but certainly human compassion was present here. Nature gave Khrushchev a strong instinct of self-preservation, which enabled him to feel the silent underground currents that were stirring among the people.

After such a disclosure, it was impossible to preserve Stalin's system unchanged. The gates to the camps were thrown open, and millions of half-dead people began to return to life. They will always be grateful to Khrushchev for this. This action will forever remain his act of heroism. Professor Burlatski, who accompanied Khrushchev on many of his international trips, remembers:

He had turned sixty at the time, but he looked very strong, active and mischievously cheerful. He would bellow with laughter at the slightest opportunity … His wide face, with its two warts and huge bald pate, his large squat nose and sharply sticking-out ears, could easily have belonged to a peasant from a Central Russian village or a worker from the outskirts of Moscow, pushing his way through a queue towards the bar. Only the eyes, the small dark eyes, either full of humour or filled with rage, either shining with good-cheer or with harsh power, these eyes gave him away as a deeply political man, who had passed through fire, water and the trumpets of Jericho ...'

It is something of a marvel that even though Khrushchev passed through the harsh school of Stalinist secrecy and reserve, spending the greater part of his life in an atmosphere of fear and suspicion, he remained a cheerful, impulsive man, not losing his essential human qualities, which could by no means be said about the other members of Stalin's retinue. He liked to invite artists to his dacha, and enjoyed singing southern Russian folk songs with them although he had no voice whatsoever. He had heard and loved these songs during his village childhood. Apparently Soviet radio, knowing the times Khrushchev usually went for a walk in the park, taking with him a portable radio receiver he had been given as a gift in America, would schedule village folk songs especially for him at these times.

According to old Chinese folk wisdom, a wart beside the nose is a sign of being chosen by fate. Khrushchev would often poke fun of this blemish on his face, and indeed never let slip an opportunity for a laugh or a wisecrack. He loved to tell and listen to bawdy anecdotes, and freely used juicy unprintable words. Similar words would often slip out during speeches. His famous curse 'Kuskin's Mother' – something midway between strong vulgarity and a folk-lore expression, untranslatable into any other language – circled the world, bringing much grief to interpreters. His Minister of Agriculture recalls how Mr Gharst, a farmer whom Khrushchev had met while visiting America, once flew to Moscow. Khrushchev invited him to his dacha. The Minister warned Khrushchev that Gharst, to put it mildly, was a man who made no excuses for himself: he would yell instead of conversing, bellow instead of laughing, loved to put his feet up on the table and was generally obnoxious. 'Don't worry,' replied Khrushchev, 'bring him along. We're no worse at being obnoxious.'

Strange as this may seem, considering his previous experiences, something childish survived in him. It was unlikely to have been childish naïveté, rather childish curiosity, aiming to explore a new and unknown world. He was fascinated by gadgets and toys. Professor Burlatski, who accompanied Khrushchev on a journey to Yugoslavia, remembers how during a meeting with Marshal Tito, while the other was making a speech, Khrushchev would occasionally fish a watch out of his pocket, recently given to him by the world famous physicist Leo Szilard, the cover of which opened like the lens of a camera, and would examine it with curiosity. He was completely oblivious of the time, he was simply compelled to play around with this amusing trinket; and he did it all under the table, thinking that no one would notice.

Military personnel would tell of the wonder with which Khrushchev would greet the testing of new technology, not so much for its utility as for its design. It can be said with almost complete assurance that his love affair with space was by no means determined wholly by strategic considerations; it was also a part of his nature. Khrushchev's son-in-law, Alexei Adjubei, chief editor of the paper *Izvestia,* remembers:

On 1 April 1961 Sergei Korolev (the chief designer of Soviet space rockets) called Khrushchev ... and yelled down the phone in a voice hoarse from weariness: 'The parachute has opened, he's going to land!' The conversation was about Gagarin's landing. Khrushchev would constantly ask: 'Is he alive? Is he signalling? Is he alive?' No one at that stage could say for certain how the flight would end. Finally Khrushchev heard: 'He's alive!' It was a moment of personal triumph for him.

Khrushchev's trips abroad were not always a result of political necessity. He would often set them up himself. It would be prudent to remember that he, like all Soviet people, had lived his whole life in a tin can sealed by Stalin. The West was for him like the dark side of the moon. And now, having escaped from under Stalin's heel, he thirsted to see this new world. He never concealed his delight in these journeys. He did not simply perform his duties; he showed his admiration for the ancient culture of India, the beauty of France, the vastness of America. The curiosity that attracted Khrushchev to playthings likewise attracted him to new places. Unlike Stalin, protected from the world by thick armour, Khrushchev was anxious to experience real life. As the historian M. Gefter correctly points out, Khrushchev made a discovery vital for himself and Soviet society, admitting that difference does not necessarily have to imply enmity.

By and large, Khrushchev was far more interested in reality than in fiction. So, for example, he liked the circus and documentary films, but was very cool towards feature films. He loved meeting simple people, villagers especially, and to chat and laugh with them. He enjoyed boasting how he had kept the case containing his old metal-working tools, which he had used as a young man in the mine. But he found it harder to communicate with intellectuals, who would often provoke his aggressive side.

It was well known that Khrushchev did not write his own speeches. He found it very difficult to put his thoughts down on paper. To write a simple letter, he had to summon a stenographer, dictate the overall intent of the letter, then get assistants to rewrite it to correct the grammar. Even in those rare orders that Khrushchev was compelled sometimes to write personally on official documents, there were numerous grammatical errors.

Despite this, he was deeply sure of himself. Although the texts of his speeches were certainly pre-prepared, when he started to speak no one knew how the speech would end. Apparently as a result of his literary difficulties, Khrushchev loved the spoken word and improvisation. He would often simply stuff the text of the prepared speech in his pocket and proceed to 'speak from the heart', sometimes in anger, sometimes with irony, perhaps hammering the podium with his fist or laughing along with the audience.

There were legends about Khrushchev's impulsiveness. To this day many authors portray him as a rowdy barbarian, capable at any moment of slamming his fist down on the table or his boot on the podium. Yet the image of Khrushchev as susceptible to sudden flashes of anger is incorrect. He had passed through the most rigorous of acting schools, the school of Stalin. Thus many of his allegedly spontaneous outbursts were premeditated performances.

The most memorable public picture of Khrushchev was when he hammered the table at the United Nations with his shoe. This certainly was no improvisation. This is what his son-in-law has to say about it:

This was the day that the thorny 'Hungarian question'* was due to be discussed. A day earlier, at breakfast, Khrushchev was told that just before the question was to be discussed he would be warned, so that the Soviet delegation had time to leave the meeting, as a sign of protest. 'Leave?' said Khrushchev in amazement. It was immediately decided that they would not abandon the meeting, but would rather create an obstruction and attempt to disrupt the speech of the orator. The next day, when the speaker announced the beginning of the discussion of the 'Hungarian question', to the amazement of the whole meeting, the Soviet delegation did not leave. Khrushchev began ceaselessly, but in accordance with procedure, to ask questions, demanding clarifications

---

* On this day the UN was discussing the savage crushing of the 1956 revolution of Hungary by Soviet forces.

and specifications, insisting that the orators present their mandates, in short, doing everything possible to disrupt the presentation. Also, members of the Soviet delegation, including Khrushchev, each in accordance with their temperament, began to hammer the hinged lids of the tables. The meeting was filled with noise and laughter. At this moment Khrushchev's watch slipped out of his hand. He started to feel under the table to find it, but his belly got in the way. Instead of the watch, Khrushchev found his own shoes, which he usually removed under the table so that his feet would not swell. Well, a shoe is a shoe, and it was even easier to hammer with it …

Incidentally, when the 'Hungarian question' was followed by the discussion of the 'Algerian question',* the French delegation, while leaving the meeting in protest, announced with some wit that they were going to buy mountain climbing boots.

Apart from such 'harmless' character traits, Khrushchev certainly inherited other traits from Stalin's school. Like Stalin, he could not tolerate strong and independent people around him. He found it easier to rely upon sycophants. Although Khrushchev could not be called malicious, rather possessing a peasant-like cunning and guile, he certainly possessed a good deal of deviousness. Take, for instance, the removal of Marshal Georgi Zhukov from the post of Defence Minister – the very same Zhukov who had been Khrushchev's main support during the liquidation of Beria. It is said that seeing off Zhukov before his flight to Yugoslavia, Khrushchev gently adjusted the man's scarf, saying: 'Georgi, don't catch cold, it's windy.' Several hours later, while the marshal's plane was still in the air, he had already been removed from all of his posts. Khrushchev could not forget a phrase Zhukov had once dropped, 'Not a single tank will move without my say-so', although those words had been spoken in support of Khrushchev.

Khrushchev governed the country for ten years. As a historian correctly noted, however, there was no such thing as a 'decade of Khrushchev', but rather two five-year periods. These two periods were reflected by the sculptor of his tombstone, a white and black side. Khrushchev lacked both the culture and the inner strength to avoid being deformed under the weight of the enormous power he possessed. If the first five 'white' years were those of Khrushchev the reformer, destroying Stalin's regime of despotism, then the

---

* The crushing of the revolution in Algeria by France.

next five 'black' years were those of Khrushchev the conservative, fearing the actions he himself had taken. This was the key to his personal tragedy.

A philosopher once said that culture is patience. Khrushchev fell victim to what has happened countless times in history with people of little culture, who find themselves at the pinnacle of power. The visible change began somewhere in 1958 when he, as the popular saying goes, 'went off the rails'. Things would often reach the point of absurdity. Meeting the afore-mentioned American farmer Gharst, who had spent his whole life growing corn, Khrushchev would give him advice as to how to grow that corn. He could demand that the nuclear physicists discover a new elementary particle in time for the latest communist celebration. Being completely ignorant of economics, he threw out the motto of 'catching and surpassing America', which immediately gave rise to hundreds of popular anecdotes and sayings, such as 'We should certainly catch them, but it wouldn't be a good idea to surpass them, since they'll see our torn trousers and bare arses.' Finally, the pinnacle of the euphoria which gripped Khrushchev was the promise, which even Lenin and Stalin had feared making in their own time, 'The Party is proud to announce ...' was blazoned on every wall, 'that the present Soviet population will live under Communism.' This was generally received as yet another joke.

A separation of the 'white' and 'black' periods of Khrushchev's rule was triggered by the events of June 1962 in the city of Novocherkassk, in southern Russia, where thousands of workers took to the streets to protest the sharp rise in meat prices. Some carried hand-made placards that read 'Khrushchev for offal'. The authorities responded with tanks and machine-guns. Eyewitnesses tell how young children, who had perched in trees out of curiosity, tumbled from the branches like ripe pears, cut down by bursts of machine-gun fire. Dozens were killed and injured, the boulevards were red with blood. Here in Novocherkassk, Khrushchev the conservative betrayed the ideals of Khrushchev the reformer.

Another dark page of the final years of Khrushchev's rule appeared with his so-called 'meetings with the intelligentsia'. As already stressed, Khrushchev was uncomfortable in his communications with the educated classes. Yet, objectively speaking, the intellectuals had been his main source of support during the democratic reforms of his first five years, since for them release from Stalin's despotism was far more important than his economic mistakes. This could not help but irritate the Party apparatus surrounding Khrushchev, which on the whole had preserved the thoughts and tendencies of Stalin's time. This apparatus endeavoured to set Khrushchev against the 'thankless intelligentsia' which told stories about him and was allegedly trying to turn the common folk against him. This is how Khrushchev's campaign against the intellectuals started.

The first loud argument, complete with yelling and stamping of feet, exploded in 1962 in the 'Manezh' (the central exhibition building of Moscow). For the first time in many decades, avant-garde artists, who had previously found themselves practically on an illegal footing, were invited to take part in an official exhibition They certainly did not realise that the invitation was a provocation, concocted by the Party apparatus against the intellectuals. The avant-garde artists were supposed to serve as a kind of detonator to set off the explosion.

As a contributor to this exhibition, the artist Boris Zhutovsky tells how they were invited to participate literally a day before Khrushchev was due to visit the show, and were allocated three rooms on the first floor ...

Over a single day, we gathered and put together the whole exhibition. We spent the whole night hammering in nails, hanging paintings, building platforms for the sculptures and generally larking about from an over-abundance of enthusiasm ... We parted around three in the morning, and had already come back at nine ... When Khrushchev arrived, I attached myself to his entourage and followed him around the ground floor (this was mostly devoted to works by the Realists), listening to the previously unknown conspiracy unfold. Khrushchev was yelling that he didn't have enough bronze for rockets (and here it is being wasted in these silly statues) ... Those who walked with him were pouring oil on the fire ... When the time came to move up to us on the first floor, I ran ahead ... Half a minute later Khrushchev arrived. He stopped, and throwing his arms around my shoulders and those of another artist, said: 'I've been told that your art is bad! I don't believe it, let's go see.' So the three of us entered the hall, arm in arm. Khrushchev looked around, his eyes fixing on a picture. 'Gentlemen, are you some kind of pederasses?' He didn't know the word, so he pronounced it as he heard it. Turning his body around, he came face-to-face with my painting, and started to turn a dark red colour. There were four of my paintings in the hall, and it so happened that God guided him to all four. By the time Khrushchev got to my last picture, a self-portrait, he was already muttering, 'If we get a piece of cardboard, cut a hole in it and place it up against your portrait, do you know what we'll get? The ladies should excuse me, an arsehole!' and his whole entourage started smiling pleasantly … Suddenly, a face belonging to one of his associates swam into view at Khrushchev's shoulder: 'They sell their paintings to foreigners, you know' (a political crime at the time). Khrushchev's eyes suddenly started to resemble those of a mad boar about to charge – completely leaden – and through the absolute silence he was looking directly at me. Gulping air, I said, 'I give you my absolute word that not one of the artists present has sold a single picture to foreigners.' Meanwhile Ernst Neizvestni (the future designer of Khrushchev's tombstone), had been stalking around the room this whole time. He was of modest height, dark eyed and very active – a leader. He stood in front of Khrushchev and said: 'You're the head of the government. I want you to see my work …' Khrushchev was somewhat dumbstruck at this manner of address, and followed him into the third hall. As soon as Khrushchev saw Ernst's works he went off the rails again and started to repeat his idea of having enough bronze for rockets. The Minister of the KGB then leapt towards Ernst, yelling, 'Where did you get the bronze? You're not going to leave here!', at which Ernst snapped back, 'Don't you yell at me! This is a matter of life and death for me! Give me your gun, I'll shoot myself on the spot!' We left the exhibition thinking that 'black crows' (prison vans) would be waiting for us at the entrance.

Conveying the atmosphere of the next two 'meetings with the intelligentsia' in my own words is impossible, since, as the famous film director Mikhail Romm put it, 'The whole thing became surreal. Something unfathomable.' So, I will use another extract, taken from the memoirs of Mikhail Romm, who was present at these meetings:

I counted myself amongst Khrushchev's admirers. I was even called a 'Khrushchevite' … I tried to forgive him everything. In truth, from time to time I would come across such strangeness as to cause bewilderment. At a meeting he would suddenly say: 'The ideas of Karl Marx are certainly very good, but if we butter them with a slice of hog fat, that would be even better'. In December of 1962 1 received an invitation to a reception … I arrived. Everyone was there, film directors, poets, writers, painters, sculptors, journalists … The whole artistic intelligentsia. The speeches began. At first Khrushchev conducted himself like an amiable host, but gradually he seemed to get more and more worked up, finally exploding at Ernst Neizvestni. He spent a long time searching for the most hurtful way to explain what Ernst Neizvestni was. Finally he found it, and became immensely happy: 'This is what your art resembles. If a body were to enter the toilet, and climb on into the bowl. Looking up from inside the bowl at what was above him, while someone was sitting on the toilet at the time ... That is what your art is.' Later, the poet Andrei Voznesenski took the podium. Khrushchev interrupted him almost immediately and, winding himself right up to boiling point started to yell:

'Gossip! What are you doing here? You like it overseas so much? You have admirers there? Then get lost and go there ...'

Voznesenski: 'I want to live here!'

'Well if you want to live here so much then why do you spread gossip?'

While Voznesenski is trying to reply, Khrushchev suddenly addresses the hall ... 'And what are you laughing at? You, four-eyes! In the last row, wearing a red shirt! What are you laughing at? Just you wait, we'll listen to you too, it'll be your turn soon.'

Voznesenski didn't know what to do. To continue, not to continue ... 'I'm honest. I support Soviet authority, I don't want to go anywhere. Allow me to read you my poem, 'Lenin ...'

Khrushchev: 'We don't need your poem,' and immediately, without drawing breath, 'So, you there, laughing-boy. You in the glasses, come down here ...'

Someone stands up in the back rows: 'Me?' 'No, not you. Him next to you.' Another man gets up: 'Me?' 'You, you, you ...'

A man wanders down the aisle, really wearing glasses, in a red shirt, without a tie ... a thinnish kind of man.

Khrushchev to him: 'Who are you?'

'Me? I'm Galitsin' (A very famous royal surname in ancient Russia.)

'What, Prince Galitsin?'

'I'm not a prince, I'm an artist. I draw sketches ... I'm a Realist. If you like, I can show you my work ...'

'We don't need your works. Go on, speak.'

'What am I supposed to talk about? I wasn't planning on speaking ...'

'Well, since you're here, then talk.'

'Maybe I could read some poems?'

'What poems?'

'Majakovski ...'

With this the hall dissolved into hysterical laughter, the nervous tension passing all endurance. The scene was becoming surreal.

Khrushchev: 'It doesn't matter, off you go.'

Galitsin started to leave and then suddenly turned around: 'Can I still work?'

Khrushchev: 'Yes, you can ...'

Several years would pass, and nursing his pension, having been ousted from all his posts, Khrushchev was to remember his 'meetings with the intelligentsia' with sorrow, saying, as if in apology to all those he once insulted and hurt: 'Why did I stick my nose into that business, that I knew nothing about? They provoked me and I waded right in. I shouldn't have done that.' He became emotional to the point of tears when Ernst Neizvestni, once berated and insulted by him, sent him Dostoyevsky's *Crime and Punishment* as a present, complete with his own illustrations. And when Khrushchev passed away, his relatives turned to Ernst, asking that he make the tombstone. Ernst agreed under one condition: he would make it as he saw fit, and no one should have the right to interfere. As the sculptor himself put it: 'While he lived, the deceased spoiled several years of my life, now he's going to do it after death as well, but I'll do the job, I want to myself. He is worth it.' This tombstone stands above Khrushchev's grave to this day.

A number of years later, meeting Ernst in New York, to where he emigrated at beginning of the 1970s, I once asked him in friendly conversation: 'Why did you leave Russia? What did you lack there? Money? Fame?' 'Well, no ...' Ernst replied, pondering '... I had far more of that than I do here. It's all rubbish. You see, when I first came face to face with our government, when I saw the Neanderthal-like nature of the people who ruled us ... I was sickened. I simply couldn't tolerate that.'

In 1964 Khrushchev turned seventy. Notwithstanding his ripe age, he remained hale and active. A rowdy celebratory dinner was held at the Kremlin. The papers were full of his portraits. During official functions, he was praised in almost exactly the same phrases as Stalin was once venerated, although the words 'magnificent' and 'genius' were avoided. There were no signs of any changes. The head of state remained busy: space rocket launches, arguments about matters of agriculture, journeys around the country and the world ... During almost nine months of the year so far, he had already spent 135 days on the road. Now, at the end of September, he was going to travel down to Baikanur, the secret space station in Kazakhstan – where tests of new types of rockets were scheduled, and then as usual onward to the Black Sea for a holiday.

Then came the unexpected turn of events, both for Khrushchev and for the country.

'The call on the government line came on a day that father was away at the space station,' Khrushchev's son Sergei remembers. 'An unfamiliar voice asked to speak to Khrushchev. It was strange, since everyone who had the rank to have access to the government line knew that Khrushchev wasn't in Moscow. It turned out that the caller was a KGB operative of middling rank, who wanted to pass on something extremely important. He had spent a lot of time trying to get to the line, which would only connect directly to Khrushchev. At that moment, he had seized an opportunity when his boss, who had access to the line, stepped out of the office. Such an opportunity might not come again.'

The man sounded worried, and asked Sergei Khrushchev to meet him. The meeting took place in a forest outside Moscow. What the caller had to say seemed highly unlikely and sounded like detective fiction. According to him, a conspiracy had long been hatching around Nikita Khrushchev, headed by Brezhnev and several other people from Khrushchev's closest circle. In other words, those same colleagues whom Khrushchev had personally plucked from anonymity to the pinnacle of power, and considered 'his people'. (He forgot a simple truth, 'Only your own people can betray you.')

Neither Sergei Khrushchev nor his confidant could at that moment even imagine that, beginning with their first telephone chat on the government line and ending with their conversation in the forest, their every word was being recorded on tape and would find its way to the desk of the KGB Minister, also a participant in the conspiracy. Nor did they know that Khrushchev's eldest daughter had received similar information but did not believe it and paid it no attention.

Khrushchev returned a few days later. His son's tale didn't make a huge impression on him. He simply refused to believe it. Moreover, asking whether it was true or not, he turned to the very same people who were suspected of the conspiracy. Was it some kind of childlike innocence, or elementary stupidity? You cannot really accuse Khrushchev of either of these. Most likely, his son-in-law thinks, he was beginning to suspect a conspiracy himself but did not want to believe it. If he wanted to act in the spirit of Stalin, he had to isolate everyone at the first rumour of conspiracy, not discriminating between guilty and innocent. He did not, however, wish to take such a step.

A few days later Khrushchev flew to the Black Sea for his holiday. On 12 October, a craft with three cosmonauts on board was due to be launched into orbit. Khrushchev knew the time of the launch and now, sitting at the pool, kept checking his watch. The rules were that immediately after the launch he would get a call and be briefed on how it had gone. Khrushchev adored these moments. He thought of the space programme as his baby, and carefully monitored every event that took place. And now, knowing that the launch had already taken place, he glanced impatiently at the telephone, awaiting news. But the telephone remained silent. Twenty minutes went by, then thirty, then forty ... It seemed they had forgotten about Khrushchev. Such a thing had never happened before. Finally, Khrushchev could stand it no longer and picked up the receiver himself. He was connected quickly, but instead of making excuses, the high-ranking Kremlin clerk at the other end of the line, who was obliged to brief Khrushchev about the launch, made a lacklustre apology, explaining that he was busy. Nor did he react to Khrushchev's explosion of anger with the appropriate amount of fear, which was also strange ...

A short time later Khrushchev was informed that in a few minutes his planned conversation with the cosmonauts would go ahead. 'Father loved these telephone conversations with the cosmonauts,' Sergei Khrushchev writes: 'With a childlike wonder, he was in awe of the technology that allowed him to get in touch with a spacecraft so easily, from his dacha office.'

After the conversation with the cosmonauts, Khrushchev and Anastas Mikoyan, who was resting at a neighbouring dacha, went for a walk along the beach. Khrushchev was tied to Mikoyan not only by old friendship, but also by a certain commonality of fate. They had both spent many years in Stalin's closest circle, often fearing for their lives, and both had turned out to be political survivors.

The walk was interrupted by the officer on duty, who announced that Brezhnev was calling from the Kremlin and asking Khrushchev to the phone. The conversation was strange and unexpected. Notwithstanding the fact that Khrushchev had only left for his holiday a week ago, Brezhnev asked him to come to Moscow the next day since, as he said, it was imperative to settle some questions regarding agriculture. Despite Khrushchev's disgruntled tones, Brezhnev continued to insist and, as Khrushchev later put it, his voice was almost hysterical. Remembering how the conspirators tried to get the cowardly Brezhnev to call Khrushchev, the then KGB Minister wrote: 'We barely convinced him, and had to almost drag him to the phone by force. In a trembling voice, Brezhnev told Khrushchev that there was a meeting tomorrow. In the end Khrushchev agreed: "All right ..." he said irritably. "Send the plane."'

Continuing his walk along the beach folowing the phone conversation, after a long silence Khrushchev suddenly told Mikoyan: 'You know, Anastas, they don't have any urgent agricultural matters. I think that call was connected with what Sergei was talking about.'

The night passed restlessly. The KGB coastguard were acting unusually. It seemed that they were blockading the dacha from the sea, as if they were afraid that Khrushchev might escape by swimming to Turkey.

Usually, every time Khrushchev departed or arrived at Moscow, he was seen off and greeted by all the members of the government at the airport. And although they could sense that he enjoyed it, he nevertheless grumbled about it: 'And why are you lot all here, as if I won't find the way without you ...'

This time, only two people were at the airport to meet him, the Minister of the KGB and the head of his personal guard. In response to Khrushchev's query, 'Where are the others?' the minister replied, 'Everyone is in the Kremlin, waiting for you.' Now at last, disembarking from the plane, neither Khrushchev nor Mikoyan, who flew in with him, could doubt any longer that the conversation in the Kremlin would have nothing to do with agriculture. Everything became clear, everything fell into place.

Those most enthusiastic of sycophants, who only yesterday had obsequiously sung his praises, now yelled out viciously from the hall: 'Put him on trial!' Khrushchev was accused of all the mortal sins. Some of the accusations were fair, others were petty and contrived; but this was not the most vital thing. He was not being deposed by people concerned about the good of the country, but by yet another clique, lusting for power.

Khrushchev was crushed, isolated, powerless to make any counter-move. 'I understand that this is to be my last political speech,' he said, 'but I would like to turn to the Party with a request ...' 'You will do no such thing!' Brezhnev cut him off roughly. 'It seems that things will now be done as you see fit,' Khrushchev replied, tears welling up in his eyes. 'Well, why not? I am ready for anything. I ask that my resignation be drafted, and I'll sign it. If you need me to, I'll leave Moscow ...'

In a sense, this was Khrushchev's second 'finest hour'. Only ten years ago, it would have been inconceivable that Stalin's heir could be deposed in such a bloodless fashion. Returning home, Khrushchev would say: 'Well there you go, I'm now retired. Perhaps the most important thing out of everything I've done, can be summed up by the fact that they could depose me with a simple vote, when Stalin would have arrested the lot of them'

Mikoyan came over that evening. The new power sent him to tell Khrushchev that he would be left the dacha, the flat in Moscow, his car and his pension. His attendants and guards would also stay, but the people would be changed. That was all. There was nothing else to say. Mikoyan stood up and headed for the door, then he stopped and they embraced. They would never meet again, even though they continued to live next door to each other. Those were the unwritten Kremlin laws of political self-preservation.

At first Khrushchev was in a state of shock. He would sit in his armchair at the dacha for hours, his eyes periodically filling with tears. When a teacher in school asked his grandson what his grandfather was doing, the boy replied: 'Grandfather is crying.'

The first two years of retirement were especially hard, but as time went on he grieved less and less for his lost power. His active nature asserted itself. He soon busied himself in the garden, and started to grow some kind of special tomatoes, each weighing around a kilogram. He would get up at four in the morning, water them, and fork the rows. He started to listen to foreign Russian-language radio stations. Sometimes he and his wife would travel to Moscow, to wander the streets or go to the theatre.

Almost none of his former colleagues ever visited him again. Instead, he was visited by those same intellectuals – poets, artists, writers – at whom he had once stamped his feet. This touched Khrushchev deeply, and he honestly regretted what had happened in the past.

He busied himself with the reading of classical literature, and discovered that art was not such a useless endeavour. He liked to wander through the fields, to talk to the peasants about the harvest, and they always treated him warmly. Peasants from another region once came to visit a neighbouring village. Having found out that Khrushchev's dacha was nearby, they decided to visit him. One old peasant put a crate up against the fence, clambered up on to it and looked over the fence. Khrushchev was fussing about in the garden at the time.

'Nikita, they ain't mistreatin' you here, are they?' the old man asked. 'No, no'. Khrushchev replied. Perhaps the attitude of the simple folk towards him could be summed up in this guileless 'they ain't mistreatin' you?'

Early in 1971 Khrushchev's memoirs were published in the West. On his son's advice, in extreme secrecy, he been dictating these on to tape over the past few years. The new rulers were enraged. Khrushchev was summoned to the very top. They threatened him, demanding that he write a retraction explaining that it was a fake, that he had not written any memoirs and was not planning to write any. Khrushchev refused.

'You're living too well!' one of the new Kremlin bosses yelled at him. 'By all means, arrest me, have me shot ...' replied Khrushchev. 'I've had enough of life ... Today the radio said De Gaulle had died, I'm envious of him. You can take away my dacha and pension. I will walk the land with my hand outstretched and people will help me, but you they never will ...'

It was said that just before his death, already on his way to the next world, his last request to his wife was to go to the market and bring back some pickled cucumbers ...

10 | A CULT WITHOUT PERSONALITY

DURING THE RULE OF LEONID BREZHNEV, a particular anecdote was going around the country: Stalin, Khrushchev and Brezhnev are sitting in the sleeper of a train called 'Communism', a train which seems utterly unable to move. 'Execute everyone!' Stalin orders. The executions are carried out, but the train refuses to budge. Stalin dies. 'Rehabilitate everyone!' Khrushchev orders. Everyone is rehabilitated, but the train still refuses to move. Khrushchev is deposed. 'Close the blinds on all the windows, and act as if we are moving!' orders Brezhnev.

This joke reflects the character of Brezhnev himself and that of his time. Hegel once said that history has a tendency to repeat itself. Farce comes to replace tragedy. The personification of this farce was Brezhnev himself. He possessed neither the ruthlessness of Stalin, nor the boundless energy of Khrushchev, but there was nevertheless something within him that allowed him to rule the Kremlin for eighteen years.

Leonid Brezhnev was born to a family of metal-workers. His father was a steel-founder, as was his grandfather Jacob. Leonid was born in the Ukraine in the town of Kamenskoye (later known as Dneprodzerzhinsk) on 19 December 1906. The town where he was born numbered 25,000 residents at the time, all of them connected in one way or another to the large metallurgical factory located there.

By the standards of the time, the Brezhnev family lived in relative plenty, although they resided in a primitive clay-brick house. This was the house that Leonid was born in, followed by his younger brother and sister. Their father spent most of his time at the factory, so raising the children was left to the mother. She was a quiet, modest woman, preserving these traits for the entirety of her long ninety-year life. Even when Brezhnev became an important government official, his mother still lived in her home town, in a small one-bedroom flat, refusing to move to Moscow. According to her neighbours, her life differed little from those of people around her. Like them, she would queue hours on end for food, and spent her evenings on a bench near her house, discussing the news of the town with her neighbours. Only when Brezhnev became leader of the country would she – against her wishes – move to Moscow.

In 1915 Brezhnev attended the only male private school in the town. Education here was not cheap. Of all the students, Leonid was the only one from a working-class family, so one must assume his parents were trying to give their son the best schooling, although this was not an easy financial burden for them. Leonid attended the school for three years, after which the Revolution started, followed by civil war, famine and ruin. Typhoid was rampant, a virulent strain of which the fourteen-year-old Leonid endured. The private school was closed, and he was compelled to attend a public one. Such were the times that not only the students, but the principal of the school as well, attended classes barefoot.

In 1921 Leonid began his working life. At first he worked in a dairy in the city of Kursk, and then became an apprentice metal-craftsman. In 1927 he learned to be a surveyor and travelled to the Urals to work. Earlier however, at a social gathering he had met his future wife Victoria. Victoria Brezhnev, whose maiden name was Denisov, was born to a Russian family in Kursk (later, rumours were that she was Jewish, which would sometimes give rise to strange situations. Once, arriving in Paris with her husband, she was be greeted by a crowd of Jews carrying placards such as 'Help Free Your People'.) Her father was an engine-driver. 'There were five kids in the family ...' Victoria recalled. 'I finished school and went to study midwifery at Medical Technical School. Leonid and I met at a dance ... He didn't know how to dance. I taught him. It all started from the dances ...' According to his wife, Leonid was very dashing in his youth – alert, active and cheerful. He would date her with flowers, and loved poetry. He was never a puritan, and paid a great deal of attention to the ladies. Life had its ups and downs, but his wife's calm and patient nature, coupled with Brezhnev's attachment to his family, always won out in the end. All in all, they lived happily together for more than half a century.

Many people only remember Brezhnev as he was during the last period of his rule, when he was already a shattered, sick old man mumbling incomprehensibly and clearly feeble-minded. But that was towards the end of his life. Even during his sixties, according to the memoirs of the German Chancellor Willy Brandt, Brezhnev '... notwithstanding his heavy-set physique, appeared to be an elegant, energetic and happy person.'

In 1931 Brezhnev returned to the Ukraine from the Urals, to his home town, and attended night-classes in the Metallurgical Institute. This is where his Party career began. At first he was chosen as the Party representative of the faculty, and then the whole institute. In 1935 he graduated with high distinction and was drafted into the army, where he served as political commissar of a tank company. His army service did not last long, however; a year later he was home again.

This was a time of Stalinist terror, when hundreds of thousands of people – including members of the Bolshevik Party – found themselves in the basements of the NKVD (KGB). Positions were suddenly becoming vacant. By the middle of 1937 Brezhnev was already a leading functionary in his town. It must be pointed out, however, that there is no evidence that Brezhnev in any way participated in the bloody bacchanalia of Stalin's purges. On the contrary, everyone who knew him at the time remember him as a good-natured and pleasant man with a lot of friends.

It was Lazar Kaganovich who, just as he had done for Khrushchev, helped Brezhnev to a high-placed Party career. Kaganovich was the leader of Ukraine's Bolsheviks, and in 1938 Khrushchev succeeded him in this post. This initiated Khrushchev's acquaintance with Brezhnev, who subsequently became 'Khrushchev's man'.

Leonid Brezhnev spent the Second World War in the Red Army, as a political commissar, ending up as a major-general. If one were to judge by his forty-eight-page booklet *Small Land*, which concerned those areas of the southern front where he fought, one might draw the conclusion that it was he – Leonid Brezhnev – who had been the main organiser of every victory. Indeed, while he ruled the country it was well-nigh the duty of all major military figures to mention the extraordinary talents of Major-General Brezhnev in their memoirs of the Second World War. It reached the point of absurdity. Thus, in the first edition of his memoirs, Marshal Zhukov – who was second to the Supreme Commander (Stalin) during the war – wrote of having paid a special visit to the division where the political commissar was the then Colonel Brezhnev, to ask his advice. Unfortunately, the colonel was then occupied at the front line.

Naturally, these are all fabrications. Brezhnev finished the war a little-known officer with very few awards compared to others of the period. He never participated in real combat. All his military duties were limited to keeping records of Party members among the soldiers and officers, conducting political discussions with them and presenting them with government medals. The officers called him 'Leo our Politboss' behind his back, and treated him like a good-natured simpleton.

Actually, Brezhnev had once been crossing the Black Sea in a sloop when the vessel hit a mine, and the colonel was thrown overboard. He was unconscious when sailors rescued him. That was as near heroism as he ever came, although one of his later biographers mentions that he was once forced to fire a machine-gun at the enemy. Thirty years later this brave deed was celebrated with an obelisk erected at the site, although in fact no witnesses to this act of heroism turned up, suggesting that it too originated in the realm of fantasy.

The famous Russian documentary film-director Roman Carmen told me once, in the mid-1960s, Brezhnev called him one evening. The leader was strongly under the influence, and asked Carmen to listen to a poem about the war he had allegedly just written. The poem was poor, but Carmen naturally praised it. The conversation turned to the topic of the war. Carmen reminisced about the 'Small Land' where Brezhnev fought, and by-the-by recalled how he still remembered him from back in those days. Brezhnev laughed: 'Why are you bull-shitting? I remember *you*, not you me. You were already famous back then, the whole country knew you, I was simply a faceless colonel. How could you have known me?'

After the war Brezhnev returned to the Ukraine, to his native land and – not without Khrushchev's patronship – became the Party head, first of the town of Zaporozhye, and then the city of Dnepropetrovsk. The distinguished historian Roy Medvedev writes that while working in these cities, 'Brezhnev showed himself to be not so much a capable leader as he was a calm one. His gentleness, the absence of the harshness and even callousness which was the norm for Party bosses of the period, attracted many to him ...' Hence the places where Brezhnev held sway 'could seem to be islands of liberalism and relative calm.'

In 1949 Stalin recalled Khrushchev from the Ukraine and sent him back to Moscow. The leader asked Khrushchev who he considered they should send to be head of the young Party organisation in Moldavia, the new republic formed just before the war. Khrushchev offered Brezhnev. Stalin agreed. So, in 1950 Brezhnev moved to the city of Kishinev, the capital of Moldavia. He liked the new post, and often travelled to Moscow, attending government functions there and 'being seen'. Large, well-proportioned, dark-browed, always dressed unassumingly but with careful attention to the latest fashions, the forty-six-year-old Brezhnev became the most dapper of all his Party colleagues. Even Stalin noticed him once at a function, asking curiously who he was. When he was told that this was the Party representative of Moldavia, the ageing leader good-humouredly exclaimed: 'What a handsome Moldavian.' It was a remark that did his prospects no harm at the time.

Everything was going well for Brezhnev. The only disappointment was his unruly daughter Galina, who at the time was a philology student at the University of Kishinev. Fellow students remembered how her father occasionally came to the university and asked them to do something about getting her to take more interest in her studies and her social life. A travelling circus then arrived in Kishinev. Galina began to attend its performances regularly, and when the circus left Galina disappeared as well. She became involved with a young acrobat, who became her first husband. She only returned home a year later, with a young daughter in her arms, the care of whom was taken on by her grandmother. Galina separated from her acrobat, but not from the circus, with which she was to maintain a close relationship for many years to come.

On 7 November 1952, the day of the thirty-fifth anniversary of the Bolshevik Revolution, Brezhnev mounted the podium of the Lenin Mausoleum for the first time. This occurred quite unexpectedly. At this stage Stalin was already frightened at the prospect of a conspiracy led by Beria. He decided to rid himself of his closest circle, which was becoming dangerous. The first step in this direction was to 'change the guard' by diluting the strength of the highest organ of the Party – the Politburo – filling it with new, relatively young members, for the moment slavishly devoted to himself. Stalin believed this would allow him to distance his old comrades with a minimum of risk, and perhaps even send them to the KGB basements.

Whether the leader himself remembered the 'handsome Moldavian', or whether Khrushchev reminded him, Brezhnev's name was unexpectedly listed among the new members of the Kremlin's top leadership.

Stalin's plans were not destined to be fulfilled, since the clock of his life was already counting down the final minutes. In four months he was gone, and two days after his death, his old comrades restored their unassailable positions, scattering the new contenders. All that changed in Brezhnev's life over these four months was that he moved to Moscow and received a comfortable flat and a government dacha.

All in all, it must be said that Brezhnev was certainly fate's spoilt child. Not a single bullet touched him during the war, and away from the front lines every single one of Stalin's purges passed him by – an exceedingly rare fact, considering his position at the time. Nor did the path to the top require any extraordinary effort on his part. High-ranking posts tumbled his way like overripe pears. The only serious 'political' act – if it could be called that – which involved him was the removal of Khrushchev. In this act as well, however, he was more an extra in another's game. Nevertheless, apart from the favours of fate, his personal qualities played a not insignificant role in his success: his good nature, his complaisance, his ability to compromise, and to some degree even his liking for people, in no way hindered his career.

After the death of Stalin, and the successful operation to liquidate Beria, Khrushchev did not forget about Brezhnev, and was merely waiting for the opportunity to use him to strengthen his team. In 1954, the latest bright idea of the volatile Khrushchev centred around the once-barren lands of Kazakhstan. Having cultivated these regions which had lain barren for centuries, and having produced millions of tons of bread, Khrushchev imagined it would not only be possible to match and surpass America in living standards, but also to ride gallantly into Communism like a conquering general on a white horse.

He appointed Brezhnev as the assistant to and later the Party head of Kazakhstan. In Brezhnev's trilogy (*Rebirth, Virgin Soil* and *Small Land*) the year and a half spent in Kazakhstan are described as the most intense of his life. He was never compelled to work harder, before or after this period – especially considering that he had to work under the bubbling pressure of Khrushchev, for whom these virgin lands were a favourite brainchild. Khrushchev not only followed events there daily, but would make lightning tours of these steppelands, choking on dust and expecting his retinue to do the same.

This was clearly not Brezhnev's milieu. He liked calm, clean work – work that could be done in a well-ironed suit, to chat with a visitor, smoke a good American cigarette, tell a fresh anecdote and not get bogged down with business. As a KGB minister later recalled, 'When I went to report to Khrushchev, I prepared meticulously. I knew that the most unexpected questions could come up ... Going to Brezhnev on the other hand, one could not prepare at all, just tell a few jokes, have a laugh, and that would be the whole report.' When there were no visitors Brezhnev would even be lonely in his office, sticking his head out from time to time to ask his secretary, 'Aren't there any more appointments?' In other words, Brezhnev was pining to leave the dust of Asia and return to Moscow, as he had already hinted at more than once to his benefactor.

By this stage Khrushchev was gripped by a new idea: space. In 1956 he returned Brezhnev to Moscow and made him his assistant in the Department of Defence and Space. In times to come, writing in his trilogy about the virgin lands and about space – after the removal of Khrushchev – Brezhnev would not mention a single word about him. Khrushchev's name was expunged from every publication. His image was even removed from film-archive reels, so that after re-editing it would appear that Yuri Gagarin and other cosmonauts – who usually celebrated the successful completion of each mission together with Khrushchev – were now standing on the podium above

Lenin's Mausoleum and reporting their triumph to an empty space. This was all done to create the impression that the organiser of these famous achievements was none other than Leonid Brezhnev.

In 1960 Khrushchev pensioned off one of his oldest Politburo colleagues, Stalin's close friend Marshal Voroshilov, who had at the time occupied the apparently prestigious, but actually lightweight and ceremonial, post of head of Parliament. An important position was vacated, and Khrushchev presented it to Brezhnev, who now received what he could only have dreamed of. Now he could preside over banquets, shake the hands of important personages and frequently travel abroad where, according to protocol, he was welcomed as the formal head of state. The German magazine *Spiegel* even called him 'the most elegant Soviet leader'.

This post was the most Brezhnev could have ever wanted. He had never craved for more. Everything would have been wonderful if Khrushchev had not expressed inordinate concern about his protégé. Considering Brezhnev utterly loyal, Khrushchev made him his Deputy Party Leader in 1963. Although this appointment was a significant step up the hierarchy, it disappointed rather than pleased Brezhnev. This position was one of real power, but it also required real work, especially since it required him to be constantly under Khrushchev's eye. As a colleague of Brezhnev's later told, having had a drink he could even squeeze out a tear and complain about the insensitivity of Khrushchev, who occasionally called him a loafer.

It was 1964. Khrushchev's popularity was already significantly shaken. It was exactly at this time that an anti-Khrushchev conspiracy was hatched within the Kremlin leadership. Was Brezhnev the organiser of this conspiracy? Opinions differ on this. Some people, well versed in life within the 'corridors of the Kremlin', doubt it. They maintain that although Brezhnev formally took part in the conspiracy, he was in no way its inspiration or organiser; he lacked the energy and courage for this. As mentioned in the previous chapter, when Brezhnev had to call Khrushchev in the south, to summon him to a meeting in the Kremlin where his removal was being prepared, he almost fainted with fright and had to be forcibly hustled to the phone. And when he was informed that Khrushchev's son had told his father something about the plot, Brezhnev seemed paralysed. Rushing into his friend's office, he started to whisper, 'It's all ruined. Khrushchev knows everything … you don't know him well, he'll have us all shot.'

Nevertheless, on 13–14 October 1964, a bloodless coup took place in the Kremlin. Khrushchev was removed and his place taken by the fifty-eight-year old Brezhnev. For a while he appeared overjoyed, arranging lavish royal banquets in the Kremlin for his colleagues and friends. As a sign of gratitude to Khrushchev for not resisting, he allowed the former leader to keep his Party privileges: the dacha, the flat, the car, the pension, although some of the conspirators – in accord with Stalinist tradition – demanded more severe retribution. Incidentally, during all the subsequent years of his leadership, Brezhnev not only never once visited his former patron, he did not even call him.

How could it have occurred that a person possessing neither a strong will, nor energy, nor courage, not to mention extraordinary intelligence and erudition – in short, displaying none of the qualities necessary in the leader of a country – nonetheless managed to occupy this position? In fact, such cases are not all that rare. By and large, during his initial rise to power, even Stalin was surrounded by people far worthier of the mantle of leader, yet history nevertheless chose him specifically.

Something similar happened with Brezhnev. Those who were the real soul of the conspiracy watched one another warily. Brezhnev was the ideal compromise for them, not posing any kind of threat. Lighthearted and good-natured, not endowed with exceptional intelligence, a good drinking companion, even if he did not enjoy a great deal of influence with the Party machine, that machine treated him with condescending goodwill. Besides, he was Khrushchev's official Party deputy, thus his succession looked legal and democratic. In short, he was the ideal figure for a transitional period.

Brezhnev's tolerant nature is illustrated by a personal recollection. Back in 1963 or 1964, when I was still a student at the film institute, I attended a government banquet Khrushchev had organised for the President of Indonesia, Dr Sukarno. Sukarno was a movie buff and knew the film stars very well. Noticing the famous film actress Tatiana Samoilova, he invited her to sit beside him. He produced a packet of dark cigarettes which were unfamiliar to us and offered one to everyone. Samoilova lit up with pleasure and began to examine the cigarette. At this point, a dark-haired man sitting opposite us remarked – in a didactic tone – to Samoilova: 'I wouldn't recommend you smoke. Smoking spoils the complexion. You're an actress, complexion is very important for you.' Tatiana looked at him in silence, stubbed out her cigarette theatrically in an ashtray, and answered coldly: 'If a member of the government advises me not to smoke, then I won't smoke, but if you were a gentleman to boot, you'd refrain from criticising a lady.' A silence ensued, and then, to give him his due, the man who had rebuked her apologised and turned it all into a joke. He was Leonid Brezhnev. He never took his revenge against

Samoilova or caused her any trouble. One can only imagine how someone from Stalin's retinue would have reacted.

No one, even Western politicians, doubted that Brezhnev was a temporary, transitional figure. Time went by, however, and he remained in power. At first Brezhnev lacked confidence in his lofty post. He made few job changes, treated everyone courteously and went out of his way to please people. Trying to portray himself as the energetic worker, he showed up to work early and stayed late. This did not last long, and soon his working day began at ten and then at eleven o'clock.

More than sitting in his office, he enjoyed American cowboy movies, which he would watch after friendly meals at dachas, with tasty food, good cognac, pretty women and anecdotes, which he loved to tell. He knew exactly how to show his gratitude to the young women who spent time with him. The then mayor of Moscow would later describe how he would often get a call from Brezhnev's 'adjutant' Constantine Chernenko, who would order him to receive so-and-so and 'settle the matter'. In other words, arrange a flat for her in Moscow.

Brezhnev's main love, however, was certainly hunting in the government reservations. He was almost a professional hunter. He loved to shoot big game: boar, elk and so forth, and then with more than a touch of pride, generously to give away their carcasses, sending them by special courier to his friends or to Soviet ambassadors overseas. Even towards the end of his life, when feebleness prevented him from hunting, when the recoil of a rifle would tear it out of his hands, often bloodying his nose, forehead and face, even then Brezhnev did not abandon the sport, albeit in a different form. He would command his huntsmen, indicating what they should do and allowing them to take the shots. The last such excursion took place a day before his death. He even awarded his main huntsman the rank of general.

In the cultural sphere, however, matters were not quite so rosy. Brezhnev would only visit the theatre out of extreme necessity, and he did not read books at all. Even more did he hate writing. Others naturally prepared his speeches; he did not touch them himself. Long words were especially difficult for him, hence the speech-writers were commanded not to use long words. Yet in the last years of his rule, he could still read a speech, phrase by phrase, and with a great deal of stammering, not deviating from the text one iota.

The intellectual quality of this leader of the superpower may be judged to some extent by the short notes contained in his diaries: 'In the morning I shaved, washed my hair and had a haircut ... Watched "Red Army" football team lose to "Spartak" (good lads, they played well) ... Got suits fitted. Continued the teeth cleaning ... Had a crack at dominoes. Breakfast – shaving – swimming. Fell asleep on top of the swing on the beach ... Washed my hair with baby-soap ... We killed thirty four geese ... Ate borscht ... Went to the circus ...' One could quote more of these pearls, but what is the point? A wise man once said that you can judge a person by a few lines they have jotted down.

Nevertheless, the first few years at the summit of power had already taught Brezhnev a great deal. At least he understood the simple truth that 'only your closest can betray you' faster than Khrushchev. Those who had recently been putting Brezhnev forward, counting on his simplicity and meekness, began to disappear from the highest echelons of power. No, they did not vanish into darkness, as they would have done under Stalin, they were merely sent on 'honourable pensions' or made ambassadors in countries far from Moscow.

No original minds or young contenders could be allowed next to the 'First' man of the nation. It was his right to be first in everything. So, if while out hunting, someone in the party shot more game than the 'First', moreover if God forbid they drunkenly bragged about it at the dinner table, then a short time later they could find themselves the Party boss in a far-flung province. Brezhnev could, for instance, tell an old friend who had disagreed with him over some trifle: 'You don't contradict me in front of people. I'm the First. Stalin himself sat in this office. When everyone leaves, then you can say what you wanted to say ...'

With people who presented no threat to him, Brezhnev was still personable and good-natured. The Party bureaucracy saw in him not only their own man, but their benefactor as well. Where Khrushchev upset their calm lives with his boundless energy and constant reforms, Brezhnev was quite the opposite, returning many privileges they had lost under Khrushchev. His trips around the country were usually accompanied by festive banquets, from which the head of the nation was often led away completely drunk. Provincial Party bosses greeted him far more happily than they had Khrushchev. There was good reason. Khrushchev would come as the auditor, while Brezhnev came as the 'kind monarch'. At one dinner in Minsk in 1968 he announced: 'Dear Comrades! It's time I moved on. I'd sit with you, I love good company, but work, what can you do? You drink, comrades, drink, and keep an eye on your neighbour to make sure they drink to the very bottom. Otherwise people pour drinks and don't drink them. What is the good of that, I ask you? It's not good for anything ...'

It is well known that power spoils a person, but absolute power spoils them completely. Having occupied a post for which he was clearly ill-equipped, Brezhnev naturally suffered from an inferiority complex. This in turn gave rise to a pathological envy of everyone who outstripped him in anything at all. To suppress these feelings, he required the constant sycophancy of those around him and an external shell of glamour, giving the appearance of power. Towards the end of his life Brezhnev had more medals and awards than Stalin and Khrushchev combined. The people joked: that Brezhnev had an operation to expand his chest, otherwise there would be no room for more medals.

On an anniversary of the victory over Germany, Brezhnev awarded himself the rank of marshal. Arriving afterwards at a meeting with members of his former regiment, he flamboyantly commanded: 'Attention! Marshal coming through!' Throwing back his cloak and lovingly stroking his new marshal's stars he added: 'There you go. I served out my dues.'

In 1981, a gigantic memorial complex commemorating the Second World War was opened in Kiev. The names of the twelve thousand heroes of the war were carved out on massive marble tablets. Heading this list was the name of the four-times hero Leonid Brezhnev. Stalin's name was hard to find, it had got lost somewhere near the bottom.

It goes without saying that all this earned concealed condescension from the public. A joke went around, which simultaneously poked fun at the leader's vanity and his misuse of words: 'When will Brezhnev attain the rank of Generalissimo? When he learns to pronounce it.'

Brezhnev's pathological vanity sometimes even exerted an influence on world affairs. In 1968 the famous 'Prague Spring' began. Czechoslovakia was a bubbling cauldron. People called for social and political reform, a complete break from the remnants of Stalinism. They demanded freedom for themselves and their country.

What was to be done, send in the army or not? Brezhnev was wracked by indecision, and for a while it seemed that he was disinclined to take action. Then the 'hawks' in his circle collected in one folder all the caricatures of him which flooded the Czechoslovak press, plus a number of less than complimentary articles, and slipped the whole lot to their arrogant leader. This thoroughly upset him, and overcame his indecision. The tanks moved in.

It is hard to overestimate the moral and material cost to the Soviet Union of this course of action. The incensed Czech population poured out their fury on the occupiers. People tore down street-signs, to hinder the movement of military hardware and even dug up the roads. In desperation, some threw themselves under tank tracks. In the cities and villages, soldiers were not only refused food, but even glasses of water. They were not permitted to use toilets. Radio-buffs jammed the airways of military frequencies. It was rumoured that there were even a few suicides among the deceived Soviet soldiers, who had been told they were simply going on a training exercise.

Let us return, however, to Brezhnev the man, the 'figure without the mask'. Broadly speaking, the mask fulfilled a role contrary to that for which it was intended. When he donned it, wishing to appear significant, he looked clownishly foolish. When he took it off, on the other hand, he could be charming. The US Secretary of State Henry Kissinger describes his visit to Moscow:

> Brezhnev came to my residence soon after my arrival and greeted me boisterously. He invited my colleagues and me to his villa, which he presented with the pride of a businessman who had traversed the road from shoe-shiner to millionaire. He asked me how much would all this cost in the US. I incorrectly and foolishly proposed a sum of four hundred thousand dollars. Brezhnev's face drooped. My aide, a more experienced psychologist, corrected: 'Two million,' he said ... Brezhnev's spirits were restored, and he continued the excursion glowing with pride.

In the official atmosphere of the Kremlin's ceremonial functions, especially in the period not long after his rise to power, Brezhnev astonished those around him with his rigidity and stolidity. It seemed he felt his inadequacy for the role he played, with every fibre of his being. When the circumstances were not so official, however, everything changed abruptly. Here he was friendly and eccentric, ready to slap his questioner on the shoulder like 'one of the lads'. Incidentally, it is said that he got his habit of shoulder-slapping from US President Gerald Ford, when they met in Vladivostok. Ford had expressed his affection and high spirits by robustly slapping Henry Kissinger on the shoulder, to the utter delight of Brezhnev.

It was precisely due to his shyness in official settings that Brezhnev tried to arrange his functions outside the Kremlin when possible, at his dacha, in a hunting reservation or on a yacht in the Black Sea. Here he was the noisy and welcoming host, loving to pull faces, chatter away and tell jokes like many southerners. Richard Nixon remembered: 'His escapades made him the centre of attention. His actions and humour were almost mischievous. As much as possible, I acted as his partner in such situations. Sometimes however, I found it hard to maintain a balance between politeness and dignity.'

In his private life, Brezhnev was open, cheerful and sentimental. He maintained his ties to old friends, often inviting them to visit him or going to see them, and tried not to create any distance between them and himself. He demanded that he simply be called Leon, as in times gone by. It was easy to gain his sympathy. At such moments he was even ready to help, and actually did help, people he did not know well. His sentimentality sometimes proved positive. For instance, while once watching a film, which was not allowed to be released on ideological grounds, Brezhnev suddenly shed a tear, remembering his wartime years. It goes without saying that these tears instantly decided the film's fate.

It would be naïve, however, to over-emphasise this bluff kindness and sentimentality. In matters of ideology he was very unyielding. As one journalist put it, this was a man with a steel jaw and iron fists, but in kid gloves. It was under his regime that the 'witch-hunts' gathered full steam. The writers Sinyavsky and Daniel ended up in prison for the publication of their works abroad. Solzhenitsyn was hounded out of the country. Unprecedented in its foolishness, the persecution of the academician Andrei Sakharov – one of the leading scientists of his time – ended in his indefinite exile in the town of Gorky, a place closed to foreigners. The Mordov camps in the Urals filled up with 'dissidents' and other 'scum', as Brezhnev himself put it. People were incarcerated in mental homes after a diagnosis that would perplex modern medicine: 'schizophrenia manifest as nonconformity'. Russians described this period as the 'freeze', as opposed to Khrushchev's 'thaw'.

Thus passed the first half of Brezhnev's leadership, until around the mid-1970s. Then, as his adviser Alexander Bovin wrote: 'Brezhnev began to fall apart, to fall apart as an individual ...' A huge Mafia web grew up around him, drawing in not only his immediate circle, but also his closest relatives. He began to accept personal gifts such as gold ornaments, jewellery and other expensive items from regional Party bosses trying to curry favour. For example, for his seventieth birthday he was given a bust of himself made out of pure gold, and from Siberia he was sent a vase manufactured from mammoth tusk, encrusted with diamonds. Incidentally, the same sycophants who gave him all this took it all back again from his family after Brezhnev's death. People close to the family say that Brezhnev's wife handed them over wordlessly, even with a sense of relief.

His private collection contained several hundred magnificently encrusted, hand-made hunting rifles, and dozens of luxury cars. Cars were his passion. Knowing about this, Western leaders virtually competed in trying to give him the best one. Even in his sixties Brezhnev was a fanatically keen driver. Speed captivated him, as the roulette wheel captivates a gambler. Someone even joked that the world lost a racing car driver in him. In Richard Nixon's words:

> I made him an official gift as a memento of his visit to America: an individually constructed, dark blue Lincoln Continental. Brezhnev, a collector of luxury cars, did not even try to hide his delight. He insisted we immediately try out the present. He got behind the wheel and enthusiastically urged me into the passenger's side. The head of my personal guard visibly paled when he saw me getting into the car. We dashed down one of the narrow roads ... Brezhnev was used to travelling unhindered down the central lane in Moscow, and I could only imagine what would happen if a secret service or marine jeep suddenly appeared around the corner on this one-way road. There was a steep downward slope at one point, with a bright sign: 'Slow. Dangerous turn.' Brezhnev was travelling at fifty miles an hour ... I leaned forward. The tyres squealed ...

Nixon ended his tale on an ironic note: 'Diplomacy is not always an easy art.'

For all his bravery, Brezhnev was not simply a passionate but also a skilful driver. Only once, driving his magnificent 'Silver Shadow' Rolls-Royce, did he collide at high speed with a dump truck that suddenly appeared on the road. As Henry Kissinger remarked about Brezhnev's driving: 'It reflected the tendency towards suicide, documented in Russian novels of the nineteenth century.'

In the context of Brezhnev's courage as a driver, it must be noted that whereas he demonstrated indecisiveness and even cowardice in his political life, he was no coward in the physical sense, as opposed to Stalin, for instance, and did not suffer from any form of danger-complex. It is enough to remember the attempt on his life in 1969. When the procession of cars containing Brezhnev and some cosmonauts approached the Borovidski gates of the Kremlin, Lieutenant Illyin opened fire on the lead-car, assuming it would contain Brezhnev. The driver was killed. No one else was harmed. One can only guess what would have ensued had the car contained Stalin. Apparently the incident made little impression on Brezhnev. Lieutenant Illyin was sent to a mental hospital.

Let us return, however, to the second half of the Brezhnev era. Naturally, if the head of the country does not refuse lavish offerings, what can be said of the subordinates? Corruption becomes the norm. Those found guilty of it rarely lose their positions, since the leader of the nation himself sees nothing unusual about it. Speaking with his aides about the low mean wage of the average citizen, Brezhnev once said: 'You don't understand life. No one lives on their salary alone. I remember back in my youth, while I was a student, we earned extra money unloading train carriages. So what did we do? Three sacks or crates over there, and one for us. That's how everyone in the country lives.'

To picture the situation that had formed around Brezhnev in more detail, it is imperative to return to his daughter, who had a strong influence on her father and personified the Kremlin atmosphere of the times. As we have already mentioned, Galina Brezhnev was an unruly individual. Roy Medvedev, the historian and researcher of Brezhnev's life, explains that she had a passion for tall men with dark hair, significantly younger than herself. She would choose them more often than not from a circus or artistic environment, with which she had strong ties. His daughter's 'loving' nature – well known throughout Moscow – caused her father its fair share of worries.

After a number of publicised affairs, this heavily set and not-quite-so-young lady finally married a lieutenant-colonel in the police force. Her father approved of the union, and the young man's career began to rise meteorically. Soon he was already a general, first deputy to the Minister of Internal Affairs. The young couple were apparently perfectly matched, similar both in character and lifestyle. The only difference lay in the fact that whereas his career wholly depended on her, she was free to do as she pleased.

Apart from a passion for handsome young men, Galina Brezhnev had one other obsession: gold, diamonds and antiques. Finding out via secret channels and through her father's friends about yet another impending rise in jewellery prices, Galina, together with her close friend, the wife of the Minister of Internal Affairs, would hurry to the stores and buy up these items in vast quantities. Sometimes the 'purchase' was rather unorthodox. These two influential ladies would hand over to the trembling store manager not money, but scraps of paper containing their signatures and promises to clear up their debt in a few days. Most often these 'few days' would turn into never. Then, after the prices went up, these valuables were sold at black market prices.

The writer Larissa Vasilieva recounts an amusing incident. While in the Georgian town of Zugdidi, Galina visited the local museum where two relics were housed: the death mask of Napoleon, and a golden diadem belonging to the legendary Georgian Czarina Tamara. Galina liked the diadem so much that she wanted to acquire it. The confused and terrified museum director called the Georgian government. They in turn, haltingly informed Brezhnev about it. 'Send Galina back home,' her father curtly decreed.

Naturally, under prevailing conditions, sooner or later challengers to Brezhnev's power would appear. In this context we must introduce a new character, the KGB Minister of the USSR, Yuri Andropov. This 'knight of the cloak and dagger' was one of the next candidates for the Kremlin throne; but since the throne was currently occupied, it had to be vacated. The head of the KGB directed his efforts to precisely such an end.

In 1976 Brezhnev suffered a serious heart attack, resulting in his clinical death. As rumour has it, he was revived with the aid of 'mysterious bio-energy' wielded by a healer from the Caucasus called Juna Davitashvilli, then enjoying some celebrity in the capital, and nicknamed in Moscow circles 'Rasputin* in a skirt'. Having met her by chance at a party she was hosting, I fully concur with the historical parallel that this nickname suggests. She was an attractive forty-year-old lady, bubbling with self-promotion and, like all magicians and miracle-workers of a similar ilk, highly versed in fantastic fabrications. Soon after we met, she immediately offered to demonstrate her supernatural powers to the assembled guests, promising to stop the beating of a mouse's heart with a single wave of her hand, and then with a similar motion to compel the heart of the unfortunate creature to beat again. The guests readily agreed to view this unusual experiment, but the hostess for some reason first decided to serve tea, and then, perhaps forgetting about her promise or having failed to catch a mouse, moved on to reading her own poetry.

Be that as it may, Brezhnev believed in the amazing abilities of the healer from the Caucasus and often sought her aid. Whoever finally brought him back from the other world, the leader's speech and thinking processes were disrupted for many months. Muscovites remember that during those times a resuscitation vehicle always trailed after the procession of government limousines. In a normally functioning power structure, a leader in such a condition

---

* A Siberian religious fanatic and hypnotist, who forged close ties with the family of the last Russian monarch Nicholas II and had a great influence on it.

would usually retire. Wallowing in corruption as they were, however, Brezhnev's immediate comrades were not interested in such a move. Quite the contrary, a weak leader incapable of functioning properly suited them even better.

His 'ability to function' at the time is well illustrated by the following episode. Brezhnev was very fond of the television series *The Seventeen Moments of Spring*, telling the tale of the Soviet spy Shtirlitz and his exploits behind German lines during the war. During the film, Shtirlitz is informed that he has been awarded the title of Hero of the Soviet Union for his courageous work. At this point Brezhnev turned to his retinue sitting with him in the theatre and asked: 'Have they already awarded the medal? I'd like to do it personally.' A few days later he really did award the medal to the actor who played Shtirlitz, utterly convinced that he was in fact the famous spy.

Although the leader's state of health was never revealed to the people, his on-going physical and mental feebleness were visible on every television screen. He now found it difficult to carry out the most basic formalities of protocol. All this appeared like clinging to power, and did not elicit human pity for old age and frailty from the people, but rather irritation and mockery. Essentially, a unique experiment was taking place: how long could a 'living corpse' pretend to be the leader of a mighty nation?

On 19 December 1981, Brezhnev's seventy-fifth birthday was sumptuously celebrated in the Kremlin. As Soloviev and Klepikov write: 'It is difficult to say how much of the surrounding proceedings got through to the awareness of the Kremlin leader. Sick and feeble after several strokes and heart attacks, with uncontrollable movements, a stumbling gait, rigid and motionless facial muscles, stammering incomprehensible speech, and laboured irregular breathing, he made a painful impression.'

From this anniversary, the aforementioned authors believe the clandestine manoeuvring of the head of the KGB against the Kremlin leader turned into a frontal assault. Apparently Andropov got tired of waiting out the protracted agonies of his master, while the age of the pretender himself – far beyond sixty already – also spurred him on.

One of the methods of 'speeding things up' was publicly to discredit the leader of the country. Soviet television had earlier attempted to portray Brezhnev in a 'softer' light, trying to emphasise every confident step, intentional smile or correctly pronounced word, and shying away from or editing out every appearance of aged dementia. Now it seemed purposefully to take delight in his weakness, intentionally montaging together an image of him as a 'living corpse'. It got to the point of direct sabotage. Once, during a speech in the city of Baku – the capital of Azerbaijan – at yet another meeting, which was being televised across the whole country, instead of the pre-prepared speech Brezhnev was slipped a completely unrelated text, which he began to read. Only a while later, when whispers and confusion started to fill the hall, did he understand that something untoward was going on and stopped. He was given the correct text. He smiled meaningfully, looked out across the hall and, with a certain dignity said: 'This is not my fault, comrades. I have to start from the very beginning.'

Was this an accidental slip? Of course not. Especially considering that the television studio, as if knowing about this beforehand, revelled in this gaffe across the whole country, showing close-ups of both the amused perplexity of the audience and the aged confusion on the speaker's face. In times gone by the transmission would have instantly been halted, now everything was reversed. Who needed this, and who could allow themselves to act this way towards the leader of the country? Only a very powerful opponent, already practically in power.

Around this time, another messy scandal ensued, the threads of which led to the Brezhnev family. This incident plainly alarmed Moscow's élite, and became known as the 'Gypsy matter'. Boris Gypsy was the nickname of a Moscow opera singer, a long-time lover of Galina Brezhnev. This extravagant young man usually walked around in a mink coat, a gold chain around his neck and a small dog in his arms.

The tale is rumoured to have begun with the Moscow circus, which was celebrating an anniversary. This celebration attracted all Moscow's artistic celebrities. Galina Brezhnev was naturally also present. For such a momentous occasion, she wore her best diamonds, hoping, it seems, to become the first lady of this ball. It turned out however, that a well-known circus performer – the lady tiger-tamer – who also attended the ball, was wearing family jewels that were both more beautiful and more valuable. We do not know how Galina Brezhnev took this blow; however, a short while later these family jewels disappeared from the performer's home. The theft was carried out cleverly. It was just before New Year, and a present arrived at the well-guarded house where the performer lived: a Christmas tree. A gift for the artist from her fans was an ordinary occurrence. She was not home, and the concierge allowed the delivery people to take the tree up to the floor where she lived. No one saw them or the stolen jewels again.

An investigation got under way. For some reason, Boris Gypsy and a few other friends of Galina Brezhnev came under suspicion. A search discovered a hidden cache of diamonds in one of their homes, among which were some of the jewels recently stolen from the performer. The suspects could not explain how they got there. However we might feel about Galina Brezhnev, it is impossible to suspect her as an accomplice to a burglary. Apparently the stolen diamonds were planted on Galina's friend so that the criminal thread would lead to the Brezhnev family. The question once again arises, who would find it advantageous to discredit the head of the government, and who could realise this operation so easily and professionally? The conclusion is obvious, the one who was reaching for power.

It would seem that after such a successful operation its 'conductor' would need to reap the fruits of his success: a noisy trial of Galina Brezhnev's friends, with repercussions for her and her father. Here, however, something came undone. The whole matter started to fall apart. Someone must have pulled unseen strings, someone even more powerful than the KGB. This 'someone', who gave the alarm in time, was most likely Yuri Andropov's second-in-command, a close friend and protégé of Brezhnev, also married to his wife's cousin, General Tzvigun. The powers that halted the process were most probably part of the pro-Brezhnev Politburo which understood that with the departure of the old master from the stage, their power would also end.

We are left only to guess at the titanic forces, grappling each other in a death-grip, secretly struggling during those few days for power in the Kremlin – how the scales were tipped first one way, then the other. Suddenly, exactly one month after the leader's seventy-fifth birthday, his relative and friend General Tzvigun was found dead in his office, shot in the head. Rumours spread across Moscow about the general's suicide. Moreover, the motive was said to be the fact that Brezhnev had forbidden him to investigate further the 'Gypsy matter'. Alleged tangential supporting evidence for this version of events was the fact that the obituary for General Tzvigun published in the central newspapers lacked Brezhnev's signature.

This was all stitched together with such bright thread that it could not fool even the most naïve. It was not in the general's interest to undermine his benefactor, and the general himself was not the kind of man to shoot himself over this. It was more likely not a question of suicide, rather one of murder. As for the absence of Brezhnev's signature in the official obituary, I believe those are in the right who claim this to be one of Brezhnev's most courageous acts – he refused to allow his signature to be used to cover up the murder of his friend.

This moment, it seems, was seminal. The 'Gypsy matter' moved forward with increasing speed. He was arrested. Finally, Galina Brezhnev herself was called in for questioning. Those who knew her well tell how this usually self-confident lady looked bewildered and even quipped, 'Now it seems, our song is sung', seemingly an allusion to the fate of the Brezhnev family. It looked as if the departing leader had no alternative but to accept the ultimatum delivered to him by the chief of the secret police, whom he himself had once raised up on high: either honourably living out his life in fictitious power, but more correctly without power, or a shameful eviction from the Kremlin.

Nevertheless, Brezhnev's supporters made a final weak attempt at a counter-strike. It may be that he recalled Khrushchev's success at disabling Beria. The direct perpetrators of this action were Brezhnev's personal friend, the Minister of Internal Affairs and his deputy, Brezhnev's son-in-law – Galina's husband. On the morning of 10 September 1982, two heavily armed groups of police left the Ministry of Internal affairs with orders to arrest Andropov. One squad headed for his office, and the other to his flat (he and Brezhnev lived in the same house but on different floors). One group was stopped and disarmed by Andropov's people while still en route. The second managed to make it to Andropov's empty flat where, over a period of half an hour, something resembling firing or brawling could be heard between the raiders and the KGB agents guarding the house. The outside world, neither Russia nor the West especially, knew hardly anything about these events. The only strange fact that day was that all phone communication between the USSR and the West was suddenly cut off. This was explained the next day as a result of technical difficulties ...

The day of 7 November 1982 – the anniversary of the Bolshevik Revolution was a cold and windy one. The armed forces paraded across Red Square, as did the 'jubilant masses of workers'. On the tribunal of the Mausoleum, in their identical hats, limply waving at the procession, stood the nation's leaders headed by our hero. In human terms, this was ill-treatment of a very sick, feeble old man. It is doubtful that standing around for four hours in the cold wind did his health any good. What was he thinking about during these hours, battling against intense weariness, trembling legs and laboured breathing? About a warm bed? About the fleeting nature of life? Or maybe about what a shame it was that he had not retired a few years ago? He had in fact mentioned stepping down then, but his colleagues had protested noisily, which was perhaps his intention. Or possibly he was thinking that all his best friends, those from his distant youth, had already passed away. He had recently buried one of them; losing control, he had thrown himself at the coffin, sobbing with grief. The whole country saw it on television.

The protracted end-game concluded after three days, on 10 November. As some wit grimly joked, Andropov did not change Brezhnev's batteries in time. At 8.30 in the morning, having breakfasted, he got up from the table and went into his office, not emerging for a long time. His worried wife went to check on him. He was lying on the floor, next to the desk. In another version, he was found in bed in the morning, already dead.

The first to hear the news was Yuri Andropov. As the head of Brezhnev's guard, General Medvedev, recalled, the news did not provoke much of a reaction from Andropov. He remained completely calm while listening to the general's report, and did not ask any questions.

Here we must go back to consider an unexplained oddity. In the last few years of his life Brezhnev was having trouble sleeping, and started to use strong sleeping pills, in higher and higher doses. He virtually could not fall asleep without them. One of his colleagues recommended that he chase them down with vodka, which increased their effect and appealed to Brezhnev a great deal. All this was actively abetted by his permanent nurse, an attractive, authoritative woman with whom the patient developed a very close and trusting relationship. In the end it all turned into a kind of drug, without which he could no longer manage. He even started to take these substances during the day, making him seem drunk or exhausted. Sometimes even television viewers would notice this – his vacant gaze, his slurred speech.

There are several strange entries in Brezhnev's diary – 19 December 1981: 'I got the yellow ones up to and including the 28th; 25 January 1982: 'Y.V. gave me some yellow ones' (Y.V. is most likely the head of the KGB, Yuri Vladimirovich Andropov.) So what are these 'yellow ones'? Why would such pills be handed out by the head of the KGB and not a doctor? Yet another secret of the Kremlin ...

Notwithstanding the fact that Leonid Brezhnev ruled the country for eighteen years, longer than anyone except Stalin, his death did not shake or disturb the people. Quite the contrary, it seemed that they had been expecting it for some time. As a politician he had died long ago, while his physical agonies were played out in front of the whole world, and people were accustomed to them. One of the journalists quipped: 'The entire history of Soviet Russia is tied up with cults of personality. There was Lenin's cult of personality, then Stalin's, then Khrushchev's; only Brezhnev invented a new kind of cult – a cult without personality.'

In conclusion it remains only to be added that after Brezhnev's death, when Andropov came to power, an unenviable fate caught up with Brezhnev's friend, the Minister of Internal Affairs. He was removed from all his posts, stripped of his rank and placed on trial. However, it never went to court. Bedecked in his full-dress uniform, replete with all his medals and honours, he shot himself through the mouth. Earlier still, his wife also closed her own account with life – that same lady who once ran around jewellery stores with Galina Brezhnev. Galina's husband later got twelve years, allegedly for corruption. Galina herself, much aged and now an inveterate drunkard, sometimes, as rumour colourfully put it, would creep out at night with a shovel into the grounds of her huge empty dacha to make sure that her hidden diamonds were safe. Larissa Vasilieva describes her visit to the Brezhnev family after his death, when Galina's apartment was being searched. She was drunk as usual, and watched the proceeding with friendly curiosity, even assisting the searchers. Later, when it was over, she invited the participants to drink with her: 'You'll remember my father and his time. How well you lived under him!' she exclaimed. Once she vanished for half a year, roaming the country with a band of gypsies. She was found and returned to the dacha. It was said that when she got very drunk she would swear like a virtuoso and declare that she wanted to divorce her husband the general because she loved the arts so much.

Postscript. Did everything happen exactly this way? We cannot discount the possibility that a number of details from the personal life of the Brezhnev family were nothing more than 'art' born in the offices of the KGB, whose chief was heading for power. After all, this is precisely how things were done in the Soviet system. The Kremlin likes secrets ...

11 | A COP IN A DINNER JACKET

'THERE GOES THE KIDNEY,' my taxi driver said, his gaze following the procession of government limousines that screamed past us – their windows tightly shuttered, under heavy guard, their warning lights flashing wildly. 'Who?' I asked, not understanding.

'The kidney; so they can hook it up,' the driver elaborated. 'They drive it every day around this time.'

It was the end of 1983. I had not been in Moscow for almost a year and did not know that this was how Moscow's cab drivers had christened the new master of the Kremlin, Yuri Andropov, the possessor of an artificial kidney which had to be hooked up to a special machine every day. My driver was mistaken, however, along with the accredited Western journalists in Moscow for whom this trick was intended. Andropov was not in any of the cars screaming past us. In fact there was no one there at all, apart from the drivers and guards. With this simple ruse, the authorities were trying to defuse rumours going around Moscow, that the new master of the Kremlin was hovering between life and death, having not left the government hospital in many days, and trying to rule the country from there.

In truth, rumours and myths, concocted more often then not in the depths of the KGB, accompanied Yuri Andropov along his entire rise to power. According to these tales, he was a soft-spoken intelligent person, an erudite man who loved art and had mastered several European languages, among them English. The *New York Times* had even revealed it to its readers with the sensational headline: 'Andropov Reads English Fluently'. In his famous book *The KGB*, John Barron described Andropov's flat, writing: 'The shelves are filled with books. Some of them are in English, which Andropov is fluent in.' Of an evening, the new master of the Kremlin would familiarise himself with the classics of world literature in their original languages, would play the pianoforte a little and dabble in writing poetry. He was pro-West, preferring whisky on the rocks to vodka, listened to Western radio stations, and collected jazz albums. He did not avoid contact with dissidents, setting them upon the path of truth, and even sending his personal limousine to collect them when he invited them for a chat. On top of all this, he was either one-quarter or one-half Jewish. In short, almost a new Lenin. In fact, all the other traits ascribed to Andropov completely corresponded to the archetypal characteristics of Lenin, which the Soviet people were taught: modesty, efficiency, simplicity, pragmatism and patience.

There was even a story going around Moscow, hinting at Andropov's loyalty and tolerance. He once invited an Abstractionist artist over for a chat. 'So what are you rebelling against?' the host asked good-naturedly, filling them up a glass of whisky each. 'Don't you understand that any system has a form of power? That power feeds you, and you must serve it.' 'Of course we understand', the painter replied. 'We want to serve it, but the Realists are thwarting us. They whisper lies to you about us. Imagine, on a pedestal stands a huge marble arse which feeds everyone. Everyone kisses it, in order to get more rewards from it. We also throw ourselves to kiss it, but the Realists have surrounded it on all sides. They kick us away with their feet and whisper, "Arse, arse, don't you believe them. They'll bite you." Think for yourself, what kind of idiot would bite an enormous marble arse?'

Without a doubt, Yuri Andropov was a far more complicated figure than his predecessor and neighbour Leonid Brezhnev. Not to fear being ascribed such characteristics as intellectual, erudite and half-Jewish, in a country where the vast majority of people never had any love for people 'in glasses and bowlers', let alone for Jews, one needed to possess the mind of a good chess player, to be able to think many moves ahead. One needed to have a very acute sense of the positive and negative effects that these rumours would create, and to predict their overall result. Even serious authors writing about Andropov, such as Volkogonov, Medvedev, Soloviev and Klepikov, Bovin and others, had very different evaluations of this figure.

Some consider him to have been the classic villain, coming far from last in the rogues' gallery, while others judged him to be an orthodox but positive figure, in comparison to the rest of the decomposing Kremlin hierarchy.

Such a difference of opinion does not seem very mysterious. Andropov was something of a record holder in a number of areas, among the people who had occupied the summit of the Kremlin hill. His path to power was the longest of any Kremlin leader. He attained it at the age of sixty-eight, while Lenin gained the post at forty-seven, Stalin at forty-two, Khrushchev at fifty-nine, Brezhnev at fifty-eight, not to mention the Czars, who sat upon the Kremlin throne as young men or even children. The length of his leadership was the shortest, a mere fifteen months. Although in intelligence and erudition he was ahead of many of his colleagues, he had received little formal education, let alone higher education. To concentrate all power in his hands, Party, government and military, Stalin had needed seventeen years,

Khrushchev five, Brezhnev thirteen. Yuri Andropov spent two months on this. And finally, in the entire history of Russia, he was the first head of the secret police who had made it to the Kremlin throne.

The boy Yuri was born in the northern Caucasus, in the Stavropol region, at the Nagudskaya station on 15 June 1914, to the family of a railway worker. His father was a Russified Greek, and it seems that his real surname was Andropolos, although there does not appear to be documentary evidence to support this. His father died when Yuri was only two years old. After finishing secondary school, Yuri Andropov found himself compelled to pay his own way. He worked as a projectionist's assistant in the railway club at the Mazdok station, a switchboard operator and a sailor on a river-boat on the Volga for about a year. In 1932, fate took him to the town of Ribinsk, where he applied to study in the River Transport School. 'I ask that you supply me with a dormitory and a stipend, since I do not have any further means by which to support myself,' he wrote to the school administrator.

Soon, however, Andropov dropped his studies and began his career in the Party, becoming the Comsomol* leader of the same school. This time coincided with another peak of Stalinist repression. Vacant positions began to appear in the Party ranks, and Andropov's career took off like a rocket. In 1938 he was already Comsomol leader of the entire Yaroslav region. The Party then moved him to the north, to Karelia, where he likewise headed the Comsomol, but this time of the entire republic. For a youth with little education to make such a dramatic career for himself in those terrifying times of unleashed terror, he had to possess not only exceptional luck, but also those specific qualities which Stalin's times demanded.

The Second World War caught Andropov in Karelia. As scarce and not very convincing documents explain, during this period, on assignment from the KGB, he was engaged in organising partisan divisions behind enemy lines. It is hard to say whether this was true. Probably these are merely 'heroic details' of his biography, created in hindsight to excuse his lack of direct participation in military activities. From 1951 Andropov worked in Moscow, in the central apparatus of the Party. In 1954 he was sent on diplomatic assignment to Hungary, first as an adviser and then as the ambassador. Andropov's 'Hungarian Period' was the cornerstone of his future brilliant path to power.

As the Hungarians who knew him during that period remember, this was not an ordinary ambassador by Soviet standards. He was always courteous,

* Communist Youth League.

elegant and attentive. He liked to invite gypsy musicians to the embassy dinners, and would sometimes even sing along with them. He served rare French wines at his table, politely kissed the hands of ladies whom he had finished dancing with, attentively listened to the men, always looking his questioner straight in the eye. His soft, quiet voice induced calm and trust, and his knowing, understanding gaze, beaming out through the slightly tinted lenses of his glasses, let people know that he was on their side. As one of the Hungarians later put it: 'He was a cop in a dinner jacket.'

What role did Yuri Andropov play in the suppression of the Hungarian revolution of 1956? A key one, it would seem. He not only carried out the will of Moscow and co-ordinated activities, which was only natural for an ambassador, but he also generally initiated such activities. His dispatches demanded swift military action from Moscow. The future master of the Kremlin was a firm supporter of the harshest measures, and remained proud of his role in 'suppressing the mutiny' throughout his life. In essence he acted not like an ambassador, but like an agent of the KGB. After the revolution was defeated, when the head of the Hungarian republic Imre Nagy hid in the Yugoslavian embassy in Budapest fearing for his life, it was none other than Andropov who formulated and executed a plan to lure him out of there. In the name of the Soviet government, he gave a written guarantee of complete safety to his former close acquaintance, with whom he had many a time, glass of wine in hand, held friendly discourses about literature and Hungarian poetry. When Imre Nagy, trusting this guarantee, left the embassy, he was immediately taken into custody by the Soviet secret police and soon executed.

Something similar happened to Colonel Kopachi, then chief of the Budapest police. Hurrying to the Yugoslavian embassy with his wife, where they wanted to hide and ask for political asylum, they were taken directly in the street by KGB agents and delivered to the Soviet embassy. The ambassador greeted his old acquaintances warmly, courteously kissed the hand of the lady with whom he had often danced at diplomatic functions, served them coffee, and calmed them down, assuring them that there was nothing to worry about. Quite the contrary, the new head of the government, Janos Kadar, wanted to see Colonel Kopachi in order to offer him a post in his cabinet. From the embassy, however, the couple were delivered not to Kadar but straight to prison, from which the colonel only emerged seven years later.

In 1957, as an apparent reward for successfully completing his Hungarian mission, Khrushchev brought Andropov back to Moscow where he was entrusted with the role of Party supervisor of the satellite states. One must assume that he performed this role admirably as well. In any case, the idea of the Berlin Wall – brilliant in its simplicity – belongs directly to him.

'Little October' – as the period of Khrushchev's fall in October of 1964 was labelled, as opposed to the 'Big October' of the 1917 Revolution – did not shake Andropov's positions, in fact it strengthened them. On 19 May 1967, the fifty-two-year-old Yuri Andropov was made head of the secret police – the KGB – by Brezhnev. Andropov succeeded his disgraced predecessor in this post, the man who failed to prevent Svetlana Stalin escaping abroad. It goes without saying that Leonid Brezhnev – blinded by his own splendour – did not have the slightest inkling that by this assignment he was creating a fearsome enemy.

Andropov occupied this post for fifteen years. Just as when he had sat in the ambassador's chair, outwardly he remained elegant and soft-spoken. Yet, in his cunning and ability to instigate convoluted intrigues, of his predecessors only Lavrenti Beria could come close to rivalling him.

One of the first tasks facing the new head of the KGB was to change the image of the organisation. It was at this time that Soviet literature, cinema and television screens were filled with images of brave and cultivated spies, clever detectives, just and likeable policemen. All this pulp was pasted together under the harsh control and on the direct orders of the KGB, either by hired authors or by agents of the organisation itself. Thus Andropov's first deputy, General Tzvigun, whom we have already mentioned, personally wrote a number of film scripts, hiding behind a literary pseudonym.

On Andropov's orders, the main emphasis of the KGB's recruitment policy shifted away from primitive functionaries, moving instead towards the best graduates of the capital's universities, people fluent in foreign languages, possessing good minds and worldly manners. The teaching of spy-craft attracted figures such as the former high-ranking British spy Kim Philby, who fled to Moscow after his discovery, and who became a close friend of Andropov.

Nevertheless Andropov's main task was not building an image, but rather raising the effectiveness of the KGB and restoring the authority (read 'fear') of the organisation, which had been somewhat rocked under Khrushchev's liberalism. The first to feel the change in the regime personally were the capital's dissidents, with whom Andropov decided to deal once and for all. He resurrected Stalin's habit of 'repeat-sentences', when a person was tried a second or even a third time, simply because they had not changed their convictions. Some never left the camps. Or they would simply get another sentence right on the spot, when their first one finished. The prison-psychiatric hospitals to which KGB doctors committed healthy people diagnosed as schizo-phrenics due to differences of opinion was no longer kept secret. It was the 'intellectual' Andropov, who resurrected Lenin's tradition of exiling undesir-ables overseas. Here, for instance, is what the head of the KGB suggested to the nation's top Party officials: 'Now his [Solzhenitsyn's] enemy activities have reached a new level ... His book *Gulag Archipelago* is not a literary cre-ation, but a political document. This is dangerous ... Hence, he must be cast out of the country ...'

Another episode, concerning the exile of yet another future Nobel Prize winner, the poet Joseph Brodsky, is described by the authors Soloviev and Klepikov. It seems that this time Andropov decided to flirt a little with the intelligentsia, as represented by the poet Yevgeni Yevtushenko, who came to see Andropov about a private matter. Finishing the business which the poet had come to see him about, and knowing that this information would travel across Moscow almost immediately, Andropov engaged the poet in the fol-lowing conversation:

'I wanted to ask you about Brodsky, not about his poetry, but about his fate. How do you imagine his future fate? Do you imagine it in our current conditions, in our country?' 'No,' replied Yevtushenko. 'Speaking honestly, I cannot imagine Brodsky's fate to lie here with us. He is a talented poet, but he would be better off overseas.' 'I think so too,' Andropov replied quickly. Andropov's agreement awoke a twinge of conscience in Yevtushenko. 'At least ease the bureaucratic formalities for him,' he quickly added.

Andropov promised to 'ease them', and kept his word. Brodsky was kicked out of the USSR within a few weeks.

All this was merely the visible tip of the iceberg, the 'legal' methods, in Soviet terms. However, there was also a hidden section. For the first time since the death of Stalin, Andropov reactivated the practice of secret political killings, both inside the country and abroad. Furthermore, while killings out-side the country were carefully masked, those within the country were carried out seemingly for show, as an example to others, to raise the shaken author-ity of the organisation and to perpetuate fear.

The famous film actress Zoya Fyodorov was killed in her Moscow flat by a gunshot wound to the head. She was getting ready to emigrate and live with her daughter in the USA – also a film actress – who lived there with her father, US Vice-Admiral Jack Tate. This story began back during the Second World War. The young US Navy captain, then serving as a military attaché to the American embassy in Moscow, met and fell in love with a charming Russian film actress at a diplomatic reception. The romance progressed torridly, and naturally under the silent eyes of agents of the KGB. The lovers agreed that if they had a son, they would name him Victor in honour of victory in the war, or Victoria if they had a daughter. Soon the captain was compelled to leave Moscow, while his beloved gave birth to a daughter. A short time later Zoya Fyodorov was arrested and sentenced to a long term of imprisonment for 'betraying the motherland' (contact with foreigners). She only gained her freedom after Stalin's death. During the period of détente, she was able to track down her captain, who was by that stage already a vice-admiral. After a stubborn struggle with the authorities she managed to send her daughter to live with him. And now, after almost thirty years, she was preparing to see her lover once more, and rejoin her daughter.

Officially the killing was listed as a simple robbery turned violent, but Moscow's intelligentsia did not believe this, guessing instead whose touch had a hand in this work. The dark forces were seemingly letting everyone know: Regardless of rank or awards, the punishment for trying to 'betray the motherland' had not been rescinded.*

A similarly mysterious death overtook the wife of the former Deputy General Secretary of the UN, Arkadi Shevchenko, who refused to return to the USSR. His wife, having been forcibly deported from New York to Moscow by KGB agents, soon apparently 'committed suicide'. And again, the signs of the crime were plain to see. Revenge for the betrayal of the husband, a warning to others.

Finally, there was the series of famous international murders, the so-called 'Bulgarian Trail' which ended with the shooting of the Turkish terrorist Mehmet Ali Agadja in St Peter's Square in Rome on 13 May 1981. The attempt against the Pope was the apotheosis of the KGB's neo-Stalinism. It is said that the list of Andropov's potential victims still contained the names of another two Poles: Zbignev Bdzezinsky and Lech Walesa.

Yuri Andropov himself remained elegant and polite. He lost neither his patience nor his good manners, and the possession of even a dark sense of humour lent a certain charm to his image. For instance, at a banquet in one of Moscow's theatres where he was present as a guest (his daughter Irina's husband was an actor), he reached forward with his glass in order to drink a toast with his neighbour across the table. The neighbour hesitated a moment, since

---

* It must be mentioned , however, that there are other versions of the killing. One of them was described in his story *Afanasich* by the writer Yuri Nagibin.

toasting with the head of the secret police was always considered shameful among the old Russian intelligentsia. 'I suggest you accept,' Andropov laughed softly, noticing what was going on. 'Remember, the KGB has long arms.'

Another 'joke' which did the rounds of Moscow's salons was made in far more dire circumstances. An English businessman of Ukrainian origin, Nikola Sharigin, was arrested in Moscow accused of espionage. His captors started recruiting him as an agent for the KGB, promising not to charge him if he agreed. Sharigin kept refusing. He was taken to Andropov's office.
'Well, are you still refusing to do a little work for the motherland?' asked Andropov. 'My motherland is Great Britain,' replied Nikola. 'Very well, in that case we'll put you on trial,' Andropov retorted. 'But he is really an English citizen,' one of the aides present quietly put in. 'That's OK. I don't believe the English queen will declare war on us because of Sharigin here,' laughed Andropov.

But Andropov's mind was not wholly occupied with the business of the KGB around this time. His age was starting to show, he had to act quickly if he was to bring about his life-long dream of rising to the summit of the Kremlin. Formally he was not among Brezhnev's heirs, but this did not daunt him. He knew their worth. All their deepest secrets lay tucked away in his safe. In truth, several individuals that were hindering his progress still needed to be removed, but this was merely a technical matter. Thus he paced, from corner to corner, lost in thought, his hands clasped behind his back out of habit, to and fro across his huge study, decorated with oriental carpets and redwood panels, with a toweringly high ceiling and equally massive, bullet-proof windows fitted with metal shutters, looking out over Lubyanka Square.

One of the men who was being predicted as the heir of Brezhnev, and who needed to be removed, was the Party head of Leningrad, sporting the dynastic Russian surname Romanov. Compared with the Kremlin elders, Grigory Romanov was almost a young man, only fifty-six years old. Although he possessed no particularly inspiring traits, he nevertheless was a serious opponent. An engineer by education, a peasant by birth, almost without defect as far as the Kremlin Olympus was concerned. Hence Andropov was pacing around his study, tying to solve a conundrum. He needed to find or create a 'defect' in this rival. Romanov's recent divorce from his wife? No, not enough. Something more controversial was needed ...

Around this time, Romanov's daughter was getting married. The matter seemed a family affair, unrelated to politics. That, however, would have been a dilettante's assessment. The wedding reception was naturally not organised by the father of the bride himself, but rather by his numerous henchmen, consisting of KGB operatives subordinate to Andropov. The banquet was in full swing, when a huge bruiser from Romanov's bodyguard cheerfully shouted at the young couple: 'Luck to the newly-weds!' and, in accordance with old Slavic tradition, smashed his glass upon the ground. 'Luck to the newly-weds!' the other KGB employees chorused, and also started breaking dishes. By morning it became evident that an expensive set of crockery had been smashed. But it was not just a matter of it being expensive, the problem was that it was no ordinary dinner set. Someone from Romanov's KGB entourage, without his knowledge but in his name, ordered that the dinner set be brought from a special vault in the Hermitage Museum. The dinner set was two hundred years old, and it had once belonged to Empress Catherine the Great herself.

This was blasphemy, ridicule of Russian history, an insult to national sentiment. A great row erupted. A day later the news was all over the Kremlin, and a short time later it spread across the nation, gathering rumours and details as it went. 'Does Romanov think he is already on the throne?' quipped the intelligentsia. In modern parlance, Romanov's approval rating plummeted. Such a man could no longer be a pretender to the highest office in the land which, as mathematicians say, is what was to be proved. Presumably Yuri Andropov now strolled around his study with a satisfied smile.

Did everything happen this way, or is the greater part of this story a well-concocted, delicately targeted fabrication? It is hard to establish. Several years ago in a private conversation, I put this question to the director of the Hermitage, Academic Boris Peotrovsky, who allegedly witnessed these events. The reply was negative. However, since the director of the Hermitage had a reputation among his co-workers as a man who, to put it mildly, was not very brave especially when facing powerful figures of authority, then taking his reply as gospel is also premature. Whatever the case, the story did what it was designed to do; the rival was removed.

We have already spoken about the relationship between Andropov and Brezhnev in the previous chapter. These two people were each other's antipodes, both in politics and in their personal lives. If Brezhnev was more partial to the trumpery of power, knick-knacks in the form of awards and titles, grand receptions and parades, then Andropov, quite to the contrary, loved real power itself, preferring to keep himself in the shadows. He did not like to talk about himself, rarely appeared on television, constantly avoided the press and once even made his interview with the German magazine

Spiegel conditional upon them not printing his photograph on the cover. Brezhnev was the sweetheart of fate, power almost falling into his lap and lasting him eighteen years; Andropov, however, was compelled to walk the longest road of all rulers of the Kremlin, in order to reach its summit. Brezhnev liked presents, tribute, sycophancy, while Andropov in that sense was absolutely above reproach. While Brezhnev was basically an open man for a politician of that level, not a grudge-holder, boisterous, sentimental, companionable, a carouser, then his upstairs neighbour was quite the opposite, closed, puritanical, even ascetic. He was disgusted by his downstairs colleague's numerous and noisy parties, which he was sometimes compelled to attend.

Their families differed just as strongly. The coarse commercialism of Brezhnev's daughter Galina, as opposed to the refined Irma Andropov, who graduated with honours from the philology department of Moscow University, loved music and literature, and who once dreamed of becoming an actress. Yuri Brezhnev, a heavy drinker like his father, who eventually drove himself to alcoholism, as opposed to the well-educated Igor Andropov, who spoke several foreign languages, and who – like his sister – had dreams of becoming an actor in his youth, but upon the insistence of his father became a diplomat. And while the narcissistic Brezhnev, who was generally good-natured in everyday life, was hardly bothered by these differences between them, within the fastidious Andropov they gave rise not merely to dislike, but to full-blown disgust.

The country did not yet know about the death of Brezhnev (unlike the rest of the world), when an extraordinary meeting of the Politburo was held late in the day of 10 November 1982. It lasted less than an hour. Andropov was calm and confident of the outcome. All the roles were already distributed, practical power was already in his hands. He delivered a complimentary eulogy for the deceased, and moved on to the matter at hand: the 'choice' of a new head of state. With more than a hint of implied threat, Brezhnev's former favourite and loyal adjutant, Konstantin Chernenko, to whom the former ruler had practically bequeathed his chair, was given the floor. Times had changed, however. Andropov's snake-like glare was having a hypnotic effect. Chernenko understood perfectly that one unwise word could cost him not just his career, but even his head. Of all people, those who sat here knew perfectly well who was behind the gunshots on St Peter's Square in Rome. After these gunshots, the old, almost forgotten fear of Stalin's days had slowly crept back into the Kremlin.

Rising heavily from his seat, eyes cast downward, Chernenko spoke in a hollow, cough-ridden voice, offering Yuri Andropov up as the new leader – an old man very much like himself, touched by a deathly pallor, frail as parchment and graced with a bouquet of incurable diseases. 'Hear, hear.' 'Indeed,' sycophantic voices rustled from around the hall, among them the voice of Mikhail Gorbachev, then a mere fifty-one years old. Andropov was sixty-eight at the time.

'Happy New Year, dear comrades!' the announcer of the central television station greeted Russians grandly, as the bells of the Kremlin chimed midnight, 'Happy 1937, comrades'. The point of this black humour, born of sharp Moscow tongues on the eve of 1983, could only be understood by a Soviet citizen. The former chief of the all-powerful KGB had ascended to the summit of Kremlin power, and the jester was predicting a return of the fearful 1937, one of the peaks of Stalin's Terror.

It must be said that Andropov's rise to power did not produce a unilateral reaction in the country. The orthodox part of the population, born and bred with a 'barracks' mentality and pining for the 'firm hand of Stalin', greeted Andropov's arrival with enthusiasm: 'Well, now he will put things in their right places.' The intelligentsia, on the other hand, grew fearfully quiet. I remember on that day I was out with a friend, a world-famous scientist. We were walking in silence, thinking about what was to come. 'What now?' I wondered. 'Back to the past?' My friend looked at me thoughtfully. 'Hopefully he doesn't have enough time left in him for that,' he said after a long pause.

Fifteen years of service in the KGB, to which Andropov gave the best years of his life, could do no other than deform the consciousness of the head of state. One of his first actions in the new post was a pure act of law enforcement, codenamed 'Trawl'. Units of police across the whole country started daytime raids of cinemas, public baths, hairdressers, department stores and other buildings, searching for skivers. There were even rumours that a Stalinesque decree was being prepared, announcing criminal liability for absence or being late for work. Articles began to appear in the papers which transparently implied that there was but one short step from a political anecdote to treason against the motherland. As a Moscow journalist correctly noted, the new head of state lived by the idea of disciplining the whole nation.

In other words, myths about the liberalism and pro-Western stance of the new leader began to evaporate like smoke. One of the first was the myth of Andropov's mastery of the English language. During his first meeting at

Brezhnev's funeral, with the then Vice-President of the United States, George Bush, it became apparent that Andropov did not understand a word of English. International relations took a sharp turn for the worse. Moscow papers began to compare Reagan with Hitler. Things got rather absurd. In the face of the impending economic catastrophe, the Politburo spent hours discussing such questions as increasing penalties against foreign diplomats for traffic and parking violations in Moscow. In other words, the cop remained a cop. The centre of power was gradually moving from the Kremlin to the KGB.

In the first months of his rule Andropov was enviably active and dedicated for his age. He would sit in his Kremlin office late into the night reading masses of paper work, having lengthy conversations with people he had invited, and giving orders to his 'second-in-command', who was unofficially considered to be Konstantin Chernenko. Once he even appeared without warning at a Moscow factory, throwing the place into a panic.

This went on for the first four months. By the spring of 1983, however, the situation had changed dramatically. The health of the head of state took a sharp turn for the worse. His kidneys, which had always given Andropov trouble, practically failed him. It became difficult to move around, his hands shook, the heart condition grew worse, his legs no longer supported him. To get to his car or conference table, he now had to rely upon the assistance of others. 'In dark glasses, flanked on each side by powerful bravos, he began to look like the Don of an all-powerful mafia which had seized power in the country.'

His appearances in the Kremlin became more and more rare. His last session there was on 1 September 1983. The Politburo meeting was over and Andropov already wanted to leave the Kremlin when the Minister of Defence approached him and reported: 'The plane that was shot down. It turned out not to be American but South Korean, moreover a civilian plane.' 'But I was told that the plane over Kamchatka was a spy-plane,' Andropov frowned. 'I'm flying out to the Crimea, to the Black Sea today. I need to rest and improve my health. Deal with the plane yourselves.'

The plane in question was the South Korean Boeing 747 with 269 passengers on board, which was shot down by a Soviet fighter on the night of 31 August in the Sakhalin region, over the Japan Sea. All the passengers perished.

It is clear from the dialogue above, found in secret Politburo documents, that Andropov was already informed about the plane in Soviet airspace while it was above Kamchatka, and while the tragedy could still be avoided. The order to destroy the 'target' was given by him personally. According to the on-board time-table, some passengers were sleeping, others were watching a film. The plane was shot down with two rockets, fired by the pilot Osipovich, who was so professionally negligent that he failed to distinguish the most famous type of passenger airliner in the world from a military plane. In response to the first queries from dispatchers in South Korea, Japan and the USA about the disappearance of the Boeing, Moscow expressed surprise and announced that it had no idea what they were talking about. A few hours later, when a wave of concern had already swept the globe, Moscow put forward the 'suggestion' that it had 'crashed by itself'. The morning edition of the newspaper *Pravda* already suggested a new version: Soviet interceptors were trying to help the lost airliner, leading it to the nearest airport, but it did not respond to their communications and flew off in the direction of the Sea of Japan.

Need we continue to list the stages of this cynical deception? The bodies of people who did not even understand why they had died were already settling on the bottom of the ocean, while the members of Andropov's Politburo continued to lie. The head of state offered no condolences or commiserations about the deaths. His reaction was cold and harsh: no concessions, formulate a counter-response ... after which he flew to the Crimea to recuperate.

On orders from the Kremlin, over ten warships were dispatched to the scene of the tragedy with all haste, so as to beat the search and rescue operations of other countries to the scene. Their task was to recover from the seabed the lost plane's black-box recorder, whose magnetic tape contained a record of every stage of the tragedy. The box was recovered, but this was kept the strictest secret, and the ships continued to prowl the waters for many days pretending that their efforts had not been successful. It was then that America took an extreme step, revealing that their secret military monitoring station had recorded the transmissions of Soviet pilots at the moment at which the 'target' was destroyed, and made these recordings freely available.

The world was first stunned, and then exploded with angry indignation. This was in a sense the culmination of Andropov's rule. It found Andropov already in the Crimea. Walks in the fresh air, bathing in sea-water and other medicinal activities were supposed to pour new life into the frail body of the aged leader. Fate however, had something other in mind. Walking in the park, Andropov sat down on a granite bench to rest, and apparently failed to notice himself getting cold. This was enough for the already frail organism, weak-ened to its limit by illness. He returned to Moscow from the Crimea on a stretcher, and was taken straight to the government hospital.

He was failing, but unlike his predecessor, who fell into aged senility a long time before his death, he was in possession of a clear mind and memory, continuing to hold power firmly in his hands. Andropov's Kremlin office was virtually moved to the hospital. Important government documents were brought for him to sign, reports and encrypted telegrams to read, while ideas, orders and memos flowed out. He was not in a condition to hold these documents himself, and asked that they be read aloud to him.

As many authors mention, the tragedy or paradox of the situation lay in the fact that although weak in body, Andropov was simultaneously at the height of his power. His empty chair in the Politburo meeting hall malevolently reminded everyone of his presence. His real state of health was unknown not just to the people, but even to his closest colleagues. So, for instance, at a grand meeting in the Kremlin in honour of the anniversary of the Bolshevik Revolution, a rumour spread that Andropov was definitely going to attend. The members of the Politburo took their places in the praesidium, leaving an empty chair in the middle and seating themselves on either side of it. It stayed empty during the whole meeting, creating an atmosphere of oppressive and worried expectation. It was precisely at this time, as described at the start of this chapter, that a government cortège started driving around Moscow, mystifying the onlookers and Western journalists.

For the last two months of his life Andropov was no longer mobile. He found it difficult even to turn from one side to another, yet his mind continued to work clearly. He read a lot and, as the hospital personnel insist, even wrote poems to his wife. The last few days before his death he spent unconscious in a coma, but the huge machine of the empire continued to function in his name. On 8 February a letter was sent to Japan in his name, although in actuality this was already a letter 'from the next world'. Andropov died on 9 February. A powerful, but cruel intellect had passed away. But what do we really expect from those who climb so high?

We are mortal in this world beneath the Moon.
Life is but a moment, non-existence – eternal.
The sphere of the Earth spins in the Universe.
People live and people disappear ...

This poem was found in the dead leader's papers.

12 | THE LEADER HISTORY DIDN'T NOTICE

IT WAS THE SPRING OF 1984. I was working with Central Russian Television at the time. We were shooting a documentary film in co-production with Italian television. The script required us to hold a small shoot in the precincts of the Kremlin. In order to receive permission for this shoot, I approached the so-called 'special department' of Moscow television, which was formally considered the department handling 'work with foreigners', but was widely known to be a branch of the KGB. Such departments existed in every large industry and institution in the country.

The director of the department – a high-ranking KGB officer – listened to my request and explained that it would not be easy to receive permission for this at the moment: 'They are currently doing some restoration work there,' he added with a smirk. 'What are they restoring?' I inquired. 'Konstantin Chernenko,' he laughed.

My jaw dropped, so unexpected was this. For a KGB worker, in an official conversation with an unknown person, to allow himself such a joke directed at the head of the Party and state, was a phenomenon I had never encountered before. There was something new here.

A term exists in ballistics which describes a projectile as 'spent', meaning that the initial energy of flight given to the projectile has dissipated, and the missile is about to fall to earth. One of the main driving forces of the Soviet system was fear. If that fear was ending, that meant the system itself was coming to an end. It was 'spent' …

No one spoke about this openly of course. Moreover, no one could even really believe it. The three-quarters of a century during which the Soviet system had endured, under which more than one generation of people had grown up, had conditioned us to think that even if this system collapsed it would not be in our time. It was too concrete to collapse on its own, just like that, without a momentous explosion and worldwide upheaval. No one, however, could fail to catch the corpse-like stench of decay. It hung in the air.

Coughing, creaking, short of breath, a new leader crawled up on to the summit of the Kremlin hill: Konstantin Chernenko. In a number of areas he even exceeded the 'achievements' of his predecessor, becoming the supreme record-holder of the Kremlin Olympus. He was seventy-three years old at the time, fate had left him a mere thirteen months to rule, and he carried with him a swag of diseases such as Andropov could not have dreamt of.

Truth be told, Konstantine Chernenko had carved himself out a spot on the edge of the Kremlin Olympus a long time ago, but not as an *éminence grise* or an all-powerful regent, but rather as a lackey, who was allowed to sit in the master's chair while he was away. In Brezhnev's time, he had replaced the 'head' when the latter got sick of routine work and had a hankering to go hunting ducks or boar. Later, when the leader was consumed with senility, Chernenko fulfilled the function of a 'surrogate president', chairing meetings of the Politburo and other secretarial work. During Andropov's reign he also spent almost half a year in that chair, giving voice in the Kremlin to his master's voice from hospital. All in all, it was as if people had become used to this stooped, outwardly personable, but poorly educated, tight-lipped old man, with his plain face, and its heavily prominent cheekbones, his mediocre intelligence and mumbling speech. Hence when on 10 February 1984, a day after the death of Andropov, the question of who was to become leader was raised before the Politburo, there was not a lot of debate. As had happened already more than once in Soviet history, the 'grey mediocrity' won. More powerful forces, fearing each other, pushed him to the top as a safe compromise for all concerned.

Konstantin Chernenko was born on the 11 September 1911, in the Siberian village of Bolshaya Tes in the Krasnoyarsk region, to a peasant family. His mother died when he was eight years old. His father got married a second time, to a mean, quarrelsome woman; thus Konstantin had to endure a good deal from his stepmother. At the age of twelve he left home and found work with a wealthy farmer. This was followed by three years of village schooling. The young lad's 'political awareness' was noted by the authorities, and he was made the Comsomol propagandist of his region, occupying this post until 1930. Next came two years serving in the border guard in Central Asia. Here Chernenko became a member of the Party, and then the head of a border detachment. That more or less was his entire 'heroic youth'.

Konstantin Chernenko did not spend the Second World War at the front, nor was he especially keen to get there, as various documents testify. In 1943–5 he studied in Moscow, in the Party propaganda school. It was at this time that he met Anna Lyubimov, his future wife. Anna was a keen, active girl – a fanatic Comsomol. Earlier, in the hungry years of collectivisation, she travelled from village to village with a 'Red Convoy', bullying hidden stores of grain away from the peasants. As she herself told, towards the end of the war in 1944 she was sent to the Volga region, to organise a 'grain-collection'. There were three men with her in the unit. One of them was a quiet, soft-spoken, shy man. When she was leaving he walked her to the station and put a note in her hand just as she was boarding the train, saying, 'Read it when the train starts moving.' She read it. Later they were married.

After Party school Konstantine Chernenko headed for the city of Penza where he worked for the Party as 'ideological supervisor' for the next three years. From 1948 he found himself in the sunny republic of Moldavia, fulfilling a similar role. It was here in July of 1950 that his 'epochal' meeting with Leonid Brezhnev occurred.

It would not be accurate to say that they hit it off immediately. Brezhnev simply noticed the helpful, slightly stooped clerk, who always appeared to be at hand, always brought him necessary paper and forms, was punctual, polite, never objected, did not ask superfluous questions and in whose eyes there always shone a dedication to authority. Simply put, he was comfortable, like old furniture. In time Brezhnev got used to this figure, and considered it indispensable, like an important possession in his office.

Some time later Brezhnev moved to Moscow. The absence of the familiar figure at his side created a certain unease, it seems, especially considering the fact that the figure would serve up reminders from time to time, in the form of servile congratulatory cards for holidays, birthdays and family celebrations. Brezhnev would then remember sunny Moldavia, bubbly wine, good and joyous times. In other words, something pleasantly sentimental.

In 1960, having received the position of head of Parliament as a present from Khrushchev, Brezhnev moved Chernenko to Moscow, making him the chief of his secretariat. For Chernenko this was the pinnacle of happiness. Now they met much more often. Brezhnev became increasingly fond of this quiet, inarticulate man, with a sheaf of papers always tucked under his arm, and eyes devotedly watching his patron.

The 'Little October' of 1964 arrived. Khrushchev was overthrown. Delirious with happiness, Leonid Brezhnev ascended the Kremlin Olympus, where he was fated to sit for eighteen long years. Konstantin Chernenko also ascended to a new clerical rung. He was now the head of the secretariat of the highest Party organ in the country, the Politburo. Like his patron, he would occupy this post for eighteen years. Even in 1978 when, on a whim of Brezhnev, he became a member of the Politburo, he would none the less remain head of the secretariat, since, second after the adoration of his patron, the office was his passion, his calling, his love. The rustle of paper, the clatter of typewriters, folders, order, secrecy ... all these were the song of his soul.

His relationship with his patron also strengthened. Not a day now went by that they did not meet. Chernenko became Brezhnev's shadow. The coughing, gasping Konstantin, incurably ill with bronchial asthma, must always be at hand. Who else would punctually hand him the medicine that the doctors prescribed, slip him paper work that needed signing, or whisper the latest gossip in his ear? Chernenko knew a great deal of gossip. He was not only a clerk, but also a 'special-department' man. 'His study contained equipment with which it was possible to listen to the telephone conversations of the highest ranked members of the Party.'

There was one more narcotic-like quality that Konstantine Chernenko possessed which warmed the soul of Brezhnev: flattery. As the Georgian proverb goes: 'Flattery will knock even a bull off his feet'. Not being a person of refined sensibilities, Chernenko naturally did not notice where flattery and servility exceeded all imaginable boundaries. The object of his adoration, however, was from a similar stable, so they matched each other perfectly. Professor Volkogonov recounts an episode which vividly illustrates both their characters. Once, while conducting a nation-wide meeting of clerks, Chernenko presuaded Brezhnev to say a few words to the audience: 'There are two important events occurring in the country at the moment, about which everyone is talking,' declared Brezhnev. 'The first is the mounting of a bust in my home town, commemorating my awards of Hero of the Soviet Union, and Hero of the Socialist Workers, and the second is my gaining the rank of Marshal of the Soviet Union ...' Chernenko got up from the praesidium table and to thunderous applause, mimicking Brezhnev's intonation, announced: 'I was hoping that you would come in the uniform of a Marshal. Since that is not the case, I will show everyone your portrait in a Marshal's dress-uniform.' A large full-size portrait was brought to the praesidium table, depicting Brezhnev wearing the gold epaulettes of a Marshal and covered with the glare of countless medals. Chernenko continued: 'Today is a great celebration ... We offer our joyous congratulations on your gaining the rank of Marshal ... After your speech we have got a second wind ... We begin every day with thought of your directives ... Your words inspire us ...'

What more could one add? The country laughed. Thank God, Brezhnev was not a tyrannical dictator, but rather a clown.

In turn, Brezhnev also treated his adjutant with kindness: 'Dear Konstantin, I got your note, thank you. I am however saddened that you have taken ill … You write that "It's nothing, I'll be better soon and back at work in a day or two." Don't take offence, but even I laughed. How nimble of him, I thought to myself, a temperature of almost 40°C. then he went to the toilet, and suddenly his temperature was 36.5°C. That's not how things work, Konstantin.'

Towards the end of 'Brezhnev's era', when the 'Head' had already fallen into deep senility, Chernenko's role grew dramatically. Now he would often give orders himself in the name of the 'Head', not even informing him. Sometimes he even beat the table with his fist at his clerks. High-ranking functionaries even begin to fawn before him.

Was Brezhnev grooming Chernenko as his successor? Doubtful. Although it might have looked that way from the outside, it is unlikely that Brezhnev thought about a successor at all. One must not forget that Brezhnev himself was not a true ruler and master of the country, a ruler-patriot, a zealous master like the Russian Czars and even like Khrushchev. Brezhnev was a 'temp', who loved to 'live it up', who had accidentally found himself in the master's comfortable chair. His aspirations did not go beyond the circle of his personal interests, hence it is doubtful that he was seriously concerned with the future of the country, and the question of succession, let alone considering someone like Chernenko, who in his eyes was not really a partner but more a servant.

Nevertheless, the habit of almost two decades of always seeing Chernenko next to the 'Head', seeing him often sitting in for the 'Head' in the chairman's seat, and of receiving orders from the 'Head' through him, all did their work. Whether they liked it or not, in the consciousness of his colleagues in the Politburo, Chernenko became the successor. Perhaps despised for his simple-mindedness, his lack of personality, his poor education, his physical frailty, but the successor none the less. Moreover, this even suited many of them to an extent. The average age of the Politburo members was around sixty-seven at the time, and some were even beyond eighty. What they wanted more than another struggle for the summit, with unpredictable results, was to live out their lives quietly and without upheaval. A successor in the form of Chernenko, without new ideas, without fire, without strength, all but guaranteed them that. He was the ideal compromise. That is the way things would have gone, had the 'Andropov factor' not interfered.

Fifteen months of Andropov's rule not only failed to unsettle Chernenko's position in the Politburo, but even strengthened it. The fear which had crawled back into the Kremlin after the assassination attempt on the Pope again reminded the Methuselahs of the Kremlin how precarious their good fortune really was. Now, after the death of Andropov, there were no obstacles to Chernenko. The 'young' Mikhail Gorbachev had not yet mustered real power, and the old men had no heart for a battle. Coughing, wheezing, gasping for breath and puffing on his inhaler, Chernenko crawled on to the Kremlin throne. As his wife remembers, he came home and said: 'They affirmed me.' 'Where did they affirm you,' I asked, ' ... into the grave? Are you in such a rush to get there?'

Subsequently, as is the norm in the Soviet system, the myth-making began, a 'heroic-biography' was woven for the new master of the Kremlin. No such biography can exist naturally, without battle, the front line and the enemy. Brezhnev as we recall, invented his heroic defence of the 'Small Land', Andropov allegedly organised partisan detachments behind enemy lines, so what did Konstantin Chernenko do during those difficult years of the war? It could not be said that in the hardest years of the war, when the battle cry of the country was 'Everything for the front! Everything for victory!' a thirty-year-old man was wearing a hole in his trousers sitting in a Party school. Thus, the poorly educated lad from a distant Asian border detachment also became a hero. The 'Song of the Border Guards' was already dedicated to him, describing how he bravely led his detachment into battle. A play was already written about him, and shooting of the film, *The Lad from the Border*, began Unfortunately, none of these projects had time to enjoy mass-consumption. Thirteen months on the throne was not long enough to get around to everything.

Chernenko started his new job with gusto. 'We will work like we did under Brezhnev,' he announced to his old colleagues from the office, not hiding his dislike of the late Andropov. This dislike was of course personal, not ideological, since Andropov's harsh methods of rule could not have raised any objections in Chernenko, who had more than once warmly reminisced about the 'order' in Stalin's day, among a close circle of friends.

Was Konstantin Chernenko a vain man by nature? It is unlikely. His whole previous life of 'service' speaks of this. It is more likely that he caught the virus of vanity from his patron. All his conscious life he had served someone, flattered someone, praised someone, and now, at the end of his life, when blind fate had thrown him into the embrace of power, he suddenly wanted to be surrounded by his own 'Chernenkos'. He sat enraptured, pathetically childlike, watching himself on the television screen, greedily read the newspapers looking for reports, opinions and comments about himself, awaited outpour-ings of flattery, smiles, compliments ...

In times gone by his patron rarely took him along on his international trips. And now, when he might have traveled, taken pleasure in the diplomatic life – the magnificence, the receptions, the fame – the doctors would not allow it. His asthma, his heart, his lungs, his kidneys ... It was hard to breathe, walk, think. In truth, he compensated somewhat for his medical ban against foreign travel by receiving high-ranking guests in the Kremlin. The king of Spain, Juan Carlos I, François Mitterand, Margaret Thatcher, Genscher, Andriotti ... Shaking the guest's hand and offering him a seat, he would then usually stick his nose into the previously prepared 'conversation pages', print-ed in a large easy-to-read font. Afraid to raise his eyes in case he lost his place or skipped a sentence, he duly recited the text, coughing, gasping, choking on the words. There was no question of adding something personal. Stringing words into sentences was always his weak point, as indeed it was among a number of his predecessors. His polite guest, in the meantime, watching the agonies of the host, might well think to himself how blind and unjust life was, burdening this old, sick man of clearly less than average intelligence with such an unbearable weight.

During the first months of his rule Chernenko worked with zeal, as much as his health would allow. He studied papers, 'decided questions', phoned around to see how things were going, demanded that things be cleared up, improved, reported upon ... His wife and three children – two daughters and a son – did not even see their father on Sundays. If the doc-tors ordered him to bed for a few days, then he would pine, fret, become depressed. It seemed he was afraid of leaving his post even for a day, wor-rying that he might lose it.

Illness and age, however, took their due. His hands shook, his legs were giving out, he was getting short of breath, his spoken words started to run together, a two- or three-minute speech came with difficulty, leaving him sweating and gasping. He now no longer appeared in his Kremlin office every day, he was simply not strong enough. A holiday on the Black Sea failed to bring relief. The master of the Kremlin was literally falling apart in front of the whole country. And he must be given his due, he fought bravely, even heroically, not for his life, however, but for the high rank which had fallen into his lap.

As Professor Volkogonov relates, Chernenko was still able to make an appearance on 7 November 1984 in the Kremlin Palace of Meetings, at a grand banquet celebrating another anniversary of the Bolshevik Revolution, and made something akin to a speech there:

> His eyes, it seemed, were skipping lines of text, since all that could be heard in the huge and hushed hall was literally gibberish. My wife who was standing next to me saw my expression change and asked me with concern: 'Are you ill?' 'I'm embarrassed,' I replied, 'embarrassed for all of us, for the country.'

On 7 February 1985 Konstantin Chernenko presided over a meeting of the Politburo for the final time. From that day his office was moved to that same hospital where his predecessor had ended his days a year previously.

How mysterious, mystical or even tragi-comical history can be. When the dying man was already unconscious, in a coma, the last letter of his life was sent in his name to Japan, to that very same person – the leader of the Japanese Communist Party – who had received an identical letter 'from the next world' one year previously from Yuri Andropov. What could this omen mean?

On 10 March 1985 Konstantin Chernenko died. His wife grieved, his children mourned their lost father. But what of the country? The country laughed, inventing stories. Regarding George Bush's subsequent arrival for the next seemingly annual funeral, the jokers wisecracked: 'In order not to bankrupt the State Department, Bush has started buying a yearly pass to Moscow.'

Postscript: Volkogonov writes: 'A locksmith was called to open Chernenko's private safe. A mute scene was to follow. Everyone was stunned. Apart from a thin folder of documents, the whole safe was stuffed full with rolls of banknotes. The drawers of the writing desk were also filled with money. Where were they from, and why did the leader need such massive amounts? Their origins can only be speculated about. But in truth, I do not feel a desire to elaborate on this topic ...'

13 | PRINCE HAMLET ON THE KREMLIN STAGE

EVEN PRIOR TO THE DEATH OF KONSTANTIN CHERNENKO, Western news-papers were writing that he would be forgotten before his funeral candles had gone out. The papers were not wrong; less than a day went by and the Kremlin was being run by the energetic young Mikhail Gorbachev. The Kremlin Olympus was in such decline that there was almost no one to battle for power. Most of the Politburo members were of such an age that malicious folk jested, 'People don't live that long!'

It is hard to write about Mikhail Gorbachev for a number of reasons. First and foremost, he is our living contemporary, about whom there is as yet no 'historically established view'. Each of us has his own deeply subjective per-spective of him, depending on which angle we view him from. A warrior for freedom of speech will always remember him with gratitude as the leader who gave the country a voice after seven decades of strained silence. A pensioner, trying to make ends meet, fondly remembers the good old days of 'overall equality in poverty', while a young businessman cannot understand how peo-ple could have lived like that. Decades will pass, time will illuminate the most important, discard the secondary, and then a future historian will be able to fashion a finished portrait of this outstanding political figure, who became one of the most influential people of the late twentieth century.

Mikhail Gorbachev was born on 2 March 1931 in the south of Russia – the northern Caucasus – in a village on the steppes called Privolnaya, in the region of Stavropol. His family, peasants for generations, lived in a hut of straw and clay, typical of the region. As his mother remembers, Mikhail came into this world with a bright red mark on his forehead which caused people to speculate. Was it the mark of one chosen by fate, or did 'the Devil mark his own'

His ancestors were Cossacks from the river Don, who had at one time set-tled here in the Caucasus in search of empty lands. The grandfather and grandmother on his mother's side were Ukrainians with the surname Gopcalo. Pantelei Gopcalo was an energetic, prosperous person of consider-able political savvy. He joined the Bolshevik Party in good time and worked his way up to the post of kolkhoz chairman. In the context of a sleepy province, this was not a minor post. In those times of collectivisation and dis-possession of the 'kulak' class, the life of a peasant depended – in the direct sense of the word – on the kolkhoz chairman. The grandfather on his father's side, Andrei Gorbachev, had a more complicated life, which was something of a family secret.

The Stavropol region, rich in land and southern sun, was always considered a comfortable corner of Russia. For more than one century the Cossacks settled there in search of 'land and freedom', a hard-working, proud and independent people. Unlike the poor northern regions of Russia, with its land-starved peasantry, Stavropol was the home of prosperous – by peasant standards – farmers, blessed with land and the skill to work it. It was clear that Stalin's collectivisation would meet with stiff resistance from the people here, and this in turn would attract repression from the authorities. The artificially created hunger across all of southern Russia and the Ukraine swept away the lives of millions of peasants – a crime comparable only to the annihilation of Jews by the Nazis. The robbing of peasants' farms, the arrest and punishment of the hardest workers, the exile to Siberia and the Far North – virtually to extinction – of hundreds of thousands of peasant families ... all of this was visited in full measure upon the Stavropol region, and on the small village of Privolnaya.

Andrei Gorbachev, Mikhail's grandfather, was a peasant of average wealth, neither rich nor poor. He had land, although no hired hands, he had cows, pigs and other livestock. One of the chores of young Mikhail was to feed this very livestock.

Grandfather Andrei did not distinguish himself with any particular political activity, nor did he join the Party. However, even this did not save him: not poor and not a Party supporter was to be an enemy. He was in the black lists of 1937. One night, they came for him. There was no need for explanation, people were just 'taken'. Eyewitnesses remember it was so frightening that even the women stood silently, fearing to cry or protest. In just this one night, in the village of Privolnaya – with its two thousand-odd inhabitants – forty people were taken. They were locked in cattle-cars, and sent to the concentration camps of the Far North. Mikhail's grandfather got ten years for allegedly hiding twenty kilograms of grain for his family, which he was obliged to hand over to the kolkhoz.

Time went by. The family were convinced that their grandfather was long since dead. Fate, however, decreed otherwise. To lay some blame on others, Stalin decided to execute the minister of the KGB, Yezhov – the 'Bloody Dwarf', as he was known among the people – accusing him of illegal repressions. For greater credibility, of the millions languishing in concentration camps, several tens of thousands of people were released. Mikhail's grandfather Andrei was one of them.

We are devoting such attention to the grandfathers of Mikhail Gorbachev, because it was they who had such a strong influence on the formation of the character of their young grandson. In these early years, when the foundations of his identity were being laid, before the child's eyes stood two examples: a prosperous 'Party' grandfather, whom he loved, and a no less beloved 'enemy of the people'. Might this not have sown the seeds of duality and indecisiveness that were to characterise the future leader? No child living at the time could fail to be affected by events such as those witnessed by young Mikhail: hunger, the annihilation of the peasantry, nighttime arrests, war, enemy occupation, Stalin's deportation of the people of the southern Caucasus ...

Mikhail had turned ten when the war with Germany started. His father was taken into the army. In August of 1942, Privolnaya was occupied by the Germans. There were no serious battles near the village. The German army passed through, leaving a garrison of sixty soldiers and a burgomaster, appointed from the local citizens.

With its first decree, the occupying force abolished the kolkhozs. Each could now work on their own field, although apart from the women and children, there was no one left. The men were at the front, the machinery had been removed, the kolkhoz livestock driven away. Yet there was no hunger. Fertile nature was all around, and a few animals were kept. Gorbachev remembers waking at dawn, to the slap of his mother's bare feet on the floor. She was returning from the yard with manure briquettes for heating the stove, and fresh steaming milk from her own cow. She was obliged to prepare food for the German soldiers quartered in their house, while young Mikhail cleaned potatoes for them.

Perhaps it was this light occupation – compared to that in other parts of the country – that later helped Mikhail Gorbachev to rid himself of the long-standing Soviet stereotype, seeing a Nazi murderer in every German. Who knows what subconscious thread connected the young Gorbachev of those times with the one on whose word the unification of Germany hinged?

In January of 1943, the occupation of Privolnaya ended. The family was fortunate, the father returning alive from the war. In the summer holiday months, the son began to work with his father in a tractor machine station, as an assistant combine operator. This continued until his eighteenth birthday.

Mikhail's father Sergei was a quiet, gentle person, with a technical slant to his mind. He spent a greater part of his life as a combine operator, and as a mechanic, repairing farming equipment. He was not the real head of the family, and had only a minor influence on his son. Mikhail's mother Maria Gorbachev, however, a strong, thick-set woman, was a chip off her father Pantelei Gopcalo, and the complete opposite of her husband. As their neighbours remember, she was active, talkative, loud and even quarrelsome. While she did not possess any particular education, and wrote with great effort, no event of even the mildest importance occurred in the village without her, and her voice was always heard first. She was pushy, and it was practically impossible to stop her train of thought and speech, or argue her down. She was the real head of the family.

People who knew the Gorbachevs well think that Mikhail followed his mother's line, in character, while his younger brother Alexander, with whom Mikhail was never close, inherited their father's side. Gorbachev himself also says that, emotionally he was closer to his mother, while intellectually he was more influenced by his father.

In 1950 Mikhail finished school with a silver medal, and attended the law faculty of Moscow University – the most élite in the country. This was a period of yet another peak of Stalinist terrors: a time of secret political murders, a rise in anti-Semitism, the annihilation of the creative intelligentsia, the 'Jewish Doctors' Plot'. It goes without saying that at this time the law faculty did not train specialists, called to defend justice and the law, but rather to mould future Party and KGB functionaries, camouflaged by a lawyer's diploma and dedicated to uphold Stalin's regime.

Did Mikhail have a talent for the legal sciences? His high-school teachers say that he was more interested in literature, theatre and art, was an excellent amateur actor, and even dreamed at one point of going to study at theatre school. He liked to speak, perform and organise, and even once announced that he wanted to become a diplomat. Indeed, there was something 'diplomatic' in his character. He learned not to quarrel, always sought to compromise, and had a knack for attracting people he needed.

For a lad from a sleepy farming province, the life of a student in Moscow was new, interesting and in a way even mysterious. The names of famous professors, foreign students, the children of leading Moscow families, flaunting their superiority and often teasing his lack of culture and provincial southern accent. But Mikhail needs to be given his due, for this did not upset him. After the first few terms, he fully acclimatised to his new surroundings.

He lived in a boarding house, in an old Moscow building, built back in the time of Peter the Great as a barracks for soldiers. Each room housed between seven and twenty-five people. There were no particular creature comforts – a toilet, kitchen and outside bath, all communal. The majority of the students were former soldiers, so Mikhail was one of the youngest. Fellow faculty member and long-time friend, the Czech Zdenik Mlinarzh, who later became a leading figure of the 'Prague Spring'*, remembers how drunkenness was widespread among the students in those days and was considered an important aspect of male pride. Mikhail eagerly participated in evening festivities, but drank little, which invariably raised suspicion among the lads as to whether he might be an informant.

The political maturity and social activities of the first-year student were valuable. He soon became the Comsomol leader of his group, and then of the whole faculty. It is interesting to hear how Gorbachev's fellow faculty members reacted to him. He seemed a happy and intelligent boy, neat, careful and reserved. He possessed a certain magnetism, attracting people and with a knack for getting them to open up and reveal the information he needed. He was hard-working, often sitting at his studies until two or three in the morning. He liked to eat and was not interested in sport. He expressed minimal interest in women and had no extra-curricular hobbies. He was a 'correct' Comsomol and never deviated from the Party line. Occasionally, in the company of friends, he might flare up and speak from the heart, even about political issues, but quickly changed to the opposite opinion. Some of the students were wary of him but by and large he was trusted. No one openly accused him of collaborating with the KGB, but many considered it impossible to be the Comsomol secretary of the law faculty and not be hand in glove with the KGB, since those were the rules of the game. But none of his fellow students saw in him the mark of a future government leader.

In 1953 Mikhail met his wife-to-be, Raisa Titorenko, who studied philosophy in the same university. Raisa was born in southern Siberia, to the family of a railwayman. The family then moved to Rostov, on the river Don. Here Raisa finished high school with a gold medal, which gave the opening to Moscow University. Mikhail and Raisa met at a dance and it was love at first sight. Raisa was an attractive, vivacious young woman with a marvellously slender figure, and a trail of suitors to whom she paid no heed. Mikhail had to spend more than a week walking around and sighing to attract her attention.

They were married in the autumn of 1953. While still in his first year, Mikhail once admitted to his friends that he only knew what opera and bal-

* The democratic movement in Czechoslovakia which led to the revolution of 1968.

let were by word of mouth. Now, after their marriage, Raisa began the cultural education of her husband, forcing him to attend the theatre and to go to museums and exhibitions. 'He grew before our very eyes,' says a fellow faculty member. Those student friends who remain close friends of the family to this day, say that their love not only did not wane with the passing of years but even grew stronger. Zdenik Mlinarzh writes that Raisa was a key factor of Gorbachev's success. In time, she would become the alter-ego of her husband, influencing his character and being involved with him in the resolution of world political questions. So, the heightened attention afforded her by the public was fully deserved.

As the end of the university days approached, Raisa and Mikhail dreamed of staying and working in Moscow. Only there could they continue their academic careers and make their marks. According to accepted practice, Comsomol leaders usually remained in the capital, but Mikhail's case was somehow an unfortunate one. Applying to the Moscow judiciary with a request for work, he received a very cold response advising him to go back home.

The Stavropol of the time, to which Mikhail and Raisa, now expecting, returned was a sleepy, dusty, one-storey town of one hundred thousand inhabitants, with a single-track railway connecting it to the outside world. As someone joked, a 'warm Siberia'. The Gorbachevs settled in a private apartment, renting a room from the landlord, where their daughter Ira was born. She would grow up to become a doctor, marry a surgeon colleague and bear her delighted parents two granddaughters.

For the time being, however, Mikhail became a junior inspector in the Stavropol judiciary. Raisa also got a job in the local medical institute, where she started to teach political science. However, Gorbachev only worked a few months in his chosen profession, and was offered a transfer to work for the Comsomol. From then on his path to the top was to be a direct one, without diversions. In 1960 he was already head of the Comsomol for the entire Stavropol region. In 1962 at the age of thirty-one, thanks to his ability to avoid controversy and please the establishment, he was already an important functionary of the upper Party élite of the region. In 1966 he was Party head of the city of Stavropol. And the point here was not 'connections'. Devotion to career, a capacity for hard work carried to the extreme, pragmatism, total loyalty to the Party line coupled with the knack of compromise, an ability to bend his point of view, sound knowledge of the provincial environment that had raised him – allied, not least, with the liberal atmosphere of

'Khrushchev's Spring' – these are the main factors which came together fortuitously to impel Gorbachev forward and upward.

At this time Gorbachev took another sensible step: he completed a local agricultural institute course by correspondence, thereby adding an agronomy diploma to his diploma in law. Granted that in his current position it was not a very difficult thing to do. Try to imagine a professor who would fail the examination attempt of the city's Party leader!

When the First Secretary of the Stavropol region was transferred to work in the Kremlin, the obvious choice to succeed him was the young, obedient Party man who was already his deputy. Mikhail Gorbachev had not yet turned forty, ludicrously young for such an important post, yet when he was proposed for the position of 'First', Moscow gave its consent.

On the regional level, Gorbachev's career had reached its peak. The post of First Secretary, which he received in April 1970, was the absolute ceiling beyond which lay only the distant heights of the Kremlin. But to get there, to the very summit, it would be necessary to gain the attention of the powers-that-be in Moscow.

For the attainment of this goal, Stavropol was the ideal place. Whoever called the Stavropol region a 'warm Siberia' must have been talking of its intellectual and cultural pretensions, not its natural assets. In that respect, this was a little corner of Heaven. The foothills of the Caucasus boasted hot sunshine and snow simultaneously. The Caucasus mineral springs, around the Black Sea, which had constituted the best resort complex of Czarist Russia and attracted the aristocracy, was now the site of numerous sanatoriums, including exclusive government ones where the 'Kremlin elders' would come to treat their aches and pains.

One of the duties of the 'master of the region' was to welcome these important guests, ensure they had every comfort, indulge them, entertain them and generally wait on them hand and foot. What better opportunity to establish personal contact? Mikhail Gorbachev used these occasions to full effect. It was here that he became close to Yuri Andropov, the Chief of the KGB who regularly travelled to the 'springs' to tend his ailing kidneys. (As a matter of fact, Gorbachev himself suffered from hereditary diabetes associated with the kidneys. It was because of this that his wife monitored his diet so strictly, while he himself was a fierce opponent of alcohol.)

The gentle sun, the relaxed atmosphere of the resorts, similar medical procedures, all this was an excellent combination for friendship and dialogue. Bored by holiday routine, Andropov was pleased to invite the intelligent and comparatively young couple Mikhail and Raisa to his government villa, where they would talk about philosophy, literature, poetry and listen to music.

Andropov and Gorbachev would together go on leisurely walks, marvelling at the beauty of the mountains, talking about topics that interested them. Although of different generations, they saw themselves as having much in common, both considering themselves intellectuals; gradually a warm father-son relationship was established, though never crossing the line of mutual politeness.

In July 1978, the former 'master' of the Stavropol region who had advanced Gorbachev's career, died suddenly in Moscow. The deceased had been a member of the Politburo, in charge of agriculture. Gorbachev travelled to the capital for the funeral. After the ceremony he called an old university friend and she jokingly said, 'Well Mikhail, there is a vacant place in the Kremlin now. Time to move to Moscow.'

The joke turned out to be prophetic. Barely two months went by, and the forty-seven-year-old Party boss from Stavropol found himself among the most influential figures of the Kremlin. This was not yet the summit of Olympus, but certainly in the foothills. Gorbachev himself was taken by surprise. Arriving in Moscow, he called his friend again and asked, 'How could you have foretold this? You're a real Cassandra!' to which she laughingly replied, 'Just you wait. Even greater success awaits you.'

Nothing unexpected had really happened, however, everything was within the bounds of logic. The 1970s were drawing to a close; the country was slowly decaying. Yuri Andropov was grappling towards the pinnacle of power and was pulling 'his' people after him. It was beyond argument that Mikhail Gorbachev was one of them. Even Brezhnev himself liked him, especially after he presented the vain leader with a beautiful album containing photographs of himself along with his 'great utterances'. That, plus two higher education diplomas – almost unheard of at that level of the Kremlin hierarchy – put the final stamp of approval in place.

And so, Gorbachev was in the Kremlin, among the thirty most powerful Party officials. The next step was the Politburo. In October 1980 he overcame this barrier as well. On Andropov's recommendation, forty-eight-year-old Mikhail Gorbachev was 'elected' a member of the Kremlin's 'super-government'.

Much changed in Gorbachev's life in these two short years. He moved to the capital from provincial Stavropol, taking with him, to be sure, his provincial accent and similar mannerisms. However, he gained a new office in the main Party building of the country, where the 'deathless ones' preside, and a huge limousine with gently purring tyres, which was deferred to courteously by all the traffic police.

Raisa, too, went up in the world, growing in self-confidence and ambition. She now lectured on Marxist philosophy in Moscow University – 'the limousine-riding Marxist,' as her students jibed. All this was pleasant, although there were some inconveniences as well. It was no longer possible as in Stavropol to take a walk with Mikhail along the street or through a park, perhaps to drop into the theatre ... The dizzy height of the post carried obligations. But there was a grand new residence, with a giant fireplace, a cinema, a huge kitchen, a winter garden with a glass roof, for relaxation and sunbathing, as well as a numerous staff.

One wonders whether Raisa, with her philosophical education, ever asked herself the question: 'What would have happened if back then, after university, Mikhail and I had stayed and worked in Moscow? Would he have then reached such heights or, like his younger brother Alexander, would he have become an official in an ordinary Moscow ministry?' Who knows? More than likely he would not even have got that far. The path to power is a complex and tangled one, and he who travels it must – like a predator – have enough space in which to run and pounce. It may be no accident that all the leaders of Russia, without exception, came from the provinces. Had Gorbachev remained in Moscow, beneath the Kremlin walls, he would probably have been lost among the horde of the capital's bureaucrats, scrabbling over the bodies of one another.

In November 1982 Yuri Andropov assumed supreme power at the Kremlin. Although officially Konstantin Chernenko was considered the number two man, in actual fact that person was already Mikhail Gorbachev. And on 11 March 1985, less than a day after the death of Chernenko, Gorbachev formally 'took' power and became master of the Kremlin.

My opinion is that while he occupied the highest post in the land, ideas of *glasnost* and *perestroika* were far from Mikhail Gorbachev's mind. Indeed, there was little to distinguish him from his predecessors. The same Party boorishness, the filthy language and impudence, the same Lenin-like mudslinging of opponents. For instance, after meeting with President Reagan, Gorbachev described him to his colleagues in the Politburo as a man 'who is characterised by profound primitivism, a prehistoric countenance and intellectual impotence ... In the persons of the representatives of the American administration we have people without moral conscience ...' This was the head of the country talking about his partner in negotiations, whose hand he had just shaken.

The only thing that the new leader seemed to sense better than his colleagues was that the country stood on the edge of an abyss, that something had to be done. This in truth was no great discovery: the fact that it was no longer possible to go on living this way was evident to any schoolboy. The only people who did not want to know about it were the Kremlin 'Methuselahs' who dreamed of finishing their life in serenity and comfort. The country in the meantime was drinking itself to death, and experiencing acute poverty. According to secret statistics of 'competent organs', up to ten million unconscious drunks a year were picked up in the streets of towns and villages by law enforcement officials. Imagine the entire population of Greece or twice that of Switzerland lying by the road in a ditch!

It is easy to say; 'something must be done'. But what? It is difficult to give advice even today, so what about back then? Gorbachev did not have anyone to learn from, nor anyone to turn to for advice. He had to act on intuition. The fact that he nevertheless decided to act was already one of his great achievements.

His first attack was directed at drunkenness. The price of alcohol jumped sharply, its production was cut back, vineyards began to be cut down. The drinking population unanimously replied with effective counter-measures. Sugar vanished from the stores as people used it to make moonshine. As in any prohibition period, underground trafficking of alcohol flourished. The poorer members of the population began to consume anything which contained even the scent of alcohol in its make-up: perfume, poisonous wood alcohol, varnish, and even highly flammable mixtures of polish. I remember a drunken refrain I overheard at the time: 'Get away from me, you bastard, or I'll breathe on you and set you on fire!' The numbers rolling around in ditches did not drop, but the hospitals overflowed with poisoned patients.

At the end of 1986 Gorbachev took a step which catapulted his approval rating in the West. He made a telephone call to the city of Gorky – a place closed to foreigners – where the academician Andrei Sakharov and his wife had lived in exile for seven years. Without apologies or explanation, Gorbachev told the disgraced scientist that the Politburo had allowed him to return to Moscow. One wonders if Gorbachev, the qualified lawyer, ever asked himself what manner of quasi-judicial organ this Politburo was, which could send a man into exile without investigation or trial, or return him from there on a whim. Probably not. In 1985, before the Twelfth Worldwide Festival of Youth and Students in Moscow, the Minister of the KGB wrote him a memo in which he proposed that a few dozen 'politically unreliable' representatives of the intelligentsia be 'isolated' (without any cause) for the duration of the festival. The lawyer Gorbachev wrote on this document 'In favour – Gorbachev 24.7.85'. And Stalin and Beria were long gone.

In any event, after the phone call to Gorky, Gorbachev's popularity in the West was greater than that of any Soviet leader over the past decades. The West saw the hand of human compassion in this act, a trait not readily associated with the 'Evil Empire'.

Gorbachev's relationship with the West is one of the brightest pages of his biography. As at one time, the audacious journey of Peter the Great into Europe opened the West to Russians, so now – shattering all Soviet stereotypes – Gorbachev's visit to England reintroduced Europeans to modern Russia. From the moment the Soviet Il-62, carrying the Gorbachevs on board, landed at London Airport, the West was seduced by this 'new Russian'. The year was 1984, Chernenko was still alive. Yet, perhaps foreseeing his rapid ascent of the Kremlin 'throne', Margaret Thatcher paid him the respect usually reserved only for heads of state.

Prior to this, the television viewer in the West might have caught a glimpse of a Soviet leader's wife at her husband's funeral, under a black veil, looking like a grandmother. This Soviet leader not only brought his wife with him, but also showed her off to the world with enthusiasm and indeed a touch of pride. A flirtatious half-length fur coat and hat, à la Cossack, fur-lined boots, tastefully applied mascara, a friendly laugh, witty responses to journalists, the ability to play up to the TV cameras – all this made her seem more the Hollywood star than the Russian grandmother. She flitted happily through the stores with an American Express credit card, even if her purchase with that card of a Cartier diamond ring worth several thousand pounds, while astonishing Western viewers, may have provoked anger among those back home.

The black Rolls-Royce with the little red flag carried the couple around the sights of London – Westminster Abbey, Parliament, the British Museum … Raisa enthusiastically discussed architecture, culture and history. Indeed it was impossible to stem the flow of her words. She knew everything about anything and better than anyone. It was hard to believe that this was her first official visit to the West. For the duration of the visit, she became the darling of British television. Just as President Kennedy once jokingly included himself in the entourage of his wife Jacqueline, so Gorbachev could include himself in Raisa's retinue. The press joked, 'Raisa is his secret weapon.' He himself once remarked wryly: 'This woman not only costs me a lot of money, but a lot of worry as well.'

As we have already said, it is hard to overestimate the influence of the First Lady on her husband. Gorbachev almost never travelled without her. She was his chief adviser, edited his speeches and influenced his decisions. A former Gorbachev aide writes: 'She was involved in the formulation of policies ... and in the distribution of portfolios. Most important of all, she formed the character of the President ...' She gave practical advice to the directors of the country's largest industries, insisting it should be carried out. When the confused director suggested that he required 'orders from the top', Raisa would reply, 'You'll get a call', and indeed that call would duly be received.

The incompatibility of Raisa's overflowing personality with that of American First Lady Nancy Reagan became a favourite topic of the world press. On her first visit to the White House, Raisa informed Nancy that it was not a home but a museum, and no one could be expected to live there. Nancy Reagan herself writes in her memoirs:

> I was nervous before my first meeting with Raisa Gorbachev ... I didn't know what we would talk about, but as it soon turned out, it made no difference. For the first minute she herself talked and talked, so much that I could hardly get a word in ... The impression that I got ... was that she never stops talking, or to put it more accurately, to lecture ... One or two times she even lectured me on the shortcomings of the American political system ... In Geneva, she impressed me as wanting to appear a woman whose word is law. She didn't like the chair she was sitting on, she clicked her fingers. The KGB bodyguards instantly offered her another. I could not believe my eyes. I've met First Ladies, Princesses, Queens, but I've never seen any of them act that way.

At a function in honour of Gorbachev, hosted by the Secretary of State George Schultz, Raisa was introduced to an intelligent lady involved with the problems of human rights. 'What do you think,' she ventured to Raisa, 'what kind of joint efforts could we make in this field? 'What is your educational background?' Raisa asked her. The lady answered bashfully that she had graduated from Geneva College. 'I am a philosopher,' answered Raisa, 'and I'll give you a philosophical answer. From the moment of birth, every human being has problems to do with human rights.' When being introduced to the Pope in Rome, the Lady Gorbachev presented herself as: 'Raisa Maximovna, from Russia!' The similarity to 'The Russian Empress Catherine the Great' called forth a smile from those present. It was not without reason that Gorbachev called her 'my general'.

All this would not warrant attention if it had not occurred at such a high level. As one wise and politically astute individual said, only half in jest: 'If you want to discern the reason for tension in one or another region of the world, pay closer attention to the relationship of highly placed wives and mothers-in-law.'

This is even more pertinent when the region in question is a country as conservative as Russia. Not yet rid of the archaic view that women should 'not be prominent', the Soviet citizen saw something anti-national and even amoral in the 'Raisa factor'. They blamed Gorbachev for this even more than for all the errors of *perestroika*. The trips overseas with her husband were to an extent forgiven by the Soviet television viewers since 'It's diplomacy', 'That's what people expect over there', 'But why the hell does she tag along after him inside the country?' As always, Soviet society responded not with anger but with sarcasm: 'Across Russia dashes a Troika* – Mishka, Raika, Perestroika ...'

So much for the diversion. Mikhail Gorbachev's week-long visit to London was his triumph. The Iron Lady told the whole world: 'I like Mr Gorbachev. We can do business together.' The papers reported that they were compatible not only in politics, but also in simple human terms. There was even speculation as to whether they were physically attracted to each other. Those close to Margaret Thatcher said that they rarely saw her in such high spirits as during her meetings with Mikhail Gorbachev. 'I have not spoken with a single Soviet leader the way I spoke with him,' announced Mrs Thatcher.

Unfortunately, Gorbachev's countrymen did not share this enthusiasm. To their eyes the leader had two faces, one for export and another for local use. The local face of Gorbachev so far differed little from those of his predecessors. If Khrushchev promised the Soviet people complete communist abundance, Mikhail Gorbachev, with similar flippancy, promised every Soviet family a separate flat. If Khrushchev had his bloody Novocherkassk, where tanks fired at protesting workers, then Gorbachev had many such 'hot spots' – witness the events of Vilnius, Baku, Alma Ata and Tbilisi.

---

* Traditional Russian holiday recreation: a sled festooned with bells, and pulled by three horses.

'During the break-up of the first rows of protestors, in the face of fierce resistance of extremists using sticks and stones, the crowd became uncontrollable ... As a result of the subsequent pressure, sixteen people died, thirteen young women and three men ...' These are lines from a telegram sent to the Kremlin by the Party head of Georgia, regarding the events of 8 April 1989 on the square in front of the Government House in Tbilisi.

I was in the square that frightening night and can personally testify that the official information was a lie. The many thousands in the crowd were young, carefree and happy. They had little in common with extremists. The purpose of the gathering was a hunger strike in front of the Government House by a dozen young people demanding 'freedom for Georgia'. The special forces were brought into the city during the day. Towards nightfall they surrounded the square, but no one could even imagine that they were preparing to attack an unarmed crowd. Everyone simply assumed that they were there just for show to intimidate and keep the peace. Not long before the start of the bloody events, the Patriarch of Georgia appeared before the crowd, pleading with the people to disperse because, in his own words, he had just become aware that something terrible might be about to happen. The crowd replied with silence.

Suddenly, this terrible event began. The headlights of military trucks flashed on, and uniformed people advanced on the crowd. These were not young, freshly conscripted soldiers, but apparently specially selected 'grizzled wolves' thirty to forty years of age. It seemed that they were all heavily under the influence. They carried short, razor-sharp sappers' shovels in their hands, with which they proceeded literally to carve up the crowd. Why did more young women die? Well, because the young girls moved up opposite the soldiers, trying to stop them, shouting, 'What are you doing? – thinking that the soldiers at least would not touch them. But they did, hacking them down with the shovels. Cans containing some sort of gas flew into the scattering, panic-stricken crowd. As doctors later explained, this was a paralysing nerve agent nicknamed 'bird-cherry'. I myself spent a day in hospital, suffering a thankfully mild poisoning from the gas. I learned, however, from the doctors that out of the many dozen admitted with a diagnosis of poisoning, some did not leave alive.

I am revealing this in order to show that the figure of the leader of *perestroika* is far more complicated and contradictory than it seemed both in the West and at home. The West attributed positive characteristics to Gorbachev that he simply did not possess, and at home, quite the contrary, he was crucified for all the evil that was inherent in the system itself and not his personal doing. Nowadays, it is not uncommon to hear that the system was already dead when Gorbachev came to power, that with or without him it was just about to collapse, that he played no special role in this, he was simply the 'favourite of history', finding himself in the right place at the right time. All this is both true and not true. As to the former allegation, somehow all of us, even the wisest, were caught totally unprepared by this collapse of the system. We all foresaw it, but only in some kind of perspective, 'not in our day'. This might have dragged on for the lifetime of our whole generation. Because of this, I feel we should accept without irony Gorbachev's words that, at his whim, had he not wished to humanise the system, he could have ruled quite comfortably for another decade without any kind of *perestroika*.

The particular quality of such a harsh totalitarian system as the Soviet one was that any change could only occur from the top. Change from below was impossible, since, as we have had countless opportunities to convince ourselves, it would be crushed by tanks. For a politician who was in favour of democratic changes to reach the top was equally unlikely, since the system only promoted people in its own image. So, when we speak of Gorbachev, it is important to understand that he was a man of the system, yet the best of those that the system could somehow allow to get to the top. Coming to power, he did not even consider dismantling the system, he only wanted to improve it, to give it a 'human face'. But moving this Sisyphean boulder, which the system had unsuccessfully attemped to roll up the hill of Communism, he could no longer hold it in place. The boulder, gathering speed, careered downward, demolishing everything in its path. The *glasnost* Gorbachev announced tore the system apart from the inside, since its foundation was a lie. Gorbachev's greatest virtue was that, having started the process of *perestroika*, and understanding that the system was no longer viable, he – after some wavering – refused to prop it up with bayonets and tanks, giving it the opportunity to self-destruct. He was the first Soviet leader to understand the wisdom of the cunning Talleyrand, who told the Emperor of France: 'You can do a lot with bayonets, but you can't sit on them.'

Gorbachev's angry refrain: 'What? You want to solve the problem with tanks again!' in answer to the hard-liners' demands to crush the anti-communist uprising in Rumania, will forever remain to his credit. When speaking about Gorbachev one must remember that, having become the gravedigger of Communism, he was simultaneously, if not an orthodox believer, then at least a practising Communist.

Every period of Soviet history had its sore points. If for Andropov, that point was the South Korean Boeing, then for Gorbachev – as if symbolising the disintegration of the system – it was Chernobyl.

On 26 April 1986, at 1:23 a.m., 130 kilometres from Kiev, an event occurred which was destined to stand alongside such historical cataclysms as the destruction of Pompeii or the Lisbon earthquake of 1755. The reactor of a nuclear power plant had exploded. Carried away by the wind, the deadly radioactive clouds spread out over the planet. Only a few hours after the catastrophe, the Western world sounded the alarm. The Scandinavian countries started transmitting information on the radioactivity situation, vegetables were quickly destroyed in northern Italy, and even in distant America, milk was tested for radiation. The whole world demanded clarification of what had happened, but the Kremlin remained stubbornly silent. The Soviet people had so far not received a single sentence of information. In the zone of the accident, children played as usual, pensioners warmed themselves in the spring sunshine and the young people celebrated weddings. It was spring, the May celebrations were nearing, with their warm days, parades and long weekends, while the unseen death spread across the vast regions of the Ukraine and Belorussia. As scientists later established, over 150,000 people were exposed to serious radiation poisoning. And the Kremlin was still silent. Only on 28 April, the Politburo gathered under the chairmanship of Mikhail Gorbachev, to decide what information to release and what not to release.

I shall never forget a certain documentary film shot somewhat later. Drunken villagers are catching fish in a river near Chernobyl. The cameraman is trying to explain to them that the fish harbours death within, that they must not eat it. 'No worries,' laugh the men, 'that there radiation won't get to us, we'll drown it with vodka.'

Nowadays this sounds incredible, but back then that was simply the way it was. The inertia of secrecy and silence still prevailed. The Politburo had already handled previous crises in just such a manner. Back in September of 1954, on the Totsk training ground in the Orenburg region, almost in the very centre of Russia, near populated villages, the first military manoeuvres in the history of humanity involving the use of a live nuclear bomb took place. Think about it, the first nuclear strike against the Russian people was carried out by their own government. Later, in October 1957, in the Chelyabinsk region of the Urals, an accident occurred at a plutonium manufacturing plant – a 'little Chernobyl' – covering an area of 20,000 square kilometres in radiation, where thousands of unsuspecting people were living. All this was kept secret from the world for decades.

The history of Chernobyl is well known and I mention it here not only because, in my opinion, it signified the last symbolic death knell of the disintegrating Soviet system, but also proved to be a severe test for Gorbachev himself, pushing him towards the impending announcement of a 'new way of thinking'. To Gorbachev's credit, it must be said that, at the meeting of the Politburo, he was the first to declare: 'We must make an announcement quickly, we can't delay.' Then after a pause he added: 'The more honestly we behave, the better.' And this was only the second year of his government.

The acme of Gorbachev's popularity in the West came during 1989–91, while the award of the Nobel Peace Prize was in essence his crowning glory. Whatever people might say, he deserved that prize more than possibly any other of its recipients, for there is no man in the twentieth century who did more for the neutralisation of the global nuclear threat to our entire civilisation than Mikhail Gorbachev. 'Gorby! Gorby!' the delighted West greeted him. All the more hurtful and unjust, then, was the fact that his countrymen at home reacted to the award in a negative and even hostile manner. The higher his political credibility rose in the West, the lower it fell in his own country. This may well be the deepest tragedy of Gorbachev the politician.

The threat of physical destruction hung constantly over Gorbachev, beginning in 1987. The duality of his actions created a paradoxical situation. He was threatened both from the left and from the right. Fanatics with democratic leanings saw him as an obstacle in the path of those reforms to which he himself gave impulse, while communist fanatics saw him as a traitor who had deceived the party. The events of Rumania and the fate of Nicolae Ceausescu seemed a very relevant example to both sides. The personal guard was strengthened many times. However, despite all precautions, shots were fired. On 7 November 1990, during the annual celebration of the anniversary of the Bolshevik Revolution, when the entire party leadership of the country stood on Lenin's mausoleum, a certain Alexander Shmonov from Leningrad, dissatisfied with the speed of democratic reforms, fired two shots meant for Gorbachev. Fortunately, a tragedy did not occur. As the previous head of Gorbachev's personal guard attests, this was not the only attempt. Although there is another version: none of these attempts was real, but staged by the Secret Service to frighten the 'reformer'.

The people have a saying: 'Do no good and you'll receive no evil.' Unfortunately, this rule seems often to be verified in political life, when the benefactor becomes the victim of the recipient. There are hundreds of such examples: we need only remember such crucial ties as Lenin–Stalin, Khrushchev–Brezhnev, Brezhnev–Andropov. Mikhail Gorbachev was also destined to be linked in this way ...

Mikhail Gorbachev and Boris Yeltsin were already acquainted from the days of their lives in the provinces, when the former was the master of a rich agricultural region – Stavropol, while the later presided over the industrial giants of the most industrialised region of the country – Sverdlovsk, in the Urals. From time to time Gorbachev would ask his colleague to assist the region with metals and machinery, while returning the favour with the bounties of the south. From time to time they would meet at Kremlin gatherings, greeting each other with a friendly handshake. When Gorbachev was transferred to Moscow, Yeltsin was the first to come by his office, offered his congratulations '... and we embraced warmly'.

They were almost the same age, although polar opposites. If Gorbachev possessed flexibility and cunning, then Yeltsin was quite the reverse – direct and even a little simple, although he distinguished himself with a dynamic temperament and unquenchable energy.

Aiming to revitalise the Kremlin inner circle, Gorbachev invited Yeltsin to work in Moscow. The acclimatisation of the hard-bitten provincial to life in the capital was a painful affair. By nature he was a populist, his forte was face-to-face contact with people, masculine directness, the long stride across the factory floor, giving orders off the cuff, hustling people into action. Now, however, he encountered the quiet, softly carpeted Kremlin corridors, rigid subordination coupled with unmistakable fawning, abasement before strong 'palace' intrigue

In December 1985, on Gorbachev's recommendation, Yeltsin was already the Party head of Moscow and a candidate for membership of the Politburo. It had been a long time since Muscovites had seen such a 'head', whom you could run into of a morning in a crowded city bus, standing in line for bread or sausages, at the cinema or in the markets. You could get an appointment with him and even air a grievance. A rumour spread among the food retailers of the city that the directors of dozens of the larger stores had already been fired, and that the delicacies hidden for decades under the counters – 'for their own use'– had been put out for sale. People whispered almost unbelievable things, that the new Party head of the city was already at work at 8 o'clock in the morning, and that you might still catch him in his office at midnight. In a word, the 'good Czar' that the Russian people always dreamed of had arrived ...

Rumours also circulated through the party bureaucracy. Yeltsin had already fired more than half the regional Party bosses of the capital. He had refused a luxurious dacha and chosen a more modest one. Nor did he want to move to a magnificent flat, more befitting his current status, but stayed in the ordinary one that he had been assigned upon moving to Moscow. He used regular medical facilities, not the 'government only' ones. When going for a holiday down south, he did not fly in the personal plane assigned to him, but took a seat on a regular flight.

This is not all for nothing, whispered the Party bureaucrats, he is playing up to the people, he wants cheap respect. But there were whispers not only in the Kremlin. Conversations about Yeltsin became a favourite topic among Muscovites. Sympathy towards him grew. Gorbachev observed all this with growing envy.

A year went by in this fashion. Yeltsin was finding his job more and more difficult. The more support Muscovites expressed for him, the more his colleagues in the Kremlin actively hated him. He had to make a decision, either to make his peace and become 'like everyone' or to head for a schism.

Time went on. The celebrations commemorating the seventieth anniversary of the Bolshevik Revolution approached. The Politburo gathered in honour of this. Everything proceeded as normal – flowery speeches, words, promises. Boris Yeltsin also got up to speak. His words did not yet contain explosive force, but there was already some veiled criticism there. He very warily talked about how it was time to clarify for the people what exactly *perestroika* was and how long it would go on, a year, two, three, twenty? The mood of the people depended on this, as did its faith in realistic results. Gorbachev carefully observed his protégé, even agreeing with him on some points, but his eyes did not carry the former light of friendship.

In October 1987 a Party plenary session convened. Everything once again went smoothly, until Yeltsin raised his hand. Expectant silence hung over the hall, since he was already considered a 'dissident' among this circle. Repeating his words about the duration of *perestroika*, Yeltsin suddenly looked in the direction of the praesidium and added: 'I am for instance deeply troubled by sycophancy from some members of the Politburo, towards the person of the General Secretary …' Now the silence in the hall became charged. Since the days of Stalin, it had not been acceptable to speak such words about the 'master'. Gorbachev looked at his opponent more with irony than anger. Who did he intend to tangle with? Yeltsin continued: 'It seems that my work is not effective as a part of the Politburo … I am obliged to ask you to release me from my duties as a candidate for membership of the Politburo' and ponderously left the podium.

So began, as they say, the persecution of the heretic. Taking the stand as a strong and confident leader, he left it as a nobody. Neither Gorbachev nor Yeltsin, of course, could then have foreseen that the moment of this 'fall' would mark the beginning of his ascent to the heights of world politics. From this day forward, an open battle was declared between the two most powerful leaders of Russia towards the end of the twentieth century, in many ways determining the future of the country.

So what was the deep divide between these two men? Only yesterday they had both been, if not orthodox, then at least practising communists. Both went through more or less the same school of Party life. Neither had ever deviated from the Party line, nor could they deviate, or they would not have found themselves at its pinnacle. So where was the point on their common road where their paths diverged? Could these just have been petty ambitions, personal quarrels, a squabble for power? Could such measly reasons have had a cardinal effect on the fate of millions? Are we so easy to fool? Unfortunately, such a version is not impossible, although we do not want to believe in it. I feel that the root of this conflict, perhaps even unconsciously, lay not only in personal but also in deeper reasons. Gorbachev's divided loyalties did not yet allow him to break completely with that ossified communist dogma which he had served for so many years. His concept of *perestroika* was tied into preserving the system, but giving it a more human face. Yeltsin, on the other hand, as a result of a more direct character and one closer to the people, was more attuned to the inhuman nature of the system which had fully exhausted its resources. Consciously or not, he was not heading for 're-structuring' so much as 'new-structuring', for the complete replacement of the existing order. Gorbachev would also come to this, but later on and too late ...

In the end both opponents were to become President. Gorbachev, as the President of the USSR, practically appointing himself to the post without general elections or a struggle, and assuming, it would seem, there to be no other alternative candidates (although as a sharp wit once remarked, 'Only Dostoyevsky has no alternatives.') Gorbachev's opponent was to act with more courage, a year later becoming the first generally elected President of Russia in her many centuries of history.

In the spring of 1991, there was a moment in the opposition of these two men (which will be covered in more detail in the next chapter) when fate handed them a chance to turn the history of the country in one essential direction. The danger of disintegration already hung over the empire. The President of the USSR felt power slipping out of his hands. One after another, former republics were declaring themselves independent. Gorbachev's holdings shrank down to the walls of the Kremlin. He was becoming a king without a kingdom, and was already being nicknamed 'The Commandant of the Kremlin'. Something had to be decided.

In May, the heads of the republics gathered in the residence of the President of the USSR, outside Moscow. The formation of a completely new union was discussed; the Commonwealth of Independent States. As Yeltsin remembers, the situation was so weighty that even he and Gorbachev found it within themselves to put aside personal matters, communicate like 'normal people' and even drink a glass of cognac. It seemed that everything was just about to fall into its required place. The country would avoid disintegration and, like the phoenix, be reborn in its better form. All that remained was to sign the Agreement of Union. Only to sign it ...

What forces drove Gorbachev to leave at this very moment for a holiday in the Crimea? Family, children, weariness? Perhaps some other zigzags of politics which remain unknown to us? There are rumours, that one would not like to believe, that he not only knew what was about to occur in the near future, but personally orchestrated the process. Whatever the case, appearing on national television on 2 August, from his Crimean residence – Foros – Gorbachev announced that the Agreement of Union would be available to sign from 20 August. On 19 August, as the whole word now knows, the unexpected occurred: the pro-communist coup began ...

If Chernobyl was the first distant keening, then the August coup became the final death knell, demolishing a mighty empire. On those fateful days, the author of this book found himself in distant Australia. I was awoken at night by a phone call from the local television station. They wanted me to take part in a television debate with a group of international political commentators. Tanks rumbled across the TV screen, surrounded by agitated Muscovites. I felt worried and ill at ease, I wanted to be in my home town. Everyone who took part in the debate with me felt that something irreparable had happened, that Russia would once again be thrown decades back, into the darkness of totalitarianism.

What was happening at the time in the Crimean residence of the President of the USSR? Let us listen to an eyewitness; the head of Gorbachev's personal guard, KGB Major-General Medvedev.

Medvedev recalls that 18 August was an ordinary day. Around 11 a.m. Gorbachev and his wife went down to the sea. She went for a swim while he read a book on the beach. They returned to the house an hour later, to prepare for the flight to Moscow which was scheduled for the next day. The general also returned to his office. Suddenly he got a call from the ranking officer on duty who informed Medvedev that the personal guard had received an order not to let anyone out of the gates. The general was amazed and proceeded to try to establish who had given such an order. At that moment, his immediate superior from the KGB walked into the office, having just flown in from Moscow.

'Who gave the order to seal the gates?' asked Medvedev.

'Don't worry. Everything is fine,' smiled the newcomer. 'A group has arrived to see Mikhail Sergeivich, go and inform him.'

'Who has arrived? Regarding what matter?'

The 'guest' named those who had arrived. These were all people very close to the President. The anxiety subsided, and the general went to see Gorbachev. Gorbachev was sitting in a warm robe, reading the paper. He had been suffering back problems for a few days. Medvedev reported, listing the arrivals by name. Gorbachev was surprised.

'Why are they here?'

'I don't know.'

The President stopped to think. After a moment he stood up and headed for his wife in the bedroom without a word – his eternal habit of consulting with her. Medvedev returned to his office and informed his waiting colleague that the President had not replied 'yes' or 'no'.

Some time later, wishing to get in touch with the President, General Medvedev picked up the receiver of the intercom. A signal should have flashed in Gorbachev's study. If the President was in, he would answer. The receiver was silent, there was no dialling tone.

'Don't touch that, the phone isn't working,' said the 'guest'.

'It was then I understood,' says Medvedev, 'the "Khrushchev variant" – a coup – the lines were dead.'

Both walked outside. The newly arrived group appeared from the guest-house. They had apparently found Gorbachev and had already talked to him.

'How did it go?' the general's 'guest' called over to them.

'Not much. He didn't sign.' The answer sounded disappointed but calm, as if that was what they expected. General Medvedev continues:

> If Mikhail Sergeivich had wanted to turn the tables, I had lads on hand.
> I also had access to a spare Tu-134 plane and a helicopter. In practice
> it would have been child's play to slap some handcuffs on them and

take them to Moscow. Once we got to the capital, we could nab whoever we wanted to. It was still the 18th ... Didn't Gorbachev catch on?
Didn't he know what would come next?

As the head of the personal guard, my main concern was whether
or not something threatened the President's life, his personal safety.
There could be no question of a physical threat or of arrest. Saying
their good-byes, the President and the visitors exchanged handshakes.
The delegation left Gorbachev upset, but mostly calm – it didn't work,
so be it, they were expecting this result. Neither Gorbachev nor those
who came to see him knew what would happen next ... I believe that
they did have some sort of preliminary conversation about declaring a
state of emergency with Gorbachev, perhaps in the most general of
terms. I mean, they didn't fly over to arrest the President but to talk to
him, to persuade him to give his signature. If they flew over, they must
have hoped to succeed. Couldn't they agree on form and method?

The guests flew back to Moscow and the President, according to General
Medvedev, 'went to the beach. Had a swim. Sunbathed. And in the evening,
as was usual watched a film. He only became troubled a day later, that is the
evening of 19 August, when the conspirators announced him "sick" at a press
conference.'

There is a great deal in this story that does not make much sense: as the
general said, they flew in to talk, not to arrest the President, but for some reason the phones were disconnected and the residence was sealed. Even the general himself realised that this was a coup.

The President's wife had this to say about those troubled days, in an interview given on 3 September 1991 to the Moscow paper *Labour*:

On 18 August, around five in the evening, a troubled-looking Mikhail
Sergeivich suddenly entered my room. He said, 'Something important
has happened, perhaps even something terrible. Medvedev told me that
a group of people has arrived from Moscow. They are already in the
grounds of the dacha, and are demanding to meet me, but I didn't invite
anyone. I tried one phone after another ... they are all dead, even the
hotline [the Commander in Chief's phone]. The intercoms have been
disabled as well. This is isolation, perhaps even arrest. That means a
conspiracy ...' Indeed, everything was dead, even the television. After a
period of silence Mikhail Sergeivich told me, 'I'm not going to go for

any deals or shady enterprises ... but we could all pay dearly for this, all of us, the whole family. We must be ready for anything. I quickly called Irene and Anatoli, our children ... it was then that we expressed our opinion – it was unanimous – 'We will stay with you.' This was a very serious decision. We know our history, its frightening pages. Perhaps this was one of its darkest moments ... Mikhail Sergeivich went to meet the conspirators. They confirmed his darkest suspicions.

The new arrivals presented their demands: the signing of a declaration instituting a state of martial law in the country and the transfer of powers to the Vice President. When this was rejected, Mikhail Sergeivich was asked to step down ... Towards the evening of the 19th, after some stubborn demands, we managed to have the television turned back on. The atmosphere around us however was constantly thickening. We found ourselves in complete isolation. No one was allowed on to or off the territory of the dacha. The cars were locked and sealed. The plane was taken. We no longer saw the traffic of civilian shipping on the sea ... however, additional military and patrol vessels began to appear ... The feeling of growing danger compelled us to act. We walked the grounds of the dacha towards the sea with a specific goal, to ensure that as many people as possible saw the President was alive and well ... since we were constantly observed from the cliffs, from the direction of the sea and from on board the ships. The more people saw us, the harder it would be later to hide the truth ...

This interview sounds a bit strange as well. How are we to understand Raisa Gorbachev's statement, for instance, that they turned off the television? This was satellite, not cable television. And what of the 'demands' to have it turned on again? To whom were such demands directed? There was no contact with the outside world, complete isolation, they were surrounded only by the remaining loyal guard. All this is not very clear.

In conclusion, one of the main designers and builders of the President's network of communications in the Foros maintains that the system is so complicated and secure that it is well nigh impossible to jam it or turn it off, it can only be destroyed. The conclusion that the expert comes to is that 'this was a case of voluntary absence of communication'.

It is easy for us today to criticise Gorbachev, to accuse him of mistakes, miscalculations and misunderstandings, but we must not forget the political débris that he encountered. He did not have exemplars or advisers who could point out the clear path. He did not even have time. The genie of *glasnost* was released from its bottle and was sweeping the country with waves of meetings and demonstrations. The worldwide acclaim, bordering on adoration – so rare in the world of politics – was overpoweringly intoxicating. Yes, perhaps he admired himself more than he should have done, spoke more than he listened, was too self-assured and not always honest, did not possess enough willpower, was a poor judge of character ... This list of faults can be continued, but are they not understandable human weaknesses? Which of us, with hand on heart, can say that we would have acted otherwise in his place. Gorbachev once said, 'A vast restructuring is under way, a restructuring of ourselves. We are not gods ...' This applied first and foremost to himself. He was and will remain a pioneer on a global scale, and pioneers, as we know, are forgiven their mistakes ...

Time will sweep aside the personal, the trivial and will preserve the most important. Then we shall see that what he did for Russian history will far exceed all his mistakes and sins. On one occasion, speaking in Paris, the ex-President of the USSR said, 'We are heading towards a new civilisation, which will not be a choice between capitalism and socialism, but will become a synthesis of our personal experience.'

God grant this to be the case ...

14 | THE GUY FROM THE URALS

ONCE, IN THE SPRING OF 1989, my son dragged me along to another meeting of democrats in Manezh Square. A truck stood beside the Hotel Moscow, a makeshift stage with microphones set up on its trailer, and behind it across the whole length of the hotel stood mothers carrying placards and mourning photos of their sons, killed by criminal elements in the Russian army. Orators jostled around the truck, speeches were made. My son hung my imposing camera around his neck, took my press card and also clambered up on to the truck, while I waited below. Yet another 'street scene' was unfolding nearby. A thug-like man with a scowling face, wearing a massive fur hat and surrounded by enraged women, was pontificating: 'Never mind, never mind,' he yelled. 'We'll shoot a hundred thousand or so, send another million into Siberia, and there'll be order.' 'You bastard, KGB swine!' the enraged women snarled at him. It seemed that the speaker was longing for a confrontation to attract attention to himself. I suddenly got the urge to intervene and have some fun. 'Citizens!' I shouted. 'Have you all gone mad? I'm a psychiatrist. This man visits my clinic for a check-up every week, and you're arguing politics with him?' Laughter rang out, and a few minutes later the orator in the hat was standing alone and giving me angry glances. Time went by, and you can understand my amazement when I suddenly saw this man on television, running for the Russian Presidency. It was Vladimir Zhirinovski.*

I was standing there waiting for my son, surrounded by a sea of people waving placards – 'Mikhail, Everyone is Sick of You', 'Communism, the People's Prison', and portraits of Yeltsin. I knew no more about Boris Yeltsin at that time than anyone else in that square: a Party official who had arrived from the Urals, headed the Moscow communists for about a year and a half, fought with Gorbachev and mutinied, was fired from all his posts, became a fighter for Russian 'justice'. That was about it. The name Yeltsin did not conjure up any other associations in my mind. What happened at that moment, what subconscious gears were activated, I do not know. I was looking at a portrait of Yeltsin which I had already seen dozens of times, and suddenly I felt as if I had received an electric shock. Could this be that same Yeltsin from Ural Technical College? Boris, who played on the volleyball team?

* An odious figure in Russia politics, usually described as a clown.

274

Images from my distant youth swam into my mind. It was 1953 and I was a first-year student in the Geophysical Department of the Mining Institute in Sverdlovsk. The Technical College and the Mining Institute were the leading further education colleges of the city, and their rivalry extended to everything. I was a fanatical sportsman at the time, playing basketball for a high-level team. The term did not exist at the time but in fact we were professionals, devoting more time to sport than to study. I was not friends with Boris Yeltsin, we had met a few times around the courts, nothing more. He was a senior at the time, the captain of Ural's best volleyball team, and, as the lads said, 'was a decent chap'. I studied in Sverdlovsk for about a year and a half, then I transferred to another university and left. That was the story, now a whole lifetime distant ...

I remembered it all again, this time sitting in a plane, flying from a distant southern region. It was early June of 1991 and I was hurrying to Moscow. The Russian presidential elections were scheduled for 12 June – a truly momentous event. The nation was choosing a head of state for the first time in the many centuries of her history.

What did my lone voice mean among millions? Nothing. But I was in a hurry, not only because I wanted to be part of a great event, but also because I also sensed, almost physically, how vicious the clash would be, between the departing totalitarian system and the as-yet weak and completely untested democracy. Many still mistook freedom for anarchy, and troubles for freedom. Each voice could be decisive. Apart from this, something personal also pushed me towards the elections. Boris Yeltsin had suddenly turned into that 'decent chap' from my distant youth whom, by the laws of male camaraderie, I was obliged to support.

A week remained before the elections. From morning to late at night I visited my friends, debated, argued, proved, persuaded, or simply begged them to vote for Yeltsin. On the day of the elections I almost got into a fight at the balloting area, where opponents of Yeltsin were doing everything in their power to keep voters who did not suit them off the electoral rolls. Then followed victory and jubilation ...

Many events have come and gone from that moment. Everything has come to pass, both approval of the new President and disappointment in him as well, but I never doubted one thing: the importance of that victory. Whatever mistakes and omissions he may have made, he has entered into the history of our country as a noteworthy figure, able to turn the rusty wheel of our lives. History has accepted him onto her pages, and his full measure will be given later, with the distance of time ...

So as not to retell the President's youthful years in my own words, I quote a passage from his own book, *Confessions on the Given Topic*, published in 1990 when the Soviet Union still existed and our hero was not yet the President. I hope that an autobiographical account will allow the reader not only to catch the flavour of the President's youth, but also to sense his character, better than any retelling could.

I was born on 1 February 1931, in the village of Butka in the Sverdlovsk Region where almost all my ancestors had lived. They ploughed the land, sowed wheat, in short – existed. My father married there. The village consisted of the Yeltsin clan and the Starigin clan – that was my mother's surname. They were married, and soon afterwards I appeared in the world – their first child. My mother told me the story of my baptism. There was only one church for the whole area, covering several villages. The birth rate was quite high and baptisms took place once a month, so the day was rather hectic for the priest. The baptisms took place in the most primitive of fashions. There was a barrel, containing some kind of holy liquid, the child was completely immersed in it, then the squealing infant was pulled out, blessed, given a name and entered into the church register. As was the custom in villages, the parents then presented the priest with a glass of booze, vodka, moonshine – whoever had what … Considering that my turn only came around in the second half of the day, the priest was by that time having trouble keeping his feet. I was passed to him, he lowered me into the barrel and forgot to take me out, instead starting to discuss and argue with the onlookers about something. My parents were some distance away, and didn't grasp the problem at first. When they did understand, my mother jumped up with a cry, caught me somewhere around the bottom and pulled me out. I was brought around … The priest was not greatly upset, saying: 'Well, since he endured such a trial he must be the strongest, we'll call him Boris …'

My childhood was very hard. There was no food. The harvests were abysmal. Everyone was herded into a kolkhoz – it was a time of mass dispossession for the kulaks. Moreover, war-bands roamed the land – almost every day there were gunfights, murders and thievery. We lived in poverty. A small house, a cow, there was a horse but it soon died so there was nothing to plough with … In 1935, when even the cow died and it became completely unbearable, father decided to find work at a construction site somewhere, to save the family. This was the so-called period of industrialisation. We hitched ourselves to the cart, threw our last few possessions onto it and headed towards the station, thirty-two kilometres away. We found ourselves in the town of Berezniki. Father enlisted as a construction worker on a site. We were housed in a barracks – wooden, made out of thin planks, draughty. A common hallway and twenty small rooms, no amenities of course, the toilet was outside, as was water from the well. We were given some clothes and we bought a goat. By this time a brother and younger sister were already born. So the six of us, including the goat, slept on the floor, all huddled together ... Mother, who learned to sew in childhood, worked as a seamstress, and father worked on the construction site. Mother had a gentle, kind disposition, she helped everyone and sewed for them. She'd sit around at night and sew, not taking any money for her work; if someone simply brought half a loaf of bread or some other kind of food, that was thankyou enough. Father had a hard-bitten character. His belt was the main way he raised us. Sometimes he'd close the door and say, 'Lie down'. I'd lie down, pulling my shirt up and my trousers down. It must be said, he didn't hold back any ... I would of course grit my teeth and not make a sound, that would anger him, but of course mother would intervene, take away his belt and interpose herself between us. All in all, she was my eternal defender ... We existed in the barracks in this fashion for ten years ... I remember how hard our lives were to this very day. Especially during winter, when there was nowhere to hide from the frost. We had few clothes, in the main we were saved by the goat. I remember when you snuggled up to it, it was as warm as a furnace. She saved us during the whole war as well. The milk was thick, even though she gave less than a litre a day, it was enough for the children to survive. All in all, that's how childhood went – mostly joyless, there was of course no question of any sweets or delicacies, simply survival, survival, survival ...

School. My activity and persistence singled me out among the children. It so happened that from my first to last grade I was always elected class prefect. My grades were always fine – all 'A's – my behaviour, however, was harder to praise. More than once, I was on the verge of having to part ways with school. There were, to put it bluntly, episodes of hooliganism as well. For instance, we would nail gramophone needles into the underside of chairs. The teacher would sit down, and a scream would echo around the school ... We also had battles, region against region, sixty to a hundred people to a side would fight. I always took part in these battles. The bridge of my nose resembles a boxer's to this day, they whacked me with a shaft ...

I started to be active in sports. Volleyball immediately attracted me. I was missing two fingers on my left hand, so there were difficulties with receiving the ball ... There is a story to go with the loss of my two fingers. Wartime – all the kids were itching to get to the front. We decided to acquire some grenades and dismantle them, so as to learn how they worked inside. I volunteered to break into the church, where a military cache was located. At night, I crawled past three perimeters of barbed wire, sawed through the grate in a window, climbed inside, took two grenades and successfully made it back out. (The guard would have shot without warning.) The other kids and I drove some sixty kilometres into the forest and started to dismantle the grenades. Kneeling, I placed a grenade on a rock and started hitting it with a hammer. However, I did not remove the detonator – I didn't know ... an explosion, and no fingers ...

I went to study at the Ural Technical College, in the Engineering Department. I played volleyball at a rather high level at that time, a member of the Sverdlovsk team in the top league, where the twelve best teams of the country played. Volleyball left a big mark on my life ... I spent about six hours a day on it.

Before I went to university I had not seen the country or the sea, I had not been anywhere really. So I decided to travel the country during my summer holidays. I mostly travelled sitting on the roof of a train, sometimes between the carriages, sometimes on the steps. I set myself the following goal: travel by night, arrive in a city and explore it for a day or sometimes two. Sleep in a park or at the train station, then off again on a carriage roof.

When I left I had a large antique watch, given to me by my grandfather. This watch, however, like all my clothes, I lost playing cards ... It was like this: there was an amnesty in the country at the time, former prisoners were returning on the roofs of trains, once a group latched on to me and suggested playing cards. I didn't know anything about cards, never played in my life. Well, I couldn't say no in a situation like that. They said, 'Let's play for clothes.' Very soon they stripped me to my shorts, they won it all. In the end they said, 'We'll play for your life. If you lose, we'll throw you off the roof of the moving train and that's all, good night. If you win, we'll return everything.' What happened next is hard to understand now, either! I started to get the hang of the game or perhaps they suddenly took pity on me ... in short, I won. They returned everything except the watch. After that game they didn't bother me any more, even started to respect me. Someone even gave me a piece of bread.

Once, my beloved volleyball almost killed me. At some point, training six to eight hours a day and studying during the night, it seems I over-exerted myself. Then I suddenly came down with angina, had a temperature of 40 degrees, but went to practice anyway; naturally my heart couldn't cope. My pulse was 150, I felt weak and was taken to hospital. I was told to lie and rest, then there would be a chance that no sooner than in about four months my heart would recover, otherwise I would have a stroke. I escaped from hospital a few days later. I have to admit in all honesty that the risk was of course colossal, since I could have ruined my heart forever. I thought, however, that I shouldn't spare it, but rather strain it as much as possible, driving out like with like ...

This is the very colourful self-portrait that the author of the *Confessions* paints. The storyteller, however, omits such tragic pages in the biography as the dispossession of his family, the death of his grandfather, and his father's two arrests. These episodes could hardly have been forgotten. More likely, it was influenced by the fact that the book was written at the height of Yeltsin's political struggle for power. Since, according to the 'ethics' of the Soviet regime, under which we were all raised, being the descendant of a fortunate, well-to-do peasant family was a mortal sin, while coming from a poor and struggling one was honourable. Yet to reveal that his relatives suffered as kulaks – how would the voters take this, including as they did many supporters of 'Stalin's firm hand'? But a few years later, in the second volume of autobiography, *The Notes of a President,* we hear a completely different voice – the confident voice of a victor: 'If we damn the past, strike it from our memories, things will not get better. Our history is both great and damned simultaneously.'

There lived in the village of Butka the solid and well-to-do peasant clan of the Yeltsins, with roots deep in the Ural soil. They laboured, sweated, bent their backs, and the land was grateful. The grandfather on the father's side was a well-known village blacksmith and a church elder. As Internal Security noted in 'Case #56-44', prior to the Revolution he had a large village house, two mills – one water, one wind – he also owned a threshing-machine, an automated harvester, five horses, four cows, and twelve hectares of land. He also kept helpers, hired hands.

By the rules of 'revolutionary morality', this hard-working farmer might well have been executed. But the law was 'merciful', the farm was confiscated and the old man – the 'bloodthirsty kulak' – was deprived of his citizen's rights and, in 1930, along with his wife and others like himself, was taken to a settlement in the dreamy, distant northern taiga.* A barracks one plank thick, and thirty below outside – you might as well have lain down and died. But the grandfather – as the grandson later tells – decided not to die, and in the best peasant tradition, 'took to the hills'. This, however, did not save him, and within about four months he did die.

All this happened just before the grandson was born. Everyone left in the village was forced into the kolkhoz. They would have died of starvation had the kolkhoz chairman not turned out to be a decent person, allowing the men into the city during the winter to earn money. Nikolai Yeltsin, Boris's father, was that self-same natural handyman that people considered to be innately gifted. Four grades of education but golden hands, a God-given builder. He always found work for himself, that is how they could afford to eat ...

Further on, there are some discrepancies in the President's accounts. In the passage quoted above, he writes that in 1935 their family moved to the Ural town of Berezniki, where his father found work on a construction site. There is no word about his father's arrest there, although in a different part of the book he says, 'When father was taken away at night, I was six years old ...' (in other words, this occurred in 1937). In *The Notes of a President*, published in 1994, when Yeltsin was already at the height of power, he tells a more complete and slightly different story about his family. In April 1934, his father was arrested along with his youngest uncle Andreian and another four workers, all accused of sabotage. This was of course pure nonsense. Stalin's engine of destruction was simply revving up. The 'sabotage' consisted of the fact that twenty-two-year-old Andreian Yeltsin poured out a keg of spoiled soup from the canteen on to the ground, accompanying this with a few strong words. Another worker also muttered something uncomplimentary. It all constituted a 'kulak' brigade. As was written in the accusation, and preserved in

---

* Siberian forests.

'Case #56-44': 'To hide their social origins, they produced good results at work.' The father and uncle were given three years each in the camps, the others five.

'I was only three years old, but I remember the terror and fear to this day,' Yeltsin writes in *The Notes of a President*. 'It is night. People walk into the barracks. Mother shouts, she is crying. I wake up and also start to cry. I'm not crying because they are taking father away, I am still little and don't understand what is going on. I can see that mother is crying, and how scared she is ... Father is taken away, mother rushes to me and embraces me. I calm down and go to sleep. Three years later father returned from the camps.' (From this one can surmise that this was the first arrest, and the second, which is described earlier, occurred in 1937.)

Why am I stopping on these overall minor omissions and discrepancies in the President's autobiography? The point of course is not in them. When the author promises the reader *Confessions* (consider the word), this is a sort of promise that before us lies the complete and even sacred truth, without secrets and silences. Its breach puts us on our guard, and drastically reduces our trust in the author.

To read the book is to experience some feeling of embarrassment. Indeed, some Western reviewers must have shared this feeling. 'A smug Siberian poser', 'A power-loving and overly self-confident braggart', 'Sly and conceited, with a huge thirst for power' – these are just a few of the accusations levelled at the author by critics in *The Economist*, *Le Monde* and *The Financial Times*, among others. Harsh certainly, but the book is undeniably infused with conceit and a kind of adolescent heroic posturing.

Judging by Yeltsin's autobiography, he surmounts every situation in life only as victor and hero. He persuades some boys to go to the taiga for three months, to look for the source of some river. They get lost, trekking across bare wilderness for several months. They find themselves in a life-and-death situation, on the verge of starvation. They fall victim to intestinal typhoid, with temperatures of more than forty degrees, fevers and loss of consciousness. Only our hero, thanks to willpower and self-control, remains on his feet. Gathering the last of his strength, he pulls the lads on to a boat, thereby saving their lives. Only afterwards does he lose consciousness himself.

And there is the episode on the roof of the train, with the pardoned criminals, who first want to beat him at cards and throw him off the train, but are foiled by our hero's self-control and willpower, who emerges victorious, even earning their respect.

Here is another example. When the young Boris was a construction engineer, working on a site manned by prison labour, a fierce bruiser of an inmate once stormed into his office, brandishing an axe and threatening to split his skull – demanding that he endorse some fabricated pay-slips. The situation was extremely dangerous. But once again, our hero did not lose his head. 'Get out!' he roared menacingly. The bruiser suddenly 'lowered the axe, dropped it on the ground, turned around and silently left, hunching his back ...' Well, what more can one say? What a rather cowardly bruiser ...

There are dozens of such episodes, scattered throughout the book. Our hero risks life and limb to save a huge construction crane, about to fall over in a strong wind. He risks his life to save a dump truck stuck on a railway crossing. He takes a flying dive out of the window of a train about to be derailed, this time saving his own life. While a student, and devoting 'six to eight hours' a day to sport, he nevertheless manages to achieve only the highest grades, studying at night and devoting no more than three or four hours to sleep. As a prominent construction director, he mingles with the common folk – staying up all night with the women's brigade, wallpapering and chatting about life. Out of his own pocket he supports a worker who has been unfairly dismissed. And having risen to the Kremlin heights, he refuses to 'eat salmon and chase it down with black caviar, because it's shameful ...', shameful in the eyes of the people who do not have such opportunities.

To reiterate, there are dozens of such episodes. Reading all this, one experiences a degree of discomfort. After all, it is generally accepted that an individual's good deeds are recounted by others, not by oneself.

On the other hand, listen to the guileless and doubtlessly truthful memories of a mother about he son. From the age of six, all the chores of the house were Boris's responsibility, one from which he never shirked. He was the first to help his mother in everything, patiently and tenderly caring for his younger siblings, cooked, washed the floors, and during the war would stand in line all night for a loaf of bread. Remembering those hungry times, his mother recalls how the ten-year-old Boris, arriving home after school, would sit in the corner and rock back and forth mumbling, 'I'm hungry. I can't stand it. I'm hungry ...' In the holidays, rather than play with children his age, he would hire himself out along with his mother to reap grass at the kolkhoz, so as to earn enough for a couple of loaves of bread. He was not shy of doing women's work – something wholly uncharacteristic for boys of the time – as for instance sewing and embroidery. (While touring the US, during a visit to a textile factory, President Yeltsin amazed the local workers with his almost professional ability to handle a sewing machine.)

So what are we to make of the 'heroic episodes' in the President's autobiography? Are they the result of difficult childhood, when a wilful and naturally impressionable adolescent – not having the opportunity to 'play hero' in his youth – subconsciously compensates for it now, in his adult imagination? Or it is a glaring case of populism, of which he was so often accused? Perhaps it is left-over youthful romanticism, which we – the children of that generation – all suffered from? I think there is a little of everything here ...

Student years at the Ural Technical College passed actively and hungrily, as was the case with many others. Unloading wagons at night to earn a little extra. A velvet jacket and military boots. Sometimes even living coat-less during the fiercest of Ural cold-snaps, but always an abundance of bubbling energy and mischief, as well as a fanatical – almost intoxicating – devotion to sport. Naturally, these years also bring love. According to Boris's friends, though forward and active as he was in a group, he was quite passive and even shy in personal contacts. (This 'collective' tendency was characteristically mapped in politics as well. He was considerably more effective in front of a crowd or audience than in a close eye-to-eye encounter, which entailed subtle diplomatic manoeuvres.)

His pull towards the crowd can also be sensed in his *Confessions*, which is littered with words and phrases such as 'lads', 'girls', 'our company', and hardly any specific individual. But with one significant exception. 'I started to notice one more and more – Naina Girina ... I remember the first time we pledged our love to one another in second year, in the gallery of the foyer in the Union House of the university, and kissed next to one of the columns ...'

This gentle, pleasant girl – hailing from an old, traditional family of Orenburg peasants – apparently reminded Boris in some way of his mother. If we take into account his deep relationship with his mother, his 'eternal protector', there is no doubt that the choice he made was the right one. Yet even here he cannot get by without 'high-minded' deeds. To test 'whether the love is strong, whether it is deep', he decided to part with his beloved for a year, and not maintain any contact with her during that time. Only after a year did he send her this 'humorous' telegram: 'Boris is having trouble with his heart. Come to him ...', unsigned.

Soon the young family acquired its first child, and some time later, a second. Although Boris longed for a son – he had put an axe under the pillow, and a service cap – he got two daughters, Lena and Tanya. The family often recalled an episode from Yeltsin's early fatherhood. One time, his wife fell ill and there was no one to look after the newborn infant. Her father took her to Orenburg, to her grandmother. In the train the infant started crying, wanting to eat. She would not be comforted. The bewildered father did not know what to do, but found the answer by opening up his own shirt and giving his daughter his breast to suckle. The baby fell asleep blissfully, while the whole female population of the carriage dabbed their eyes out of tenderness.

Then begin the years of the 'young specialist'. After gaining his diploma in 1955 he declined the engineering post offered and worked on construction sites for a year as an ordinary labourer. He learned the professions of stonemason, cement worker, carpenter, glazier, plasterer, painter and crane operator ... a month on each, only then considering himself worthy of accepting the role of a foreman.

Yeltsin writes in his book, not without obvious relish, that he was never anyone's second, he was always the boss, even if the responsibility was a small one. According to his mother, this tendency began in her son's schooldays. Once, he accidentally found himself in a 'closed-shop' for Party bosses, where he saw items of food of which he had never even heard. This first and concrete contact with social inequality had such a strong impact on the imagination of the adolescent, that returning home he gloomily but firmly announced, 'Mother, I'm going to be a boss.'

The working day of the young engineer began at seven in the morning and ended around eleven at night, prior to which it was also necessary to walk twelve-odd kilometres from his boarding house to the construction site. He handled individual relationships in various ways, exploiting his natural style of leadership and often crossing the line between harshness and viciousness. He handed out fines and sackings more or less at random. Obviously, this did not earn the sympathy of his subordinates, who could not understand why the hell he was driving himself and others so hard. Did he want it more than anyone else, or something?

Yeltsin's difficult character extended not only to his subordinates but also to his bosses. He had one 'original', to say the least, supervisor who – at the slightest provocation – would scream curses and grab a chair, threatening to throw it at him. He, in turn, would also pick up a chair: 'Bear in mind, if you make the slightest move, I have quicker reactions, I'll hit you first anyway.'

At the age of thirty, very late for such a career, Boris Yeltsin joined the Party. Although he says that he 'honestly believed the ideals of fairness that the Party promoted', it is difficult to believe the sincerity of these words.

According to the recollections of his teachers, Boris – unlike Mikhail Gorbachev – was not simply indifferent to Comsomol affairs, but even avoided them. Again this may have been caution associated with the past fates of his father and grandfather. Filling out the countless forms, Boris never mentioned in them that his close family had been repressed. This would have closed the doors of university for him. Perhaps it might also be true that 'Khrushchev's Thaw' created an illusion of cleansing for him, the Party's penance for the past.

Although I was never a member of the Party, it was at about this time I nearly became one. I remember how once the university Party representative visited our group of students, a tank commander crippled in the war and a person we knew to be decent, with democratic ideals. He began to encourage us to join the Party. We sat silently, our mood very sceptical. Finally one of the braver souls could stand it no longer: 'Who needs this Party, full of bastards and the architect of so much misery?' The face of the tank commander lost its colour. He sat for a long minute, supporting his head with the stump of his crippled hand, then rose, closed the door more tightly and turned to us. 'Can't you understand?' he said, his voice trembling. 'If decent people don't join the Party, we'll stay in this crap forever.' Remembering this episode I catch myself thinking that it was good Yeltsin joined the Party after all.

After fourteen years of work in construction, Boris Yeltsin was offered the post of supervisor of the construction department of the Sverdlovsk Regional Party Committee. The Party leadership had long since noticed this ambitious engineer, able to squeeze the maximum out of his subordinates. His harsh style of leadership was in keeping with Party norms, and his unquenchable energy was precisely what was needed to force at least some motion into the rusty wheels of the bureaucratic machine.

Yeltsin served at this post for a further seven years, and in November of 1976 Leonid Brezhnev himself approved him for the role of First Secretary of the Sverdlovsk Regional Party Committee. 'In those times the First Secretary is a God, Czar – the master of the region ... The power of the First is practically limitless. The feeling of power intoxicates ...' writes Yeltsin. How did his character change over the ten years of ruling Sverdlovsk? It would seem to have become harder. If the style of his leadership was harsh on the construction site, among workers, then here among the Party clerks it became almost dictatorial. After a number of years, when Yeltsin was running for President of Russia, his opponents and foes – citing Sverdlovsk – were to call him a 'Stalinesque leader', scaring the voters with 'bloody dictatorship' and 'people hanging on poles'.

As for his personal life, the new post did not seem to bring about any particular changes. The same love of pelmeni*, and meat-patties with fried potatoes. During the holidays the all-powerful master of the region preferred to spend his time either in country hikes, or in his native village of Butka with his parents, where he fussed about in the garden, chopped wood, carried water and all in all became a real peasant for short time. The depth of the peasant vein in the Yeltsin clan could at least be seen by the fact that after more than thirty years away from the land, somewhere in the 1970s Boris's father would abandon city life, buy a plot of land and a house and return to his native village.

Yeltsin's wife continued to work as a construction engineer in the Project Institute until the day of their departure for Moscow. Socially, she and her husband were different people. If Boris Yeltsin was typically public-spirited, largely indifferent to family matters, then Naina Yeltsin was quite the opposite – home, family and hearth remained her priorities, regardless of what posts her husband occupied. Unlike Raisa Gorbachev, for instance, politics and her husband's business never attracted Naina, and more likely bothered her. Yet it is reasonable to think that had it not been for Naina, Boris Yeltsin's political career would not have flourished, since it required strong motherly support, which she gave him. As Naina's former university classmate noted: 'Boris was her young son.'**

There was one incident in Yeltsin's Sverdlovsk period, however, which was to remain a dark stain on his biography. This was the destruction of the old 'Ipatiev House' in Ekaterinburg (the old name for Sverdlovsk), also known as 'The Special House', in which the last Russian emperor Nicholas II and his family had been kept under arrest.

There are many dirty deeds in Bolshevik history, but the thuggish murder of the Czar's family became a symbol of villainy. On direct orders from the Kremlin, on the night of 16 July 1918, the Czar and his family – his wife, four young daughters, gravely ill fourteen-year-old son, personal physician and three servants who willingly remained with him – were exe-

---

* Siberian meat dumplings.

**There is a curious episode from her life. In Orenburg, where she was born, there is a pilot school where Yuri Gagarin studied at one time. Yuri and Naina met in a dance-hall, and for a while he even courted her. Several years later, when she was already the wife of the engineer Yeltsin, she was sitting with a friend in front of the television watching the newscast about the first manned flight into space. Suddenly she saw her suitor from Orenburg, who had become the world's first cosmonaut. 'There's who you should have married,' Naina's friend exclaimed. 'Imagine who you would have been now!'

cuted in the basement of this house. Here are some extracts from the report of the executioners:

> I woke doctor Botkin and told him that it was imperative that every-one quickly get dressed as there was trouble in the city and I was obliged to transfer them to a more secure place. Nicholas carried Alexei [his sick son] in his arms. The others, some carrying pillows, some carrying other possessions, descended into the basement.

> The Romanovs were completely calm, they suspected nothing. The Czar looks around questioningly. The Czarina crossed herself ... but I was already pulling the trigger and putting the first bullet into the Czar. Along with my shot, the first volley rang out. I saw Botkin falling, a servant slid down the wall and the cook fell to his knees ... nothing could be seen in the room through the smoke. We were now firing on barely visible falling silhouettes. A joyous female yell could be heard from the right corner of the room: 'Thank the Lord, God has saved me!' The unharmed maid got to her feet unsteadily ... the maid was run through with bayonets ... the wounded Alexei moaned ... we examined the rest and finished off those still alive.

Naturally, the house where this horrific deed occurred would become a 'special' place in the eyes of the people. People came to visit it for decades, stood there, looked, and reflected. At the time Sverdlovsk was a city closed to foreigners, so the authorities did not give this much significance. However, the sixtieth anniversary of the martyrdom of the Czar's family approached. The world community's interest in this crime was revived. In July 1975, a memo arrived in the Politburo from the KGB chief Yuri Andropov: 'Recently, foreign specialists have begun to visit Sverdlovsk. In the future the circle of foreigners could grow significantly, and the "Ipatiev House" could become an object of their serious attention. In connection to this, it seems expedient to charge the Party's Sverdlovsk Regional Committee with the question of demolishing this house, in line with the planned reconstruction of the city.'

'I read and did not believe my eyes,' Yeltsin writes. 'A closed motion of the Politburo to demolish the "Ipatiev House". Not to obey was impossible. A few days later, at night, machines approached the "Ipatiev House" and by morn-ing there was nothing left of the building. Later, the spot was asphalted over.'*

The day of 3 April 1985 was pivotal in the political career of Boris Yeltsin. The phone call from the Politburo found him in his car. The offer being made was unexpected, and came directly from Mikhail Gorbachev, recently ascended to the highest Kremlin post. Yeltsin was being invited to move to Moscow, to the Party Central Committee, to head the Department of Construction.

According to Yeltsin, at first he refused without hesitation. The Urals were his homeland, where he lived, studied and worked – people knew him there, he felt at home there. Those, according to him, were the motives for his refusal. The same memoirs, however, also reveal other motives. 'What's this, I've served ten years as the master of a five-million-strong industrial region and I'm being offered simply to head a department! They could offer me something higher. Look at Gorbachev himself, for instance, look where he leapt from a post like my own? And compared to Ural, Stavropol is an industrial backwater. In other words, I'm not willing to take such a post.'

This was the first weak signal of the future confrontation with Gorbachev. People say that just before his departure from Sverdlovsk, Yeltsin dropped a comment to his colleagues: 'You'll see, I'll be the General Secretary …'

On 12 April he had already begun work in Moscow. Half a year later Gorbachev, compelled by fate, was to raise his future enemy almost to the heights. Now he was a candidate for membership in the Politburo and the Party head of Moscow.

Yeltsin's work as head of the capital's Party organization has been covered in the previous chapter. With his 'descent among the people' – travel by public transport, appearing in public places, noisy battles against bureaucratic privileges – Yeltsin conquered the hearts of Muscovites. Truth to tell, wicked tongues whispered that he would transfer on to the tram from a limousine, one or two stops away from the factory he was heading for, and that he only appeared in the stores once or twice, and did not even buy anything. But that was not important. The main thing was that rumours were already flying around the capital.

---

* Everything is not as simple and straightforward as Boris Yeltsin would have us believe. The order from Moscow to demolish the 'Ipatiev House' was given in July 1975, during the stewardship of the previous Party head of the Sverdlovsk region. For some reason he did not hurry to carry out this order. It was only two years later, after Boris Yeltsin became the Party head of Sverdlovsk, that the order was carried out. The job was done efficiently and quickly. Under the cover of night, on 27 July 1977, under a heavy army escort, bulldozers and excavators arrived at the house. Even the foundations were torn out and taken away, and so as finally to obliterate all memory of the tragedy, asphalt rollers flattened the area.

Whatever people said, Yeltsin's popularity grew very rapidly, moreover in two directions. While the people saw him as their defender, trying to re-establish social equality, rein in the 'starving bureaucracy', put an end to corruption and close down the secret Party stores, the Moscow Mafia saw him as bitter enemy. 'Get back to your Sverdlovsk, before it is too late ...' they threatened in letters and on the phone. 'Khrushchev tried to put us all in prison, he got nowhere and neither will you. We've stolen and will keep on stealing.'

They continued stealing, of course, but to a lesser degree. During an incomplete two years as the reigning Party head of the capital, Yeltsin managed to put more than a thousand directors of Mafia-run trading establishments around the city behind bars. 'We are having such a *perestroika* here in Moscow, that there isn't enough room in prison for everyone we would like to put there,' he said in an interview.

It goes without saying that Yeltsin could not have possibly have allowed himself such 'revolutionary' actions under Brezhnev, let alone under Khrushchev or Stalin. So it is only fair to give credit to Gorbachev's *perestroika*. As La Rochefoucauld said: 'Whatever advantages nature has endowed a man with, it can only make him a hero with the help of Fate.' Thus it can be said with almost complete certainty, that without Gorbachev, the 'Yeltsin phenomenon' would simply have been impossible. That is one of the paradoxes of the conflict between Gorbachev and Yeltsin.

The higher Yeltsin's popularity grew with the citizens of the capital, the more his conflict with his Party colleagues intensified. Even Gorbachev was finding it harder and harder to restrain his own envy towards a contender he himself had raised up. The climax of the conflict, as already related in the previous chapter, occurred on 21 October 1987 at a Party conference, where Yeltsin made a speech cautiously criticising the stalling process of *perestroika*, and alluding to the cult of Gorbachev himself. No one, Yeltsin included, could have begun to imagine that this four-minute performance – ending in a request to relieve him of the Party posts he held – would become a turning-point in the history of Russia. Whether this step was the result of a sudden emotional outburst, or a carefully calculated decision, we do not know. One thing, however, is unarguable; it was a brave and unprecedented announcement. For someone willingly to step down from the Kremlin's Olympus – such a thing had never happened before.

The arrow of 'war' had been launched. At a directorial gesture from Gorbachev, the whole Kremlin hierarchy gathered, like the ancient Greek

Areopagus court, to trample the heretic. He was accused of slandering the Party, of treason, 'a blow from behind'. Three hours of such manhandling was enough to string out any nervous system. Yeltsin held on for two more weeks, and was then taken to hospital by ambulance, suffering a major heart attack. His condition was so serious that the doctors did not even let his wife see the patient, telling him – as they once did in his youth – to lie there and keep lying there.

On the third day, as if nothing had happened, Gorbachev called the hospital. He asked Yeltsin personally to attend his formal removal from Party posts. In reply to the sick man's protests, that he was not even allowed to get up from bed, let alone go anywhere, Gorbachev responded quite jovially, 'Don't worry, the doctors will help', and hung up the phone. 'I won't ever be able to understand that,' Yeltsin writes. 'To take someone out of hospital, just to officially fire them ... it's inconceivable. However badly Gorbachev might have felt towards me, to act that way is inhuman, immoral.' Those who saw Yeltsin that day say that he left the impression of being a crushed man, stumbling over his words, losing his train of thought, speaking nonsensically ...

Why was Gorbachev in such a hurry? He quite understood that such an unpleasant act would become common knowledge, and would certainly not enhance his authority. He could have left the thing for a week later, what was the difference? Moreover, formally they did not even need to relieve him, since Yeltsin himself had asked to be removed from the Party positions he occupied.

The fact that 'he himself asked' is where the whole twist in the affair is hidden. In the whole history of Soviet rule, there was not a single instance of anyone willingly leaving that Party 'holy-ground' known as the Politburo. Voluntary departure implied a challenge, doubt in the 'heavenly purity of Olympus', its fall from grace. According to the unwritten but brutal laws of the Kremlin, there were only two possible ways down from the Party heights: feet first or banishment. It was impossible to delay. Rumours of Yeltsin's offer could not be allowed to spread across the country. They needed to be quashed, and replaced by a public lynching of the heretic. This is why Gorbachev was in such a hurry. This is why, when on the evening of 31 October TASS* got a bulletin that Yeltsin had quit, they received another government telegram a quarter of an hour later, forbidding the publication of the first. There could be no mention of any kind of voluntary departure, there could only be shameful expulsion.

* Telegraph Agency of the Soviet Union, the principal news agency.

Expulsion, however, requires a reason. What reason could be presented to the public? Criticism of the stalled process of *perestroika*? The people themselves were grumbling. Criticism directed at Gorbachev? The people themselves were already reviling him on every corner. Legends started to form around the name of the exile. Rumours began to circulate in Moscow about Yeltsin's 'brave speeches' – which he never gave. He was ascribed deeds which he never performed. The people begin to 'mould a hero'. As has happened many times in history, the individual whom the people raise up on a pedestal becomes a hero. It is already irrelevant what he is really like, he is a national symbol.

In his conflict with Yeltsin, Gorbachev made at least two significant actions that hastened the end of his career. The first he could not have foreseen, it was fate: the transfer of Yeltsin to Moscow. The second, however, was a blatant miscalculation. Knowing the mentality of the Russian people, their love of the underdog, there was no better gift to Yeltsin than to be loudly condemned and banished. As we have already said, Yeltsin was no master of 'close combat'. His strength was battle at a distance, in the squares, on the barricades, where he was in his natural element. Like the mythological Atlas, regaining his strength by touching Mother Earth, so Yeltsin was revitalised by the crowd. Gorbachev roughly threw him aside, thereby giving him an ally: a weary people, long since disenchanted with the Kremlin rulers. Simply put, Gorbachev created the 'Yeltsin phenomenon' with his own hands.

For the time being, however, an exiled and mauled Yeltsin returned to hospital. Seemingly directed from above, the doctors started carefully to suggest a pension. Yeltsin refused. Several days later, Gorbachev called again. He graciously offered his defeated rival the post of Minister of Construction, and ended the conversation with a wholly unambiguous phrase: 'But keep in mind, I'll not let you near politics again.' In actual fact, this was political death.

Why did Gorbachev not deal with Yeltsin more harshly? As one experienced Kremlin survivor said, 'Our Politburo is like the mysterious Bermuda Triangle. Whoever is cast out of it, disappears without a trace.' Firstly, times were already different, and Gorbachev himself was not a Stalin-type sadist. More importantly, however, *glasnost* had loosened tongues and a powerful wave of protest had washed over the country. Soviet and Party departments and newspapers received an enormous number of letters in support of Yeltsin. In the post offices of Sverdlovsk there were even signs saying that letters addressed to Yeltsin would not be delivered. In reply to this, leaflets appeared around the city, calling on the citizens to support their countryman. In simple terms, a confrontation with the people was not part of the ruler's plans – this matter had to be calmed down softly, gently applying the brakes. That is why Gorbachev offered Yeltsin a minister's post.

The next few months in a minister's chair were a time of great loneliness and deep reflection. Here is how he himself describes the period:

> I looked around – no one ... some kind of emptiness, a vacuum ... a frightening feeling of being trapped. Like a leper ... It's hard to describe the state. A real battle with myself started. An analysis of my every word, every deed – an analysis of my principles, my views of the past, present and future – an analysis of my relationships with people and even my family, a constant analysis, day and night, day and night. In such situations, people often look for an outlet in God, others become drunkards ... I sifted hundreds of people through myself – friends, comrades, neighbours, co-workers. Sifted through my relationships with my wife, my children, my grandchildren. I sifted through my faith. What was left in place of my heart? It had turned to coal, burned out ... Migraines tormented me constantly. Almost every night. Often the ambulance would come, I would be given an injection, the pain would recede for a while, and then come back. Naina and my daughters constantly spent sleepless nights by my bed. When the fearsome migraine attacks came I barely stopped myself from crying out. Later, I heard some rumours about me expressing thoughts of suicide. I don't know where these rumours came from ... Although of course, the situation I had found myself in was conducive to such an outcome.

The way up from the bottom of the political well was slow and difficult, but nevertheless it began. Interviews began to appear here and there, and the American TV company SBS even made a show about him.

On 28 June 1988, a nationwide Party conference was due to begin in the Kremlin, which would be televised to the whole country. To speak at it would mean taking a step towards political resurrection. But how to become a conference delegate? Gorbachev no longer had any intention of letting him near a political podium. A strict directive was handed down from the Kremlin: Yeltsin was not to be nominated to go to the conference.

But times were now different. Many factories in the Urals supported and nominated their disgraced countryman as a conference delegate. Unrest begun in Sverdlovsk, the capital of the Urals. People were demanding to be heard, threatening strikes. The situation was heating up. So the authorities decided to give ground, calculating that a confrontation with the people was more dangerous than a prickly delegate. Immediately prior to the opening of the conference, Yeltsin was informed that he would be 'chosen' as the delegate for the Republic of Karelia – a place where he had never been.

Yet to be chosen, and to sit silently in an auditorium of five thousand accomplished little. He had to take the stand. Days passed, the conference was nearing its end, but he was still not called upon to speak, although he had been sending notes to the praesidium from the very first day. Finally, on the last day, when it became clear to him that he would not be allowed to speak, Yeltsin saw that he had no other option but to go for broke – to take the podium 'by direct assault'.

The Karelian delegation, of which Yeltsin was a member, was seated in the highest balcony, right below the ceiling. To enter the hall, you had to go downstairs and enter through the doors to the stalls, which were closed and guarded by KGB agents. Yeltsin went. Recognising his face, the guards let him through without hindrance. Raising his delegate's red identification above his head, Yeltsin approached the table of the praesidium, followed closely by the gaze of television cameras (the broadcast was being beamed to the whole nation). The hall became still. Everyone understood what was going on. Walking up to the praesidium and looking Gorbachev in the eye, Yeltsin announced that he demanded the right to speak, or to allow the conference to vote on whether he should or not. Gorbachev became confused. 'Sit down in the front row,' he snapped.

A few minutes later a guard approached Yeltsin and told him that Gorbachev was asking him to step into the praesidium room to have a talk. Yeltsin stood and slowly headed towards the exit, glancing over at the praesidium to see which of them would rise to meet him. No one was getting up. People were whispering to him from the front rows, 'Don't leave the hall, you won't get back in.' He understood that himself. Right by the very doors, Yeltsin suddenly turned around and returned to his seat in the front row.

To reiterate, all this was happening in front of millions of people following everything on television. I remember how in those days the country came to a virtual standstill for two weeks. Everyone – from office staff to factory workers – sat glued to their TV screens from morning till evening, as they watched for the first time their country's rulers becoming actors in a political play. The situation was getting out of control. Not to let Yeltsin speak was already impossible ...

It is now no longer particularly important to recall the denunciatory words Yeltsin spoke, once he got to the podium. What was important was that he had won, and before the eyes of the whole nation, transformed from victim to conqueror. The isolation had ended, the people now stood behind him. From that moment on, the Gorbachev–Yeltsin conflict came out into the open.

The podium 'assault' cost the victor another heart attack. The conference had not yet ended, when doctors were already labouring over him. Recovery was assisted – better than any medicine – by the bags of letters pouring in from all corners of the country. Unknown people were expressing their love, offering the patient honey, herbs, jam. He was now surrounded by a wall of nation-wide protection. Any rumour – even if it happened to be the truth – which could besmirch the idol was rejected by the people. He was in their keeping and they demanded only one thing from him: to go forward, in their name.

The country was preparing for the election of People's Deputies, from which the Parliament would then be formed. Common sense told Yeltsin that be should lodge his candidacy in the Urals, where his election was all but guaranteed. Yeltsin would not be Yeltsin however, if, having caught the sporting scent of battle, he did not hurl himself into its very heart. He thirsted for revenge right here in Moscow, from where he had been thrown out two years before.

Despite his outward impulsiveness, however, sober calculation and the need for extra insurance did not desert him. Understanding that the authorities would use all manner of cunning tricks to stop him becoming a deputy, he responded in like manner. According to law, to become a candidate for the post of deputy, you had to pass the Regional Voter Council. But the authorities had the right to select a council of people obedient to them, ready to thwart any candidacy of which they did not approve. In case of failure in Moscow, Yeltsin decided simultaneously to register as a candidate for the post of deputy in his own home town of Berezniki in the Urals as well, where his chances of being selected were extremely high. The local authorities there, however, on instructions from the capital, were aware of this possibility and prepared for it.

On the day of the Regional Voter Council in Berezniki, Yeltsin pretended that he had changed his mind and remained in Moscow. When the last scheduled plane from the capital to the Urals had departed, and Yeltsin's arrival at the council seemed impossible, he flew to Leningrad. There he was met by friends who secretly ferried him to the Urals in an old propeller-driven military transport plane, 'hugging a rocket', as the passenger himself quipped. Yeltsin's sudden appearance in Berezniki was a shock to the local authorities who had neglected to carry out the necessary preparations. His countrymen, however, greeted him with jubilation; the triumph was complete.

In the end none of these tricks were necessary. On 26 March 1989, having avoided the numerous pitfalls and gathered 86 per cent of the Muscovites' votes, Yeltsin received the deputy's mandate. However, being elected as a people's deputy did not yet solve anything: it could merely pander to vanity. The deputies still had to choose a Parliament from among their number. Only if he got into Parliament did Yeltsin have a realistic chance of getting back into politics.

Three-quarters of a century of the Soviet regime had halted the development of political culture in the country. It existed at an embryonic level. The people had not yet learned to express their opinion without prompting from the Party. Hence, a crushing majority of the 2,250 people's deputies were Party protégés. For an undesirable deputy to pass through this sieve and end up in Parliament was almost impossible. And Yeltsin did not make it through ...

After receiving more votes from the Muscovites than anyone else, after the conference deputy Yeltsin found himself out on the street. Not for nothing, however, was he popularly called 'The Lucky One'. Political fortune once again did not abandon him. A deputy from Siberia who got into Parliament – a professor from the University of Omsk – decided to give up his place in favour of Yeltsin. This was so unexpected that even Gorbachev was at a loss.

Apart from this surprise, the conference threw up another for Gorbachev. For the first time since the times of Stalin's show-trials, an official opposition to the ruling regime appeared in the Soviet parliament. It was organised by a group of deputies, including such famous figure as Academician Andrei Sakharov, and Boris Yeltsin became one of its leaders.

The most important task of the opposition was to legalise itself, that is, to force the political world to acknowledge its existence. The best way to achieve this was to attain international recognition for its leader, by such figures as the President of the United States, or instance. With this in mind, in September 1989, Yeltsin set off for America.

This was his first trip across the ocean. The days went by in a frenzied rhythm of meetings with businessmen, students and politicians. The main goal however, remained a meeting with the President, who it seemed was in no hurry to see the disgraced guest from Russia, not wishing thereby to upset Gorbachev. Hence the guest decided to employ the already tried and tested partisan tactic, to 'take the White House by direct assault'.

Before the 'assault' on the White House however, an incident occurred which threw the hosts into mild shock. Here is how James Garrison, the coordinator of Yeltsin's trip in America, recalls the event:

> At 11 pm Yeltsin and his delegation ... flew out of New York to Baltimore on David Rockefeller's private plane ... In the airport (in Baltimore) Yeltsin was awaited by a number of high-ranking individuals from Johns Hopkins University ... where Yeltsin was supposed to speak the following day, before leaving for Washington ... When the plan landed, Yeltsin came down the ramp but instead of greeting the delegation that awaited him he walked down the runway to the tail of the plane, and turning his back to us started to relieve himself on the rear wheel of the plane. We stood shaken, in awkward silence, not knowing what to think. Yeltsin came back, not saying a word he shock hands with the dignitaries, received a bouquet of flowers from a young woman and got into the limousine which awaited him. Everyone pretended that nothing happened.

On the third day of his tour Yeltsin arrived in Washington, where he was scheduled to have a meeting with a presidential aide. Having already driven up to the White House, however, he flatly refused to leave the car unless he was given a chance to meet President Bush. An uncomfortable situation was forming, one for which the White House was not prepared. This 'frighteningly stubborn peasant from the Urals' sat sulking in his car and did not want to get out. Finally, a compromise was reached. The President would not receive him in his office, but would 'accidentally' pop into his aide's office while Yeltsin was there. The meeting took place and lasted fifteen minutes, after which the President described his guest as 'an amusing chap'.

It would seem that everything went well, the trip was a success and the goal was reached. All that remains was to consolidate the victory. However, one peculiarity of Yeltsin's 'sportsmanlike' character was that as soon as the 'game' is over and the referee's final whistle sounds, he would let himself go.

After a week of touring, *The Washington Post* suddenly ran an article about a 'Russian bear' who loved whisky and never sobered up from drinking. As an example, Yeltsin's appearance at at that very same Johns Hopkins University was cited where, according to the paper, he appeared tongue-tied after a heavy night of drinking. A few days later, a similar article appeared in the Italian newspaper *Repubblica* to the effect that all the money earned for public appearances by the Russian guest were spent on bars and clothes, so the sick would have to wait a long time for the disposable syringes which he promised to give his country. The writer even reported details of how much Yeltsin drank – four bottles of whisky and two bottles of vodka in the first week. (To which Yeltsin replied something like this: 'The author of the article is just a sissy. If a peasant from the Urals drinks, then it isn't in such pitiful doses.')

On the last day of the tour, an issue of *Pravda* came out in Moscow, containing an article about Yeltsin's trip around the United States, reprinted from *Repubblica*. The effect was one of shock. The fact that the Russian man was no saint was self-evident, but nevertheless ... Rumours started to spread. To believe or not to believe? Finally, the people's trust in their idol won out. As a sign of protest, they started burning copies of *Pravda* in the centre of Moscow. The people were angered, and the result ended up being the opposite of of what may well have been intended: Yeltsin's popularity rose even higher.

The publicity had not yet died down when Moscow Central Television screened an hour and a half-long programme filmed by Americans about Yeltsin's visit to the States. The crux of the programme was that same ill-fated university visit, where Yeltsin had allegedly arrived after a heavy night's drinking. Indeed, the screen showed a man with obviously uncoordinated reflexes, tripping over his words and perpetrating what might charitably be called 'abnormal acts'. (As a 'joke', he grabbed the text of the speech from in front of the person speaking at the podium.) In other words, as the Russians say, the lad was as 'senseless as a fly'.

What reaction could be expected from the viewers after such a programme? Disappointment? Concern? A fall in popularity? Nothing of the sort. It seemed to be some sort of miracle, mass hypnosis and mass psychosis. Yeltsin's popularity and the people's belief in him were already so high that the viewers did not believe what they saw on the screen. They didn't believe their own eyes, suspecting yet another lie ...

Later, Yeltsin would explain his state at that university meeting as a result of extreme fatigue, due to an overbooked schedule of meetings and receptions. According to him, arriving at his hotel late, he immediately took several strong-acting sleeping pills. Early in the morning, when he went to yet another meeting, their effect had not yet worn off; he was in a sluggish state, 'not himself'.

Furthermore, as Yeltsin announced, he was able to find out that the American video material had also been tampered with by Moscow montage editors. Speeding up the tape in some places, slowing it down in others, and thereby creating a further impression of slurred speech and uncoordinated movement. All this, according to Yeltsin, was nothing more than yet another provocation against him by Mikhail Gorbachev.

I have no desire to enter this debate, but would nevertheless like to point out the following. I did personally see this material on Western television, where Soviet montage scissors could not yet have touched it. The impression was that he was inebriated. Apart from this, other people in the same shots were not slurring their speech; so to suggest a version of events where the tape was creatively edited is technically unsustainable.

It would seem that after such a flood of compromising material its 'hero' would need to step forward and say something, explain himself. Nothing of the kind, in fact he completely disappeared from view for several weeks. Rumours spread across Moscow that he had been killed, had a heart attack, been in an accident ...

Suddenly, he found himself at the centre of yet another row. This story was told to the whole country by the Minister of Internal Affairs, speaking at a parliamentary session that was being screened on television. Obviously this was done under the guidance of Mikhail Gorbachev, who was chairing the session.

The minister explained that several days after returning from America, late at night, Yeltsin appeared – wet from head to toe – at a police station outside Moscow near the government dachas. He informed the policemen that an attempt had just been made on his life. Unknown persons had put a sack over his head, and thrown him off a bridge into the Moscow River.

It was late autumn, the temperature was approaching zero Celsius. Their guest, wet through and through, was shivering from the cold. The police gave him tea to drink. Soon his wife and daughter arrived to take him home. Before leaving, Yeltsin asked the police not to tell anyone about this incident, not to inform their superiors, since he did not want to take any official action regarding the incident.

According to Yeltsin, he had gone to the government dacha settlement to see an old friend. He left the car a few hundred metres from the destination in order to get some fresh air. As soon as his car drove off, some other car pulled up behind him. Several unknown people got out, threw a sack over his head, and suddenly he was falling off a five-metre bridge into the river below. He barely managed to swim to shore. The victim considered this a political provocation, orchestrated by the authorities.

According to the Minister of Internal Affairs, prior to his appearance at the police station, Yeltsin was seen in the dacha area with a bouquet of flowers. In the minister's opinion, there was no attack – the victim's version was made up

– since the height of the bridge was not five metres as he said, but fifteen. Had he been thrown from such a height, he would have been severely injured. In other words, as the minister implied, all this was nothing more than the wanderings of a drunken philanderer, finding himself in a compromising position.

The height of the bridge seems immaterial. What puzzles me is why, having thrown all this in the faces of millions of viewers, neither the victim, nor the police, bothered to take this investigation to its conclusion. Was there or was there not an attack ? If there was, then by whom and why, who stood behind it? If not, then why did the victim need to make it up?

Yeltsin himself presents a very 'original' – to put it lightly – version as to why he did not take this matter further. He writes: 'I easily foresaw the reaction of people, who were making a great effort to tolerate the moral provocations against me, but would be unable calmly to accept the news of an attempt to physically annihilate me. As a sign of protest ... (the largest defence facilities of the country might come to a standstill) ... half of Moscow would come to a halt. After this, due to the strikes at strategic installations, martial law would be declared throughout the country ... Hence, because Yeltsin allowed himself to succumb to provocation, *perestroika* in the country could have 'come to a "fortunate" end'. For this reason, the victim informs us, he decided to stay silent.

While the victim gave such a strange – to put it lightly – explanation for his silence, the authorities gave none at all. However, the curious masses looked for an explanation. Here is one version, put forward from second-hand accounts by the respected authors Soloviev and Klepikov. That evening Gorbachev's Prime Minister, whom Yeltsin knew well from their work together in the Urals, was celebrating some kind of family event. Considering Gorbachev's and Yeltsin's relationship, the latter naturally was not invited. Then Yeltsin decided to spring a surprise on them. Grabbing a bouquet of flowers, he arrived to wish his countryman well, without an invitation. With his arrival, the atmosphere at the table started to get heavy. Gradually an unpleasant conversation ensued between him and Gorbachev, passing first into name-calling and then possibly to the grabbing of lapels. Yeltsin slammed the door and left. Inflamed by the wine and the argument, Gorbachev signalled to the trained lads from his guard, telling them to catch up with him and teach him a lesson. So they taught him one.

However enraged both sides were, having the row out in public was something neither of them wanted. This did not add to anyone's authority, and both leaders understood this. However, rumours of the incident had already spread and both sides wanted to present themselves in a more favourable light. Yeltsin argued that this was provocation by the authorities, while Gorbachev painted it as the amoral activities of his adversary ... *

* After the chapter about Boris Yeltsin had been written, new information appeared about this mysterious event, which continues to trouble Russian minds to this day. I present it here, leaving the above-mentioned versions intact as well, since what is finally important is not this specific incident but how the 'leader's face' is formed in the consciousness of society.

This information was revealed by KGB general and sitting member of parliament Alexander Korzhakov – Yeltsin's old friend and the former head of his personal guard. On the evening in question he got a call from Yeltsin's daughter who informed him in worried tones that her father had just been thrown from a bridge into a river, and that he was currently in a ghastly state, in a police post not far from where the incident occurred. Korzhakov jumped into a car and raced down there. Boris Yeltsin was lying on a bench in the police post, looking pitiful, wet, in only his underwear, covered with a police jacket. Korzhakov notes that his body was blue with cold. Seeing his friend run in, Yeltsin burst into tears and said, 'Look what they have done to me ...' After Korzhakov forced him to drink several glasses of vodka, the victim regained some of his strength. His wet clothes were hanging on a nail, and Korzhakov noticed some river weeds clinging to them. In other words, there was no doubt that Yeltsin had taken a dip in the river. Korzhakov began to question the victim about how this had happened. Yeltsin recounted an already familiar version: he was walking, a car stopped behind him, several large men jumped out, a bag was thrown over his head and he found himself in the river.

'I found almost everything in this story to be strange ...' Korzhakov writes. 'If they really wanted to kill him, then they would have definitely hit him over the head before throwing him in, to be sure. And in any case, how did these people know that Yeltsin would go on foot? He was always driven to the very door. So then I asked him: "Did they tie up the bag?" He replied "Yes"... This information perplexed me even further – strange thugs we have here, can't even tie a bag over someone's head properly.'

Let us remember that Korzhakov is a KGB general, and is very familiar with the methods of the KGB, so his expert evaluations can be trusted.

Also, Moscow journalists recently decided to carry out their own independent investigation of this incident. Their method was simple – jumping into the river from that same bridge. Thank god that a local girl walking past stopped them. The height of the bridge turned out not to be five metres like Yeltsin said but closer to fifteen, while the depth of the water under the bridge was less than a metre. So, if Boris Yeltsin had really been thrown from this bridge, then the history of Russia would have unfolded a different way.

Nevertheless, who needed this spectacle? Korzhakov does not give a straight answer to this question, but the way he titled the episode – 'A Flight Through Dreams and Reality' – speaks volumes. In his interviews and memoires, the general explains that Boris Yeltsin – with whom he spent ten years 'from sunrise to sunset' – would sometimes experience nervous episodes, with a tendency towards suicide. In other words, the classical Russian malaise after a bender. Korzhakov recalls several incidents where Yeltsin tried to do away with himself. One occurred when Gorbachev removed Yeltsin from political life, and transferred him to the post of Minister of Construction. Sitting in his ministerial office, Yeltsin tried to stab himself in the heart with scissors. Another incident, this one after the 'flight from the bridge', occurred when parliament threatened President Yeltsin with impeachment. He then locked himself in the sauna and decided to suffocate to death, but Korzhakov broke down the door and dragged him out. In other words, the 'flight from the bridge' was another nervous episode. Boris Yeltsin didn't jump from the bridge of course, but he did go under it, and he did throw himself into the river ...

The word 'charisma' is a popular one today in the Russian political lexicon. It assumes the possession of certain qualities by an individual, without which he could not possibly be a true chief, leader, governor, hero or dictator. These qualities are: a highly visible desire to gain authority, strong will, decisiveness, cunning, harsh rationality, and the readiness to spill blood – both their own and that of others – if the need arises. What is absent from this list is a powerful intellect. A charismatic leader does not need one, and may even find it harmful. A sensitive emotional make-up is anathema to a ruler, and has always been viewed by the people as a negative quality. Andrei Sakharov, for instance, could never have become leader of Russia even in the most favourable of circumstances. This phenomenon is universal, in the East as in the West, and if there are the occasional exceptions, they are very rare indeed. No one knows this better than we Russians.

In the eyes of the people Yeltsin was certainly a charismatic leader at the time. All the polls showed him to be the most popular political figure in the country. All the roads to power, however, were firmly closed by Gorbachev. Here – Yeltsin must be given his due – he found a loophole that would only have been visible to a very shrewd politician.

In the mass-consciousness of the time, the concept of the Soviet Union was always assumed to be equivalent to Imperial Russia, forcibly holding and exploiting the other Republics. They were the slaves and she was the master. Yeltsin turned this scheme in another direction: the Republics, including Russia, were all under the whip of the Kremlin Centre. They must not fight among themselves, but pool their efforts and attempt to free themselves from the rule of the Centre. All power must pass to the Republics, the Kremlin only retaining the role of co-ordinator.

Such a concept could not help but appeal to both Russians as well as the citizens of other Republics. The latter always felt themselves to be second-class citizens, vassals of Russia, and hated her for this. The Russians, on the other hand, saw them as parasites and hangers-on. But everyone loathed the Kremlin, which was generally associated with the hated System.

Whether this idea was born in the mind of Yeltsin, or was the fruit of a collective effort, the 'Achilles' Heel' in Gorbachev's defences had been found. Yeltsin's next step became clear: to become the head of the Russian Parliament, and then begin the struggle for Russian independence from the Centre, which was led by Gorbachev.

At the end of May, preparations began in the Russian Parliament for the election of a new chairman. The battle promised to be brutal. The whole country followed every move with great intensity. Even the most popular football matches did not keep people so thoroughly glued to their television screens. In essence this was already a battle between the Kremlin and the People, the battle for Russian democracy. Already familiar slogans were wheeled out: 'Yeltsin is Russia's Gravedigger', 'Power-hungry', 'A Dictator to Rival Stalin' ... The voting was conducted three times. The first two times, none of the candidates managed to gather the required number of votes. The third voting session was moved to the following day.

Emotions around the Kremlin – where the Parliamentary sessions were taking place – were running high. Hundreds of slogans were everywhere: 'Boris! We are with you!', 'An exhausted Russia believes only Yeltsin!', 'If you don't choose Yeltsin, there will be a Civil War!' ... The people surrounded deputies trying to get into the Kremlin and demanded they vote for Yeltsin. Russia had not seen such a political storm for a very long time. The hall of Parliament that next day was not the same place it had been the day before. The fifty-nine-year-old Boris Yeltsin won by a majority of four votes, and on 29 May 1990 became the chairman of the Russian Parliament. The people celebrated, this was their victory.

One and a half months later, under the watchful eyes of millions of television viewers, Yeltsin executed another effective and even theatrical gesture, which all in all was no longer a risky one for him. Climbing up to the podium during a Party conference in the Kremlin, he informed Gorbachev that, as the head of the Russian Parliament bringing together, in his post, people of many political views and persuasions – he no longer considered it possible for himself to be a member of any one political party and carry out its directives. Therefore, he was leaving the Party. Then, leaving his Party identification ticket – from which he had never parted during the past thirty years – on the table of the praesidium, to the jeers of the orthodox in the hall, he walked out of the conference. This was not simply a member leaving the Party, it was a demonstration of Russia's independence from the System, a demonstration that three-quarters of a century of fear and obedience were coming to an end. Needless to say, Yeltsin's approval rating went through the roof that day.

The country was jubilant. The Baltic Republics announced their departure from the USSR. National tensions flared up in the Central Asian Republics and the Caucasus. The Empire was cracking along the seams. Power was slipping out of the Centre's hands, whose embodiment was Gorbachev. According to those near Gorbachev, he almost went mad on account of Yeltsin at the time. At any conference he would return to the 'Yeltsin

Question', labelling him with all manner of rude epithets: '... sucked down half a bucket of vodka, and now he's setting his cronies on to me ... they need a good smack in the gob ...' Whatever the topic of conversation at home or abroad, it came back to Yeltsin. Yeltsin became his *idée fixe*, his nightmare, his point of madness ...

Seeing the impending fragmentation of the USSR and hoping to avert it, in March 1991 Gorbachev announced a nationwide referendum. One question was being put forward: do the citizens of the Soviet Union wish to continue living in a united nation? In turn, Russia's Parliament – headed by Yeltsin – announced an additional referendum: do the citizens of Russia want the head of their government to be a President? The people answered both questions emphatically.

On 12 June 1991, as already mentioned, Russians elected the first President in the history of their country: Boris Yeltsin. Even today, we are not able to comprehend fully what this event meant for Russia. It will require a historical distance of at least several decades.

And so, the Kremlin suddenly acquired two masters: the President of the USSR, Mikhail Gorbachev, and the President of Russia, Boris Yeltsin. But why? Why would the Kremlin need two Czars? In its many centuries of history, the Kremlin had already experienced similar situations, which always ended in blood. Any Russian peasant knows that two bears cannot live in the same lair, while the eastern nations – of whom we are a part – have their own aphorism for the situation: 'The world is too small to be ruled by two tyrants at once.'

As already mentioned, there was a moment at this point where, it seemed, tensions between Gorbachev and Yeltsin might be lessened, saving a great nation from disintegration. We are talking about the formation of the Commonwealth of Independent States, to replace the Soviet Union. The Republics would be headed by their own presidents, and the Centre would be headed by a federal president – Mikhail Gorbachev. 'Gorbachev and I suddenly and clearly felt that our interests had finally coincided,' Yeltsin writes, ' ... these roles suited us fully. Gorbachev maintains his seniority, while I maintain my independence.' (One can only be astonished by the author's outspokenness, and particularly by his cynicism: 'I ... We ... Gorbachev's and my interests ... Gorbachev and I were satisfied ...' And where are We – 300 million people – and Our interests? Did this satisfy Us?)

The tense preparations for the 'Agreement' regarding the Commonwealth of Independent States were finally complete. Towards the end of July, it seemed a fragile balance that appeared to satisfy everyone had been achieved. It remained only to finalise it with signatures. But at that moment Mikhail Gorbachev left for a holiday in the Crimea. What was this, 'Russian Fate' or foul play? History will one day tell us.

On 19 August Yeltsin was at his dacha outside Moscow. Early in the morning, his daughter burst into the bedroom yelling, 'Wake up Dad! It's a coup!' At that moment, blanketing the city with the sound of caterpillar-tracks, columns of tanks and armoured cars were already driving through the streets of Moscow. The capital was rubbing its eyes in disbelief: 'Is it a war?'

A major-general, the commander of a famous KGB brigade codenamed 'Alpha', tells how he was aware of Yeltsin's every move and every word, as well as those of every member of his family. The President of Russia was even observed in the sauna. Early in the morning on the day of the coup, all accesses to the President's dacha precincts were secretly blockaded by KGB cars. The general received an order from the coup leaders to isolate Yeltsin. A plane was allegedly prepared, on which the Russian President was supposed to be taken 'in an unknown direction ...' According to the general, however, neither he nor his people wished to be part of a coup. Hence they delayed, doing everything they could to get nothing done. The general misinformed his superiors, saying that taking Yeltsin in the dacha was dangerous – there would be needless witnesses and a lot of bloodshed. In actual fact, Yeltsin's guard was weak, and the 'Alpha' soldiers were so well trained that the operation would last only a few minutes, during which no one would notice a thing.

Meanwhile, courses of action were being debated at the President's dacha. Finding out about the coup, aides and people close to the President flocked to his side. Some thought that a resistance headquarters should be established right here, at the dacha. Others advised going to Moscow, to the White House (Government House). But how to make it through into Moscow? All the roads were blocked by tanks.

It was decided, nonetheless, to try to break through. Yeltsin was dressed in a bullet-proof vest. Escort cars drove ahead and to the sides, while the limousine containing the President was in the centre, flying the Russian government flag.

How did the President's cortège manage to make it through to the capital? Why did tanks drive off into ditches to make way for them? 'What saved us?' Yeltsin asks rhetorically. 'We could have been shot from ambush as we drove out, or taken on the motorway ... I later found out that Special Operations Unit was observing our movements from the forest. The group leader had 'administered 200 grams", for courage. He was expecting to receive a kill or capture order at any moment. These lads observed our every move for over four hours. When they understood that we were heading for Moscow, for the centre of the city, they settled down. We were not hiding, quite the opposite, throwing ourselves into the heart of the fire. I will never forget those exhausting minutes, the endless columns of military hardware ...'

In reply to the President, the commander of 'Alpha' says that they did not have orders to kill Yeltsin. There was an order to arrest him but, if the general is to be believed, they were even reluctant to carry that one out. Hence they allowed the President's cortège to leave the dacha, although its capture or even destruction was a mere matter of a minutes.

Not long before the coup, Yeltsin visited a division barracked not far outside Moscow. He was shown around by the commander of the Airborne Infantry (the future Minister of Defence) General Pavel Grachov. Half joking and half serious, Yeltsin asked him: 'If the lawfully elected authorities are threatened, could you be counted on, General?' The general replied: 'Yes, I could be.' And now, that time had come. Before leaving the dacha, Yeltsin called the general and reminded him of that conversation. A long silence ensued and the general finally said: 'I'll send Scout Company.'

Exactly a quarter of an hour after the President's procession left for the capital, a group of eight men in military fatigues drove up to the dacha. Their leader presented documents identifying him as a colonel of the Airborne Infantry, explaining that they were here on General Grachov's orders, to defend President Yeltsin. It was then that something unforeseen happened. One of Yeltsin's guards who had remained at the dacha had recently taken some KGB courses and recognised this colonel as one of his instructors. The instructor did not remember the student. The fake infantryman was a KGB officer. Everything became clear: having intercepted his phone conversation with General Grachov, the KGB had sent their own team ahead of the Scouts, meaning to take Yeltsin quietly and calmly without the use of force. They were too late, however; he had already departed for Moscow. The President's family, who were still at the dacha, pretended they did not know about the deception, and 'guests' likewise pretended that nothing had happened.

Yeltsin made it to the White House around ten or eleven o'clock in the morning. The White House is the first government building after the Kremlin to be built specifically for that purpose. Hundreds of offices, many departments, kilometres of corridors, underground bunkers, secret exits connected to a system of underground communication. A real citadel.

The peaceful countenance of the building was disturbed that day. Tanks and armoured personnel carriers had taken up positions along the whole façade. A sea of people milled all around, bodily preventing the further advance of the armoured units. They blocked streets with trolley-buses, shoved girders into the tracks of stationary tanks, erected barricades. As Yeltsin writes:

> I looked out the window on to the square again. A crowd of people had surrounded an armoured car. The driver poked up out of the hatch. I felt it like a blow, like an inner pull – I have to be there right now, with them ... I went down. I climbed up on to a tank's turret, straightened up ... A feeling of complete clarity, absolute unity with the people standing around me. There are many of them, cries and whistles sound from the crowd ... I take out the piece of paper with my speech. I read loudly, my voice almost breaking. I then speak to the tank commander, to soldiers. Seeing their faces and eyes I know they won't shoot at us ...

This was no more than an emotional impulse on the part of the President. It was already completely clear that the coup could not succeed without storming the White House. Starting from three in the afternoon, communication was already cut off, snipers with night-scopes took up positions on the roofs of neighbouring buildings. Airborne Infantry assault forces were approaching ...

In turn, the defenders of the White House were also preparing. Their numbers grew by the hour. More and more people came. Russian Parliamentary deputies, students, journalists, Kazakhs, ordinary citizens. Even the pregnant wife of Moscow's vice-mayor refused to stay at home and was there with her husband. Stopping this flood of volunteers – which broke through every cordon – was impossible.

The approaching night promised not to be an easy one. The main concern for the President's guards was to protect their charge in the event of an assault. Several plans were formulated. One of them was to spirit him away via the underground communications tunnels spanning the whole of Moscow. A wig, beard and moustache were even prepared for the President in one of the capital's theatres. Perhaps the simplest and safest of plans was to shelter in the American Embassy located next to the White House, especially since the Americans themselves lent their unequivocal support. However, this was not acceptable from a moral point of view. The interference of foreigners in 'our business' was never viewed kindly in Russia.

The coup-leaders were also preparing for nightfall. The assault was scheduled for three o'clock in the morning. Responsibility was entrusted to the commander of 'Alpha' brigade. To this end, fifteen thousand specially prepared soldiers were ready to go. In the opinion of the commander of 'Alpha', the assault on the White House would not have presented any extraordinary difficulties, and would have taken from fifteen to thirty minutes. Late in the evening, together with General Lebed, they examined the barricades surrounding the White House, finding them to be 'toylike'.

The plan for the assault was as follows: at three in the morning infantry would blockade the building. Specialised armoured transports would hack a path through the barricades. Tanks would then stun the defenders of the White House with a barrage from their cannons. Special forces units would scatter the crowds, using gas and water cannon, forming a corridor through which brigade 'Alpha' would enter.

It is hard to say if everything was as clear and simple as the commander of 'Alpha' explained. The thousands of defenders positioned around the White House also had their own instructors. The people were broken up into groups and divisions. They were ordered, as soon as the assault began, to give ground, allow 'Alpha' to enter the corridor thus formed, then press down upon them bodily and disarm them. On paper this looks simple, but what would it have been like in reality?

The commander of 'Alpha' considers everything to have hinged on his decision in this situation. He thanks God that he decided not to go ahead with this business, that he refused to participate in the assault, otherwise there would have been a slaughter in a sea of blood. This decision by the commander of 'Alpha' is verified by General Grachov, who was told on the phone, 'I will not take part in the assault.'

It is interesting to follow the actions of another general, Alexander Lebed. On the one hand he, along with his immediate superior General Grachov, carried out the orders of the Minister of Defence, who participated in the coup. On the other hand, it seems that both generals did not have their hearts in the coup. That night, having examined the defenders' barricades and finding them to be 'toylike', General Lebed met Yeltsin and informed him that he had ordered eight armoured transports to take part in the defence of the White House. Here is how Yeltsin describes the general: 'Lebed is an interesting individual. A general who served in Afghanistan, meeting the physical requirements of a infantryman better than any soldier. A straight-talking man, unusually abrupt in his mannerisms, who places a military officer's honour above all else.'

The night ended and morning came. The crowds around the White House grew, but the coup-leaders still did not begin the assault. Why were they so indecisive? Even a blind man could see that time was working against them. The longer the soldiers interacted with the people, the less the chances that they would then fire on them. The whole thing started to turn into a huge show – a theatrical coup, as it was later called. Girls joined soldiers in their tanks to 'warm' them, young men brought along something bracing to drink, while mothers and grandmothers brought thermoses of hot food.

There are different explanations for this indecision. One of them is that the coup did not have a true leader, someone willing to take responsibility. Another is that the whole thing was not a real coup, but a deception. It has been hinted that the instigator of the coup was Gorbachev himself, who lost his nerve at the last moment. Finally, there are more simple explanations. The coup-leaders were not tyrants nor butchers, but merely orthodox Party bureaucrats. Hence the coup was more a bureaucratic one than a bloody one.

The final version is, I feel, closer to the truth. It is enough to remember an episode when, on the night of 20/21 August three young people died in one of the city's underpasses. They wanted to halt the advance of a tank column. To blind the leading vehicle, thus creating a traffic jam, they threw a tarpaulin over it. One of the lads jumped up on to the tank. A shot rang out, the young man fell. Two others leapt forward to help their friend. The 'blinded' vehicle jerked forwards and backwards. One boy was crushed by a track, the other was also shot. It is said that when the Minister of Defence found out about this 'first blood' he was horrified. The final blow was delivered by his wife, herself a survivor of a recent car accident, who, in tears broke into her husband's office and started yelling: 'Who have you got yourself involved with?'

All this occurred a day later. For now, however, the tension was growing. The coup-leaders found themselves in the grip of circumstances they themselves had created. An assault was already well-nigh impossible. Thousands of people, in several concentric rings, had surrounded the White House. The assault plan prepared earlier was already unsuitable. Now, it would mean shooting and crushing unarmed people at point-blank range. It was rumoured that the assault was being delayed from hour to hour.

Finally, exactly at midnight on 21 August, a column of some twenty armoured personnel carriers filled with troops approached the barricades.

People tried to stop it. The soldiers fired live rounds into the air. Ignited trolley-buses started going up in flames, one armoured car had already started to burn. Half an hour later, the above-mentioned tragedy took place in an underpass – three young people died …

It is hard to say what role the wife's tears played, but they definitely played some part. By morning, the Minister of Defence had given the troops the order to leave Moscow.

This was a victory. The leaders of the coup were scattering. The President of Russia declared them fugitives. On the evening of the same day, the President of the USSR returned from his Crimean 'captivity'.

'An inordinately huge crowd of people, stretching from the White House to the cemetery. A heavy, oppressive atmosphere and an intolerable feeling of shame for us all … I was left with the mothers – blackened with grief – I couldn't leave. Who could know that these funerals would not be the last?' That is how Boris Yeltsin describes the last chord of these events, bidding farewell to the boys killed in the underpass.

That would seem to be all. The ravaged country deserved some peace. Now, it would finally be possible to sign the 'Commonwealth Agreement', to save the country from disintegration and begin fundamental restructuring.

Considering that the people had voted for it in a referendum, what impeded the preservation of a united country? Unarguably, the most important impulse towards disintegration was the coup. If, prior to it, the leaders of the Republics had treated Gorbachev with the respect due the leader of a nation, then the coup and the residual ambiguity of Gorbachev's role in it, ruined the President of the USSR's image. Gorbachev's sentimental tale of his 'captivity' at the Crimean dacha elicited sarcasm rather than sympathy from the members of Parliament. There was a feeling that he had somehow failed, even allowing for his captivity. The President of the country had not become the moral leader of the resistance, but instead had distanced himself from events. To go bathing in the sea while the country was collapsing was a hard position for a head of state to justify. Leadership during the days of the coup had passed firmly from the Kremlin to the Republics – to Russia in the first instance – and returning it to the Kremlin was something the Republics were not prepared to do. One after the other, they proclaimed sovereignty, declaring their independence from the Kremlin. Presidential elections started to be held through all the Republics.

It was not only this, however, that determined the final disintegration of the Soviet Union. The confrontation between Gorbachev and Yeltsin flared up with renewed vigour, but now the attacking party was President of Russia. If Gorbachev had once promised Yeltsin not to let him near politics, now the situation was reversed. Yeltsin was actively pushing his opponent overboard, out of the political vessel. It seemed that he thirsted to initiate a new chapter in the history of Russia from a clean slate.

'It was a marvellous winter's evening. A light frost lay upon the air. A light snow fell. A real crisp December.' With this lyrical phrase, Yeltsin begins the chapter of his book in which he tells of the final days in the life of the world's last empire.

On 8 October 1991, in a sable reservation called Beloveshskaya Forest, in a hunting cabin belonging to the head of the Byelorussian parliament, the leaders of the three largest Republics – Russia, Ukraine and Byelorussia – gathered: 'the Three Lads', as the Belorussians will later call them. The object of the meeting was the signing of a document declaring the full independence of these Republics, their exit from the USSR and their transformation into independent nations, which effectively marked the liquidation of the Soviet Union. 'The meeting took place in secrecy. The residence was even guarded by the Special Forces', Yeltsin writes.

A question immediately arises: why the secrecy? What was threatening them? Logic dictates that such a meeting, if it is legal and does not harbour any hidden agendas, should not need to be highly secret, but on the contrary, highly visible. What, other than a nationwide referendum, could answer the question of whether or not 300 million people – of whom tens of millions had given their lives for its unity – should or should not live together? Especially considering that the people had recently already answered the question emphatically in the affirmative.

In his memoirs, President Yeltsin tries to convince us that the liquidation of the USSR was the only method of keeping together Republics that were scattering in all directions. Attaining unity, not through a slavish obedience to the Kremlin, but through a voluntary gathering of a people who had lived side by side for many centuries. This thought has a rational seed, but far more in the way of guile. The imperial form of government under which the Soviet Union existed had certainly outlived its usefulness, and was in need of change, but not by way of Bolshevik methods of 'tear it down to the foundations and then ...' This rapid collapse of the Soviet Union inflicted a terrible blow upon the people – especially the Russians. With one swipe of the pen, Russia was hurled back almost to the borders of Peter the Great, depriving her of one-third of her territory and even the

southern seas, which she had battled for over the centuries. Most importantly, in the name of what?

'I understood,' Yeltsin writes, 'that I would be accused of settling the score
with Gorbachev. That the separatist agreement was merely a tool for pushing
him out of power. I knew that this accusation would now sound for the
remainder of my life. This made the decision doubly difficult ... But I felt in
my heart, that big decisions must be made lightly. Thus, this wasn't a "secret
coup" but a legal change in the existing order of things ...'

The matter is not in the words, but in what is read between the lines,
namely the President's burning desire to prove to himself and his readers that
the events in 'Beloveshskaya Forest' were not illegal, and the 'secret coup' that
took place there and resulted in the ruin of a great nation was for the good
of Russia. Although the Russian people had quite recently voted against disintegration, as was the custom in Russia for centuries, the leaders knew best
what was good for the people. 'An act of worldwide significance,' writes
Professor Burlatski, 'the disintegration of a great Euro-Asian nation, took
place under circumstances typical to the communist "meeting of chiefs", convinced that they were right to decide anything at all, not stopping to think
about the will of the people or their accountability to history.'*

'There was another possibility, another way out of the existing situation,'
Yeltsin continues, 'to try legally to take Gorbachev's place. To stand at the
head of the Soviet Union, and begin its reform anew, from the "summit" ...
This path, however, was closed to me. Psychologically, I could not take
Gorbachev's place.' Elsewhere Yeltsin adds: 'What in the main, is President
Yeltsin personally dependent upon? In the first place it would seem, on his
inner "ego".'

A thoughtful silence is appropriate here. Could a dislike of Gorbachev
have outweighed a leader's responsibility for his country? What then is the
difference between the president of a great nation, and a tribal chief, ruled
only by his own ambitious 'ego'?

Let us return however to the forests of Byelorussia. It seems that the light
frost, the gentle snowfall, and a good sauna with cold beer, put the three leaders into a good mood. The 'Beloveshski Agreement' was signed. Russia, the
Ukraine and Byelorussia left the USSR. Awakening the next morning, millions

---

* By the way, after the Beloveshskaya Agreement was signed, having called Gorbachev to
arrange a meeting, Yeltsin cautiously asked him: 'Will I be arrested...?' In other words, he
understood perfectly that the secret meeting in the forests of Belorussia was nothing other than
a political coup.

of amazed people discovered that they were living in a different country and that many of them had even become foreigners. Their nation no longer existed; all that remained of it was the Kremlin and a lonely President – without a country or people.

On 25 December 1991 – having delivered his farewell address to his countrymen – the first and last President of the USSR, Mikhail Gorbachev, went into retirement. He did not leave to a fanfare, as would befit a President, but rather to quiet gloating and revelling.

Here is how Gorbachev himself describes the moment:

> In the first few days after my retirement ...I came face to face with the uncivility of those who had come to power. On the 27th of December I had a meeting scheduled with Japanese journalists. In the morning however I was called and informed that Yeltsin and his coterie had occupied my office, raucously celebrating and drinking a bottle of whiskey ... A pack of carnivores was reveling, I can find no other comparison. I was ordered to vacate the country residence and the President's apartment within three days ..."

All this is saddening. Once again we missed a chance to demonstrate dignity and nobility.

Time will go by, the euphoria will pass, and somewhere in the depths of our souls a nostalgia will stir about the loss of the great nation in which we were born. Naturally we are not talking about the System, but about a mighty country, with its huge territories and many-faceted culture, deserts and snows, desolate peaks and warm seas. A citizen of tiny Switzerland might not understand this, just as a staid, provincial town-dweller might not understand the soul of a romantic drifter. Yet a question, now irrelevant, still nags: could not the 'Evil Empire' have been liquidated while the mighty country was preserved?

Thus the Kremlin gained a new master. For the first time in a long history, he was a freely elected President. In truth, many considered that the new Russian government should not move into the Kremlin, but stay in the White House, which had become the symbol of its victory. It was time to let the Kremlin rest, turn it into a historical reserve, a monument to Russian and world history. Supporters of this view thought that the enchantment of autocratic power which the Kremlin possessed needed to fade away, to sink into oblivion. In a democratic government, power should not cause fear. In moving the capital from Moscow to St Petersburg, Peter the Great was trying to make Russian government more civilised, close to European models. When Lenin moved power back to the Kremlin, he restored its autocratic grandeur, elevating it over the people. The time had come to correct this mistake. The Kremlin, as proponents of this viewpoint maintained, should remain a symbol of our history and culture, not a symbol of power and fear.

The President, however, decided to the contrary. Along with the symbols of power, Yeltsin inherited from Gorbachev its chattels, from the 'nuclear button' to the most secret of secret archives. The 'button' turns out to be a small suitcase full of special communications equipment. As for the Party archives, its files will prove to be just as explosively dangerous, containing the truth about many of the System's dirty deals – from lies and secret murders to international terrorism. Many of the secrets in these files have not been made public to this day.

As is well known, even fictitious literary characters often live and act outside the will of the author. What then can be said about our documentary protagonist! My intention in this book has been to reveal the personal, everyday aspects of the various individuals who have occupied the Kremlin 'throne'. I realise with some annoyance that Yeltsin is here too politicised, although I did not want this. I wanted instead to paint him in a more down-to-earth, day-to-day aspect. However, what is there to be done if his personality is more the 'rabble-rouser' than the 'personal-achiever'? His professional working environment is the crowd, not the silence of an office. The essence of Boris Yeltsin's character is risk, struggle and, of course, victory. Victory no matter what, at any price, victory in everything, from sport to politics or personal affairs. By his psychology and worldview, he is a sportsman ('... he threw himself into a Party career like he once threw himself into spiking the ball ...' '... he takes the blow well ...'), and like any sportsman, the loss of the opponent is the loss of purpose, spirit, stimuli for the will. Yeltsin standing on the barricades in front of the White House, and Yeltsin sitting in a quiet minister's chair are two different people. The former is confident, active, driven; the latter is broody, sulky, irritable. And now fate had lifted him up to the pinnacle of power. What would he be like on the Kremlin throne, in the role of 'Czar Boris'?

The role he had been handed was certainly not an easy one. The country lay in economic ruins, having slammed into the dead-end of the Communist road. As one wise author commented, it not only seemed that the Russian empire was ending, but that Russian history was drawing to a close. The country needed to be dragged out of a deep chasm, and placed on the road of a wholly new system of development. All this would require heroism, struggle and victories, but not in the style of the barricades. Would Yeltsin cope with this?

Earlier, before the disintegration of the USSR, as head of the then Russian republican Parliament, Boris Yeltsin – on his own insistence – had been granted broad, extraordinary powers, mainly with the aim of challenging central power, namely Gorbachev. After Yeltsin became President of Russia, and another person took on the post of Head of Parliament, these extraordinary powers were not repealed and automatically passed to the new head. The already familiar situation of the 'two bears' recurred, when two leaders, possessing roughly the same powers, commanded the same territory. The story of Gorbachev versus Yeltsin was repeated, but now the struggle for leadership flared between the President and the Parliament.

On 20 March 1993 Yeltsin appeared on television and informed the citizens of Russia that he had prepared a decree, according to which the country would be governed under 'special circumstances'. The decree would be in effect until such a time as the country overcame the 'crisis of dual-leadership'. Several days later, the Constitutional Court announced its verdict, declaring the decree illegal since it breached the country's constitution. This was an excellent reason for impeachment. The hastily reconvened Parliament now had to decide whether or not to impeach the President.

On 22 March Yeltsin summoned the Commandant of the Moscow Kremlin and ordered him to prepare for the arrest of Parliament if the deputies voted for impeachment. As General Korzhakov, Yeltsin's closest aide at the time, recalls, canisters of chloropicrin – a highly aggravating chemical compound – were secretly installed in the balcony of the hall where the Parliament was meeting. This compound was usually used to test gas-masks. If a gas-mask had the slightest hole in it, the wearer would vacate the testing area like a cork coming out of a bottle.

The plan was simple. If Parliament voted to impeach the President, then the President's earlier decree would come into effect, dissolving the Parliament. If the delegates did non obey the decree willingly and vacate the hall, then force would be employed. The plainclothes secret-service officers on the balcony would pour the prepared canisters into the hall. Naturally panic would ensue. People would try to leave the building as quickly as possible. Each of the officers participating in the operation knew 'his' deputy, whom he had to arrest. Buses were already waiting for them outside.

However, the decree never had to be enforced and no one had to be arrested. The motion to impeach fell short by several dozen votes. 'This is victory!' Boris Yeltsin joyously announced to his comrades. Everyone gathered in the Kremlin, 'toasted their victory, had a hearty bite to eat and peacefully dispersed,' writes General Korzhakov . 'So even if the impeachment went ahead, the President would not have relinquished power anyway."

Nevertheless, this confrontation could not go on indefinitely. Sooner or later it was bound to end in an explosion; it was only a question of time. Something had to be decided.

On 21 September 1993, in his television address to the people, Boris Yeltsin announced that he had signed a decree dissolving the Parliament. This decree again breached the acting constitution of the country, although it was possibly the only way out of the dead-end situation that had arisen between President and Parliament.

Out of the thousand deputies of the dissolved Parliament, most accepted the decree, but around 150 refused, declaring the decree illegal and themselves the last defenders of freedom. Barricading themselves in the White House, they refused to leave and voted in favour of impeaching the President.

On the surface the situation was very reminiscent of the August coup of 1991. History seemed to be repeating itself, except for one difference. If the uprising of 1991 had been an unequivocal farce, there was now the sense of a brewing tragedy capable of plunging the nation into civil war.

There was another palpable difference. Whereas the coup of 1991 had caught the White House unprepared, almost undefended, now it had turned, literally, into a fortified citadel. Now as then, it was surrounded by volunteer defenders but now they mingled with hundreds of armed men wearing army fatigues, veterans of more then one 'hot-spot'.

Days went by, the stalemate dragged on. The nation split into two camps. From the White House, surrounded by barricades of their defenders and rows of police blocking them in turn, incitements to armed resistance rang out, to topple the 'Presidential clique'. I managed to get inside the White House on the last evening that it was still possible to do so. The overall impression was one of a military camp during a civil war, as shown in films. Cooking-fires were burning, strange people stood around, some wearing padded jackets and wreathed in cigarette smoke, some in paramilitary uniform, others in warm Cossack hats, having obviously travelled far. Many were armed, more than a few were drunk. Hostile tension hung in the air, threatening to grow into a pogrom at any moment. The blister of violence was virtually swelling before our eyes.

It burst on Sunday, 3 October. Units loyal to the White House, sweeping aside the police cordons, plunged on to assault the Moscow Mayor's office. The President received this news while at his residence outside Moscow. In another half an hour a helicopter was taking him to the Kremlin by a secret route. Secret, '... so they don't waste us with a Stinger, or something of that kind,' Yeltsin was later to remark.

Buoyed by the sacking of the Mayor's office, the leaders of the rebels called upon their supporters from the balconies of the White House, not to lose momentum and go on to storm the television centre and the Kremlin. 'We need the airways!' they cried. Muscovites remember these terrifying hours spent in front of their televisions. Evening. Fierce exchanges of gunfire. The assault. The glass wall of the Television Centre, shattered by a truck. The glow of fires. The dead video-engineer, spread-eagled in the vestibule next to the lift. The feral cries of the leader of the assault, not suspecting that his words are being broadcast: 'Now this scum (the television centre) won't be talking for a long while.' Hundreds of bodies. Suddenly, the chilling silence of a black screen. The nationwide television centre had ceased transmitting ...

Deep into the night, speaking via a secret back-up transmitter, the Prime Minister addressed the capital. His face a mask, voiced laced with tragedy. His words made it clear that we were standing upon the edge of an abyss. The speaker implored Muscovites to stand and defend the President and democracy, right now, straight away, at night. The meeting-place was the centre of Moscow – the square outside the Mayor's office ...

I remember gunning the car through an empty city, not paying any attention to traffic lights. It was late at night, but the massive city did not sleep. It did not go to bed. The glow of television screens shone in every window. Everyone was tensely watching the only channel, transmitting in secrecy. People were waiting for the President to speak. Why was he remaining silent? Was he stunned? Had he lost his nerve? Was the government preparing to defend the citizens, or must we defend ourselves, with our bare hands? The President's silence was becoming worrying. He would write later that rumours of his confusion and cowardice were not based on reality. 'I understood clearly, that the fate of the country hung on a thread ... It was not the time for speeches. I was trying to bring my generals out of their state of shock and paralysis.'

It was not of course a matter of shock or paralysis. The Army – like the rest of the country – had divided into two opposing camps. Not long before, during the coup of 1991, the President himself proclaimed the slogan: 'The

Army is outside politics!' A soldier does not have to carry out criminal orders. For the first time in the history of Soviet rule, the Army was given an opportunity to consider its role. And now this slogan came boomeranging back.

The picture was more than simply disturbing. Here was a huge city, and divisions of armed rebels not meeting any resistance. The kind of men in these can be gauged by some graffiti left on a wall: 'I killed five people and am very happy.'

Three in the morning. A meeting continued in the Ministry of Defence, which the President was attending. He was pale and tense. Everyone understood that the situation could only be defused by the taking of the White House. 'What are the suggestions?' The only answer was the grim silence of the generals.

Muscovites, it seems, will never fully know what kind of night they lived through on 3/4 October 1993. An assault plan was finally worked out. Tanks would need to shell the rebels, infantry would break through the barricades, and following them the assault would be carried out by the same old ubiquitous 'Alpha'. It seemed to be a mirror image of the events of 1991.

Five in the morning. The head of the President's guard appealed to the President, asking that he meet in the Kremlin with the officers of the élite 'Alpha' and 'Pennant' divisions, which were supposed to participate in the assault. 'A feeling of danger and disquiet, a kind of hopeless melancholy clung to me,' Yeltsin writes. 'Are you ready to carry out the orders of the President?' he exclaimed, entering the hall where the officers had gathered. He was met with silence.

The strong lads sat silently, not willing to obey their commander-in-chief. One could understand them. Once again they were being sent to attack the White House. Back then, one set of politicians was quarrelling, now it was another, but the killing and dying were being left to them. Finally a voice rose from the ranks: 'We didn't go through training to end up shooting at unarmed seamstresses.' The final point was made, there was nothing further to talk about.

Looking ahead, it may be pointed out that only a tragic incident pushed them into participating in the assault. The commander of 'Alpha' persuaded a few soldiers to get in an armoured transport and at least approach the White House. Their very presence nearby was intended to have a fear-inspiring effect upon the besieged. It was here that a tragedy took place. One of the officers of 'Alpha' jumped out of the transport to help a wounded person lying on the road, but himself fell victim to a sniper's bullet. The death of their comrade ended the hesitation of the 'Alpha' commandos. (This story is lacking one vital and unknown piece of information. Whose sniper was it?)

By morning, tanks were already assuming battle-positions – training the muzzles of their weapons at the White House. The remaining events of that day were seen by the whole world. They were shown by American television, transmitting this drama from the roof of the neighbouring building.

I was there with a group of journalists. The whistle of bullets, cutting through tree branches. The dull thud of cannon. Tongues of fire, licking the white walls of the Parliament. And the Muscovites, frozen in a stupor ... All this seemed unreal – the filming of some action movie. People, however, were dying for real, and it did not matter on whose side. These were all Russians. This was Russia's tragedy ...

◆　◆　◆　◆　◆

On 9 January 2000 the Bolshoi Theatre was full. Moscow's entire élite had gathered here. The annual 'Triumph' prize for outstanding achievement in literature and art was to be awarded. The floodlights flared on and in the 'Czar's booth', built two centuries ago specially for the Russian monarch, appeared Russia's first President, Boris Yeltsin. Everyone in the hall stood. Speaking from the huge stage, a world-famous dancer, currently the director of the theatre, appealed to the illustrious guest with words befitting this grand occasion: 'You came to power in triumph, and left it just as triumphantly.' The audience stood once again.

What was this? Forgiveness of past sins or a theatrical production? Nine days earlier, on 31 December 1999, at the threshold of a new century, Boris Yeltsin shocked Russia a final time, willingly passing on the mantle of power.

◆　◆　◆　◆　◆

But this was still to come. For now, it is late 1995 and the first term of his presidency will be coming to an end the next year. Yeltsin's approval rating was approaching zero. He was hated by everyone, even his recent comrades who defended the White House with him shoulder-to-shoulder. He was hated for the catastrophic destitution of the country, for the explosion of crime and corruption, for lost hopes and shattered illusions. This general dislike was in no small measure the aggravation Russians felt towards themselves. For we ourselves broke an ancient biblical law – 'Do not build an idol for yourself.'

On the eve of 1996, the approaching new year, Yeltsin suffered yet another heart attack. 'Yet another' because he had already had several. A year earlier, a similar heart attack occurred in his plane, when the President was flying from the USA and was supposed to stop in Dublin for a meeting with the Prime Minister of Ireland. The Prime Minister and a guard of honour waited for him on the tarmac for half an hour, but Yeltsin was unable to leave the plane. He later invented another not very imaginative version for journalists: he was tired. He fell asleep. While his guards, you see, would not allow him to be woken, announcing that, 'Our President's rest is more valuable than some diplomatic formalities.' In front of the cameras, Yeltsin promised to 'smack his guards one' for this, showing the whole country his heavy fist.

Another serious heart attack came several months later, after a heavy night's drinking in June 1995. Entering the President's bedroom at night to check on his sleep, the doctor on duty did not find his patient in bed. The search led to the bathroom. The locked door was forced open. The President lay unconscious on the tiled floor. The next attack came in October, and now – on the eve of the approaching elections – a new heart attack.

Under great secrecy, the President was once again hidden away in a government rest-home outside Moscow. The people were informed that he had gone on holiday. His closest circle was nervous – what to do about the elections? Is it worth putting a seriously ill person up for a second term, when his rating is almost non-existent anyway? The head of the President's guard, General Korzhakov, recalls that during one of his visits to his ailing boss the latter '...lifting his head up from the pillow with difficulty, quietly said, "I have decided to stand for re-election"'. His whole life was dedicated to one goal: power. And for its sake he was ready to do anything.

Despite the fact that the doctors – having pumped the President full of drugs – once again managed to prop him up on his feet, everyone understood that going to an election with such a low rating and in such poor health was not only disaster, but simply suicide. General Korzhakov then proposed that the elections simply be cancelled. Cancelling the elections and extending Boris Yeltsin's presidency for an indefinite period under the pretence of say, the war in Chechnya, was a very attractive proposal. Formally this would be called 'postponing the elections', informally, however, it would be taking power by force.

Korzhakov soon shared the idea of a postponement with journalists. Publicly, Yeltsin condemned the idea; in reality, however, matters were moving in that direction. One night the President summoned all the ministers of the armed forces. They discussed what to do if the people, tired of promises, did not accept the 'postponement of elections' and took to the streets. 'I felt that we could not wait for the result of the elections,' Yeltsin himself writes in his latest memoirs. '... A number of decrees were secretly prepared: the banning of the Communist Party, the dissolution of the Parliament, the post-ponement of presidential elections to a later date.'

It is hard to say what would have been in store for the country if these decrees were announced and enforced. Many analysts – including the Minister of Internal Affairs at the time – think that the result would have been a bloody civil war and the complete disintegration of Russia.

Here the President must be given his due. Despite the overwhelming desire to hold on to power, despite the sycophantic entourage which insisted that 'The people don't want elections, they have grown accustomed to you', Yeltsin found the courage to listen to the outnumbered voices of the opposi-tion. 'I protested, raised my voice, almost yelled ... but in the end abandoned the almost-finalised decision,' he writes.

I do not think that moral considerations played a key role in this turn-around. More than likely, the main motivator was a sober analysis of the sit-uation. This isn't important however. What is important is that the President did not cross that line beyond which another bloody chapter of Russian his-tory could have started.

◆　◆　◆　◆　◆

Now is the time to say a few words about General Korzhakov. Why did the head of the President's guard, an officer with very limited responsibilities when all is said and done, gain such prominence in the system of power? He offered solutions upon which the fate of the country rested; he advised Prime Ministers; the highest bureaucrats in the land sought to curry his favor. In actual fact he was the second most influential person in the country after the President.

Alexander Korzhakov was born in Moscow, in a working-class family. Like Boris Yeltsin, his childhood wasn't an easy one. 'I was born in an eight-metre-square-room (where the whole family lived),' he writes in his memoirs. 'An oven stood in the corner. The floor was earthen. The kitten didn't go out-side. He'd do all his business on the floor and bury it on the spot.' His par-ents worked hard to earn enough to eat, so Alexander was raised by the street. After school he went to university, but dropped out. He then worked in a factory and served in the army. Handsome, tall, athletic – a member of one of the best volleyball teams in Moscow – Alexander stood out among his peers. It was exactly this type of lad which was needed in the élite battalion guarding the Kremlin. After finishing a tour of duty in the Kremlin battalion, Alexander was invited to work in the KGB, as a member of the secret bodyguard. He served in the personal guard of the then-President of Afghanistan, the Soviet placeman Babrak Karmal, then in the personal guard of Leonid Brezhnev, Yuri Andropov and Mikhail Gorbachev. At the end of 1985, when Boris Yeltsin became the Party Head of Moscow, Alexander Korzhakov became his personal bodyguard.

Thus began their friendship. Its initial foundations were a love of sport and a matching Russian mentality, common to people of similar origins and upbringing.

The fight with Gorbachev, and the subsequent loss of all Party positions, deprived Yeltsin of his personal guard, but did not deprive him of his friendship with his former bodyguard. They continued to meet even during the hardest months of Yeltsin's life. This could not have gone down well with the KGB, which honoured the unspoken rule that a fallen boss is deprived of everything, including personal friendships. Major Korzhakov's departure from the ranks of the KGB followed soon after. Formally this occurred due to poor health; informally, however, it was because of his unsanctioned meetings with the fallen chief.

Naturally, their common grievances against the powers-that-be drew them even closer together. Korzhakov resumed acting as Yeltsin's bodyguard, but no longer as an agent of the KGB. Now he was not simply a bodyguard, he was a friend and member of the family. They were to move ahead side-by-side for many years, one as the symbol of the new Russia, the other as his shadow. Having become President, Yeltsin was to tell Korzhakov: 'I want you to create a small KGB, my own personal mini-KGB.'

'In some ways, Korzhakov was closer to him than his wife,' writes a biographer of Yeltsin. As Korzhakov himself will later say: 'When we were left alone Yeltsin was no President to me. We considered each other "blood brothers" and as a sign of faith we twice cut our palms and mixed blood. The ritual signified friendship till the grave.'' *

---

* The first time this occurred was during Yeltsin's visit to Siberia. The mayor of Yakutsk organised a good old Siberian sauna for his guests. After a drink, sitting in the steam-room, the President was kidding around and jokingly cut his bodyguard on the hand. It seems he miscalculated and cut a little deeper than he had wanted to. Blood started to flow. Yeltsin felt ashamed, and forced Korzhakov to cut him on the palm as well. They mixed blood, hugged, kissed and drank a glass each of good Siberian vodka, swearing friendship to the grave.

I think it is now clearer what weight and influence General Korzhakov had in President Yeltsin's administration.

◆　◆　◆　◆　◆

Let us return however to the elections of 1996. By proposing that the elections be cancelled, Korzhakov showed concern not only for the health of his 'blood-brother' but for his own interests as well. He understood perfectly that if the President gained power without an election he would not need any 'egghead' analysts, but he would need General Korzhakov and the military forces that stood around him.

So, the President's decision to hold on to power by way of elections was all the more praiseworthy. Without any fanfare, a group of American election campaign specialists were invited to Moscow for the first time. The strategy of the President's camp was simple. The voters had to be convinced that they were not deciding between candidates, but between systems, between old and new. The message was to be: it doesn't matter what Yeltsin is like as a person. It doesn't matter that he is sometimes rude and cynical. It doesn't matter that he drinks and dissembles. It doesn't matter that you don't like him, because if not him, then Communists will come to power. Do you want to go back to Communism?

The fear of Communism was rooted deeply in the subconsciousness of the people, so the strategy was chosen wisely. At any rate, more than half the voters were ready to vote for the devil himself as long as it was against Communism. Nevertheless, the election campaign was difficult. On meeting the President, people openly said that he was old, sick, feeble, that it was time to choose someone younger and healthier. Yeltsin however, did everything he could to prove them wrong.

The whole world has seen the footage shot at Rostov on the Don River, when, throwing off his coat, the President jumped up on stage and started dancing something akin to a cancan. What an overwhelming thirst for power must have possessed a man to do this, when only the other day he had been put back on his feet with great difficulty after a heart attack. As members of the election campaign who witnessed this recall: 'We prayed that the presidential candidate not fall over dead right there on the stage ...'

It wasn't just a thirst for power that drove the President. There was an element of self-preservation here too. Yeltsin understood very well that if the Communists won he would not be able to avoid standing trial. They would bring up many things: the intentional dismantling of the USSR, plundering the country, the attack on Parliament in 1993, the tens of thousands dead in Chechnya, the attempt to outlaw the Communist party. All this was visible on the horizon ...

To re-elect Boris Yeltsin, the powers-that-be spent huge amounts of money – billions of dollars – 'black cash' as it was called. This was illegal, but the oligarchs were going for broke. They understood that with the return of Communists to power, this bottomless well of natural wealth called Russia would be closed to them. Their secret motto was: better a half-dead Yeltsin than a living Communist. The most famous popular artists toured the country organising concerts and urging people to vote for Yeltsin. They had to be paid for this, and paid well. They were paid 'under the counter' with 'black cash'. As one analyst observed, if Yeltsin had listened to Korzhakov then 'he could have gotten all the votes for free, using tanks and Special Forces. Instead, he was trying to buy all the votes.'

The miracle came to pass. On 16 June 1996, Boris Yeltsin won the first round of voting by a minimal lead of a few percent. A Communist was breathing down his neck. In two weeks the second round was to take place.

Suddenly, a catastrophe occurred. A few days before the second round the President suffered yet another heart attack. Shock gripped his closest circle. It was clear to everyone that if the people found out about his heart problem, everything was finished. No one would vote for a seriously ill man. 'What will we do if Grandpa dies?' they whispered in the Kremlin corridors. Had the President made a mistake when he refused Korzhakov's plan?

The doctors insisted on absolute quiet and hospitalisation, but Yeltsin refused. 'After the elections do what you want, even cut me, but for now leave me be ...' he said. The thirst for power was stronger than his desire to be healed.

Everything had to be done to ensure that information about the illness didn't seep through to the people. Naturally, all meetings and appearances were cancelled. Yeltsin's entourage gave out the impression that the President was confident of success and did not consider it necessary to engage in further pre-election campaigning.

If this had happened two weeks before the second round of elections, not two days before, it would have been impossible to keep the information secret. But it happened almost on the eve of the election, and the pre-election marathon had already gained momentum ... 'This was a fantastic, amazing victory!' writes Yeltsin. 'I won, although at the start of the year no one – including my closest people – believed I could. I won despite all predictions, despite a minimal rating, despite a heart attack and political crises ...'

The presidential inauguration, shown nationwide on 9 August, shocked everyone. The oath to serve the people was being taken by a gravely ill man who could barely stand on his feet. The President's daughter, who was sitting in the hall, wept on looking at her father. The people even resurrected a joke from Leonid Brezhnev's time, reworking it slightly: 'Today, after a long and serious illness, not regaining consciousness, the President of the country ... assumed his official duties.'

It was pointless – and impossible – to hide it any more. A month later the country was officially informed that the newly elected President was suffering a serious heart condition and required an operation. The people sighed in disillusionment. They had been fooled once again.

On 5 November, brigades of Russian and foreign surgeons operated on the President's heart. His heart was switched off for 68 minutes, while the whole operation lasted from eight in the morning until two in the afternoon. At seven am, practically on the operating table, Yeltsin signed a decree temporarily transferring power to the Prime Minister, and 23 hours later, as soon as he opened his eyes after the anaesthetic, he signed a second decree, returning power to himself. Knowing Yeltsin's lust for power, however, even these 23 hours elicited numerous cynical jibes among the people.

The next four years of Russia's history were a history of President Yeltsin's illness. Despite the successful operation, he was dogged by ill health. In the words of the radio station 'Liberty', the Russian President '... comes to life every month for three days.' His recently mighty organism seemed to suddenly grow old and decrepit. Now the main function of the Kremlin administration was to create the impression that the President was working. In some ways these years were reminiscent of the sunset years of Leonid Brezhnev. The people felt no pity or compassion for the gravely ill man, but rather brimmed with cynicism and sarcasm. The blind clinging to power annoyed them. The country overflowed with jokes.

Every awkward step or unfortunate word created an ever stronger backlash. In Sweden the President of Russia got that country confused with Finland; he called Germany and Japan nuclear states; he acted less than tactfully to the Swedish Queen, and at one point even decided that he was in Norway. At home he told his countrymen that to that very day he maintained a correspondence with his first schoolteacher, that he planted potatoes in his garden himself and ate them all year long, that 38 specially trained snipers were keeping an eye on the Chechen guerillas so there was nothing to worry about ...

At another time all this might all have been taken for unfortunate jokes, but now it was taken seriously. Russian and foreign press started to discuss the President's mental capacity, arguing that it could have been diminished as a side effect of the coronary bypass operation. There was even talk of Alzheimer's Disease.

However, as someone close to him said, 'Yeltsin has many flaws, but he was never a fool.' At some point it seems he understood that his strength was spent. A successor must be chosen.

Once, thrusting Gorbachev out of power, Yeltsin refused outright to grant the retiring President of the USSR immunity from prosecution. He announced that there could be no question of immunity: 'If Gorbachev wants to admit to something, let him do it now ... [while he is still President]'. Now the boomerang was flying back. Yeltsin himself was in dire need of guaranteed immunity. For this he needed to find a successor whom he could trust as surely as himself.

According to the constitution, if the President is taken ill or retires early he is replaced by the Prime Minister. So, a secret search began for a suitable candidate for the job. Prime Ministers changed with kaleidoscopic speed. The country became feverish. The people became agitated.

We won't guess what criteria Boris Yeltsin used to find his successor, but we would like to believe that they were not only the criteria of self-preservation, but included concern for the future of the country as well.

So who is he, Boris Yeltsin? 'He is an endlessly talented man,' says his aide. 'You have done much harm to the people,' an old war veteran tells him to his face. 'Yeltsin is poison for Russia,' say the Communists. Some might even remember that on 30 May 1990, the day after Boris Yeltsin was elected chairman of the Soviet Parliament of Russia, an exceedingly rare event occurred in Moscow – an earthquake. What was this, a warning from above?

His opponents accused him of primitivism and incompetence, but he beat them in every political battle. They used his name to try to frighten the people, saying that he threatened dictatorship and 'people hanging from lampposts', but Russian society was never as free as it was under him. The only people who didn't put the boot into him were those who were too bone-idle to do so, but he maintained a dignified silence. He could have easily become a dictator, but he conquered himself and did not become one.

So who is he, Boris Yeltsin? It seems that after ten years of rule we never did find out everything about him ...

Although he was old and sick, and seemed to be half-asleep, this was the sleep of a crocodile. He retained his instinct for power completely, and bore little resemblance to a man who would be willing to let it go without a fight. Thus the words he spoke to the whole nation on 31 December 1999 sounded all the more deafening: 'I have completed the main work of my life. Russia will never again return to the past ... I am leaving. I have done all I can.'

When the television screen went dark the President started crying. His last words in the Kremlin were directed at the new President: 'Preserve Russia!'

A new epoch started in the Kremlin, the epoch of Putin. The first decree of this new ruler was to guarantee immunity from prosecution to the departing President. That same decree which Boris Yeltsin refused his predecessor so rudely and cynically.

So who is he, Boris Yeltsin? To answer this question, it seems we have to look behind us, deep into Russian history – a history of bloody civil revolts, which started as struggles for freedom and ended in theft and banditry, a history of impostors and False-Kings, and of spirited Cossack freebooters. Yeltsin is the quintessence of the flaws and virtues of the Russian people. He is us ...

The Kremlin has entered a new century. What will it be like for Russia?

BIBLIOGRAPHY

Adjubey, Alexei. *Those Ten Years*. Moscow, Sov. Russia (Soviet Russia), 1989

Alexinsky, Tatiana. *1917*. Novi zurnal (New magazine), #90–94, 1968

Alliluyev, Svetlana. *Twenty Letters to a Friend*. Moscow, Sov. Pisatel (Soviet Writer), 1990

Annenkov, Yuri. *Remembering Lenin*. Novi zurnal (New magazine), #65, 1963

Antonov-Ovseenko, Anton. *The Career of an Executioner*. Moscow, Zvezda (Star), 1988/9

Barron, John. *KGB*. London, Corgi Books, 1975

Bazhanov, Boris. *The Memoirs of Stalin's Former Secretary*. Moscow, Sofinta, 1990

Beria, Sergo. *My Father – Lavrenti Beria*. Moscow, Sovremennik (Contemporary), 1994

Burlazki, Feodor. *Russian Lords*. Moscow, Shark, 1996

Chernov, Victor. *Lenin through the Eyes of an Opponent*. Ogonek, #17, 1991

Essen, M. *Inessa Armand*. Moscow, Gosizdat, 1925

Fisher, L. *The Life of Lenin*. London, 1970

Gnedin, Evgeni. *The Catastrophe and the Rebirth*. Amsterdam, 1977

Ioffe, Z. *Was Lenin poisoned by Stalin?* Moscow. Za rubezom (Abroad), #40, 1990

Khrushchev, Nikita. *Khrushchev Remembers*. New York, Chalidze, 1979

Khrushchev, Sergei. *A Pensioner of National Importance*. Moscow, Pravda (Truth), 1989

Korzhakov, Alexander. *Boris Yeltsin: From Sunrise to Sunset*. Moscow, Interbook, 1997

Kostomarov, Nikolai. *The History of Russia*. Petrograd, 1915

Kostomarov, Zabelin. *Of the Lives, Welfare, and Morals of the Russian People*. Moscow, 1996

Krupskaya, Nadezhda. *Memories of Lenin*. Moscow, 1972

Lombroso, Cesare. *Genius and Madness*. Moscow, TAMP, 1990

Malkov, Pavel. *Memoirs of the Commandant of the Kremlin*. Moscow, Molodaia Gvardia (Young Guards), 1967

Medvedev, Roy. *The General Secretary from Lubyanka*. Moscow, 1993

Medvedev, Zhores. *Andropov*. Oxford, 1983

Mlechin, Leonid. *The Formula of Power: from Yeltsin to Putin*. Moscow, Centropolifraf, 2000

Mlinarzh, Zdenek. *A Cold Wind Blows from the Kremlin.* New York, 1988

Orlov, Aleksander. *The Secret History of Stalin's Crimes.* New York, 1983

Prushinskii, K. *A Night in the Kremlin.* Sov.sekretno (Top Secret), #3, 1989

Reagan, Nancy. *My Turn.* Moscow, The Foreign Literature, #9, 1991

The Russia of XV–XVII Centuries through the Eyes of Foreigners. Leningrad, 1986

Sheehy, Gail. *The Man Who Changed The World.* New York, HarperCollins, 1990

Shturman, Dora. *V. I. Lenin.* Paris, 1989

Skrinnikov, R. G. *Russia on the Eve of the Troubled Times.* Moscow, Misl (Idea), 1985

Solomon, G. *Lenin and his Family.* Moscow, 1992

Solouhin, V. A. *In the Light of Day.* Moscow, 1992

Solovyiov, V., Klepikov, E. *Yuri Andropov: The Secret Passage into the Kremlin.* St. Petersburg, 1995

—*Boris Yeltsin.* Moscow, 1995

Stalin's Correspondence with the President of the USA and the Prime Minister of Great Britain. Moscow, 1976

Sudoplatov, Pavel. *Spies in the Kremlin.* Moscow, Geia, 1996

Tarle, E. *Napoleon.* Moscow, Progress, 1992

Tolstoy, Aleksei. *The Silver Prince.* Moscow, Molodaia Gvardia (Young Guards), 1986

Trotsky, Leon. *Stalin.* 1–2 v., Moscow, EPL, 1990

—*Lenin,* Moscow, EPL, 1991

Ulyanov, M. I. *About V. I. Lenin and the Ulyanov Family.* Moscow, 1989

Valentinov, N. V. *Meetings with Lenin.* New York, 1981

Valishevskiy, K. *Troubled Times.* Moscow, IKPA, 1989

Vasilieva, Larissa. *Kremlin Wives.* Moscow, Novosti (News), 1995

Volkogonov, Dmitri. *Triumph and Tragedy. I. V. Stalin.* Moscow, Novosti (News), 1989

—*Lenin.* 1–2 v., Moscow, Novosti (News), 1994

Wittlin, Thaddeus. *Commissar.* NY, Macmillan, 1972

Yeltsin, Boris. *Confessions on the Given Topic.* Vilnius, 1990

—*Notes of a President.* Moscow, 1994

—*The Presidential Marathon.* Moscow, ACT, 2000

Zabelin, I. E. *The History of the City of Moscow.* Moscow, Stolitza (Capital), 1990

Zenkovich, Nikolai. *Boris Yeltsin: Different Lives.* Moscow, Olma-Press, 2001

INDEX

A

Acropolis, the, 10
Adjubei, Alexei, 192
Afghanistan, 308, 321
Agadja, Mehmet Ali, 233
Ahmat, Khan, 18
Ahmatov, Anna, 77
Alexander III, Czar, 96
Alexander's Settlement, 27–9
Alexandria, 20
Alexei, Czar, 63–7, 68–72
Alexei, Czarevich, 74, 76, 85
Alexinsky, Tatiana, 109
Alliluyeva, Nadezhda, (Nadya), 130,
  135–7, 177
Alliluyeva, Svetlana, 125, 135–7,
  140–1, 143–5, 151, 162–3, 171–2,
  180, 231
Alma Ata, 261
Anastasia, Czarina, 60
Andreiev, Boris, 1634
Andriotti, 247
Andropov, Igor, 236
Andropov, Irina, 233
Andropov, Irma, 236
Andropov, Yuri, 220–40, 242, 246,
  248, 255–7, 264, 266, 287, 321
Annenkov, Yuri, 117
Annunciation Cathedral, 21, 87
Antonov-Ovseenko, 179, 181, 185
Apraxin, Marfa, 72
Archangel Cathedral, 21, 41, 53–4,
  87
Armand, Alexander, 105
Armand, Inessa, 105–6, 122
Assumption Cathedral, 21, 55, 67,
  83, 89
Astrakhan, 95, 116
Athens, 10
Azerbaijan, 222

B

Bagration, General Prince Peter, 88
Baikanur, 200
Baku, 222, 261
Balobanov, Angélique, 106
Baltic Sea, 81, 86
Baltimore, 296
Barron, John, 227
Bdzezinsky, Zbignev, 233
Bedni, Dimyan, 111, 150
Belorussia, 110, 264, 311
Beloveshskaya Forest, 310–11
Berezniki, 277, 280, 294–5
Beria, Lavrenti, 142, 159, 162,
  169–72, 179–87, 190, 194,
  209–10, 224, 231, 259
Beria, Sergo, 142, 186–7
Berlin, 78, 158, 159, 161, 187, 231
Bernstein, Edward, 108
Bhati, Khan, 14
Black Sea, 126, 200–1, 207, 216,
  238, 247, 255
Blanc, Alexander, 95, 97
Blanc, Maria Alexandrovna, 95, 105
Bliukher, Marshal, 180
Blok, Alexander, 17
Bobruisk, 110
Bogdanov, 115
Bologna, 21
Bolshaya Tes, 242
Borbius, André, 123
Boris Godunov, Czar, 15, 40–53, 52,
  56–8, 60, 62, 313
Borodino Field, 88
Botkin, 287
Bovin, Alexander, 217, 228
Bozhanov, Boris, 131–2, 136, 177
Brezhnev, Galina, 208–9, 219–20,
  222–4, 226, 236
Brezhnev, Leonid, 145, 200–2,

205–26, 228–9, 231, 234–6, 238,
242–6, 256, 266, 285, 289, 321,
324
Brezhnev, Victoria, 206
Brezhnev, Yuri, 236
Brodsky, Joseph, 232
Budapest, 152, 230
Bukharin, Nikolai, 166
Burlatski, Professor, 190–1, 311
Bush, George, 238, 248, 296
Butka, 276, 279, 286
Byelorussia, 154, 310–12
Byron, 103
Byzantium, 19–20, 22, 25, 58

C
Caligula, 24
Calvin, John, 19
Calvus, Caius, 20
Caplan, Fanny, 110–12
Carmen, Roman, 208
Caspian Sea, 13
Catherine I, Empress, 78, 81, 83
Catherine II, the Great, Empress, 235,
261
Caucasus, the, 106, 119, 124–6,
130–1, 133, 151, 158, 174, 180,
220, 229, 249, 251, 255, 302
Ceausescu, Nicolae, 265
Chaliapin, Fyodor, 50
Chaureli, Mikhail, 161
Chavchavadze, Illiya, 174
Chechnya, 319, 323
Chelyabinsk, 264
Chernenko, Constantine, 213
Chernenko, Konstantin, 236–8,
241–9, 257, 259
Chernobyl, 264–5, 269
Chernov, Victor, 113, 120
Chet, 15
Churchill, Winston, 124, 152, 158,
160, 174
Cicero, 20
Circassia, 27

Constantinople, 19
Copenhagen, 80–1
Cracow, 102
Crimea, the, 151, 168, 238–40, 269,
304, 309
Czechoslovakia, 215, 253

D
Daniel, 217
Danil, Prince, 14
Davitashvili, Juna, 220
Debosis, 22
Demunt, Helen, 137
Denisov, Victoria, 206
Denmark, 63–4, 75
Diderot, Denis, 87
Didi-Lilo, 124–5
Dimitri, Czarevich, 39, 46, 49–51,
53, 57, 59
Dimitri, the False, Czar, 50–60, 70
Dneprodzerzhinsk, 205
Dnepropetrovsk, 208
Dolgorukaya, Maria, 38
Dolgoruky, Maria, 63
Donskoy, Dimitri, Prince, 15–17
Dostoyevsky, 50, 58, 103, 199, 268
Draule, Milda, 147
Driver-Rabbit, 112
Dublin, 319
Dumas, Alexander, 98
Dzhugashvili, Galya, 138
Dzhugashvili, Jacob, 127, 137–140
Dzhugashvili, Joseph, see Stalin,
Joseph
Dzhugashvili, M., 142
Dzhugashvili, Visarion, 124–5

E
Egypt, 135, 148
Ehrenburg, Ilya, 178
Eisenstein, Sergei, 31, 168
Ekaterinburg, see Sverdlovsk
Elizabeth I, Queen of England, 37,
39

England, 32, 37–9, 75, 145, 259
Estedt, Karl Frederic, 95
Estomin, Valentina, 137
Estonia, 115
Execution, Place of, 30, 57, 61

F
Filaret, *see* Romanov, Fyodor
Finland, 108–9, 324
Fiorovanti, Rudolfo, 21–2
Fischer, Louis, 105
Fletcher, Giles, 34–5
Ford, Gerald, 216
Foros, 269, 272
France, 32, 59, 70, 75, 88, 192, 194, 263
Frederick the Great, 79
Fyodor I, 'the Bellringer', Czar, 36–7, 40–1, 44–6, 48–9, 53, 72
Fyodor III, Czar, 70–1, 79
Fyodorov, Zoya, 232–3

G
Gagarin, Yuri, 210, 286
Galitsin, 198–9
Garrison, James, 296
Gaulle, Charles de, 204
Gefter, M., 189, 192
Geladze, Katherine, 124–5
Geneva, 19, 102–3, 260
Genoa, 112
Genscher, 247
Georgia, 104, 125, 142, 145, 180, 262
Gerasimov, Mikhail, 41
Germany, 75, 107–8, 113, 139, 150, 159, 215, 251, 324
Gharst, Mr, 191, 195
Ghengis Khan, 13
Glinskaya, Helena, 23–4
Gnedin, Evgeni, 181
Godunov, Boris, *see* Boris Godunov, Czar
Godunov, Fyodor, 52–3

Godunov, Irene, 40–1, 43–5
Goethe, Johann W., 102–3
Gopcalo, Pantelei, 249, 252
Gorbachev, Alexander, 252
Gorbachev, Anatoli, 272
Gorbachev, Andrei, 250–1
Gorbachev, Irene, 272
Gorbachev, Maria, 252
Gorbachev, Mikhail, 113, 186, 237, 246, 249–74, 285–286, 288–295, 298–304, 308–314, 321, 325
Gorbachev, Raisa, 253–254, 256–257, 259–261, 272, 286
Gorbachev, Sergei, 251
Gori, 124–5
Gorky, Maxim, 148
Gorsei, John, 39–40
Grachov, General Pavel, 305, 307
Granavitaya Chamber, 21, 53, 87
Greece, 258
Grosskopf, Anna, 95
Grossman, Vasili, 120
Grozni, 115
Grushetski, Agafia, 72
'Gypsy, Boris', 222–3

H
Hastings, Mary, 39
Hegel, Georg Friedrich Wilhelm, 102, 205
Hidznak–Gurevich, Major Mikhail, 187
Hitler, Adolf, 112, 132, 138, 153–5, 174, 238
Hlopov, Maria, 62–3
Hofburg, 10
Holland, 73, 75, 80

I
Ignatashvili, Jacob, 124
Illizarov, Professor Boris, 128
Illyin, Lieutenant, 218–19
India, 144–5, 192
Indonesia, 212

Inessa, 105–7, 122
Ioffe, Professor, 119
Ipatiev House, 286–8
Iremashvili, Joseph, 127–8
Irena, Czarina, 63–4
Islam, 19
Italy, 21–2, 94, 104, 264
Ivan II, 15
Ivan III, the Great, Czar, 17–22, 25, 89
Ivan IV, the Terrible, Czar, 9, 18, 20, 23–45, 48–9, 52–4, 57–60, 62, 68, 83, 112, 136, 148, 150, 156, 168
Ivan Romanov, Czarevich, 72–3, 75
Ivan, son of Ivan the Terrible, 36–7, 43–4
Ivanov, General, 165

J
Jacob-Wallet, 112
Japan Sea, 238–9
Japan, 239–240, 248, 324
Joan of Arc, 58–9
Joseph, Stalin's grandson, 144
Juan Carlos I, 247

K
Kabulov, 181
Kadar, Janos, 230
Kaganovich, Lazar, 176, 207
Kalesnik, Alexander, 139
Kalinin, Mikhail, 148
Kalinovka, 175
Kalita, Ivan, 14–15, 21
Kamchatka, 238–9
Kamenev, 131, 133–4, 167
Kamenskoye, 205
Kant, Immanuel, 102
Kapler, Alexander, 143–4
Karelia, 229, 293
Karmal, Babrak, 321
Katherine, Princess of Poland, 37
Katya, Stalin's granddaughter, 144
Katyn Forest, 157

Kazakhstan, 200, 210
Kazan, 33
Kazivetter, A., 88
Kennedy, Jacqueline, 260
Kennedy, President John F., 259
KGB, 99, 111, 128–9, 131, 133–4, 137, 140, 142, 144, 146–52, 156, 159–60, 168–9, 172, 175, 179–80, 182, 185–8, 197, 200, 202, 207, 209–10, 220–1, 223–7, 229–35, 237–8, 241, 250, 252–3, 255, 259–60, 269–70, 274, 287, 293, 300, 304–5, 321
Khazan, 96–7, 142
Khrushchev, Leonid, 176
Khrushchev, Yulya, 176
Khrushchev, Nikita, 60, 123, 128–30, 136–7, 142, 144–5, 147, 152, 154, 161–3, 167–8, 170–2, 175–205, 207–12, 214–15, 217, 224–5, 228–31, 243, 245, 255, 261, 266, 270, 285, 289
Khrushchev, Sergei, 200, 202
Khrushchev, Yefrosinya, 176
Kiev, 154, 215, 264
Kirov, Sergei, 145–7
Kishinev, 208–9
Kissinger, Henry, 216, 218
Klepikov, 221, 232, 299
Kobila, Andrei, 60
Kollontai, Alexandra, 106
Koltovskaya, Anna, 38
Kopachi, Colonel, 230
Korea, South, 239
Korolev, Sergei, 192
Korzhakov, Alexander, 300, 314–15, 319–23
Kostomarov, Nikolai, 16, 48, 57
Krasnoyarsk, 242
Krupskaya, Nadezhda, 97–103, 107, 118–9, 121–2, 134
Krupsky, Constantine, 97
Kuharchuk, Nina, 176
Kulikov, 16, 17

Kureika, 128–9
Kursk, 175, 206

L
Laletin, 129
Lapuhina, Evdakia, 74
Latvia, 115
Lazovski, Solomon, 168
Lebed, General Alexander, 307
Lena, river, 94
Lenin, Vladimir, 84, 93–123, 128,
    131, 134–5, 148–50, 154, 173,
    181, 195, 198, 209, 211, 225,
    227–8, 232, 257, 265–6, 313
Leningrad, 136, 138, 145–8, 151,
    154, 156, 234, 265, 294
Léon, 22
Leon-Bootmaker, 112
Leonov, Leonid, 166
Lisbon, 264
Lithuania, 29
Litvinov, Maxim, 168–9
Litvinov, Professor, 111
Livy, 20
Lobrozo, Professor, 115
Lombroso, Cesare, 32
London, 45, 87, 102–3, 158–9, 261
Louis XVI, King of France, 25
Lubjanka, 180
Luther, Martin, 19
Lyubimov, Anna, 242

M
Machiavelli, Niccolo, 179
Malkov, Pavel, 111
Mamai, Khan, 15, 16
Mao Tse-tung, 164, 166
Maria Nagoy, Czarina, 39, 44, 46,
    51, 54, 57
Marina, 51, 54–5, 58–9
Marx, Karl, 137, 197
Massa, 61
Maykop, 115
Mayranovski, Professor, 180

Mazdok, 229
Mdivani, Buda, 148
Medvedev, General, 225, 228, 269–71
Medvedev, Roy, 208, 219
Melentieva, Vasilisa, 38
Meltzer, Yulia, 138–9
Menshikov, Alexander, 76, 82
Mikhail III Romanov, Czar, 59, 61–4
Mikhoels, Solomon, 168
Mikoyan, Anastas, 154, 201–3
Miloslavsky, Maria, 67, 69
Minin, 59
Minsk, 168, 214
Mitterand, François, 247
Mlinarzh, Zdenik, 253–4
Mnishek, Marina, 51, 54, 58
Moldavia, 208, 243
Molière, 70, 103
Molotov, Vyacheslav, 168
Mongol-Tatar, 13–20, 22, 33, 28
Moroz, Gregory, 144
Morozov, Boris, 67–8
Morozov, Ivan, 105
Morozov, Savva, 105
Moscow River, 15, 22, 298
Moscow, 9, 14–15, 17–22, 25–8, 30,
    38–40, 45, 47, 49, 52, 55–7, 60,
    63–4, 66, 73, 75–7, 85–90, 93,
    100, 105–6, 109–12, 117, 119,
    121, 130, 135, 138, 140–1, 144–7,
    150–1, 153–5, 157, 159–60, 163,
    169, 173, 175, 177, 178, 180–3,
    185–6, 189–91, 196, 200–3, 205,
    208–10, 213–14, 216, 218–20,
    222–23, 227–34, 236–43, 248,
    252–59, 266–7, 269–71, 274–5,
    286, 288–9
Mozart, Wolfgang Amadeus, 48
Munich, 102
Mussorgsky, Modest, 50

N
Nagibin, Yuri, 233
Nagudskaya, 229

Nagy, Imre, 230
Naina Girina, see Yeltsin, Naina
Napoleon, 10, 88–90, 120, 220
Narishkin, Natalia, 69–70
Natalia, Czarina, 73–4
Neizvestni, Ernst, 197–9
Nero, 24, 58
Nevski, Alexander, 13–14
Nevsky Avenue, 84
New York, 155, 199, 233, 296, 327–8
Newton, Isaac, 76
Nicholas II, Czar, 61, 107, 220, 286–7
Nikolaiev, 146, 147
Nixon, Richard, 216, 218
Nizhny Novgorod, 59
North Sea, 35
Norway, 324
Novgorod, 13–14, 31, 59
Novocherkassk, 195, 261

O
Oranienburg, 139
Orda, 14
Orenburg, 264, 283–4, 286
Orlov, Alexander, 152–3
Osipov, Professor, 116

P
Palestine, 9
Paris, 89, 102–6, 206, 273
Pauker, 152
Paulus, Field Marshal, 139
Penza, 114, 243
Peotrovsky, Boris, 235
Peter and Paul, Fort of, 84
Peter I, the Great, Czar, 49, 58, 69, 71–86, 93, 252, 259, 311, 313
Peters, Olga, 145
Petrograd, see St Petersburg
Philby, Kim, 231
Poland, 39, 50–1, 54, 57–8, 159
Pompeii, 264

Pope, the, 19, 233, 246, 261
Popov, Ivan, 106
Portugal, 58
Potresov, Alexander, 97
Potsdam, 158–9
Pozharsky, Prince, 59
Privolnaya, 249, 250, 251
Protopopov, 111
Prushinski, 155
Pushkin, Aleksander Sergeyevich, 50, 53, 58, 88, 102
Pushkino, 105
Putin, Vladimir, 327

R
Rasputin, Grigori Efimovich, 220
Reagan, Nancy, 260
Reagan, Ronald, 238, 257
Red Square, 26, 30, 56–7, 59, 61, 77, 87–8, 109, 121, 123, 155, 224
Ribin, Major, 182
Ribinsk, 229
Riga, 82
Rochefoucauld, François, duc de la, 289
Rockefeller, David, 296
Romanov, Fyodor (Filaret), 60, 62–3
Romanov, Grigory, 234–5
Romanov, Nikita, 60
Romanov, Sophia, 72–7
Rome, 9–10, 19–21, 25, 58, 135, 233, 236, 261
Romm, Mikhail, 197
Roosevelt, Franklin D., 124, 152, 158, 160
Rostov, 106, 253, 322
Rostov, Natasha, 106
Russell, William Howard, 87

S
Saardam, 75
Saburova, Solomonia, 23
Sachsenhausen, 139
Sakhalin, 238

Sakharov, Andrei, 217, 258, 295, 301
Salieri, 48
Samoilova, Tatiana, 212
Saratov, 114
Schiller, 103
Schultz, George, 260
Semeon, 15
Serebrianny, 28–9, 32
Serov, Ivan, 129
Shakespeare, William, 70, 103
Sharigin, Nikola, 234
Sheremetieva, Yelena, 37
Shevchenko, Arkadi, 233
Shmonov, Alexander, 265
Sholokhov, Mikhail, 145
Shtirlitz, 221
Siberia, 45, 47, 64, 67, 100, 128,
    137, 146, 217, 242, 250, 253–5,
    274, 295, 321
Sikorski, General, 156–7
Simbirsk, 94
Singh, Radj Bridj, 144
Sinyavsky, 217
Smidt, Nikolai, 105
Sobakina, Martha, 38
Solomon, G., 115
Soloviev, 221, 228, 232, 299
Solzhenitsyn, Alexander, 102, 174,
    217, 232
Sophia Palaeologus, 19–21, 25
Spain, 32, 247
St Petersburg, 10, 80–1, 83–4, 86–8,
    93, 95–101, 108–9, 112, 130, 313
St Helena, 89
Stalin, Joseph, 24, 31, 33, 77, 83, 94,
    99–100, 104–5, 107, 112–19, 121,
    123–174, 176–85, 187–95, 199,
    201–3, 205, 207, 209–16, 218,
    225, 228–9, 231, 233, 237, 246,
    250–2, 259, 266–7, 279–80, 289,
    291
Stalin, Nadezhda, 141
Stalin, Svetlana, see Alliluyeva,
    Svetlana

Stalin, Vasili, 137, 140, 142–3, 171
Stalingrad, 134, 139, 187
Stamenov, Ambassador, 154
Stavropol, 229, 249–50, 254–7, 266,
    288
Stephan, Natalie, 105
Stephan, Théodore, 105
Stephen Bathory, king of Poland, 39
Streshnov, Yevdakiya, 63
Sudoplatov, Lieutenant General Pavel,
    147
Sukarno, Dr, 212
Surikov, 77
Svanidze, Alioshka, 167
Svanidze, Katherine, 127
Sverdlov, Jacob, 111, 128, 136
Sverdlovsk, 61, 266, 275–6, 278,
    285–9, 291–292
Svetoslav, Prince, 9
Sweden, 324
Switzerland, 98, 106–7, 258, 312
Szilard, Leo, 191

T
Tacitus, 20
Talleyrand, Charles-Maurice de, 263
Tamara, Czarina, 220
Tatar see Mongol-Tatar
Tate, Vice–Admiral Jack, 232
Tbilisi, 261–2
Teheran, 152, 158–9
Temrukova, Maria, 27, 37
Thatcher, Margaret, 247, 259, 261
Tiflis, 104, 124, 126, 138
Tistrov, Elizabeth, 97
Tito, Marshal, 191
Titorenko, Raisa, see Gorbachev,
    Raisa
Tolstoy, Count Alexei K., 28–9, 32, 34
Tolstoy, Count Leo, 50, 58, 89, 98,
    106
Totsk, 264
Trotsky, Leon, 108–9, 114, 118–19,
    131–3, 138, 147, 174

Truman, Harry S., 159
Turkey, 202
Tzvigun, General, 223, 231

U
Uglich, 45–7
Ukraine, 154, 175, 178, 205–8, 250, 264, 310–12
Ulyanov, Alexander, 96–7
Ulyanov, Anna, 96, 99
Ulyanov, Ilya Nikolayevich, 95
Ulyanov, Maria, 96, 118–19, 134
Ulyanov, Vladimir, see Lenin
United Nations, the, 193
United States of America, 145, 168, 191–2, 195, 210, 218, 232, 238–9, 264, 295–8
Urals, 206, 217, 264, 266, 274–7, 279, 281, 283, 285, 287–9, 291–7, 299, 301, 303, 305, 307, 309, 311, 313, 315, 317, 319, 321, 323, 325
Usovka, 175–6

V
Valdemar, Prince of Denmark, 63–4
Valentinov, Nikolai, 102–4
Varconi, Frans, 188
Varkuta, 143
Vasilchikova, Anna, 38
Vasilieva, Larissa, 101, 106, 220, 226
Vasily 'the Dark', 17
Vasily III, Czar, 22–4, 39
Vasily, Prince, 17
Vatican, the, 10
Vedenin, Professor, 186
Venice, 19, 22, 76, 85
Versailles, 10
Vienna, 10, 19, 45
Vilnius, 261
Vladimir, 27
Vladivostok, 216
Volga, 94–5, 98, 134, 151, 229, 243
Volkhov River, 31
Volkogonov, Professor D., 95, 114, 117, 157, 170, 228, 244, 247–8
Voroshilov, Marshal, 162, 211
Vorovsky, 94, 103
Voznesenski, Andrei, 198

W
Walesa, Lech, 233
Wartburg Castle, 19
Washington, 296
Watermann, Johann, 20
Wright, Frank Lloyd, 145

X
Xenia, 52–3, 55

Y
Yagoda, Henrich, 146, 149, 150, 169
Yakubov, Apollinariya, 97
Yakutsk, 321
Yalta, 158
Yaroslav, 229
Yeltsin, Boris, 266–9, 274–326
Yeltsin, Naina, 283, 286, 292
Yeltsin, Nikolai, 280
Yeltsin, Tanya, 283
Yevtushenko, Yevgeni, 232
Yezhov, 250
Yudenich, General, 114
Yuri 'Longarms', Prince, 9
Yuri, the Great Prince, 14

Z
Zaharina, Anastasia, 26, 36
Zaporozhye, 208
Zbarsky, Professor, 122
Zhdanov, Yuri, 144
Zhemchuzhina, Polina, 168, 169
Zhirinovski, Vladimir, 274
Zhukov, Marshal Georgi, 183–4, 194, 207
Zhutovsky, Boris, 178, 196
Zinoviev, 131, 133–4, 153
Zugdidi, 220
Zurich, 102